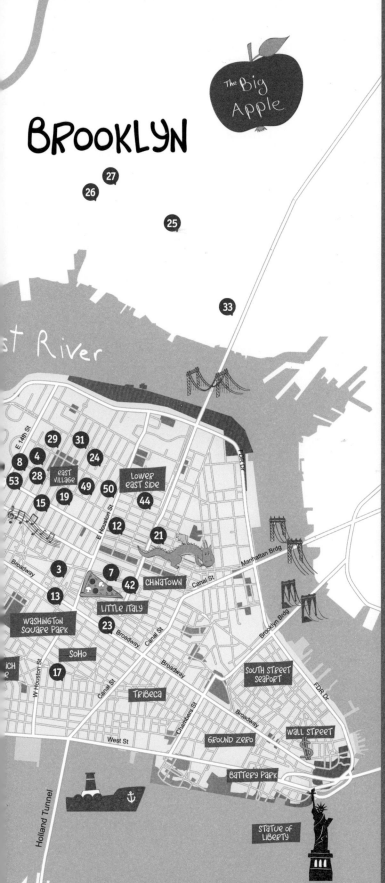

BROOKLYN

The Big Apple

MW00910399

1   21 Club (p. 53)

2   A Voce (p. 57)

3   Acme (p. 63)

4   Au Za'atar (p. 69)

5   Awadh (p. 75)

6   Bagatelle (p. 81)

7   Balaboosta (p. 87)

8   Balade (p. 91)

9   Benoit (p. 97)

10 Betony (p. 103)

11 BLT Prime (p. 107)

12 Blue Ribbon Sushi Iz. (p. 111)

13 Bond Street (p. 115)

14 Brio (p. 121)

15 Café Mogador (p. 127)

16 Catch (p. 131)

17 Charlie Bird (p. 137)

18 Cherry (p. 141)

19 Desnuda (p. 145)

20 Dovetail (p. 149)

21 Dudleys (155)

22 Eataly (p. 161)

23 Ed's Lobster (p. 165)

24 Edy & the Wolf (p. 171)

25 El Almacen (p. 177)

26 El Born (p. 183)

27 Five Leaves (p. 185)

28 Flinders Lane (p. 189)

29 Gnocco (p. 195)

30 Jacob's Pickles (p. 201)

31 Kafana (p. 207)

32 La Masseria (p. 213)

33 Landhaus at the Woods (p. 217)

34 Laut (p. 221)

35 Lexington Brass (p. 223)

36 Luzzo's (p. 229)

37 Masseria dei Vini (p. 233)

38 Mira Sushi Izakaya (p. 237)

39 Molyvos (p. 243)

40 MP Taverna (p. 247)

41 Oceana (p. 253)

42 Oficina Latina (p. 257)

43 Periyali (p. 261)

44 Pig & Kao (p. 267)

45 Pizzetteria Brunetti (p. 271)

46 Pure Food and Wine (p. 275)

47 Salinas (p. 279)

48 Seasonal (p. 285)

49 Som Tum Der (p. 289)

50 Supper (p. 295)

51 The Cecil (p. 299)

52 The Red Cat (p. 305)

53 The Redhead (p. 309)

54 Wallflower (p. 315)

"In New York,
concrete jungle where dreams are made of,
there's nothin' you can't do,
now you're in New York,
these streets will make you feel brand new
big lights will inspire you
Let's hear it for New York, New York, New York"

Empire State Of Mind
Alicia Key and Jay-Z

"In New York freedom looks like
Too many choices
In New York I found a friend
To drown out the other voices"

New York
U2

"I wanna wake up, in that city that doesn't sleep,
to find I'm king of the hill, head of the list
cream of the crop at the top of the list
My little town blues are melting away
I'll make a brand new start of it, in old New York
if I can make it there, I'd make it anywhere
it's up to you, New York New York"

New York, New York
Liza Minelli - Frank Sinatra

"It comes down to reality
and it's fine with me
'cause I've let it slide
don't care if it's Chinatown
or on Riverside
I don't have any reasons
I've left them all behind
I'm in a New York state of mind"

New York state of mind
Billy Joel

"Dear New York I hope you're doing well
I know a lot's happen and you've been through hell
So, we give thanks for providing a home
Through your gates at Ellis Island we passed in droves
Brooklyn, Bronx, Queens and Staten
From the Battery to the top of Manhattan
Asian, Middle-Eastern and Latin
Black, White, New York you make it happen"

An open letter to NYC
Beastie Boys

"It's easier to leave than to be left behind,
leaving was never my proud.
Leaving New York never easy,
I saw the life fading out"

Leaving New York
R.E.M.

NEW YORK

publisher › editore

www.NextBook.it

ITALY
Via Rosmini 21 - 72100 Brindisi
tel. +39 (0) 389 7965 348

info@nextbook.it

author › autore

fabio mollica

ISBN
978-88-906709-3-0

First published in USA, Canada, UK, Italy in September 2015
Pubblicato per la prima volta in USA, Canada, UK, Italia nel Settembre 2015

Design:
Salvatore Antonaci

Translations / Traduzioni:
Mariann Grace Lotesoriere

Printed by / Stampa:
Locopress, Italy

Printed in August 2015
Finito di stampare ad Agosto 2015

Many thanks to those who generously participated
in this project, the newyorkers:

› Sivan Askayo
pag. 10

› Trisha Krauss
pag. 14

› Ornella Fado
pag. 45

› Albin Konopka
pag. 48

› Daniela Kucher
pag. 50

› Chiemi Nakai
pag. 328

› Bobby Seeger
pag. 318

› Jeryl Brunner
pag. 346

› Mo Foulavand
pag. 361

› Jessi Colasante
pag. 46

dedicated to... / dedicato a...

Christine (2 years), the youngest victim of 9/11, and the other childs that lost their life in that tragedy: David, Juliana, Zoe, Dana, Bernard, Rodney, Asia.

A Cristina (2 anni), la vittima più giovane dell'attentato alle Torri Gemelle, e agli altri bambini che hanno perso la vita in quella tragedia: David, Juliana, Zoe, Dana, Bernard, Rodney, Asia.

All the dreamers.
Tutti i sognatori.

contents

(sommario)

11
100 things to do in New York
(100 cose da fare a New York)

329
Cheap Eats
(mangiare con meno di 15 dollari)

15
Portraits of New York
(ritratti di New York)

337
Shopping in New York
(dove comprare)

51
Restaurants & Recipes
(ristoranti e ricette)

347
Family Attractions
(attrazioni per famiglie)

319
Where to Stay
(dove dormire)

352
Angel of Harlem
(un romanzo breve)

366
Index of Recipes
(indice ricette)

editoriale
foreword

This book has been published in 2015, but it started to take shape in 1996, the year I arrived in New York for the first time. Admiring the skyline from the taxi was enough to understand that I'd fallen in love with this city. After my first walk in Manhattan I realized that it was a different kind of love, stronger than the one you feel for the city where you were born. It wasn't only the beauty of the Big Apple that was striking my heart, because as much as New York is wonderful, it's certainly not a paradise on Earth. It was rather for its ability to surprise, for the energy springing out of every corner and every neighborhood, for the friendliness of the New Yorkers, who are always ready to hug and help a stranger, even if he has his mysteries, risks and diversities.
I love London; I would happily live in Sydney; I love Barcelona; Shanghai and Singapore excite me, but what I feel here is completely different. The vibes I feel when walking the streets in Harlem, the joy that I experience when I jog in Central Park, the curiosity to know the stories and lives of those who pass by, are all things that only happen to me nowhere else in the world but here. I can't explain it, but this is it, and it happens to me every time I return: the excitement before the departure, the feeling that in this city anything can happen and come true, the tears I can't ever stop the day I leave. I know, I might seem stupid, but New York has this effect on me. But mind you, New York isn't America. It's more, it's magic, it's exaggeration, it's madness and desire. New York is the world. It's the heart that beats like a drum, the hope for change, the incubator and the container of the dreams of millions of people. Even yours.
I hope this book can convey to you a part of my endless love for this city, because at least, I'll be able to say that I have returned the love that New York has given me.

Questo libro è uscito nel 2015, ma ha iniziato a prendere forma nel 1996, l'anno in cui arrivai a New York per la prima volta. Bastò ammirare lo skyline dal mio taxi per capire che mi sarei innamorato di questa città. E dopo la prima passeggiata a Manhattan compresi che era un amore diverso, più forte perfino rispetto a quello che si prova per la città in cui si è nati. E non era solo la bellezza della Grande Mela che mi stava colpendo al cuore, perché per quanto New York sia meravigliosa, non si tratta certo di un paradiso sulla Terra. Era invece per la sua capacità di stupire, per l'energia che sprizza in ogni angolo e in ogni quartiere, per la disponibilità dei newyorkesi, sempre pronti ad abbracciare e aiutare lo sconosciuto, perfino quando porta con se misteri, rischi e diversità.
Vedete, adoro Londra, vivrei volentieri a Sydney, amo Barcellona, mi eccitano Shanghai e Singapore, ma quello che sento qui è completamente diverso. Le vibrazioni che provo camminando per le vie di Harlem, la gioia che vivo quando corro a Central Park, la curiosità di conoscere le storie e la vita di chi mi passa accanto sono cose che mi accadono solo qui e in nessun'altra parte del mondo. Non so spiegarvene il perché, ma è così, e mi succede ogni volta che ci torno: l'eccitazione prima della partenza, la sensazione che in questa città tutto possa accadere e realizzarsi, le lacrime che non riesco mai a fermare il giorno in cui vado via. Lo so, vi sembrerò stupido, però a me New York fa questo effetto. Ma badate bene, New York non è l'America. È altro, è magia, esagerazione, follia e desiderio. New York è il mondo. È il cuore che batte a mille, la speranza di un cambiamento, l'incubatore e il contenitore dei sogni di milioni di persone. Anche del vostro.
Spero che questo libro riesca a trasmettervi almeno un po' del mio infinito amore per questa città, perché così potrò dire di aver ricambiato l'amore che New York mi ha donato.

fabio mollica
author of the book

Sivan Askayo
Travel Photographer

sivanaskayo.com

What do you like about NYC and New Yorkers?
I Love New York City's dynamics and energy. It is such a fast-paced city and so many things are happening at the same time, that you can't always follow up. It fits well my personality and my profession as a Photographer as I am always in search of visual stimulation. I can never get bored in New York and I am always inspired. This is where the things are happening. And this is what I actually like about New Yorkers; We have seen it all but we never get tired of new adventures.

What do you dislike about NYC and New Yorkers?
I would like to say that I love everything about New York. I even got used to the cold winters, but then again, I don't like these vortex snow storms we just had last winter. The only time I don't like New Yorkers is when they are crammed next to me in the Subway.

What's your favorite restaurants?
I have few favorite locations spread out in the city. Cafe Gitane in Mott street, Nolita, is a French Moroccan restaurant I always love going. I usually take my friends who come to visit me for a brunch there. I like their avocado, lemon juice, olive oil, chili flakes on seven grain toast and the Moroccan couscous with red peppers, potatoes, raisins, toasted pine nuts, hummus and eggplant. Buvette Gastrotheque in West Village is a french feel bistro in such a leafy street in the West Village. There is a French New Yorkish atmosphere, great selection of wine and a chocolate mousse dessert to die for. I always enjoy passing through Eataly in the Flatiron district. This store is spread out on one block and

I always like walking through it from one end to another. I go through the cheese section to the pasta restaurant, the bakery and the gelato, and I feel like I've been transferred to Italy in no time. For a really fun and quick bite I like Wesville (various locations in the city). I wait in line and I don't care how long it takes to get the corn on the cob topped with lime, cumin butter and cotija cheese. It is such a 'licking-fingers' dish. Sushi: I love to go to Kawa Sushi in the Meat Packing/West Village area. They serve fresh sushi and sashimi. It is like eating in Nobu without fearing your bank clerk will call you the next day.

A place for shopping?
B&H, for camera and photography equipment. McNally Jackson in Prince street for books. J. Crew and Anthroplogie for clothes.

Your favourite place/area in the city?
West Chelsea-Hands down. All the area of the Meat Packing District and the High Line is my favorite area at the moment. I always find what to shoot there. I like going there mostly on Thursday evenings for Gallery Hopping and Openings. I've been shooting two hotels in that area too so been spending a lot of time there lately.

A place that tourists can't miss?
'Sleep No More' and I won't say more about it. Trust me, it is a "must see".

Your next project/dream?
My dream project is probably traveling to Italy to shoot a book about Hotels and Food.

(italian text at page 362)

100 things
to do in New York
100 cose da fare a New York

1) Go running in Central Park without headphones and listen to the birds sing. **2)** Go Kayaking on the Hudson River (Pier 40, 72nd Street). **3)** Have a picnic on Governors Island at the weekend. **4)** Visit the 9/11 Memorial Museum, to not forget the horrific actions humans are capable of. **5)** Attend a gospel mass in Harlem. **6)** Take a walk on the High Line. **7)** Take a tour of the museums. **8)** Stroke the Wall Street bull for good luck (its testicles or nose). **9)** Go ice skating in Central Park or at Rockefeller Center. **10)** Play basketball in the Tompkins Square Park playground in the East Village. **11)** Go walking along the charming Spring Street. **12)** Eat hot dogs from the street vendors scattered around the city. **13)** Have fun with the coolest dancers in New York, every weekend in Union Square. **14)** See a Broadway musical! **15)** Buy the New York City Pass to save on tickets to six famous tourist attractions. **16)** Request a Metrocard or make a temporary subscription to save money on the subway. **17)** Experience the East Village nightlife on Friday nights. **18)** For women: get your nails done in one of the hundreds of nail-shops in Manhattan. **19)** For men: getting a haircut in New York is expensive (usually not less than $ 40) but it's an experience. **20)** Go shopping in Times Square: you can't resist the temptation and the sight of the giant advertising screens. **21)** Take a view from the sky: from the terrace of the Empire State Building or from Top of The Rocks. The panorama is breathtaking. **22)** Visit the Statue of Liberty. **23)** New York is the most beautiful city to photograph, so take your camera and enjoy! There is even a two and a half hour tour that will make you discover the most photogenic city sites (citifari.com). **24)** Admire the majesty of the Grand Central Station hall. **25)** Spend an hour in Washington Square Park. **26)** Spend money, lots of money, wandering around shops and shopping centres. **27)** Enjoy the view of the large and small mural art on the city's buildings. **28)** Take part in the New York City Marathon (even if you don't complete it, it will still be an unforgettable day). **29)** Listen to Jazz music at Minton's, the famous jazz club in Harlem (mintonsharlem.com). **30)** Have a doughnut (or donuts) indigestion for breakfast! **31)** Have lunch and dinner by trying all the street-food that you see whilst walking around the city. **32)** Walk across the Brooklyn Bridge. **33)** If you want to take a ride on the rickshaws, ask the price per minute before getting on to avoid unpleasant and expensive surprises. **34)** Use the City Bikes to save

1) Correre a Central Park senza cuffie, ma ascoltando il cinguettio degli uccelli. **2)** Fare Kayak sull'Hudson River (Pier 40, 72th Street). **3)** Un pic-nic a Governors Island nel fine-settimana. **4)** Visitare il 9/11 Memorial Museum, per non dimenticare l'orrore che l'uomo è in grado di causare. **5)** Assistere ad un messa-gospel ad Harlem. **6)** Passeggiare sulla High-Line. **7)** Fare il tour dei musei. **8)** Accarezzare i testicoli o il naso del toro di Wall Streets: dicono che porti fortuna. **9)** Pattinare sul ghiaccio sulla pista di Central Park o del Rockefeller Center. **10)** Giocare a basket al playground del Tompkins Square Park, nell'East Village. **11)** Passeggiare e fare shopping nell'incantevole Spring Street. **12)** Mangiare gli hot dog ai carretti sparsi per la città. **13)** Divertirsi con i ballerini più cool di New York, in scena ogni week-end a Union Square. **14)** Vedere un musical a Broadway! **15)** Acquistare la New York City Pass per risparmiare sui biglietti d'ingresso a sei famose attrazioni turistiche. **16)** Richiedere una Metrocard o sottoscrivere abbonamenti temporanei per risparmiare denaro in metropolitana. **17)** Vivere la movida dell'East Village il venerdì sera. **18)** Per le donne: farsi le unghie in uno delle centinaia di nail-shop disseminati per Manhattan. **19)** Per gli uomini: un taglio di capelli a New York costa caro (generalmente non meno di 40 dollari) ma è un'esperienza da vivere. **20)** Shopping a Times Square: non potrete resistere alla tentazione. E allo spettacolo del megaschermi pubblicitari. **21)** Uno sguardo dal cielo: dalla terrazza dell'Empire State Building o da Top of The Rocks. Panorami mozzafiato. **22)** Visitare la Statua della Libertà. **23)** Non ce ne voglia il resto del mondo, ma New York è la città più bella da fotografare, quindi armatevi di fotocamera e divertitevi! C'è perfino un tour di 2 ore e mezza che vi farà scoprire gli angoli più fotogenici della città (citifari.com). **24)** Ammirare la maestosità del salone di Gran Central Station. **25)** Trascorrete un'ora in Washington Square Park. **26)** Spendere soldi, tanti soldi, girovagando per negozi e centri commerciali. **27)** Godersi lo spettacolo dei murales, piccoli e grandi, che adornano i palazzi cittadini. **28)** Correre la New York City Marathon (anche se non arriverete al traguardo, sarà un giorno indimenticabile). **29)** Ascoltare musica Jazz al Minton's, lo storico locale jazz di Harlem (mintonsharlem.com). **30)** Fare colazione con una indigestione di doughnuts (o donuts)! **31)** Pranzare e cenare provando tutto lo street-food che vi si presenta davanti passeggiando per la città. **32)** Attraversare a piedi il ponte di Brooklyn. **33)** Se volete fare un giro sul risciò, chiedete il prezzo per minuto prima di salire a bordo: eviterete spiacevoli e costosissime sorprese. **34)** Sfruttate le City Bike per risparmiare denaro e muoversi agevolmente senza perdersi nemmeno un angolo della città. **35)** Per le donne:

money, and move around easily without missing any parts of the city. **35)** For women: admire the most handsome men in the world. **36)** For men: admire the most attractive and sexy women in the world. **37)** You'll spend a fortune in tips. **38)** Take part in one of the many national parades organized through the streets of Manhattan: whether it's Puerto Rican, Irish or Italian, it's always a feast of colours, culture and music. **39)** Find a taxi driver that was born in New York. **40)** Take photos of the giant Christmas tree at Rockefeller Center and Diker Lights in the Italian neighbourhood of Brooklyn (12th Ave & 84th St). **41)** Celebrate the New Year in Times Square. **42)** Go shopping in the Union Square Holiday Market, one of the most beautiful Christmas Markets in New York. **43)** Are you searching for a personal shopper to guide you on a tour of the trendiest stores? Contact Roxy Hauldren: shopwithrox.nyc **44)** Street-food, shopping, restaurants, beautiful people: at Chelsea Market you will find all this, and much more. **45)** Take your children to the magical world of M & M's or Toys-R-Us. **46)** Celebrate the Chinese New Year (February) in Chinatown: better-chinatown.com. **47)** Do you like beer? Don't miss the New York City Beer Week (at the end of February): newyorkcitybrewersguild.com. **48)** Dine in great restaurants without emptying your wallet during the NYC Restaurant Week: $25 for lunch and $38 for dinner. Starred restaurants too (www.nycgo.com/restaurantweek). **49)** Sip some of the best cocktails in the world in bars and restaurants. **50)** Take your children to a dream land in the Coney Island Luna Park fun-fair. **51)** Queue to get your own plate of chicken rice from the Halal Guys (53 street, avenue 6). **52)** Buy your beloved a bouquet of flowers, choosing from one of the many on display at every street corner. **53)** Take your children to the carousel in Dumbo, right under the Brooklyn Bridge. **54)** Watch a Knicks game at Madison Square Garden. **55)** Dive into the Central Park North swimming pool (in the summer). **56)** Go to the Statue of Liberty by ferry. **57)** Enjoy the many shows and open-air cinemas in the summer that bring the parks to life at night (they are often free). **58)** Bargain with the Chinese people in the Chinatown shops (if you want to get good deals, always offer half of what they ask for). **59)** Play chess with the New Yorkers in Union Square (usually $ 5 per game, or

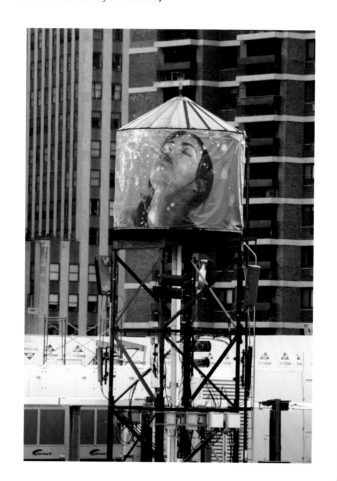

you can take classes for a fee). **60)** Visit the MoMA (Friday afternoons the admission is free but "with an offering"). **61)** Go on a crazy shopping spree and get lost in the largest and most interesting stores (Macy's, Urban Outfitter, Uniqlo, H & M, Abercrombie...). **62)** Take your children to the American Museum of Natural History. **63)** Spend a Friday or Saturday night in one of the clubs in the Meatpacking District. **64)** Go to the Pier 25, Hudson River Park, and spend an afternoon doing one of the many activities including mini-golf, beach-volley, skateboarding, ice skating and more. **65)** Buy vintage clothes, jewellery and antiques at the Brooklyn Flea Market

ammirare per strada gli uomini più belli del mondo. **36)** Per gli uomini: ammirare le donne più attraenti e sexy del mondo. **37)** Spenderete una cifra (una grossa cifra!) in mance. **38)** Partecipate ad una delle tante parate nazionali organizzate per le strade di Manhattan: che si tratti di portoricani, irlandesi o italiani, è sempre una festa di colori, valori, musica. **39)** Riuscire a trovare un tassista nato a New York. **40)** Fotografare l'albero di Natale gigante al Rockefeller Center e le Diker Lights nel quartiere italiano di Brooklyn (12th Ave & 84th St) . **41)** festeggiare il Capodanno a Times Square. **42)** Fare acquisti all'Union Square Holiday Market, uno dei mercatini di Natale più belli di New York. **43)** Cercate una personale-shopper che vi guidi in un tour dei negozi più trendy? Contattate Roxy Hauldren: shopwithrox. nyc. **44)** Street-food, shopping, ristoranti, bella gente: al Chelsea Market troverete tutto questo, e molto altro ancora. **45)** Portare i vostri bambini nel magico mondo di M&M's o Toys-R-Us. **46)** Festeggiare il Capodanno cinese (febbraio) a Chinatown: betterchinatown.com. **47)** Vi piace la birra? Non perdetevi la New York City Beer Week (a fine febbraio): newyorkcitybrewersguild.com. **48)** Mangiare in grandi ristoranti senza svuotare il portafogli? È possibile, durante le Nyc Restaurant Week: 25 dollari a pranzo e 38 a cena, anche in ristoranti stellati (www.nycgo.com/restaurantweek). **49)** Sorseggiare i migliori cocktail del mondo, in giro per bar e ristoranti. **50)** Far sognare i vostri figli al luna park di Coney Island. **51)** Fare la fila per avere il proprio piatto di chicken rice dagli Halal Guys (53 strada, 6 avenue). **52)** Regalare un mazzo di fiori alla propria amata, scegliendo tra le decine di soluzioni in esposizione ad ogni angolo di strada. **53)** Portare i figli alla giostra di Dumbo, proprio sotto il ponte di Brooklyn. **54)** Vedere una partita dei Knicks al Madison Square Garden. **55)** Tuffarsi nella piscina di Central Park Nord (d'estate). **56)** Andare in traghetto alla Statua della Libertà. **57)** Godersi i tanti spettacoli notturni e i cinema all'aperto che d'estate fanno vivere i parchi anche di notte (spesso sono gratuiti). **58)** Contrattare con i cinesi nei negozi di Chinatown (se volete fare buoni affari offrite sempre la metà di quanto chiedono). **59)** Giocare a scacchi con i newyorchesi a Union Square (solitamente ci si gioca 5 dollari a partita, oppure si possono prendere lezioni a pagamento). **60)** Visitare il MoMa (il venerdì pomeriggio l'ingresso è gratuito "con offerta libera"). **61)** Darsi allo shopping sfrenato perdendosi negli store più grandi e interessanti (Macy's, Urban Outfitter, Uniqlo, H&M, Abercrombie...). **62)** Portare i bambini all'American Museum of Natural History. **63)** Trascorrere il venerdì o il sabato notte in uno dei club del Meatpacking District. **64)** Andare al Pier 25, sull'Hudson River Park, e trascorrere un pomeriggio scegliendo tra mini-golf, beach-volley, skate, pattinaggio sul ghiaccio e molto altro ancora. **65)** Acquistare abiti vintage, gioielli e pezzi d'antiquariato al "mercato delle pulci" di Brooklyn (www.broklynflea.com). **66)** Pregare nella cattedrale di St. Patrick. **67)** Fotografare il Flatiron e chiedersi come faranno a muoversi nelle stanze con

(www.broklynflea.com).

66) Pray in St. Patrick Cathedral. **67)** Photograph the Flatiron and wonder how people move in the rooms with the narrower angle. **68)** Have fun finding places where the most famous films and the most popular TV series have been filmed. **69)** Eat pastrami in Katz's, the oldest and most famous deli in New York. **70)** Visit the wonderful New York Botanical Garden in the Bronx. **71)** Devour a burger from Shake Shack! **72)** Take a break and eat a slice of pizza for 99 cents. **73)** Watch a tennis match at the US Open. **74)** Visit the Brooklyn Brewery, the oldest and most popular brewery in New York. **75)** Go to a concert at the Lincoln Center. **76)** If you are passionate about books and reading, you can't miss the New York Public Library hall, it's wonderful. **77)** Take a night tour on one of the many boats that sail around Manhattan. **78)** Savour a cupcake or some chocolate desserts from one of the many bakeries and pastry shops in the city. **79)** Drink a cocktail at the Standard Hotel rooftop. **80)** Take photographs with the street performers, like the Naked Cowboy or the topless girls in Times Square. **81)** Eat in a steakhouse. **82)** Photograph the Chrysler Building, for many, the most beautiful skyscraper in the world.

83) Ask someone to take a photograph of you and your partner in front of the word "Love" (between Sixth Avenue and 55th Street). **84)** Spot celebrities in restaurants, bars or simply in the street. **85)** Get a photo with the New York policemen or firemen. **86)** Take a step back in time in the Ellis Island Museum, where millions of immigrants arrived between 1892 and 1954. **87)** Have a "Passion and Love" in the Oficina Latina, in the East Village: a glass of rum, and a few "sniffs" of coffee, brown sugar and cinnamon. **88)** Indulge in ocean oysters and lobster rolls. **89)** If you like folk music, don't miss the Brooklyn Folk Festival (brooklynfolkfest.com). **90)** Have a film feast at the Tribeca Film Festival (tribecafilm.com/festival) or the Brooklyn Film Festival (brooklynfilmfestival. org). **91)** Relax in Bryant Park, by doing tai chi or yoga, or by taking part in literature and poetry reading groups, piano and guitar performances, watching films. **92)** Spend a couple of hours at the South Street Seaport (Pier 17, southstreetseaport.com), among shops, restaurants and various attractions: but you'll have to wait until the finish of the renovations. **93)** Go running along the East River promenade, under the Williamsburgh, Manhattan and Brooklyn bridges, where the Chinese exercise in the early morning. **94)** If you want to deepen your knowledge of New York, visit the Museum of the City of NY (mcny.org) on Fifth Avenue. **95)** Get to know more about Mr. Jazz, Louis Armstrong, by visiting his house-museum in Queens (louisarmstronghouse.org). **96)** Take a trip back to the medieval times by visiting The Cloisters, a monastery located in Fort Tryon Park (metmuseum.org/visit/visit-the-cloisters). **97)** Take a walk around Little Italy and Chinatown. **98)** Play golf at the Chelsea Pier. **99)** Decide whether you love or hate New York. **100)** Return to New York!

l'angolo più stretto. **68)** Divertirsi a scovare i luoghi in cui sono state girate le scene dei film più famosi e delle serie tv più popolari. **69)** Mangiare il pastrami da Katz's, il deli più famoso e antico di New York. **70)** Visitare il meraviglioso New York Botanical Garden, nel Bronx. **71)** Divorare un hamburger da Shake Shack! **72)** Ristorarsi mangiando un trancio di pizza a 99 cents. **73)** Guardare una partita di tennis agli US Open. **74)** Visitare la Brooklyn Brewery, il più vecchio e popolare birrificio di New York. **75)** Assistere ad un concerto al Lincoln Center. **76)** Se siete appassionati di libri e letture, non perdetevi il salone della New York Public Library: è meraviglioso. **77)** Fare il tour notturno su uno dei tanti battelli che navigano intorno a Manhattan. **78)** Assaporare un cupcake o qualche dolce al cioccolato in uno dei numerosi negozi-pasticcerie della città. **79)** Sorseggiare un drink sulla terrazza dello Standard Hotel, con vista su downtown. **80)** Farsi immortalare con gli artisti di strada, the Naked Cowboy o le ragazze in topless a Times Square. **81)** Mangiare in una steak-house. **82)** Fotografare il Chrysler Building, per molti il più bel grattacielo del mondo. **83)** Farsi fotografare con la compagna o il compagno davanti la scritta Love (tra la sesta Avenue e la 55esima strada). **84)** Scovare qualche celebrità nei ristoranti, nei bar o semplicemente per strada. **85)** Farsi una foto con i poliziotti o con i vigili del fuoco di New York. **86)** Fare un salto indietro nel tempo al museo di Ellis Island, il luogo in cui - tra il 1892 e il 1954 - arrivarono milioni di immigrati. **87)** Farsi un "Passion and Love" all'Oficina latina, nell'East Village: un bicchierino di rum e delle sane "sniffate" di caffè, zucchero di canna e cannella. **88)** Abbuffarsi di ostriche oceaniche e panini all'aragosta. **89)** Se siete appassionati di musica folk, non perdetevi il Brooklyn Folk Festival (brooklynfolkfest.com). **90)** Fare una scorpacciata di film al Tribeca Film Festival (tribecafilm.com/festival) o al brooklyn Film Festival (brooklynfilmfestival.org). **91)** Rilassarsi a Bryant Park, facendo tai chi oppure yoga, o partecipando a reading di letteratura e poesia, performance di pianoforte e chitarra, programmazioni di film. **92)** Trascorrere un paio d'ore al South Street Seaport (Pier 17, southstreetseaport.com), tra negozi, ristoranti e attrazioni varie: ma dovrete attendere che finiscano i lavori di ristrutturazione. **93)** Correre lungo la East River promenade, passando sotto i ponti di Williamsburgh, Manhattan e Brooklyn, dove i cinesi fanno esercizi ginnici al mattino presto. **94)** Se volete approfondire le vostre conoscenze su New York, visitate il Museum of the City of NY (mcny.org) sulla Quinta Strada. **95)** Conoscere meglio Mr Jazz, Louis Armstrong, visitando la sua casa-museo nel Queens (louisarmstronghouse.org). **96)** Tuffatevi nell'era Medioevale visitando The Cloisters, un monastero situato a Fort Tryon Park (metmuseum.org/visit/visit-the-cloisters). **97)** Fare un giro a Little Italy e Chinatown. **98)** Giocare a golf al Chelsea Pier. **99)** Decidere se amate o odiate New York. **100)** Tornare a New York!

NEWYORKERS
Trisha Krauss
Illustrator

(www.trishakrauss.com)

What do you like about NYC and Newyorkers?
The best thing about New Yorkers is the New York sense of humour. I also admire and enjoyed New Yorkers' ability to work and play equally hard. New York is the funnest city I have ever lived in and it is the place I have worked the most. There is a great atmosphere of promise, hope, optimism, enthusiasm and that any thing is possible in life. I also love the drama of a big snow storm and of a day that is 100 degrees in the shade with 100 percent humidity. It brings out the true survivors in life. New York is full of survivors. I love the food, bars and restaurants in New York.

What do you dislike about NYC and Newyorkers?
After many years in New York I began to dislike all of the things I loved most about it (the extremes, the pace, the enthusiasm). However I never stopped liking toe food or the people. I met some of the best people in my life in New York City and I stay in touch with them after 10 years of being away. I love New Yorkers unconditionally and I am so grateful that I was one for so many years.

What is your favourite restaurant?
Bar Piti. It is a classic and it is such a wonderful place to be on a hot summers night. It is also very close to where I use to live in the West Village.

The best place for shopping?
Century 21 has great designer bargains. Bergdorf Goodman is where I prefer to shop because of the old style department story charm and service. It comes at a very high price but it is worth it.

Where is your favourite place in the city?
West Village.

A place or thing that tourists can't miss?
The High Line in the Meat Packing District, The Tenement Museum in the Lower East side. A walk across the Brooklyn Bridge. Grocery shopping at Zabar's on the upper West side, followed by a picnic in Central park.

What is your next project/dream?
My biggest project at this very moment is to finish my book that I am illustrating for Random House US. My dream is to write and illustrate many more books for Random House and other publishers. My non-work dream is to restore and decorate an old doll's house that I purchased. I also would like to have a month without a project just to see how it feels.

(italian text at page 362)

Portraits of
NEW YORK

BRIDGES

CENTRAL PARK

BUILDINGS

NEW YORK

SKYSCRAPERS

HUMANS OF NEW YORK

COLORS OF NEW YORK

NYPD·ENY

A LOGO FOR
AMERICA

WE PRAY FOR PEACE
IN THE MIDDLE EAST!

"I EARN
I GO TO SCHOOL"

"...ARE ME T....NOTHER"

PLACES

GELA REED KYTE   SUSAN M. SAUER   EDWARD

MAS DEAN   TIMOTHY E. REILLY   ALAN JAY

CE ROBERT PASSANANTI

JANIC

NEWYORKERS
Ornella Fado
Creator, Author and Host
of the TV Program
"Brindiamo" on NYCTV

What's your favourite area in NY?
I've been living on the Upper West Side for the past 20 years, and I love it. I'm very close to Lincoln Center (I adore ballet and opera), Central Park, Riverside and Museums such as the Natural History Museum. I have been very lucky because the schools here are really good; my daughter for example went to La Guardia High School and the School of American Ballet, both of wich are in the area.
What do you dislike of New York and New Yorkers?

I like everything about NY, I truly love the energy that I feel when I walk around the city... I feel at home.
Any favourite restaurants?
I have many favourite restaurants, thanks to my work, wich brings me to some of the best restaurants in the city. I would suggest "SD26" (at 26 street and 5th) and "Buddakan" (in the Meatpacking district). While "La Masseria" is perfect before or after going to a Broadway show.
A place for shopping?

I love to shop at Saks, on 5th Avenue: they also provide me with wardrobe for the show. I also adore "Michael's", the arts and craft shop. I really enjoy painting and scrapbooking.
Your next project/dream?
In 2015 I celebrated 10 years of Broadcasting, so let's think to the next 10!.

(italian text at page 362)

NEWYORKERS
Jessi Colasante
Singer

What do you like about NYC and Newyorkers?

There is no place like it in the world. There is an honest air about it and the people in it. I am a born and bread New Yorker therefore NY has always been my home in every sense. Folks here are real whether you want them to be or not and that is something I adore!

What do you dislike about NYC and Newyorkers?

I dislike gentrification which has moved at an extremely rapid pace over the last 15 years. Neighborhoods are no longer communities as the people who once inhabited them were forced to move. Rent is through the roof even in areas which used to be affordable, and often I feel like a stranger in my own home. The "transplants" as I call them often bring an "attitude" of what New Yorkers are supposed to be like which we aren't at all. There is a general lack of respect for what and who were once here. .

What is your favourite restaurant?

Pizzetteria Brunetti West Village NYC

The best place for shopping?

Astoria Queens - Steinway Street

Where is your favourite place in the city?

That's a tough one. Really depends on my mood. East Village some days, West Ville another,... Can't say there is a favorite.

A place or thing that tourists can't miss?

Stay away from the tourist attractions! Go to different neighborhoods and sample cuisine from all over the world, for example Chinatown, Williamsburg etc... If you are into the arts, do your homework before coming! There are always great musical acts, exhibits and live performances of all kinds to see.

What is your next project/dream?

To continue pursuing music. I am enjoying collaborating with other bands and producers.

Our Bests

BEST DINNER
Cherry - Salinas - Dovetail

BEST LUNCH
A Voce - Benoit - MP Taverna

BEST LOCATION-DINING ROOM
21 Club - Catch - Jacob's Pickles - Oceana- Cherry

BEST CHEFS
Bryce Shuman (Betony) - Mads Refslund (ACME) - Pino Coladonato (La Masseria-Masseria dei Vini)

THE CHEF'S CHOICE
Gnocco - Kafana - Au Za'atar

BEST SERVICE
Betony - Cherry - Balade

BEST BRUNCH
Five Leaves - Lexington Brass

BEST BURGER
Benoit - 21 Club

BEST ITALIAN RESTAURANT
La Masseria dei Vini

BEST ETHNIC RESTAURANT
The Cecil

BEST APPETIZER
Lobster roll (Ed's Lobster)
Croquetas de txipiron (Salinas)
Octopus & chikpeas (MP Taverna)

BEST ENTREES
Gumbo (The Cecil)
Low country shrimp (The Redhead)
Grilled lamb rack (Flinders Lane)

BEST DESSERT
Fuji apple goya (Cherry)
Vanille millefouille (Benoit)
Malva pudding cake (The Cecil)

BEST PASTA
Lobster Ravioli (Ed's Lobster)
Uovo in Raviolo (SD26)
Agnolotti (A Voce)

BEST PIZZA
Tartufata (Gnocco)
Margherita (Pizzetteria Brunetti)
Quadrata (Luzzo's)
Frutti di mare (Masseria dei Vini)

BEST STEAK
Entrana (El Almacen)
Kansas city steak (BLT Prime)
Wagyu on a rock (Catch)

BEST SUSHI & SASHIMI
Omakase chef's selection (Cherry)
Spicy tuna pizza (Mira Sushi)
Soft Shell Crab (Bond St)

BEST FISH
Smoked Trout (Dovetail)
Crispy Whole Snapper (Catch)
Sardines (Kafana)

BEST COCKTAILS
Oficina Latina
Wallflower
MP Taverna

Albin Konopka
Music Director, Composer

What do you like about New York and New Yorkers?
Who said I liked New Yorkers? I'm only partially kidding. Although they aren't warm and friendly, in general New Yorkers are happy to talk to you if only to give you their opinion on anything. Just read this interview if you don't believe me!
New York is still the capital of the world. I enjoy the ethnic diversity you find here. Because the city is actually quite small physically, the diffe-

rent ethnic groups often mix, as well as having their own neighborhoods. I love going to Chinatown both in Manhattan and Queens, or Little Russia by the Sea in Brighton Beach, I live in the remnants of Spanish Harlem and I love my little bodega grocer that actually has butchers that grind my ground beef in front of me and carve me a steak out of a side of beef. There is a grocer in Little India that has literally hundreds of herbs, spices as well as exotic oils and some things I

have no idea what they are. You want baked goat heads? Go to Greek town in Queens. Nicaraguan tamales wrapped in banana leaves-no problem! Turtle blood soup-try Chinatown. It's delicious! Finally, we have what must be the largest theater center in the whole world. If you love musical theater, this is the place. Apologies to London's West End.
What don't you this like about New York and New Yorkers?

About New York, there's too much trash on the street. The sanitation department can't keep up with the amount of trash we make. The city is very noisy. Ambulances and fire trucks abuse, not use, their sirens. I've seen a fire truck, sirens blaring, park and shop at West Side market. I've seen an ambulance run through a red light with it's siren on, pull up to a Five Guys and get a burger. It's funny because it's one of the largest cities in the world but New Yorkers are very provincial and jingoistic. If you think everything you do is the best-then there's no reason to try to improve. New Yorkers think everything here is the best! Ask a New Yorker and they will tell you our subway system is the best in the world! It's not. It might be one of the largest and one of the few that run all night, but it's dirty, noisy and antiquated. Most metro systems today run on rubber tires which last longer, are cheaper to replace, and most importantly for me, so much more quiet. Ours is still metal wheels scraping against metal rails. When they break....!

I remember when I first went to London in the 70's, the "tube" had these displays that told you how long before the next train arrives, ...we haven't even finished installing this system in our trains in 2015! That's roughly 40 years later!

Your best restaurants?
Don Antonio's for pizza. Thai Market for Thai, The Curry Club for Indian, Gallagher's for Steaks. Edi and The Wolf for Fusion Austrian

A place for shopping?
The Internet!

What's your favorite place in the city?
The High Line and The North Woods section of Central Park. We have some great museums: Met, Moma, The Frick, Natural History. And then there's Times Square.

A place or a thing that tourists shouldn't miss?
Well, you have to see the 9/11 Memorial if only to pay your respects. The High Line is unique. Basically, I would say see the things I listed as my favorites.

Your next project/dream?
I do what I love to do. I am a musician. It's a struggle but I'm glad I don't have an office job. I have a great family and I am loved. I'm living my dream! *(italian text at page 396)*

NEWYORKERS
Daniela Kucher
Blogger
and Photographer

(www.firstgenerationfashion.com)

What's your favourite area in NY?
I love that NYC is always changing. It's impossible to get bored living here because there is always something new and exciting to discover. I also love the diversity in New York City. I am very passionate about travel and culture and feel very fortunate to have friends who originate from all over the world.
What do you dislike of New York and New Yorkers?
New Yorkers are always in a rush. I enjoy walking around the city and taking photographs, but in certain areas people are always bumping into me.
Any favourite restaurants?
I usually choose my favorite places in NYC based on ambience; I love a place with good energy and great drinks. My favorite is La Esquina -- it's a Mexican restau-

rant hidden beneath a taqueria in Nolita. It's kind of like a speak easy. They offer the perfect combination of delicious cocktails, fun music, and dancing, so I always have a great time there.
A place for shopping?
NYC is the only place in the world that offers so many amazing sample sales. Sample sales are a good way to get your hands on designer one-of-a-kind pieces for a bargain. If you need help finding sample sales, you should check out Racked.com
Your favourite place/area in the city?
One of my favorite places to go to in the summer is Prospect Park. There is a bandshell where many musicians perform during the summer. You can bring a picnic basket filled with food and drinks and listen to the music under

the trees. When you're there, you forget you're in the middle of the busiest city in the world.
A place or a thing that tourists can't miss?
Try to talk to the locals to find out the best places and restaurants. There is so much to explore about New York City that doesn't appear on Trip Advisor or Yelp. I started First Generation Fashion to help people discover the cultural side of New York City from the NYC native perspective. If that appeals to you, our website is filled with tips and a city guide for dining.
Your next project/dream?
To grow my website First Generation Fashion into my full time career.

(italian text at page 363)

Restaurants &
Recipes
Ristoranti e Ricette

21 CLUB

Owner / Titolare › Belmond Group • **Chef** › Sylvain Delpique

21 West 52nd Street • Ⓜ 5 Av/53 St • +01 212 582 7200 • **www.21club.com**

There are several things to know before going to 21 Club. The first is that this is not a restaurant, it's an institution: dozens of movies have taken shots in this place, and hundreds of State leaders, actors and celebrities have sat at these tables. The second is that here there is a no jeans or sneakers policy, and for men, suit jackets are required. The dining rooms are elegantly casual (sporty even), and leave you stunned. Third and last thing: If you wonder why Americans spend so much money to eat an hamburger, you'll find the answer in 21 Burger. Whether you like American cuisine or not, 21 is worth a visit, because it embodies the soul of New York, it is a wonderful place with excellent service and a spectacular wine list. As for the food, we were pleasantly surprised by the tuna tartare and the meat one, by the burger (really top level) and by the desserts, they are all great.

Ci sono diverse cose da sapere prima di entrare al 21 Club. La prima è che questo non è un ristorante, ma una istituzione: decine di film hanno ripreso questo posto, e centinaia di capi di Stato, attori, celebrities si sono seduti a questi tavoli. La seconda è che qui non sono ammessi jeans e sneakers, e per gli uomini è richiesta la giacca; ma le sale sono di una eleganza informale (e perfino sportiva) che lascia di stucco. Terza ed ultima cosa: se vi chiedete perché gli americani spendono così tanti soldi per mangiare un hamburger, la risposta la troverete nel 21 Burger. Che siate amanti o meno della cucina americana, il 21 merita una visita, perché incarna l'anima di New York, perché è un posto meraviglioso con un servizio eccellente ed una lista visti spettacolare. Quanto al cibo, noi siamo rimasti piacevolmente sorpresi dalla tartare di tonno e da quella di carne, dal burger (davvero di livello superiore) e dai dolci, tutti ottimi.

Wine List › Carta dei Vini	**Cuisine** › Cucina	**Lunch** › Pranzo	**Dinner** › Cena
1500 Labels › Etichette	**American** › American	$ 50	$ 65-100

New York cheesecake with passionfruit coulis and almond struesel

INGREDIENTS FOR 8-10 INDIVIDUAL CHEESECAKES:

Graham Crust:
- 15 graham crackers (crushed)
- 2 tbsp melted butter

Cheesecake:
- 8 oz. cream cheese (soft)
- 3/8 c sugar - 2 eggs (at room temperature)
- 1 vanilla bean (scraped)
- ½ tsp vanilla extract
- 1 lemon juice (fresh)
- graham crust (recipe below)

Passion Fruit Coulis:
- 8 oz passion fruit purée
- 1 ½ c orange juice
- 1 c sugar
- 2 tbsp pectin

Almond Streusel:
- 1 c butter (at room temperature)
- 1 c confectioners' sugar
- ½ c all purpose flour
- ½ c almond flour
- ½ c sliced almonds

Graham Crust:

Crush the graham crackers (you can use a food processor, or just place them in a plastic bag and go to town with a rolling pin) and place in a bowl. Melt the butter, pour over the crushed grahams and, using your hands, mix until the crumbs are slightly damp. If you squeeze a small amount with your hand, they mix should clump up. Prepare a 9" cake round (spring form if you have it: if you are using a spring-form pan, tightly wrap the outside of the pan with foil to avoid leakage from the water bath you'll be baking in) by greasing the bottom and placing a round of parchment paper down. Dump the graham cracker mixture on top and, using your hands or a glass, pack down the mixture to form the crust. Set aside and make the cheesecake batter.

Cheesecake:

Pre-heat your oven to 325°F, and set a kettle to boil water for your water bath. Make sure that all the ingredients are at room temperature; this will ensure that there are no lumps in the final batter.Beat cream cheese with the paddle attachment in a stand mixer (or with a hand mixer) to soften it. Scrape the bowl with a spatula, then add the sugar and the vanilla scrapings.Scrape the bowl again to make sure all ingredients are well-combined, then add in the eggs, lemon juice, and vanilla extract. Beat until well-mixed, then pour onto the prepared crust. Place the pan in a larger baking dish (a casserole or brownie pan works nicely), then pour the boiled water (carefully) around the cheesecake tin. Place in the oven, and bake for 35-45 minutes, or until the center of the cake is no longer soupy (there will be a slight jiggle when you shake the pan, but it shouldn't appear to be liquid). Remove the pan from its water bath and allow to cool completely at room temperature, then refrigerate for at least two hours before attempting to remove it from the pan.

Passion Fruit Coulis:

This has a couple of specialty ingredients that are relatively easy to find these days: passion fruit puree can be found in the frozen food section of most grocery stores, usually near the international section (Goya makes a great option, and they have a whole section in most freezer aisles); pectin is available in most baking aisles, near the sugar, and is usually surrounded by products to make jams and jellies. Look for "classic pectin" or "apple pectin", rather than "instant"... you'll get a much better texture and flavor this way. In a small bowl, combine the sugar and pectin and mix together well (this will avoid lumps in your final product). In a pan, combine the passion fruit puree and orange juice over medium heat. Whisking constantly, slowly stream in the sugar/pectin mixture. Make sure not to just dump it in: you'll end up with clumps of uncooked pectin in your final sauce and no one wants that. Continue cooking, whisking constantly, until the mixture reaches a boil. The mixture will start to thicken nicely; keep whisking while at a boil, counting to 30 in your head. When you hit 30, cut the heat, and transfer the sauce to a small bowl. Cool the sauce quickly by placing that bowl into a larger bowl filled with ice water. Be careful that none of the ice bath drips into your sauce.

Almond Streusel:

Pre-heat the oven to 325°F. Using the paddle attachment, beat the softened butter with the confectioners' sugar until well-combined. Add in the all-purpose flour, almond flour, and sliced almonds. Mix until just combined, then spread the dough over a parchment-lined sheet tray, crumbling it with your hands.Bake for 15-20 minutes, until nicely golden brown. Depending on your oven, you might want to turn the tray halfway through baking to avoid burnt spots. Allow to cool completely before crushing up the streusel. You can make the pieces are large or small as you want, but we aim for pea-sized crumbs, using the "plastic bag and rolling pin" trick.
Store in a container with a tight-fitting lid and reserve.

A VOCE
Owner / Titolare › Marlow Abela • **Chef** › Bew Lee

41 Madison Avenue (at 26th Street) • **M** 28 St • +01 212 545 855 • **www.avocerestaurant.com**

Us Italians, when it comes to food, think we are superior to all, and always fear going to an Italian restaurant abroad: there are too many fakes around the world. Also, if the Italian restaurant is American-owned and the chef is not from the Bel Paese, many doubts arise. But once the threshold of "A Voce" is crossed, all fears dissolve: the place is beautiful, refined, elegant and romantic. The food is great, definitely worthy of the best Italian restaurants. In the menu, you can find specialties from different regions of the country that is famous for its good food. Do not miss the burratina and the quail, the cassoncini and gnocchetti, as well as tuna and lamb. The agnolotti are outstanding, and the desserts admirably end an unforgettable meal. The service is excellent. What else to say: one of the restaurants in New York where you will always want to return to again.

Noi italiani, che sul cibo pensiamo di essere superiori a tutti, abbiamo sempre qualche timore quando entriamo in un ristorante italiano all'estero: troppi fake in giro per il mondo. Se poi il ristorante italiano è di proprietà americana e lo chef non è del Bel Paese, i dubbi aumentano. Ma una volta varcata la soglia di "A Voce", tutti i timori si dissolvono: il posto è bellissimo, raffinato, elegante e romantico. Il cibo è strepitoso, sicuramente degno dei migliori ristoranti italiani. E nel menù si ritrovano specialità di varie regioni del paese famoso per la sua buona cucina. Da non perdere la burratina e la quaglia, i cassoncini e gli gnocchetti, così come anche il tonno e l'agnello. Gli agnolotti sono eccezionali, e i dolci chiudono egregiamente un pasto indimenticabile. Il servizio è eccellente. Che dire: uno dei ristoranti newyorchesi dove avrete sempre voglia di tornare.

Wine List › Carta dei Vini	**Cuisine** › Cucina	**Prix-fixe Lunch** › Pranzo a prezzo fisso	**Dinner** › Cena
750 Labels › Etichette	**Modern Italian** › Italiana	$ 40 (three courses) › 3 portate	$ 55-75

Agnolotti, lemon ricotta, shrimp, salsa verde pesto

Agnolotti, ricotta al limone, gamberi, pesto salsa verde

INGREDIENTS FOR 6 SERVINGS:
Pasta Dough: - 2 lb of flour - 1 cup of canola oil - A drop of water **Lemon Ricotta:** - 4.5 lb of ricotta - 4 ea lemon zest - 2 cups of parmesan - 1 ea egg **Salsa Verde Pesto:** - 1 qt of picked parsley - 1 qt of picked basil - ½ qt of picked tarragon - 1 qt of picked mint - 1 qt of spinach - 1 garlic clove - 2 ea anchovy fillet - 1 tsp of dijon mustard - ¼ cup of extra virgin olive oil **Method::** - 14 ea agnolotti - 3 oz of shrimp - ½ oz of pine nuts - ½ oz of pansito - ½ oz of butter - 1,25 oz of pesto - ¼ oz of grated parmesan - 1,25 oz pesto - ¼ oz grated parmesan

INGREDIENTI PER 6 PERSONE:
Impasto pasta: - 907 g di farina - 1 cl di olio di canola - una goccia d'acqua **Ricotta al limone:** - 2041 g di ricotta - scorza di 4 limoni - 2 tazze parmigiano (200 g circa) - 1 uovo **Pesto Salsa Verde:** - 1 parte di prezzemolo fresco - 1 parte di basilico fresco - ½ parte di dragoncello fresco - 1 parte di menta fresca - 1 parte di spinaci - 1 spicchio d'aglio - 2 filetti d'acciuga - 1 cucchiaino di senape di Digione - ¼ cl di olio extravergine d'oliva **Piatto:** - 14 agnolotti - 85 g di gamberetti - 14 g di pinoli - 14 g di pansito - 14 g di burro - 35 g di pesto - 7 g di parmigiano grattugiato

Pasta: Put the flour into a kitchen aid bowl, add the eggs and mix at speed 2. Mix until the dough looks smooth, for about 6 minutes. Remove from bowl and put into a large ziploc bag. Leave to rest at room temperature for 20 minutes.
Lemon Ricotta Filling: Mix all ingredients together, season with salt and pepper to taste.
Roll out the pasta dough. Pipe the lemon ricotta filling and make agnolotti shapes. Put in a parchment-lined sheet tray with semolina flour on the bottom and place in the fridge until ready to use.
Salsa Verde Pesto: Blanch herbs and shock in ice water. Squeeze remaining water out of herbs. Mince the garlic and puree all the ingredients in a blender with extra virgin olive oil. If necessary, add a touch of ice water.
To cook: Heat the pesto and spoon it onto a plate. Bring a pot of water to boil and cook pasta until 90% done. In a sauté pan, combine some butter and pasta water, then add the cooked pasta. Add the shrimp, and cook until just pink. Finish off with chopped parsley and parmesan.
Plate agnolotti and shrimp on top of pesto. Sprinkle with breadcrumbs, pine nuts and parmesan.

Pasta: Mettete la farina in una ciotola, aggiungete le uova e mescolate a velocità 2. Mescolate per circa 6 minuti, fino a quando l'impasto è liscio. Togliete l'impasto dalla ciotola e ponetelo in un sacchetto sottovuoto grande. Lasciate riposare a temperatura ambiente per 20 minuti.
Ripieno di ricotta al limone: Mescolate tutti gli ingredienti e aggiungete sale e pepe quanto basta.
Stendete l'impasto. Adagiateci sopra il ripieno di ricotta al limone con un tubo e date la forma agli agnolotti. Poneteli su un vassoio ricoperto di carta da forno e spolverato con farina di semola. Mettete tutto in frigo fino al momento di cottura.
Pesto Salsa Verde: Scottate le erbe e raffreddatele in acqua ghiacciata. Strizzatele per rimuovere l'acqua in eccesso. Tritate l'aglio e frullate tutti gli ingredienti con l'olio extra vergine d'oliva. Se necessario, aggiungete un tocco d'acqua ghiacciata.
Riscaldate il pesto e mettetelo sul fondo di un piatto con un cucchiaio.
Portate una pentola d'acqua ad ebollizione e cuocete la pasta al 90%. In una padella, unite il burro con dell'acqua della pasta e aggiungete la pasta. Aggiungete i gamberi e lasciate cuocere fino a quando si colorano di rosa. Infine aggiungete prezzemolo tritato e parmigiano. Adagiate la pasta e i gamberetti sopra il pesto. Aggiungete una spolverata di pangrattato, pinoli e parmigiano.

TALÒ › Verdeca Puglia IGP
CANTINE SAN MARZANO

Colore giallo paglierino con riflessi dorati; al naso rivela sorprendenti profumi di fiori bianchi e vaniglia; al palato è fresco e giustamente minerale con una buona persistenza sapida.
Abbinamenti: Frutti di mare, crostacei e pesci lessi con salse leggere.

Straw yellow colour with green reflections; Scotch broom notes and a hint of citrus and tropical fruits on the nose. Lively in acidity, fresh and mineral.
Best served with: Excellent with starters and fish soup, fresh cheese and pasta with light sauces.

Cassoncini, portobella filling, prosciutto

Bomboloni

INGREDIENTS:
Bomboloni Dough (about 60 pieces): - 240 gr of milk - 16 gr of dry yeast - 110 gr of sugar - 120 gr of sour cream - 4 eggs - 775 gr of all purpose flour - 7 gr of salt - 70 gr of shortening - vanilla sugar
Pastry Cream: - 1 qt of milk - 220 gr of sugar - 50 gr of cornstarch - 120 gr of egg yolks - 1 Vanilla Bean Salted Caramel **Sauce (2 Quarts):** - 500 gr of sugar - 250 gr of water - 500 gr of glucose - 225 gr of butter - 1 qt of cream- 1 t salt

INGREDIENTI:
Impasto Bomboloni (circa 60 pezzi): - 240 g di latte - 16 g di lievito secco - 110 g di zucchero - 120 g di panna acida - 4 uova - 775 g di farina - 7 g di sale - 70 g di grasso - zucchero alla vaniglia **Crema pasticcera:** - 950ml di latte - 220 g di zucchero - 50 g di amido di mais - 120 g di tuorli d'uovo - 1 baccello di vaniglia
Glassa di caramello salata (2 lt circa): - 500 g di zucchero - 250 g di acqua - 500 g di glucosio - 225 g di burro - 950 ml di panna - 1 cucchiaino di sale

Pastry Cream Filling: Mix sugar and cornstarch together in a pot. Whisk in the egg yolks. Add a small amount of milk to make a slurry, then continue whisking in the rest of milk. Add the vanilla bean. Bring to a boil and thicken for 1 minute. Strain and chill.
Bomboloni: Heat milk to about 100°F. Bloom yeast for 3-4 minutes. Mix in sour cream and eggs. Combine flour, sugar, and salt in a Kitchen Aid. Add the wet ingredients. Mix for 2 minutes until dough is formed. Add shortening in increments. Mix for another 2 minutes. Proof for 2 hours and punch down dough. Let rest for 10 minutes, then roll out.
Salted Caramel Sauce: Cook the sugar, water, and glucose until a very dark caramel. Add diced butter gradually. Once emulsified, slowly add the cream. When the mixture is homogenous, remove from heat and add salt.
To cook: Fry 5 pieces of bomboloni dough. Fill them with pastry cream. Toss in vanilla sugar. Serve with 1 oz of salted caramel sauce.

INGREDIENTS FOR 4 SERVINGS:
Cassoncini Dough: -4 lbs italian 00 flour - ½ lb butter, cut - ½ pt. water (add more as needed) - salt, handful
Filling: -1 lb. portobello mushrooms - 3 shallots - 4 sprigs of thyme - ¼ C butter - ½ lb spinach - 2 teeth of garlic - 5 oz ricotta cheese - 2 oz parmesan cheese - 1 lb mozzarella fresh - 1 lb straccino cheese - 2 eggs - 1 tsp chilli pepper - 1 dash colatura

Cassoncini Dough: Put all the ingredients in a mixer, except water. Mix for 2-3 minutes. Add water, mix until dough comes together. **Mushrooms:** Clean Portobello and cut into 1-inch squares. In a pot with oil and butter, stew mushrooms, thyme, and shallots at low heat for 30 min reserve. Mix in food processor.**Spinach:** Blanch spinach in salted water and refresh. Chop spinach and then sauté in olive oil and garlic. Reserve. **Cheese:** Mix the ricotta, eggs parmesan and straccino in the food processor. Grate mozzarella cheese and reserve. **Cook:** In a bowl mix mushroom, spinach, cheese, chili, colatura, salt and pepper. Roll out Cassoncini dough. Fill with mixture and seal. Fry the Cassoncini at 350 degrees Fahrenheit for about 2 minutes. Season as they come out of fryer. Serve with sliced Prosciutto di Parma

Ripieno di crema: In una pentola, unite zucchero e amido di mais. Aggiungete i tuorli d'uovo sbattuti. Aggiungete una piccola quantità di latte alla volta e continuate a mischiare fino ad averlo aggiunto tutto. Aggiungete il baccello di vaniglia. Portate il tutto ad ebollizione e fate addensare per 1 minuto. Filtrate e lasciate raffreddare.
Bomboloni: Scaldare il latte a circa 38°C. Ravvivate il lievito per 3-4 minuti. Aggiungete la panna e le uova. Unite la farina, lo zucchero e il sale con un mixer. Aggiungete gli ingredienti umidi. Mescolate per 2 minuti, fino ad ottenere un impasto. Aggiungete il grasso in piccole quantità. Mescolate per altri 2 minuti. Lasciate lievitare per 2 ore e infine lavorate ancora l'impasto con le mani. Lasciate riposare per 10 minuti, poi stendetelo.
Glassa di caramello salata: Cucinate lo zucchero, con l'acqua e il glucosio fino ad ottenere un caramello molto scuro. Aggiungete il burro a dadini gradualmente. Una volta emulsionato, aggiungete lentamente la panna. Quando la miscela è omogenea, togliete dal fuoco e aggiungete il sale.
Procedimento: Friggete 5 pezzi di impasto per bomboloni. Riempite con la crema. Passateli nello zucchero vanigliato. Servite con 28 gr di glassa di caramello salata.

ACME

Owner / Titolare › Jean-Marc Houmard, Huy Chi Le, Jon Neidich • **Chef** › Mads H. Refslund

9 Great Jones • M Bleecker St • +01 212 203 2121 • **www.acmenyc.com**

 Ten years ago, nobody would have bet a dollar, a euro or a pound on the success of the north Europe-an cuisine: the popularity of Noma in Copenhagen, of René Redzepi, has caught everyone off guard and today even in America, the land of meat eaters for excellence, restaurants offering an incredible amount of dishes based on herbs, tubers, flowers and roots in their menu are very popular. The cuisine of Mads Refslund, co-founder of Noma is today the soul of Acme, it's also substance, and above all ta-ste, as well as experimentation. We really liked everything about Acme, except for the entrance, which is more suited to a bar than a high quality restaurant: the interior is very well cared for, the ambience - and the customers - very cool. And the dishes offer extraordinary flavors, that enhance poor and very often overlooked ingredients. Just for the record: Mads, despite the successes, has remained a friendly lad and is always helpful. And this increases the good vibes towards him and his restaurant.

Dieci anni fa nessuno avrebbe scommesso un dollaro, un euro o una sterlina sul successo della cucina nordeuropea: la popolarità del Noma di Copenaghen, di René Redzepi, ha colto tutti in contropiede e oggi perfino in America, terra di carnivori per eccellenza, spopolano i ristoranti che propongono in menù una incredibile quantità di piatti a base di erbe, tuberi, fiori e radici. Ma la cucina di Mads Ref-slund, cofondatore del Noma e oggi anima dell'Acme, è anche sostanza, e soprattutto sapore, oltre che sperimentazione. Dell'Acme ci è piaciuto davvero tutto, eccezion fatta per l'ingresso del ristorante, che si addice più ad un bar che ad un ristorante di qualità: gli interni sono molto ben curati, l'ambiente - e la clientela - very cool. E i piatti offrono sapori fuori dal comune, che esaltano ingredienti poveri e mol-to spesso trascurati. Giusto per la cronaca: Mads, malgrado i successi, è rimasto un "ragazzo" alla mano, sempre disponibile. E questo aumenta la simpatia nei suoi confronti e nei confronti del suo ristorante.

Wine List › Carta dei Vini	**Cuisine** › Cucina	**Brunch**	**Dinner** › Cena
100 Labels › Etichette	**New American**	$ 25-35	$ 50-65

Summer Strawberries

**INGREDIENTS
FOR 4 SERVINGS:**
Creme fraiche parfait:
- 100 g of crème fraiche
- 50 g of sugar
- 40 g of heavy cream
- 7 g of lemon juice
- 7 g of water
- Zest of one lemon

Put sugar, crème fraiche and heavy cream into a bowl and wisk until the volume has doubled. Fold in the lemon juice, water and zest. Place in plastic container and freeze.

Strawberry powder:
Blend freeze-dried strawberries and mix with tapioca maltodextrin (5:1 strawberry to malto). Scoop out the inside of 5 large strawberries with a melon baller. Scoop out some balls of parfait with same size scoop. Place balls inside the strawberries and arrange on a plate. Scatter with strawberry powder.

Smoked salmon tacos
Tacos di salmone affumicato

INGREDIENTS FOR 4 SERVINGS:
Taco dough: - 8 ea eggs - 400 g "00" flour - 600 g of rye flour - 500 g of corn meal - 200 g of sagamite - 60 g of kosher salt **Taco filling:** - 1 qt of cold smoked salmon - 1 pint of chopped pickled cauliflower - 1 cup of yolk custard (egg yolks cooked in a water bath at 65°C for 35 minutes) - 2 tbl of chopped chives - 1 tbl of chopped capers - 2 tbl of blis brand fish sauce

Roll dough out on pasta machine to about 1/8 in thickness. Punch out circles with a number 80 cookie cutter. Fry dough in taco baskets at 350° until dark brown.
Add lemon juice and salt to taste.
Fill 3/4 of the taco shells with the filling and finish with a spoonfull of trout roe.

INGREDIENTI PER 4 PERSONE:
Impasto tacos: - 5 lt di acqua - 8 uova - 400 g di farina "00" - 600 g di farina di segale - 500 g di farina di mais - 200 g di Sagamite - 60 g di sale kosher **Farcitura tacos:** - 950 g di salmone affumicato - 470 ml di cavolfiore sott'aceto tritato - 240 g di crema di tuorlo (tuorli d'uovo cotti a bagnomaria a 65°C per 35 minuti) - 2 cucchiai di erba cipollina tritata - 1 cucchiaio di capperi tritati - 2 cucchiai di salsa di pesce BLIS

Stendete l'impasto con la macchina per pasta a circa 1/8 di spessore. Tagliate dei cerchi con un coppa pasta da 80. Friggeteli in cestini per tacos a 350 gradi fino a quando diventano marrone scuro.
Aggiungete succo di limone e sale qb.
Riempite i tacos a 3/4 con la farcitura e finite aggiungendo un cucchiaio di uova di trota.

Fermented corn sauce

Salsa di mais fermentato

Take 1000 g of corn kernels and cover with 20 g of salt. Place in a plastic or non-reactive container and press. Let sit for two weeks at room temperature.
Take one cup of fermented corn and blend until smooth in a vita prep. Mix with two cups of crème fraîche and lemon juice to taste.

Take one cup of fermented corn and blend until smooth in a vita prep. Mix with two cups of crème fraîche and lemon juice to taste. Roast chanterelles and corn in sauté pan. In a separate small cast iron pan, fry a duck egg. Season the duck egg and cover with the roasted mushrooms and corn. Spoon the fermented corn sauce over the dish. In a small bowl, mix a small handfull of nasturtium leaves, sunflower leaves, pea tendrils and sea purslane with lemon juice and thyme oil. Cover the egg dish with the small herb salad. Finish off with black pepper.

Ricoprite 1000 g di chicchi di mais con 20 g di sale. Mettete il tutto in un contenitore di plastica per alimenti e pressate. Lasciate riposare per due settimane a temperatura ambiente. Frullate una parte di mais fermentato. Aggiungete due parti di crème fraîche e succo di limone a piacere.

Scottate i funghi chanterelle e il mais in una padella. A parte, friggete un uovo d'anatra in una piccola padella in ghisa. Condite l'uovo con sale e pepe qb e copritelo con i funghi e il mais. Aggiungete la salsa di mais fermentato. In una ciotola, frullate una piccola manciata di foglie di nasturzio, foglie di girasole, viticci di pisello e della porcellana di mare con del succo di limone e olio di timo. Terminate il piatto con l'insalata di erbe e del pepe nero.

AU ZA'ATAR

Owner / Titolare › Tarik Fallous • **Chef** › Tarik Fallous

188 Avenue A • **M** 1 Av [L] • +01 212 254 5660 • **www.auzaatar.com**

Au Za'atar is a nice restaurant in the East Village that offers an interesting French-Arabic cuisine at very attractive prices for what the New York standards are: a lunch and a dinner from $14 to $24 are a really good deal in this area. If you are wondering what Arabic cuisine has to do with French cuisine, the answer is: very little, but Beirut was a French colony, and this is enough to justify some pleasant mingling. The other thing that we loved is that all the dishes in this restaurant have a high quality standard: from the tabouli salad to the hummus, from the baba ghanoush to the couscous royal, the lamb shank and the grilled meat, it is a succession of good food. If there is an ideal place where a New Yorker could eat, even every day, Au Za'Atar is perfect.

Au Za'Atar è un ristorante carino nell'East Village che propone una interessante cucina araba-francese a costi davvero interessanti per quelli che sono gli standard newyorchesi: un pranzo a 14 dollari e una cena a 24 sono davvero un gran bell'affare da queste parti. Se vi state chiedendo cos'abbia a che fare la cucina araba con quella francese, la risposta è: davvero poco. Ma Beirut fu colonia francese, e questo basta a giustificare alcune piacevoli commistioni. L'altra cosa che ci è piaciuta molto è che tutti i piatti del ristorante hanno uno standard di qualità elevato: dal tabouli salad all'hummus, dal baba ghanoush al cous-cous royal, fino al lamb shank e alla carne grigliata, è tutto un susseguirsi di buone portate. Ecco, se c'è un posto dove un newyorchese mangierebbe tutti i giorni, quello sarebbe Au Za'Atar.

Wine List › Carta dei Vini	**Cuisine** › Cucina	**Lunch** › Pranzo	**Dinner** › Cena
22 Labels › Etichette	**Arabian/French** › Araba/Francese	$ 14-20	$ 24-35

Hummus

Braised lamb shank
Stinco d'agnello brasato

INGREDIENTS FOR 4 SERVINGS:
- 2 tbsp of extra-virgin olive oil - 4 one pound lamb shanks - salt and freshly ground pepper - 5 garlic cloves, peeled - 4 medium carrots, sliced 1/4 thick - 4 medium celery ribs, sliced ¼ inch thick - 1 large onion, coarsely chopped - 1 750ml bottle of dry red wine - 1 cup of water - 3 bay leaves - 2 oranges diced - 3 dried prunes

Preheat the oven to 325°. In a large enameled cast-iron casserole, heat the olive oil. Season the lamb shanks with salt and pepper and brown them on 3 sides over moderately high heat, for about 4 minutes per side. Add the garlic, carrots, celery and onion to the casserole. Add the red wine and boil for 3 minutes. Add the water and bring to a simmer. Add the bay leaves and prunes. Cover the casserole tightly and transfer to the oven. Braise the lamb shanks, turning once, for about 1 1/2 hours, or until very tender. Transfer the lamb shanks to an ovenproof serving dish. Using a fine sieve, strain the braising liquid into a medium saucepan, pressing on the solids. Boil the braising liquid over high heat until reduced to 1 1/2 cups, for about 20 minutes. Season the sauce with salt and pepper and pour about 1/2 cup over the lamb shanks. Keep the remaining sauce warm. Cover the lamb shanks with foil and reheat them in the oven for about 10 minutes. Serve the lamb shanks with the remaining sauce.

INGREDIENTI PER 4 PERSONE:
- 2 cucchiai di olio extravergine di oliva - 4 stinchi d'agnello da 450 g l'uno - sale e pepe macinato fresco - 5 spicchi d'aglio sbucciato - 4 carote medie a rondelle da 6 mm - 4 gambi di sedano medi tagliati in pezzi da 6 mm - 1 grande cipolla tritate grossolanamente - una bottiglia da 750 ml di vino rosso secco - 235 ml di acqua - 3 foglie di alloro - 2 arance a dadini - 3 prugne secche

Riscaldate il forno a 160°C. Scaldate l'olio d'oliva in una grande casseruola in ghisa. Condite gli stinchi con sale e pepe e fateli rosolare su 3 lati a fuoco abbastanza alto per circa 4 minuti per lato. Aggiungete l'aglio, le carote, il sedano e la cipolla, infine il vino rosso, ch lascerete bollire per 3 minuti. Versate l'acqua e lasciate cuocere a fuoco lento. Aggiungete le foglie di alloro e le prugne. Coprite bene la casseruola e mettetela in forno. Brasate gli stinchi, girandoli una volta, per circa un ora e 1/2, o fino a quando la carne diventa molto tenera. Ponete gli stinchi in una pirofila da portata. Usando un setaccio fine, filtrate il liquido della brasatura in una padella media e fate pressione sulle parti solide. Lasciate bollire il liquido per circa 20 minuti a fuoco alto fino a ridurre a 350ml. Condite la salsa della brasatura con sale e pepe e versatene circa 118ml sugli stinchi. Mantenete in caldo la parte rimanente della salsa. Coprite gli stinchi con carta di alluminio e metteteli riscaldare in forno per circa 10 minuti. Servite gli stinchi con la salsa rimanente.

INGREDIENTS FOR 4 SERVINGS:
- 2 cups of drained well and cooked chickpeas, liquid reserved
- ½ cup of tahini (sesame paste) - ¼ cup of extra-virgin olive oil
- 2 cloves og garlic, peeled - Salt - Juice from 1 lemon
- Chopped fresh parsley leaves to garnish

INGREDIENTI PER 4 PERSONE:
- 400 g di ceci ben cotti scolati (tenete da parte il liquido) - 112 g di tahini (pasta di sesamo) - 59 ml di olio extra vergine di oliva - 2 spicchi d'aglio sbucciato - sale - succo di 1 limone - foglie fresche di prezzemolo tritato per guarnire

Put everything except thåe parsley in a food processor and begin to process, add the chickpea liquid or water as needed to allow the machine to produce a smooth puree.
Taste and adjust with parsley and olive oil. Serve.

Unite tutto tranne il prezzemolo in un robot da cucina e aggiungete il liquido dei ceci o l'acqua necessaria per consentire che si formi una purea liscia. Assaggiate e condite quanto basta con il prezzemolo e un filo di olio evo. Servite.

ANNIVERSARIO 62 › Primitivo di Manduria DOP Riserva
CANTINE SAN MARZANO

Colore rosso rubino molto carico ed elegante, profumo ampio e complesso, fruttato con sentori di prugne, confettura di ciliegia e note di tabacco, leggermente speziato. Vino di grande corpo, morbido e ricco di tannini nobili, con un finale che regala note di cacao, caffè e vaniglia. **Abbinamenti:** Carni rosse, selvaggina, primi piatti robusti. Vino da meditazione.

Intense ruby red colour, wide and complex to the nose; fruity, with a prune and cherry jam aroma, with notes of tobacco, slightly spicy. A full-bodied wine, soft and rich in fine tannins, with notes of cocoa, coffee and vanilla in the end.
Best served with: Red meat, game, savoury first courses. Meditation wine.

Tabouli salad
Insalata Tabouli

Namoura

INGREDIENTS FOR 4 SERVINGS:
- 2 cups of semolina
- 2 cups of sugar
- 1 teaspoon of baking soda
- 72 blanched almonds
- 1 tablespoon of butter
- 2 cups of yoghurt
- 1 cup of coconut
- 2 tablespoons of tahini

INGREDIENTI PER 4 PERSONE:
- 334 g di semola
- 450 g di zucchero
- 1 cucchiaino di bicarbonato di sodio
- 72 mandorle sbucciate
- 1 cucchiaio di burro
- 490 g di yogurt
- 100 g di cocco
- 2 cucchiai di tahin

Grease a 9x13 baking pan with tahini to avoid sticking. Put all ingredients (except maple syrup) together in a bowl and blend until the batter is smooth. Spread the batter smoothly and flatly into the pan. Place almonds to cover the surface. Bake in the oven at 250° for one hour. Check it after 45- minutes, it should be a light golden brown colour. Let the namoura cool for 10 minutes before pouring one cup of maple syrup over the pan. With a watered knife, cut the Namoura with evenly spaced diagonal lines across the long end and then across the short end to create diamond shaped pieces.
Be sure to cut around the almonds if possible so that each piece has one almond in the centre. Also, when cutting, use an up and down motion as you would when cutting a cake.

Ungete una teglia da 9x13 con il tahini. Mettete in una ciotola tutti gli ingredienti (tranne lo sciroppo d'acero) e mescolate fino a quando l'impasto è liscio. Stendete l'impasto uniformemente nella teglia. Mettete le mandorle sulla superficie. Mettere in forno a cuocere a 120°C per un'ora. Controllate dopo 45 minuti, dovrebbe essere di un marrone dorato chiaro. Lasciate che il Namoura si raffreddi per 10 minuti prima di versarci sopra 230ml di sciroppo d'acero. Con un coltello bagnato, tagliate il Namoura con linee diagonali equidistanti prima da un lato e poi dall'altro per creare pezzi a forma di diamante. Assicuratevi, se possibile, di tagliare intorno alle mandorle, in modo che ogni pezzo abbia una mandorla al centro. Inoltre, durante il taglio, utilizzate un movimento in su e giù come quando si taglia una torta.

INGREDIENTS FOR 6 SERVINGS:
- 3 bunches of finely chopped flat leaf parsley - 1 cup of chopped fresh mint - 2 or 3 tablespoons of fine bulgur - 1 chopped firm tomato - ½ onion or 2 scallions chopped - ½ cup of extra Virgin olive oil - ¼ cup of fresh lemon juice - salt to taste

INGREDIENTI PER 6 PERSONE:
- 3 mazzetti di prezzemolo a foglia piatta tritati finemente - 25 g di menta fresca tritata - 2-3 cucchiai di bulgur fino - 1 pomodoro duro tritato - ½ cipolla o 2 scalogni tritati - 118 ml di olio extra vergine di oliva - 59 ml di succo di limone fresco - sale qb

Prepare the chopped parsley and mint and set aside.
In a large bowl, mix chopped onions/scallions, Bulgur, chopped tomatoes with fresh lemon juice and salt.
Add to them the parsley and mint and olive oil and mix.

Lavare e tagliare il prezzemolo e la menta, quindi mettere da parte. In una coppa mischiare la cipolla, il Bulgur, i pomodori tagliati a pezzettini, il succo di limone. Salate quanto basta. Aggiungere il prezzemolo, la menta e l'olio: girare e servire.

AWADH

Owner / Titolare › Gaurav Anand • **Chef** › Gaurav Anand

2588 Broadway (97/98 St.) • Ⓜ 96 St • +01 646 861 36041 • **www.awadhnyc.com**

Chef/Restaurateur Gaurav Anand of the 2-star Moti Mahal Delux and Bhatti Indian Grill brought unique regional Indian cuisine to the Upper West Side. The restaurant showcases the cooking traditions of its namesake northern Indian region along with a sophisticated wine and cocktail program, and tea selection from an estate in the foothills of the Himalayas. Anand, known for his delicately balanced spicing and melt-in-your-mouth kebabs, has immersed himself in the dum pukht practice of Awadhi cooking, traveling to Lucknow, "the city of the Nawabs" or India's rulers, in the center of the Awadh region in state of Uttar Pradesh. Dum pukht involves slow cooking in a traditional sealed handi over a low flame for many hours, allowing deep, complex flavors to develop. Although an occasional dum pukht-cooked dish can be found at other New York restaurants, Awadh will be the only one highlighting the cuisine and techniques of the region.

Lo chef e proprietario Gaurav Anand, già due stelle al Moti Mahal Delux and Bhatti Indian Grill, ha portato la cucina dell'India del Nord nell'Upper West Side e la propone in un ristorante davvero carino progettato da Laura Weatherbee. La particolarità della sua cucina sono le cotture prolungate e a fuoco basso, effettuate nei tipici recipienti utilizzati nella regione dell'Uttar Pradesh. Piatti speziati, ricchi di sapori e profumi, accompagnati da una buona selezione di vini e di the. Questi ultimi provengono da una piantagione ai piedi dell'Himalaya. Awadh è il posto più adatto, anche in considerazione dell'ottimo prezzo, per avvicinarsi alla cucina indiana e farsi un'idea di quanto essa sia variegata e ricca: una esplosione di profumi, colori e sapori che infiammano il palato.

Wine List › Carta dei Vini	**Cuisine** › Cucina	**Prix-fixe Lunch** › Pranzo a prezzo fisso	**Dinner** › Cena
50 Labels › Etichette	**Indian** › Indiana	$ 12	$ 40

Lamb Biryani

Agnello Biryani

INGREDIENTS FOR 4 SERVINGS:
For the Lamb and Gravy: - 1 lb of lamb - ¾ cup of ghee - 2 green cardamom seeds, whole - 2 pieces of whole mace - 2 bay leaves - 2 cinnamon sticks - 1 cup of onion, julienned - 2 tbsp of ginger and garlic paste - 1 tsp of degi mirch (red chile powder) - 3 ½ tbsp of milk curd - 2 cups of hot water - 1 tsp of mace powder - ½ tsp of cardamom powder - 1 tbsp of kewra water - 1 tbsp of rose water - 1 pinch of saffron, soaked in 2 tbsp of warm water for 10 minutes - salt to taste
For the Rice: - 6 cups of water - 2 cups of basmati rice - 5 cardamom seeds, whole
For the Lamb Dum Biryani: - ginger, peeled and cut into 10 strips - 10 coriander leaves - 6 mint leaves - 1 tbsp of saffron water - ½ cup of melted butter - 3 ½ tbsp of heavy cream - 1 ½ tbsp of yellow onion - 6 green chiles, seeds removed and sliced - salt to taste

INGREDIENTI PER 4 PERSONE:
Per l'Agnello e il Sugo: - 450 g di agnello - 170 g di burro ghi - 2 semi interi di cardamomo verdi - 2 pezzi interi di macis - 2 foglie di alloro - 2 bastoncini di cannella - 150 g di cipolla a julienne - 2 cucchiai di zenzero e pasta aglio - 1 cucchiaino di Degi mirch (polvere rossa chile) - 3 ½ cucchiai di latte cagliato - 500 ml di acqua calda - 1 cucchiaino di macis in polvere - ½ cucchiaino di cardamomo in polvere - 1 cucchiaio di acqua kewra - 1 pizzico di zafferano lasciato in 2 cucchiai di acqua tiepida per 10 minuti - sale qb
Ingredienti Riso: - 1500 ml di acqua - 400 g di riso Basmati - 5 semi di cardamomo interi
Ingredienti Agnello Dum Biryani: - zenzero, sbucciato e tagliato in 10 pezzi - 10 foglie di coriandolo - 6 foglie di menta - 1 cucchiaio di acqua di zafferano - 115 g di burro fuso - 3 ½ cucchiai di panna - 1 ½ cucchiaio di cipolla gialla - 6 peperoncini verdi, tagliati a fette e senza semi - sale qb

How to cook the meat:
Melt ghee in a pan. Add cardamom, mace, bay leaves and cinnamon and sauté for few seconds over medium heat.
When the spices start to brown, add onion and cook it on low flame until golden brown.
When the onions are well cooked, add meat pieces along with ginger and garlic paste, salt, degi mirch and cook for 20 minutes until the meat has browned.
Add milk curd and hot water and let cook on moderate heat untill the meat is tender, for about 35 - 45 minutes. Once the meat is almost done remove from flame and allow it to cool.
When it cools down, take the meat pieces out and cook the gravy again for 5 minutes and add the mace and cardamom powder, kewra and rose water and one tablespoon of saffron water. Reserve the remaining saffron water.

How to cook the rice:
Wash the rice thoroughly in water and soak for about 30 minutes. Heat 6 cups of water in a large pot and when the water starts boiling, add the rice and cardamom seeds.
Cook the rice over medium heat for 12 to 15 minutes.
When the rice is halfway done, strain all the water and allow it to cool.

How to cook Lamb Dum Biryani:
In a heavy bottomed copper pot, spread an even layer of rice and lamb along with lamb gravy, ginger, coriander and mint leaves.
Add another layer of rice, add the remaining tablespoon of saffron water, the melted butter, the cream and the brown onion. Top with sliced green chiles.
Cover the pan and seal the sides with aluminum foil or a flour dough and cook over a very low flame for 10 minutes making sure not to release the steam.

Come cucinare la carne:
Fate sciogliere il burro in una padella. Aggiungete il cardamomo, il macis, le foglie di alloro e la cannella e lasciate rosolare per qualche secondo a fuoco medio. Quando le spezie iniziano a colorarsi, aggiungete la cipolla e fate cuocere a fuoco basso fino a doratura. Quando le cipolle sono ben cotte, aggiungete i pezzi di carne con lo zenzero e la pasta d'aglio, il sale, il degi mirch e lasciate cuocere per 20 minuti fino a quando la carne risulta dorata. Aggiungete il latte cagliato e l'acqua calda e lasciate cuocere a fuoco moderato per 35-45 minuti, fino a quando la carne diventa tenera. Una volta che la carne è quasi cotta del tutto, togliete dal fuoco e lasciate raffreddare. Quando si è raffreddata, togliete i pezzi di carne e cuocete ancora il sugo per 5 minuti aggiungendo il macis e il cardamomo in polvere,il kewra, l'acqua di rose e 1 cucchiaio di acqua di zafferano. Tenete da parte la restante acqua di zafferano.

Come cucinare il riso:
Lavate il riso accuratamente e lasciatelo a bagno per circa 30 minuti. Scaldate l'acqua in una pentola capiente e quando inizia a bollire, aggiungete il riso e i semi di cardamomo. Cucinate il riso a fuoco medio per 12-15 minuti. Quando il riso è a metà cottura, scolate tutta l'acqua e lasciatelo raffreddare.

Come cucinare l'agnello Dum Biryani:
In una pentola di rame dal fondo pesante, create uno strato uniforme di riso e agnello, aggiungete il sugo d'agnello, lo zenzero, il coriandolo e le foglie di menta. Aggiungete un altro strato di riso e condite con la parte rimanente di acqua di zafferano, il burro fuso, la panna e la cipolla dorata. Infine, aggiungete le fette di peperoncini verdi. Coprite la padella e sigillate i bordi con dei fogli d'alluminio o con un impasto di farina e lasciate cuocere a fuoco molto basso per 10 minuti, avendo cura di non fare uscire il vapore.

Nali Ki Nihari (Lamb shank)

INGREDIENTS FOR 4 SERVINGS:
- 2 lbs of lamb/goat meat leg pieces - ¾ cup of mustard oil - 2 bay leaves - 3 ½ tbsp of ginger and garlic paste - 2 cinnamon sticks, ½ inch each - 2 cloves, whole - 2 cardamom seeds, whole - 1 cup of onion, julienned - ¾ cup of fried onion - 1 tbsp of turmeric powder - 1 tsp of degi mirch (red chile powder) - salt to taste - 2 cups of water (divided) - ¾ cup of milk curd - 2 cups of lamb stock - 1 ½ tbsp of coriander powder - 3 tbsp of ghee - ½ tbsp of garam masala powder - 1 tbsp of gaham flour - 1 pinch of saffron, soaked into 2 tbsp of warm water for 10 minutes - 1 tbsp of kewra water - Coriander leaves (for garnish) - Green chile (for garnish) - Ginger strips (for garnish)

INGREDIENTI PER 4 PERSONE:
- 907 g di coscia di agnello/capra - 175 ml di olio di senape - 2 foglie di alloro - 3 ½ cucchiai di zenzero e pasta d'aglio - 2 bastoncini di cannella da 12mm - 2 chiodi di garofano interi - 2 semi di cardamomo interi - 150 g di cipolla julienne - 115 g di cipolla fritta - 1 cucchiaio di curcuma in polvere - 1 cucchiaino di degi mirch (polvere rossa chile) - sale qb - 470 ml d'acqua (diviso in due) - 175 ml di latte cagliato - 470 ml di brodo di agnello - 1 ½ cucchiaio di coriandolo in polvere - 3 cucchiai di burro ghi - ½ cucchiaio di garam masala in polvere - 1 cucchiaio di farina graham - 1 pizzico di zafferano lasciato in 2 cucchiai di acqua tiepida per 10 minuti - 1 cucchiaio di acqua kewra - foglie di coriandolo (per guarnire) - peperoncini verdi (per guarnire) - strisce di zenzero (per guarnire)

In a large bottom pan, heat the mustard oil and add the ginger and garlic paste, the cinnamon, bay leaves, cloves, cardamom, onion, fried onion, turmeric, degi mirch, meat, and salt with 1 cup of water and cook the meat until brown. Cover the pan and seal the sides with aluminum foil or flour dough and steam for 40 minutes over a low flame. After 40 minutes, open the lid, remove the meat, strain and set aside. Add the milk curd to the remaining gravy and cook for 10 minutes. Add the coriander, cumin and garam masala power with the remaining cup of water and cook for another 5 minutes. Add lamb stock and simmer for another 8 to 10 minutes. Heat the ghee in a separate pan and fry the graham flour with 1 tsp of gravy to make a thick paste (making sure there are no lumps). Mix into the remaining gravy and simmer untill it thickens. Now strain the gravy and add saffron and kewra water. Add the meat pieces to the gravy and sprinkle with coriander leaves, ginger and green chile strips and serve hot.

Scaldate l'olio di senape in una padella dal fondo largo, aggiungete lo zenzero e la pasta d'aglio, la cannella, l'alloro, i chiodi di garofano, il cardamomo, la cipolla, la cipolla fritta, la curcuma, il degi mirch, la carne, e il sale con metà dell'acqua e cuocete la carne fino a doratura. Coprite la padella e sigillate i lati con fogli d'alluminio o con un impasto di farina, e lasciate cuocere a vapore per 40 minuti a fuoco lento. Dopo 40 minuti, aprite il coperchio, togliete la carne, lasciate colare il liquido e mettetela da parte. Aggiungete il latte cagliato al sugo e cuocete per 10 minuti. Aggiungete poi il coriandolo, il cumino e la polvere di garam masala, con l'altra parte d'acqua e continuate a cuocere per altri 5 minuti. Aggiungete il brodo d'agnello e lasciate bollire per altri 8-10 minuti. Riscaldate il burro Ghi in una padella a parte e friggete la farina graham con 1 cucchiaino di sugo per creare una pasta densa (assicurandovi che non ci siano grumi). Aggiungete il resto del sugo e lasciate cuocere a fuoco lento fino a quando si addensa. Filtrate il sugo e aggiungete lo zafferano e l'acqua di kewra. Aggiungete i pezzi di carne e cospargete di foglie di coriandolo, zenzero e strisce di peperoncini verdi. Servite il tutto caldo.

Shahi Tukda
(Awadhi Saffron
Bread Pudding)

INGREDIENTS FOR 4 SERVINGS:
- 2 slices white bread - 1 cup ghee - 4 cups milk - 1 cup sugar - 1 tsp green cardamom powder - 1 tbsp rose water - pinch of saffron, soaked in 2 tbsp warm water for about 10 minutes - 1 tbsp almonds (sliced) - 1 tbsp pistachios (sliced)

Cut bread slices into 8 circular shaped pieces by using a mold. Heat ghee in a frying pan over high heat then lower the flame to medium-low and deep fry the pieces of bread until they are golden brown. Over medium heat, boil the milk in a pot for 10 to 15 minutes, stirring continuously until it thickens. Add the sugar, cardamom, rose and saffron water to the milk and boil for another 5 minutes Place bread pieces at the bottom of dish, at least 1 inch deep. Pour milk preparation equally over the bread slices and let it absorb completely. Garnish with almonds and pistachio flakes over the soaked bread.
Shahi Tukda is ready to be served warm or cold

BAGATELLE

Owners / Titolari › Aymeric Clemente & Remi Laba • **Chef** › Sebastien Chamaret

One Little West 12th Street • **M** 8 Av [L] • +01 212 488 2110 • **www.bagatellenyc.com**

If, like me, you love contemporary art, especially if offered in traditional or unexpected contexts, you will love the Bagatelle hall, with its brightly colored paintings in contrast to the white tablecloths and classic chairs. A really nice place, spacious, bright, in a wonderful area, full of bars and restaurants. The French cuisine with Mediterranean influences is in the hands of chef Sébastien Chamaret, who landed in New York after 15 years of experience all around the world. It's hard to find something you don't like in the menu: we couldn't, despite having tasted a dozen dishes. Among the things that we liked there are the "steak frites", the tartare Bagatelle and the "codfish Nicoise". And then, after dinner, we sat at the table outdoors, enjoying a banana cheesecake and admiring the world running in front of us.

Se, come me, amate l'arte contemporanea, specie se proposta in contesti tradizionali o inaspettati, la sala del Bagatelle vi piacerà tantissimo, con i suoi quadri coloratissimi a fare da contrasto al bianco delle tovaglie e alle sedie classiche. Davvero un bel locale, ampio, luminoso, in una zona meravigliosa, piena di bar e ristoranti. La cucina francese con contaminazioni mediterranee è nelle mani dello chef Sébastien Chamaret, giunto a New York dopo 15 anni di esperienze in giro per il mondo. Difficile trovare qualcosa che non piaccia nel menù: noi non ci siamo riusciti, pur avendo degustato una decina di piatti. Tra le cose che più ci sono piaciute ci sono le "steak frites", la tartare Bagatelle e il "codfish Nicoise". E poi, fine cena seduti al tavolo all'aperto, assaporando un cheesecake alla banana e ammirando il mondo che ti scorre davanti. È anche in questi momenti che ti rendi conto di quanto la vita sia bella.

Wine List › Carta dei Vini	**Cuisine** › Cucina	**Lunch** › Pranzo	**Dinner** › Cena
250 Labels › Etichette	**French** › Francese	$ 30-50	$ 80-100

Baby artichokes salad

Insalata di carciofini

INGREDIENTS FOR 4 SERVINGS:
- 1 dozen of peeled and roasted baby artichokes
- 3 roasted plum tomatoes
- 6 cups baby arugula
- ½ cup shaved parmesan

Tomato vinaigrette:
- 12 oz plum tomatoes, halved lengthwise and cored
- 1 tbsp chopped garlic
- 1 tbsp extra-virgin olive oil
- 1 tbsp italian seasoning mix
- 1 tsp kosher salt freshly ground pepper, to taste
- 2 tbsp sherry vinegar, or red-wine vinegar

INGREDIENTI PER 4 PERSONE:
- una dozzina di carciofini puliti e scottati
- 3 pomodori arrostiti
- 120 g di rucola
- 100 g di parmigiano grattugiato

Vinaigrette al pomodoro:
- 340 g di pomodori, tagliati a metà per lungo e con il torsolo rimosso
- 1 cucchiaio di aglio tritato
- 1 cucchiaio di olio di oliva extra vergine
- 1 cucchiaio di mix di condimento italiano
- 1 cucchiaino di sale kosher e pepe macinato fresco qb
- 2 cucchiai di aceto di sherry o di aceto di vino rosso

Preheat the oven to 300°F. Coat an 8-inch-square glass baking dish with cooking spray.
Toss the tomatoes, garlic, oil, Italian seasoning, salt and pepper in a medium bowl.
Spread the tomatoes in the prepared baking dish. Bake until the tomatoes have broken down and the juices are thick and syrupy, from 1 hour and 20 minutes to 1 hour and 35 minutes.
Transfer the tomatoes to a blender. Add vinegar and puree (use caution when blending hot mixtures). Cool completely before using.

Riscaldate il forno a 150°C. Ungete una pirofila di vetro quadrata da 20cm con dello spray da cucina.
Unite i pomodori, l'aglio, l'olio, il condimento italiano, e del sale e pepe in una ciotola media.
Stendete i pomodori nella pirofila. Fate cuocere per 1 ora e 20 minuti - 1 ora e 35 minuti, fino a quando i pomodori sono appassiti e il succo è denso e sciroppposo.
Poi, mettete i pomodori in un frullatore. Aggiungete l'aceto e fate una purea (fate attenzione quando frullate ingredienti bollenti). Lasciate raffreddare completamente prima dell'utilizzo.

Roasted chatham codfish nicoise

Merluzzo arrosto, spinaci e olive

INGREDIENTS FOR 4 SERVINGS:
- 4 x 7oz chatham codfish fillets (skinless)
- salt, cayenne pepper
- ¼ cup white wine
- 4 cups baby spinach
- 2 tbsp olive oil
- 2 plum tomatoes
- 3 tbsp pitted Nicoise olive
- 1 tbsp chopped basil
- 1 tsbp chopped red onion

INGREDIENTI PER 4 PERSONE:
- 4 x filetti di merluzzo Chatham da 200 g (senza pelle)
- sale, pepe di cayenna
- 60 ml di vino bianco - 960 g di spinaci baby
- 2 cucchiai di olio d'oliva - 2 pomodori
- 3 cucchiai di olive nicoise snocciolate
- 1 cucchiaio di basilico tritato
- 1 cucchiaio di cipolla rossa tritata

Preheat the oven to 400°F.
Place the 4 pieces of fish in a roasting pan, season, pour the wine over the fillets and splash with olive oil.
Cook for 15 minutes at 400°F. Sautee the baby spinach in hot olive oil and put aside.
Chop the tomatoes, mix them with the diced olives, basil and red onion.

Riscaldate il forno a 200°C. Mettete i 4 filetti di pesce in una teglia, condite, e versateci sopra il vino e qualche goccia di olio d'oliva. Fate cuocere per 15 minuti a 200°C. Saltate gli spinaci in olio di oliva bollente, e metteteli da parte. Tagliate i pomodori, aggiungete le olive a dadini, il basilico e la cipolla rossa. Impiattate posizionando sulla base del piatto prima gli spinaci, poi il merluzzo e infine un cucchiaio di olive.

Banana cheesecake

INGREDIENTS. Serve in 8-10 inch cake mold:
- 2 cups mashed ripe bananas - 1 lb cream cheese - 1 ¼ cup sugar - 1 cup sour cream - 2 tbsp corn starch - 1 tsp vanilla extract - pinch of salt - 3 eggs **Crust:** - 2 cups graham cracker crumbs - 4 tbsp sugar - ½ cup melted butter **Toffee sauce for cheesecake:** - 13 g dark brown sugar - 30 g dark corn syrup - 50 g butter - 200 g heavy cream

INGREDIENTI. Servire in tortiera 8-10 pollici:
- 500 g di banane mature schiacciate - 450 g di crema di formaggio - 280 g di zucchero - 235 ml di panna acida - 2 cucchiai di amido di mais - 1 cucchiaino di estratto di vaniglia - Un pizzico di sale - 3 uova **Per la crosta:** - 170 g di Graham cracker sbriciolati - 4 cucchiai di zucchero - 118 ml di burro sciolto **Per la glassa toffee per cheesecake:** - 13 g di zucchero di canna scuro - 30 g di sciroppo di mais scuro - 50 g di burro - 200 g di panna da montare

Crust: Combine all the ingredients in a food mixer until smooth (or in a blender at a low speed).Pour the mixture into a prepared crust tin and bake at 350°F for 50 minutes (until the centre has set). Chill and serve. It can be made up to 3 days in advance.**Toffee sauce for cheesecake:** Combine the sugar, corn syrup and butter in a pan and slowly bring to boil. Let the mixture bubble for 2 minutes. Carefully add the cream and cook for 2 more minutes until the sauce thickens.

Preparazione crosta: Unite tutti gli ingredienti in un mixer fino a quando l'impasto risulta liscio (o in frullatore a bassa velocità) .Versate il composto nello stampo per crosta preparato e fate cuocere a 175°C per 50 minuti (fino a quando anche la parte centrale si è indurita). Lasciate raffreddare e servite. Può essere preparato anche con 3 giorni di anticipo. **Glassa toffee per cheesecake:** Unite lo zucchero, lo sciroppo di mais e il burro in un tegame, e portate lentamente ad ebollizione. Lasciate bollire per 2 minuti. Aggiungete con cautela la panna e fate cuocere per altri 2 minuti finché la glassa non si addensa.

BALABOOSTA

BOLD MEDITERRANEAN RE

to Feed the People You Love

BALABOOSTA

Owners / Titolari › Einat Admony & Stefan Nafziger • **Chef** › Einat Admony

214 Mulberry • Ⓜ Spring St • +01 646 861 36041 • **balaboostanyc.com**

A name for a restaurant was never more appropriate: Balaboosta is the Yiddish term to indicate the "perfect housewife". Einat Admony, creator and chef of the restaurant, is really a Balaboosta: simple, sociable, open, smiley. Her dishes reflect her character and her smile. Food that we would like to eat every day, without ever getting bored. Easy recipes, not elaborated, that have two goals only: to emphasize the quality of the ingredients used and kill the customer's hunger. Add the fact that Mulberry Street is one of the prettiest streets of Nolita, that the place is thought to socialize and feel good, that the prices are really competitive, and Balaboosta will become one of your favourite restaurants in New York. So much that you will want to buy Einat's book, who quotes: "Mediterranean recipes for people you love."

Mai nome fu più appropriato per un ristorante: Balaboosta è il termine Yiddish per indicare la "casalinga perfetta". Einat Admony, creatrice e chef del ristorante, appare davvero una Balaboosta: semplice, socievole, aperta, sorridente. I suoi piatti rispecchiano il suo carattere e il suo sorriso. Sono le cose che vorremmo mangiare ogni giorno, senza mai stancarci. Ricette facili, poco elaborate, che hanno due unici obiettivi: sottolineare la qualità degli ingredienti usati e ammazzare la fame del cliente. Aggiungete il fatto che Mulberry Street è una delle strade più carine di Nolita, che il posto è pensato per socializzare e star bene, e che i prezzi sono davvero interessanti, e Balaboosta diventerà uno dei vostri ristoranti preferiti di New York. Tanto che vi verrà voglia di acquistare il libro di Einat, che propone "ricette mediterranee per le persone che amate".

Wine List › Carta dei Vini	**Cuisine** › Cucina	**Lunch** › Pranzo	**Dinner** › Cena
80 Labels › Etichette	**Mediteranean** › Mediterranea	$ 25	$ 45

Shakshuka

INGREDIENTS FOR 4/6 SERVINGS:
- 3 tbl canola oil - 2 medium yellow onions, chopped
- 1 large green bell pepper, cored, seeded, and chopped
- 1 large jalapeño chile, cored, seeded, and chopped
- 7 garlic cloves, finely chopped - ¼ cup tomato paste
- One 28-ounce can whole peeled tomatoes, crushed by hand
- 1 bay leaf - 2 ½ tbl sugar
- 1 ½ tbl kosher salt
- 1 tbl sweet Hungarian paprika
- 1 tbl ground cumin
- 1 ½ teaspoons freshly ground black pepper
- 1 teaspoon ground caraway - ½ bunch Swiss chard, stemmed and chopped, or spinach - 8 to 12 large eggs

Heat the oil in a large skillet. Add the onions and sauté over medium heat until translucent, 5 to 10 minutes. Add the bell peppers and jalapeño and cook just until softened, 3 to 5 minutes. Stir in the garlic and tomato paste and sauté for another 2 minutes.

Slowly pour in the tomatoes. Stir in the bay leaf, sugar, salt, paprika, cumin, pepper, and caraway and let the mixture simmer for 20 minutes. Layer the Swiss chard leaves on top.

Crack the eggs into the tomato mixture. Cover and simmer for approximately 10 minutes or until the whites of the eggs are no longer translucent.

Cold eggplant salad
Insalata fredda di melanzane

INGREDIENTS FOR 4/6 SERVINGS:
- 3 large eggplant, stem end trimmed - Kosher salt - Canola oil for frying - 1 cup of distilled white vinegar - 5 garlic cloves, thinly sliced - ¼ cup of coarsely chopped fresh dill - 1½ tbl of sugar - ¼ teaspoon of red chili flakes

INGREDIENTI PER 4/6 PERSONE:
- 3 grandi melanzane pulite e tagliate - sale Kosher - Olio di canola per friggere - 235ml di aceto bianco distillato - 5 spicchi d'aglio affettati sottilmente - 5 g di aneto fresco tritato grossolanamente - 1½ cucchiaio di zucchero - ¼ cucchiaino di fiocchi di peperoncino rosso

Slice the eggplant into 1 inch thick rounds and sprinkle generously with salt. Place them in a colander and let them sit for 45 to 60 minutes. The salt will help purge the excess water and bitterness from the eggplant, so be sure to place a dish underneath the colander if it's not in the sink. Pat the eggplant slices dry with paper towels. Heat 1 inch of oil in a deep skillet until the temperature reaches 375° F. Fry the eggplant until golden brown, for about 7 minutes. - I suppose you could grill or boil them in the oven as a healthier option, but that's for another chapter. - Remove the eggplant with a slotted spoon and place them on a few sheets of paper towels to drain the excess oil. Whisk the vinegar, garlic, dill, sugar, and chili in a large bowl. Slice the eggplant into 1 inch cubes and add them to the bowl. Toss all the ingredients together to coat evenly. Place the salad in an airtight container and refrigerate overnight or for at least 6 hours before servings.

Tagliate le melanzane a rondelle con spessore di 2.50cm e salate abbondantemente. Mettetele in un colino e lasciate riposare per 45-60 minuti. Il sale aiuterà a spurgare l'acqua in eccesso e a togliere l'amarezza della melanzana, quindi mettete un piatto sotto il colino se non lo avete posizionato nel lavandino. Asciugate le melanzane delicatamente con carta assorbente. Scaldate 2.50 cm di olio in una padella profonda fino a quando la temperatura raggiunge 190°C. Friggete le melanzane fino a doratura per circa 7 minuti. (Si potrebbero grigliare o cuocere in forno come opzione più sana, ma questa è un'altra ricetta.) Rimuovete le melanzane dall'olio con un mestolo forato e ponetele su alcuni fogli di carta assorbente per togliere l'olio in eccesso.
In una ciotola grande frullate l'aceto, l'aglio, l'aneto, lo zucchero e il peperoncino. Tagliate le melanzane a cubetti e poneteli nella ciotola. Saltate il tutto per condire bene. Mettete l'insalata in un contenitore ermetico e lasciate riposare per una notte in frigorifero o per almeno 6 ore prima di servire.

balade

EASTERN MEDITERRANEAN

BALADE
Owner / Titolare › Roland Semaan • **Chef** › Micheline Wakim

208 1st Ave • **M** 1 Av [L] • +01 212 529 6868 • **www.baladerestaurants.com**

You can't not love the Lebanese cuisine, especially if it's in the Balade and there is a nice guy serving the dishes explaining what you're about to eat, how the dish was cooked and what the story is behind it. This is Balade, one of the many little restaurants that make you fall in love with the East Village. One of those places where you eat well and feel good because they offer an experience that goes beyond what you order and enrich your culinary culture. One of those places where you can find a nice atmosphere and nice people. Enjoy the hummus, the tabuleh, the meat, the simple desserts and the after dinner tea. And above all, listen to that waiter and trust him.

Non si può non amare la cucina libanese, soprattutto se è come quella del Balade e se a servirti i piatti è un ragazzo simpatico che ti spiega cosa stai per mangiare, come è stato cucinato il cibo e qual è la storia che quel piatto si porta dietro. Ecco, Balade è uno dei tanti ristorantini che ti fanno innamorare dell'East Village. Quei posti dove mangi bene e stai bene, perché ti offrono un'esperienza che va oltre ciò che ordini e arricchiscono la tua cultura gastronomica. Quei posti in cui trovi una bella atmosfera e bella gente. Godetevi l'hummus, il tabuleh, la carne, i dolci semplici e il thè di fine pasto. E soprattutto, ascoltate quel cameriere. E fidatevi di lui.

Wine List › Carta dei Vini	**Cuisine** › Cucina	**Lunch** › Pranzo	**Dinner** › Cena
30 Labels › Etichette	**Lebonese** › Libanese	$ 15-20	$ 30

Kebbe krass

INGREDIENTS FOR 4 SERVINGS:

Outside layer:
- 1 lb of crack wheat
- 1 lb of ground beef
- 1 tbs of salt
- 1 tbs of all spices
- ½ teaspoon of black peppers

Inner layer:
- 1 lb of ground beef
- 2 chopped onions
- ½ cup of fried pine nuts
- 1 tbs of all spice
- 1 tbs of salt
- ½ tbs of black pepper

INGREDIENTI PER 4 PERSONE:

Strato esterno:
- 453 g di grano macinato
- 453 g di manzo macinato
- 1 cucchiaio di sale
- 1 cucchiaio di spezie
- ½ cucchiaino di pepe nero

Ripieno:
- 453 g di manzo macinato
- 2 cipolle tritate
- 80 g di pinoli fritti
- 1 cucchiaio di spezie
- 1 cucchiaio di sale
- ½ cucchiaio di pepe nero

Outside layer:

Soak cracked wheat for 1 hour in cold water, mix the crack wheat with the ground beef and grind them in the food processor.

Inner Layer:

Sauté the meat and onions until cooked, then add all spices and nuts.

When the outside layer is ready, make it into a shell shape and add the inner layer into that shell. Fry at 300°F until cooked. Serve with yogurt dip.

Strato esterno:

Mettete a bagno il grano macinato per 1 ora in acqua fredda, aggiungete il manzo e macinare con un robot da cucina.

Ripieno:

Fate rosolare la carne e le cipolle fino a cottura completa, poi aggiungete tutte le spezie e i pinoli.

Quando lo strato esterno è pronto, formate una conchiglia e mettete il ripieno all'interno del guscio. Friggete a 150°C. Servite con salsa yogurt.

COLLEZIONE CINQUANTA › Vino Rosso d'Italia
CANTINE SAN MARZANO

Colore rosso rubino con riflessi porpora. Bouquet intenso e complesso in cui spiccano note fruttate riconducibili alla prugna e alla confettura e sentori terziari speziati che richiamano la vaniglia e la liquirizia. Palato intenso, di grande struttura e morbidezza; finale lungo.
Abbinamenti: Carni rosse, selvaggina, primi piatti robusti. Vino da meditazione.

Ruby red colour with purple reflections; intense and complex bouquet with fruity notes of prune and red jam and spicy scent of vanilla and licorice. Intense on the palate, full-bodied and soft with a long aftertaste.
Best served with: Red meat, game, savoury firs courses. Meditation wine.

Chocoba

INGREDIENTS FOR 4 SERVINGS:

Dough Preparation:
- 1.40 lb of flour
- 0.20 cup of milk
- 0.25 cup of soya been oil
- 0.40 tbs of salt
- 0.40 tbs of sugar
- 0.60 tea of spoon yeast
- 0.40 qt of cold water

INGREDIENTI PER 4 PERSONE:

Impasto:
- 635 g di farina
- 47 ml di latte
- 59 ml di olio di soia
- 0,40 cucchiaio di sale
- 0,40 cucchiaio di zucchero
- 0,60 cucchiaino di lievito
- 400 ml di acqua fredda

Mix everything and then leave to rest for about 1 hour, cut the dough thin and in a round shape and bake in the oven at 400°F.

As soon as the dough is baked, top it with Nutella chocolate and fresh slices of banana, then garnish with pistachio.

Unite tutti gli ingredienti e poi lasciate riposare per circa un'ora. Stendete l'impasto e cuocetelo in forno in una casseruola circolare a 200°C.

Appena è pronto, cospargetelo di Nutella e rondelle di banana. Guarnite con pistacchio.

Mouhamarra

INGREDIENTS FOR 4 SERVINGS:
- 10 pieces of fresh red peppers
- 20 pieces of ground crackers
- 300 g of fresh ground walnut
- 1 tbs of salt
- 2 tbs of cumin
- 2 teaspoon of cayenne pepper
- ½ cup of pomegranate Molasses
- ¼ cup of lemon juice
- ½ cup of olive oil

INGREDIENTI PER 4 PERSONE:
- 10 pezzi di peperoni rossi freschi
- 20 pezzi di cracker macinati
- 300 g di noci fresche macinate
- 1 cucchiaio di sale
- 2 cucchiai di cumino
- 2 cucchiaini di pepe di Caienna
- 80 g di melassa di melograno
- 59 ml di succo di limon
- 118 ml di olio d'oliva

Cut the red peppers into small pieces, grind them in the food processor, then strain them until all the juices come out.
Grind crackers finely.
Grind the walnut into chunk pieces and then mix everything together.
Bon appetit!

Tagliate i peperoni rossi in piccoli pezzi, usate un robot da cucina per macinarli e poi filtrate tutto il liquido.
Macinate finemente i crackers.
Macinate le noci in pezzi più grandi e poi unite il tutto.
Buon appetito.

BENOIT

Owner / Titolare › Alain Ducasse • **Chef** › Philippe Bertineau

60 West 55th St • Ⓜ 57 St [F] • +01 212 529 6868 • **www.alain-ducasse.com**

Benoit offers everything you'd expect from a restaurant owned by a sacred monster of the cuisine world, Alain Ducasse from France: a magnificent and elegant hall (French brasserie-style), delicious food, very high level service and prices above average (but not inaccessible). The Ducasse bistro evokes the charm and elegance of Benoit in Paris, which opened its doors in 1912 thanks to the work of Benoit Matray, and remained property of his family for 93 years and for three generations, until the great-grandson of the founder, Michel Petit, sold it to the multi-starred French chef in 2005. The biggest surprise was to eat the best hamburgers in New York here, which is not exactly what one expects from a French restaurant, but the traditions are still respected, because the menu is not short of escargot and other specialties from the country of cockerels.

Benoit offre tutto ciò che ci si aspetta dal ristorante di un mostro sacro della cucina mondiale, il francese Alain Ducasse: una sala magnifica ed elegante (in puro stile brasserie francese), cibo delizioso, servizio di altissimo livello e prezzi al di sopra della media (ma non inaccessibili). Il bistrot di Ducasse evoca lo charme e l'eleganza del Benoit di Parigi, che aprì le sue porte nel 1912 per opera di Benoit Matray, restò di proprietà della sua famiglia per 93 anni e tre generazioni, finché il pronipote del fondatore, Michel Petit, non lo vendette al pluristellato chef francese nel 2005. La sorpresa più grande è stata mangiare proprio qui il miglior hamburger di New York, che non è propriamente ciò che uno si attende da un ristorante francese. Ma la tradizione è comunque rispettata, perché nel menù non mancano le escargot e altre specialità del paese dei galletti.

Wine List › Carta dei Vini	**Cuisine** › Cucina	**Lunch** › Pranzo	**Dinner** › Cena
500 Labels › Etichette	**French** › Francese	**$ 34 (three courses)** › 3 portate	**$ 60-75**

Cucumber and yogurt gazpacho with fresh mint and a crisp garnish

Gazpacho di cetriolo e yogurt, con menta fresca e finitura croccante

INGREDIENTS FOR 4 SERVINGS:
The gazpacho
- 2 cucumbers - 1 avocado - 1 garlic clove - 2 inches of ginger - 1 cup of yogurt - ¾ cup of lowfat milk - 5 tbs of sherry vinegar - 2 to 3 tbs of tamarind puree - 1 pinch of piment d'espelette or hot paprika (2 pinches required in total for recipe) - 1 ½ cups of cold water - 3 tbs of olive oil
The crisp garnish:
- 1 granny smith apple - salt and freshly ground pepper
- 1 pinch of piment d'espelette or hot paprika

INGREDIENTI PER 4 PERSONE:
Gazpacho:
- 2 cetrioli - 1 avocado - 1 spicchio d'aglio - 5 cm di zenzero - 240 g di yogurt - 177 ml di latte scremato - 5 cucchiai di aceto di sherry - 2 o 3 cucchiai di purea di tamarindo - 1 pizzico di paprika piccante (in totale 2 pizzichi per tutta la ricetta) - 353 ml di acqua fredda - 3 cucchiai di olio d'oliva
Finitura croccante: - 1 mela Granny Smith - sale e pepe nero appena macinato - 1 pizzico di paprika piccante

Prepare the gazpacho:
Peel 2 cucumbers and remove all the seeds. Cut off about a third of one of them and set it aside. Chop the rest into small pieces. Halve 1 avocado, remove the pit, and scoop out the flesh with a small spoon. Peel and mince 1 garlic clove and 2 inches of ginger. Chop the leaves of a small bunch of mint and set aside 2 tablespoonfuls. Blend all these ingredients with 1 cup of yogurt, ¾ cup of lowfat milk, 5 tablespoons of sherry vinegar, 2 to 3 tablespoons of tamarind puree, 1 pinch of Piment d'Espelette or hot paprika (2 pinches required in total for recipe), 1 ½ cups of cold water, and 3 tablespoons of olive oil for 1 to 2 minutes. Add salt and freshly ground black pepper and keep cold.

Prepare the crisp garnish:
Peel 1 Granny Smith apple. Cut in half, remove the core and chop the flesh into very small dice (brunoise), approximately 1/8 inch. Cut the reserved piece of cucumber in the same way. Put in a large bowl with the reserved chopped mint leaves. Add salt and freshly ground black pepper. Pour the soup into a tureen or soup plates. Scatter the crisp garnish over. Then sprinkle 1 pinch of Piment d'Espelette or hot paprika on top. Serve nice and cold.

Preparazione del gazpacho:
Pulite i cetrioli e rimuovete tutti i semi. Tagliate circa un terzo di uno e mettetelo da parte. Tritate la parte restante in piccoli pezzi. Tagliate a metà l'avocado, togliete il nocciolo ed estraete la polpa con un cucchiaino. Sbucciate e tritate uno spicchio d'aglio e lo zenzero. Tritate le foglie di un mazzetto di menta e mettete da parte 2 cucchiai. Frullate tutti questi ingredienti con lo yogurt, il latte, l'aceto di sherry, la purea di tamarindo, 1 pizzico di Piment d'Espelette o paprika piccante, l'acqua fredda, e l'olio d'oliva, per 1-2 minuti. Aggiungete sale e pepe nero appena macinato e conservate in frigorifero.

Preparazione della finitura croccante:
Sbucciate la mela e tagliatela a metà, togliete il nocciolo, e tagliatela a dadini piccoli (brunoise), spessi circa 3mm. Tagliate allo stesso modo il pezzo di cetriolo messo da parte precedentemente. Mettete la mela e il cetriolo in una grande ciotola con la menta messa da parte precedentemente. Aggiungete sale e pepe nero appena macinato. Versate la zuppa in una terrina o in ciotole. Cospargete la parte superiore di finitura croccante. Infine, date una spolverata con un pizzico di Piment d'Espelette o paprica piccante. Servite freddo.

IL PUMO › Sauvignon Malvasia Salento IGP
CANTINE SAN MARZANO

Colore giallo paglierino dai riflessi verdolini; profumo floreale riconducibile alla ginestra e fruttato riconducibile agli agrumi e alla frutta esotica. Vino dalla buona spalla acida, fresco e minerale.
Abbinamenti: Ottimo con antipasti e zuppe di pesce, formaggi giovani a pasta tenera, pasta con sughi leggeri.

Straw yellow colour with green reflections; Scotch broom notes and a hint of citrus and tropical fruits on the nose. Lively in acidity, fresh and mineral.
Best served with: Excellent with starters and fish soup, fresh cheese and pasta with light sauces.

Twice baked, upside down comte cheese soufflé

Soufflé capovolto di formaggio comte cotto due volte

INGREDIENTS FOR 4 SERVINGS:
Cheese Soufflé: - 6 oz of butter - 3 ½ oz of flour - 3 ½ oz of parmigiano, grated - 1 ¾ oz of comte cheese, shredded - 1 ¾ cup of milk - 1 clove of garlic, lightly crushed - 1 pinch of nutmeg, freshly grated - 6 eggs - salt, to taste - white pepper, to taste
Cheese Sauce: - 1 ¾ cup of cream - 3 ½ oz of milk - 1.8 oz of parmigiano, grated - 1.8 oz of comte cheese, shredded - salt, to taste - white pepper, to taste

INGREDIENTI PER 4 PERSONE:
Soufflé di formaggio: - 170 g di burro - 100 g di farina - 100 g di parmigiano grattugiato - 50g di formaggio comte tagliato a striscioline - 412 ml di latte - 1 spicchio d'aglio tritato finemente - 1 pizzico di noce moscata grattugiata fresca - 6 uova - sale qb - pepe bianco qb
Salsa di formaggio: - 412 ml di panna - 103 ml di latte - 51 g di parmigiano grattugiato - 51 g di formaggio comte grattugiato - sale qb - pepe bianco qb

For the cheese sauce, bring the cream and milk to a boil and pour into a blender, add the grated parmigiano and the comte cheese. Blend until smooth and season with salt and pepper. Reserve for later (the cheese sauce can be made ahead of time and refrigerated for up to 3 days). Preheat the oven at 350°F, and bring about 2 quarts of water to a boil.

In a small pot, put the milk with the garlic and season with salt, pepper, and nutmeg. Bring to a boil.

In another pot, melt the butter and whisk in the flour to make a roux. Cook it for 3 to 4 minutes and then strain the milk into the pot with the roux. Bring back to a simmer, whisking continuously.

Place the cooked mixture into a mixer with a paddle. Mix on low speed and add the parmigiano and comte cheese. Meanwhile, whip the egg whites in a small bowl with a whisk, until they reach stiff peaks.

When the cheeses are incorporated, add the egg yolks. Fold the whipped egg whites into the mixture using a wooden spoon.

Spray some aluminum cups generously with cooking spray and place them about 1 inch apart in a pan with high sides. Fill the cups with the cheese mixture using a spoon or pastry bag. Place the pan in the preheated oven and fill with hot water ¾ of the way to the top of the ramekins. Bake in the oven for 8-10 minutes.

The soufflé should be firm on the outside when cooked, but very soft and springy to the touch on the inside. Carefully turn the cheese soufflé upside down into soup bowls and gently remove the aluminum cups.

Place the soufflé under a broiler for 1-2 minutes, until they turn brown on the top. Warm the cheese sauce and pour around the sides of the soufflé.

Salsa di formaggio: Portate la panna e il latte ad ebollizione e versate il tutto in un frullatore, aggiungete il parmigiano e il comte grattuggiato. Amalgamate bene e condite con sale e pepe. Mettere la salsa da parte (la salsa di formaggio può essere fatta in anticipo e può essere refrigerata per 3 giorni). Riscaldate il forno a 175°C, e portate circa 2 litri d'acqua ad ebollizione. Mettete il latte con l'aglio in un pentolino, condite con sale, pepe e noce moscata e portate ad ebollizione.

In un'altra pentola, fate sciogliere il burro e aggiungete la farina usando la frusta per fare un roux. Fate cuocere per 3-4 minuti e poi aggiungete il latte. Riportate ad ebollizione mescolando continuamente.

Mettete il composto in un mixer. Mescolate a bassa velocità e aggiungete il parmigiano e il comte.

Nel frattempo, con una frusta, montate gli albumi a neve in una piccola ciotola. Una volta che i formaggi si sono amalgamati bene aggiungete i tuorli d'uovo. Poi aggiungete delicatamente con un cucchiaio di legno gli albumi montati. Spruzzate delle ciotole di alluminio con abbondante spray da cucina e posizionatele a circa 2,5cm l'una dall'altra in una teglia con il bordo alto. Riempite le ciotole con il composto di formaggio con una sac à poche o un cucchiaio. Mettete la teglia in forno e riempitela con acqua calda a ¾ dell'altezza delle ciotole. Cuocete in forno per 8-10 minuti. I soufflé cotti dovrebbero essere sodi all'esterno ma molto morbidi ed elastici al tatto all'interno. Capovolgete con attenzione i soufflé di formaggio su dei piatti fondi e rimuovete delicatamente le ciotole di alluminio. Infine, lasciate cuocere i soufflé alla griglia per 1-2 minuti, fino a quando non diventano dorati sulla parte superiore. Riscaldate la salsa di formaggio e versatela intorno ai lati del soufflé.

BETONY

Owner / Titolare › Andrey Dellos • **Chef** › Bryce Shuman

41 West 57th Street • 🅜 57 St [F] • +01 212 465 2400 • **www.betony-nyc.com**

 It's hard to find a more impressive, elegant, original place. For its refined cuisine, the price (which is justified anyhow), the beauty of the premises and the impeccable service, Betony is one of those restaurants for special occasions and dinners to remember. Its owner, the Russian businessman Andrey Dellos, wanted to create an unforgettable place. The "modern American" cuisine of the chef Bryce Shuman (formerly executive sous-chef at Madison Park) does nothing to hide the French and Italian influences: the result is represented by very beautiful dishes that accompany form with a lot of substance. We appreciated very much the Pig's Head Terrine, the Lobster and the Roasted Beef Tenderloin. The sweet-savory dishes are for demanding palates and perhaps also a little too refined, but they emphasize the willingness to go beyond what has already been seen and eaten.

Difficile trovare un posto più imponente, elegante, originale. Per la ricercatezza della cucina, il prezzo (che comunque è giustificato), la bellezza del locale ed il servizio impeccabile, Betony è uno di quei ristoranti per le grandi occasioni e le cene da ricordare. Il suo proprietario, il businessman russo Andrey Dellos, ha evidentemente voluto creare un posto indimenticabile. La cucina "americana moderna" dello chef bryce Shuman (già executive sous chef al Madison Park) non fa nulla per nascondere le influenze francesi e italiane: il risultato è rappresentato da piatti molto belli che però accompagnano alla forma anche molta sostanza. Ci sono piaciuti tanto la Pig's Head terrine, l'aragosta e il Roasted beef tenderloin. I dolci-salati sono per palati esigenti e forse un po' troppo raffinati, ma sottolineano la volontà di andare oltre il già visto e il già mangiato. Uno sforzo che non si può certo biasimare.

Wine List › Carta dei Vini	**Cuisine** › Cucina	**Lunch** › Pranzo	**Dinner** › Cena
750 Labels › Etichette	**Modern American** › Americana Moderna	**$ 48 (3 courses)** › 3 portate	**$ 95 (4 courses)** › 4 portate

Lobster with summer beans and dill

INGREDIENTS FOR 4 SERVINGS:
Fava bean puree: - 1000 g fava beans, peeled - 10 g extra virgin olive oil - salt. **Lobster minestrone:** (yield: 1000 g)- 50 g olive oil - 250 g tomatoes - 150 g onions - 100 g green zucchini - 75 g leeks - 75 g celery - 50 g carrot - 25 g garlic - 30 g tomato paste - 200 g white wine - 1 l lobster stock - 10 g basil - 20 g dill - 300 g butter - 5 g roe butter - lemon - salt - cayenne pepper. **Lobster:** (yield: 300 g) - 600 g whole lobster - 2 ea thick wooden skewer. **Lobster orange butter:** (yield: 645 g) - 300 g orange juice - 300 g white wine - 800 g butter - 12 g salt - 7 g allepo pepper.
To finish: - 80 g fava puree - 4 pcs snake beans - 60 g blanched fava beans - 8 pcs long purple beans - 16 pcs yellow wax beans - 16 pcs haricot verts - 40 g cranberry beans - 4 pcs lobster tail - 4   pcs lobster claws - 4 pcs lobster knuckles - 400 g minestrone - 4 pcs dill bundle

Fava Bean Puree:
Blanch the peeled favas in salted boiling water. Shock in salted ice water and transfer to a blender.
Blend and emulsify with olive oil.

Lobster Minestrone:
Heat a large rondeau with the olive oil on high heat. Once hot add the vegetables to the pan and reduce the heat to medium low. Sweat the veggies on medium low until they are tender. Add the tomato paste to the pan and sweat for another 5 minutes being careful to not get any browning. Add the white wine to the pan and cook out the alcohol. Add the lobster stock to the pan and bring to a simmer over high heat. Lower the heat and simmer the sauce for 45 minutes. Strain and emulsify with the butters. Add the herbs and steep for 5 minutes. Strain and season the sauce with lemon, cayenne pepper and salt.

Lobster:
Be sure to keep the lobsters calm and free of stress and twist the tails off of the bodies. Proceed to twist the claws and knuckles off as well. Skewer the tails with two skewers, starting from the base of the tail and going through to where it once connected to the body. Make sure that the tails are straight. Set the combi oven to 70C full steam. Cook the tails for 6 minutes. Cook the knuckles and claws for 15 minutes. Be sure to shock in ice water immediately after cooking.

Lobster Orange Butter:
In separate pots reduce both the orange juice and wine by ¾. Dice the butter into cubes and place in the fridge so it is very cold. Combine the reduced liquids and bring to a simmer. Turn the heat off and add the butter one cube at a time. Use a large whisk to slowly emulsify the butter into the liquids. If the butter is getting too cool, turn the heat back on to low. Season the final emulsified butter sauce with salt and allepo pepper.

To Finish:
Heat the puree in a small pan and spoon the puree in the middle of the plate. Place the glazed lobster tail on the right hand side of the puree. Place the beans and lobster claws to the right of the tail. Cover the lobster and garnish with the dill bundle, flash the whole plate in the oven and then serve the sauce table side. Pour the sauce over the dill to infuse the flavor of the herbs. Remove the bundle once it has been poured.

BLT PRIME

Owner / Titolare › ESQuared Hospitality • **Chef** › Coby D. Farrow

111 East 22nd Street • Ⓜ 23 St [6] • +01 212 995 8500 • **www.e2hospitality.com/blt-prime-new-york**

To be a steak house, this place is really very nice, it's all about elegance and a dark wood colour. It has soft lighting and a fashion-club environment. After all, we are in Gramercy, and you must maintain certain standards. But we would like to add that, even if it's a steak house, we also enjoyed some excellent fish and really interesting desserts. It certainly isn't a cheap place, but the bill is not exaggerated compared to the quality of what you eat. Beginning with the bread and the chicken liver pate, followed by the popovers (all courtesy of the house), the giant bread and cheese muffins that arrive to the table still warm: good, but not recommended for those on a diet. One cannot miss "the must eat dish" of Blt Prime: the grilled bacon, a delicious fat-meat bomb. To lighten up a little and refresh your mouth, there is nothing better than a lobster salad. Then you have to give in to the charm of a Kansas City Steak, it's superb. We also tried the filet of Dover sole, basically a soft steak, outstanding! Among the desserts, you can't go wrong if you order the mini doughnuts and the carrot cake.

Per essere una steak house, il locale è davvero molto bello, tutto all'insegna dell'eleganza e del colore legno scuro. Luci soffuse e ambiente da fashion-club. Del resto siamo a Gramercy, e certi canoni vanno rispettati. Ma aggiungiamo anche che, per essere una steak house, abbiamo gustato anche del pesce eccellente e dolci davvero interessanti. Non è certo un posto a buon mercato, ma il conto non è esagerato rispetto alla qualità di ciò che si mangia. A cominciare dal pane e dal chicken liver pate, seguito dai popovers (tutto offerto dalla casa), dei muffin giganti di pane e formaggio, che arrivano sul tavolo ancora caldi: buoni, ma sconsigliati per chi è a dieta. Non si può non provare il must del Blt Prime, il bacon alla griglia, una deliziosa bomba di carne grassa. Per alleggerirsi un po' e rinfrescarsi la bocca, niente di meglio che una insalata di aragosta. Poi bisogna per forza sottomettersi al fascino di una Kansas City Steak: superba. Abbiamo provato anche il filetto di sogliola di Dover: praticamente una bistecca soffice, eccezionale! Tra i dolci, non sbagliate se ordinate i mini donughts e il cake alle carote.

Wine List › Carta dei Vini	Cuisine › Cucina	Lunch › Pranzo	Dinner › Cena
600 Labels › Etichette	**American Steak House**	**No lunch** › Chiuso a pranzo	**$ 70**

Appetizer › Antipasto

Grilled bacon
Bacon alla griglia

INGREDIENTS FOR 4 SERVINGS:
Dressing: - 1 cup chopped parsley - 1 tbsp chopped garlic - 1 tbsp chopped shallots - 1 cup extravirgin olive oil - fine sea salt - freshly cracked black pepper
Bacon: - 4 ea 1/8 inch thick slices applewood smoked bacon - sherry vinegar to finish

INGREDIENTI PER 4 PERSONE:
Condimento: - 25 g di prezzemolo tritato - 1 cucchiaio di aglio tritato – 1 cucchiaio di scalogno tritato – 236 ml di olio extravergine di oliva - sale marino - pepe nero appena macinato
Bacon: - 4 fette da 3 mm di bacon affumicata - aceto di sherry per finire

Whisk together all the dressing ingredients and set aside.
Grill the four slices of bacon on both sides.
Plate and top with two tablespoons of the dressing.
Finish with a drizzle of sherry vinegar.

Unite tutti gli ingredienti per il condimento e mettete da parte.
Grigliate le fette di pancetta su entrambi i lati.
Impiattate e aggiungete due cucchiai di condimento.
Terminate con un filo di aceto di sherry.

Dessert › Dolce

Carrot cake
Tortino alle carote

INGREDIENTS FOR 4 SERVINGS:
To make the cake: - 6 oz all purpose flour - 5 oz dark brown sugar - 2 oz granulated sugar - 1½ tea baking soda - 1 tea baking powder - 1 tea ground cinnamon - ½ tea ground cloves - ½ tea ground allspice - ½ tea grated nutmeg - 1 tea salt - 2/3 cup vegetable oil - 3 ea large eggs - 1½ cups finely grated, peeled carrots - ½ cup canned crushed pineapple, lightly drained
To make the Cream Cheese Sauce: - 8 oz cream cheese - 1 ea vanilla bean, seeds only - 1 tbsp butter, softened - 2 tbsp sour cream - superfine sugar, to taste - lemon juice, to taste

INGREDIENTI PER 4 PERSONE:
Per la torta: - 170 g di farina multiuso - 141 g di zucchero di canna scuro - 56 g di zucchero semolato - 1½ cucchiaino di bicarbonato di sodio - 1 cucchiaino di lievito in polvere - 1 cucchiaino di cannella in polvere - ½ cucchiaino di chiodi di garofano in polvere - ½ cucchiaino di pimento in polvere - ½ cucchiaino di noce moscata grattugiata - 1 cucchiaino di sale - 157 ml di olio vegetale - 3 uova grandi - 135 g di carote sbucciate e grattugiate finemente - 115 g di ananas in scatola schiacciati e drenati leggermente
Per la salsa di crema di formaggio: - 226 g di crema di formaggio - 1 baccello di vaniglia, solo i semi - 1 cucchiaio di burro ammorbidito - 2 cucchiai di panna acida - zucchero superfine qb - succo di limone qb

Preheat the oven to 325°F. Mix all the ingredients together in the order they are listed in the ingredients. Be careful to not over mix. Pour into your baking dish of choice and bake until the skewer comes out clean.
Cream cheese sauce: Mix the cream cheese and vanilla bean seeds, by hand or with a stand mixer, in a bowl, until smooth. Gradually add the other ingredients until they are all combined and there are no lumps. Do not over mix.

Riscaldate il forno a 160°C.
Unite tutti gli ingredienti nell'ordine in cui sono elencati (negli ingredienti). Fate attenzione a non mescolare troppo. Versate tutto in una teglia e lasciate cuocere fino a quando lo stecchino esce pulito.
Crema di salsa di formaggio: a mano o con un mixer mescolate in una ciotola la crema di formaggio e i semi di vaniglia fino a quando il composto risulterà liscio. Aggiungete gli altri ingredienti a poco a poco, fino a quando non sono tutti combinati e non ci sono più grumi. Anche in questo caso non mescolate troppo.

BLUE RIBBON SUSHI IZAKAYA

Owners / Titolari › Bruce and Eric Bromberg • **Chef** › Bruce Bromberg

187 Orchard Street • **M** 2 Av [F] • +01 212 466 0404 • **www.blueribbonrestaurants.com**

The Blue Ribbon Sushi Izakaya is one of the many restaurants in the Blue Ribbon Restaurant Group, founded in 1992 by chef Bruce and Eric Bromberg, who over the years have won many awards, recognitions, stars and hats. The Sushi Izakaya is a great place divided into three areas: the main room, with the chefs who prepare sushi in full view, it's characterized by long communal tables and informal seating. Then there are more reserved tables, with leather sofas and large, very beautiful, bell chandeliers. The bar lounge is where they serve lunch. Finally there is the terrace, perfect for parties and for warm evenings. The dishes are presented very well, and bring to the table lots of substance and authentic flavors. Whether you choose sushi, fish specialties or meat dishes, the quality always remains high.

Il Blue Ribbon Sushi Izakaya è uno dei tanti locali del Blue Ribbon Restaurant Group, fondato nel 1992 dagli chef Bruce ed Eric Bromberg, che negli anni hanno fatto incetta di premi, riconoscimenti, stelle e cappelli. Il Sushi Izakaya è un locale stupendo diviso in tre aree: la sala grande, con gli chef che preparano a vista il sushi, è caratterizzata da lunghi tavoli comuni e sedute informali. Ci sono poi i tavoli più riservati, con divani in pelle e grandi lampadari a campana molto belli. La sala bar è quella in cui si serve il pranzo. Infine c'è la terrazza, ottima per party e per le serate calde. I piatti sono presentati molto bene, e portano in tavola anche molta sostanza e sapori autentici. Che si scelga il sushi, le specialità di pesce o i piatti di carne, la qualità resta sempre elevata.

Wine List › Carta dei Vini	Cuisine › Cucina	Lunch › Pranzo	Dinner › Cena
200 Labels › Etichette	**Japanese** › Giapponese	$ 25-35	$ 35-50

Chocolate Bruno
Mousse al cioccolato

INGREDIENTS FOR 6 SERVINGS:
5 oz of white chocolate, chopped - 2 oz of graham crackers (½ a sleeve, or 4 full crackers), crushed (1 cup) - 18 oz of semi-sweet chocolate, chopped - 1 cup + 3 tbsp of unsalted butter - 3 tbsp of brewed espresso - 8 large egg yolks - 8 large egg whites - 1 tbsp of sugar

INGREDIENTI PER 6 PERSONE:
- 140 g di cioccolato bianco tritato
- 56 g di cracker graham (½ pacco o 4 cracker sani) tritati
- 510 g di cioccolato semidolce tritato
- 225 g + 3 cucchiai di burro non salato
- 3 cucchiai di caffè espresso
- 8 tuorli grandi - 8 albumi grandi
- 1 cucchiaio di zucchero

Line 6 (8-ounce) ramekins with parchment or wax paper. In a double boiler or in a bowl set over simmering water, melt the white chocolate and stir in the graham crackers. Divide equally among the prepared moulds, using a spoon to spread evenly on each base. Refrigerate until firm, for about 2 hours. In the top of a double boiler or in a bowl set over a pan of simmering water, melt the semi-sweet chocolate and butter with the espresso. Leave to cool for 2 minutes. Stir in (do not whisk) the yolks until just incorporated.
In a mixing bowl fitted with the whisk attachment, beat the whites until foamy. Slowly add the sugar and increase the speed. Beat until the whites form soft, floppy peaks.
Fold a little bit of the whites into the chocolate mixture to lighten it, then gently fold in the remaining egg whites. Spoon the mousse into the moulds and level the tops with an offset spatula or spoon. Chill until set, for about 3 hours or overnight.
To serve, gently dip the bottoms of the ramekins in a bowl of hot water for 30 seconds to 1 minute. Run a spatula along the edges of the ramekin (outside the wax paper) and pop the mousse out. Remove the paper. Transfer the desserts to plates and serve.

Foderate 6 pirottini con carta da forno o carta oleata. Sciogliete il cioccolato bianco a bagnomaria e aggiungete i cracker tritati. Dividete in parti uguali nei pirottini preparati precedentemente, usando un cucchiaio per spargere in modo uniforme sulla base. Poneteli in frigorifero ad indurire per circa 2 ore.
Sciogliete a bagnomaria il cioccolato semidolce, il burro e il caffè. Lasciate raffreddare per 2 minuti e poi incorporate i tuorli (senza sbattere).
In una ciotola, sbattete gli albumi con una frusta. Aggiungete lentamente lo zucchero e aumentate la velocità. Sbattete fino a quando gli albumi risultano montati a neve.
Aggiungete un po' di albumi al composto di cioccolato per alleggerirlo, e poi aggiungete delicatamente la rimanenza. Mettete la mousse nei pirottini e livellate la parte superiore con una spatola o un cucchiaio. Poneteli in frigorifero ad indurire per circa 3 ore o per tutta la notte.
Per servire, immergete con cautela il fondo dei pirottini in una ciotola d'acqua calda per 30 secondi-1 minuto. Passate una spatola lungo i bordi del pirottino (all'esterno della carta da forno) ed estraete la mousse. Rimuovete la carta e servite.

Oxtail Oden
Coda di bue Oden

INGREDIENTS FOR 8 SERVINGS:
- 12 cups beef stock - 1 lb oyster mushrooms, diced - ½ lb daikon, peeled and chopped into 1" thick rounds - 1 lb oxtail bones - 1.5 lb bok choy, rough chopped

Reinforce your beef stock with oxtails: Add oxtails and daikon to the broth, bring to a boil, and simmer for 1 hour. Remove the oxtail bones and separate the meat from the bones. Return the meat to the broth and discard the bones. Put the flame to high heat, add the oyster mushrooms and bok choy, bring to a boil and then lower the heat back to a simmer. Allow oden to cool slightly, and serve hot.

INGREDIENTI PER 8 PERSONE:
- 2,8 lt di brodo di manzo - 450 g di funghi ostrica a dadini - 225 g di daikon pelati e a rondelle da 25 mm - 450 g di ossa di coda di bue - 680 g di bok choy tritato

Insaporite il brodo di manzo con le ossa di coda di bue: aggiungete le ossa e il daikon al brodo, portate ad ebollizione, e lasciate cuocere per 1 ora. Rimuovete le ossa e separate la carne dalle ossa. Aggiungete la carne al brodo. Alzate nuovamente la fiamma a fuoco alto, aggiungete i funghi ostrica e il bok choi, portate ad ebollizione e poi lasciate cuocere a fuoco basso. Fate raffreddare leggermente l'oden e servite caldo.

BOND STREET

Owner / Titolare › Jonathan Morr • **Chef** › Marc Spitzer

6 Bond Street • Ⓜ Bleecker St • +01 212 777 2500 • **www.bondstreetrestaurant.com**

 Bond Street is the twin restaurant of Cherry, so we expected blazing performance and great food. We were not disappointed. The only thing we did't like was the anonymous little door which you have to buzz to access. The restaurant offers a stylish dark first dining room, a sushi hall where you can see the chefs at work, and finally a lounge made for long, highly alcoholic nights. The kitchen is coordinated by chef Marc Spitzer, as we were saying, it is top quality, as well as the Sake list. We very much liked the crab roll and the lobster tempura. The lamb chops were fantastic. Among the desserts, an applause for the "bread pudding", closely followed by the "green tea mille crepes", but be aware that the dessert menu will give you a crisis, because you'll have to choose between 13 sweet dishes (and 6 sweet wines). Needless to mention, the sushi is great.

Bond Street è il ristorante gemello del Cherry, dunque ci attendevamo una performance strepitosa e cibo ottimo. Le aspettative non sono andate deluse. L'unica cosa che non ci è piaciuta è stata l'ingresso del locale: un anonimo portoncino a cui bisogna suonare per accedere. Il ristorante è composto da una prima sala elegante e dark, una seconda sala sushi dove si possono ammirare gli chef all'opera, e infine una lounge per notti lunghe e ad alto tasso alcolico. La cucina coordinata dallo chef Marc Spitzer, dicevamo, è da numeri uno, così come la Sakè list. Ci sono piaciuti tanto il roll al granchio e l'aragosta in tempura. Le costolette di agnello erano fantastiche. Tra i dolci, un applauso per il "bread pudding", seguito a ruota dal "green tea mille crepes", ma sappiate che la carta dei dessert vi manderà in crisi, perché dovrete scegliere tra 13 dolci (e 6 vini dolci). Il sushi è strepitoso. Che te lo dico a fare.

Wine List › Carta dei Vini	**Cuisine** › Cucina	**Lunch** › Pranzo	**Average Price** › Prezzo Medio
50 Labels › Etichette	**Japanese** › Giapponese	**No lunch** › Chiuso a pranzo	$ 60-75

TALÒ › Verdeca Puglia IGP
CANTINE SAN MARZANO

Colore giallo paglierino con riflessi dorati; al naso rivela sorprendenti profumi di fiori bianchi e vaniglia; al palato è fresco e giustamente minerale con una buona persistenza sapida.
Abbinamenti: Frutti di mare, crostacei e pesci lessi con salse leggere.

Straw yellow colour with green reflections; Scotch broom notes and a hint of citrus and tropical fruits on the nose. Lively in acidity, fresh and mineral.
Best served with: Excellent with starters and fish soup, fresh cheese and pasta with light sauces.

Lobster tempura
Tempura di aragosta

INGREDIENTS FOR 4 SERVINGS:
- 2 each lobster, 1 ¼ lb each **Creamy Japanese Mustard Sauce:** 1 egg Yolks - 3 cups vegetable oil - 1 t cold water - 1 t japanese mustard powder - 3 oz rice wine vinegar - salt - 0,25 teaspoon cayenne - 2 oz sugar **Tempura Batter:** - 1 each egg yolk - ¼ cup vegetable oil - ¾ cup club soda - 1 cup all purpose flour **Garnish:** - 1 head Lola Rosa - 2 heads Frisse - 1,4 lbs Celery root, julienne

INGREDIENTI PER 4 PERSONE:
- 2 aragoste a persona, 560 g **Salsa di senape giapponese cremosa, a persona:** 1 tuorlo - 710 ml di olio vegetale - 1 cucchiaino d'acqua fredda - 1 cucchiaino di senape in polvere giapponese - 88 ml di aceto di riso - sale - 0,25 cucchiaino di Caienna - 56 g di zucchero **Per la pastella tempura:** - 1 tuorlo - 60 ml di olio vegetale - 175 ml acqua frizzante - 125 g di farina **Per guarnire:** - 1 testa di Lola Rosa - 2 teste di frisse - 635 g di radice di sedano a julienne

Blanch each lobster in boiling water for 2 minutes for the tail and 3 minutes for the claws. Shock in ice water to ensure they stop cooking and stay half raw. Clean from shell. Take each tail and cut it in half lengthwise and then each half into three. Remove the claw and knuckle from the shell and reserve. **Creamy Japanese Mustard Sauce:** Whip the egg yolks in a food processor or by hand and slowly drizzle in the oil. Make sure that not too much is added at once or you will break the sauce. Keep adding oil until it becomes extremely thick. Add water, then add the mustard poder, rice wine vinegar, salt, sugar and cayenne pepper. **Tempura Batter:** Beat the yolk with a fork. Whisk in the oil. Add the chilled club soda. Next add the flour and mix with chopsticks but be careful not to over mix. There should be some chunks of unincorporated flour. **Garnish:** To assemble mix the celery root, frisse and lola rosa with some of the Japanese mustard sauce. Arrange on the plate. Take the lobster meat and lightly dredge in all purpose flour and then dip into the cold tempura batter. Fry at 350° until crispy but not overcooked for about 3 minutes.

Sbollentate le aragoste in acqua bollente per 2 minuti per le code e 3 minuti per le chele. Immergetele in acqua ghiacciata per interrompere a metà il processo di cottura. Pulite i gusci. Tagliate le code per lungo a metà e ogni metà in tre. Togliete chele e nocche dal guscio e mettete da parte. **Salsa di senape giapponese cremosa:** Montate i tuorli a mano o con un mixer e aggiungete lentamente un filo di olio. Assicuratevi di non aggiungerne troppo in una volta per non rovinare la salsa. Continuate ad aggiungere olio fino a quando diventa molto spesso. Aggiungete l'acqua, poi la polvere di senape, l'aceto di riso, il sale, lo zucchero e il pepe di Caienna. **Pastella Tempura:** Montate i tuorli con una forchetta. Aggiungete l'olio e l'acqua frizzante fresca. Poi aggiungete la farina e mescolate con le bacchette facendo attenzione a non mischiare troppo. Dovrebbero esserci alcuni grumi di farina non incorporata. **Per guarnire:** Unite del sedano, del Frisse e della lola rosa con un po' di salsa di senape giapponese e sistemate sul piatto da portata. Prendete la carne di aragosta, passatela nella farina e poi nella pastella di tempura fredda. Friggetela per 3 minuti circa a 175°C finché non diventa croccante ma non troppo cotta.

Green tea mille crepe
Millecrepes al tè verde

INGREDIENTS FOR 4:
Crepe batter: - 70 g all purpose flour - 100 g sugar - 6 whole eggs - 2 c heavy cream - 1 tbsp vanilla extract
Green tea cream: - 1 q. heavy cream - ½ c sugar - 2 tbsp green tea powder - ½ sheet gelatin

INGREDIENTI PER 4:
Per la pastella crepes: - 70 g di farina - 100 g di zucchero - 6 uova - 470 ml di panna - 1 cucchiaio di estratto di vaniglia
Per la crema al tè verde: - 945 ml di panna - 112 g di zucchero - 2 cucchiai di tè verde in polvere - ½ foglio di gelatina

Crepe batter: Place all the ingredients in a container and mix well until there are no lumps. Let it rest in the fridge for one hour before you use it. Lightly butter a non-stick pan. Over low to medium heat, cook the crepe until lightly browned in spots. Flip it over for ten seconds. Reserve. **Green tea cream:** Bloom the gelatin in cold water. Mix the sugar and green tea powder. Whip the heavy cream to soft peaks and add the green tea powder and sugar and keep whipping to medium peaks. Melt the gelatin and add It to the cream mixture, keep mixing until stiff. **To assemble:** Take a crepe and spread just enough green tea cream to cover it as thinly as possible. Take another crepe and repeat. Do this for about 24 layers. Sprinkle the top with fine sugar and caramelize. Chill the cake.

Per la pastella: Unite tutti gli ingredienti in una ciotola e mescolate bene fino a quando non ci sono più grumi. Lasciate riposare in frigo per un'ora prima dell'utilizzo. Imburrate leggermente una padella antiaderente. Cuocete le crepes a fuoco basso -medio fino a quando si iniziano a scurire in alcuni punti. Capovolgete per dieci secondi e poi mettete da parte. **Per la crema al tè verde:** Sciogliete la gelatina in acqua fredda. Unite lo zucchero e il tè verde in polvere. Montate la panna e aggiungete il tè verde e lo zucchero. Aggiungete infine la gelatina mentre continuate a montare la panna. **Per assemblare:** Spalmate sottilmente sulla crepes la crema al tè verde tanto quanto basta per ricoprirla. Prendete un'altra crepes e ripetete questo procedimento fino a sovrapporre circa 24 strati. Cospargete l'ultima crepes con zucchero a velo e fate caramellare. Conservate il dolce al fresco.

Crispy softshell crab
Granchio croccante

INGREDIENTS FOR 4 SERVINGS:
- 4 each soft shell crab - 4 oz potato starch - 1 togarashi spice
Summer Bean Salad: - 4 oz french beans - 4 oz wax beans - 4 oz green beans
- 4 oz snow peas - ¼ cup edamame - 3 each radish, sliced - 3 oz miso vinaigrette
Miso Vinaigrette: - 2 oz miso paste, brown - 1ea shallots minced - 1 knob ginger,
grated - 1 ea thai chili minced - 2 ea garlic, mashed and minced - 2 oz rice vinegar - 2 oz soy sauce - 5 oz sesame oil - 8 oz canola oil - pinch of sugar
Yuzu kosho Sauce: - 4 t yuzu kosho - 3 oz soy - 2 cups mayonnaise
- 2 oz rice vinegar

INGREDIENTI PER 4 PERSONE:
- 4 granchi Softshell - 113 g di fecola di patate - 1 Togarashi
Insalata di fagioli estiva: - 113 g di fagiolini francesi - 113 g di fagioli cera
- 113 g di fagiolini verdi - 113 g di piselli snow - 38 g di edamame
- 3 ravanelli, affettati - 85 g di vinaigrette di miso
Vinaigrette di miso: - 56 g di pasta di miso marrone - 1 scalogno tritato - una
noce di zenzero, grattugiata - 1 peperoncino tailandese, tritato - 2 spicchi di
aglio, schiacciati e tritati - 56 g di aceto di riso - 56 g di salsa di soia - 226 g di
olio di canola - 141 g di olio di sesamo - un pizzico di zucchero
Salsa Yuzu Kosho: - 4 cucchiaini di yuzu kosho - 85 g di soia
- 260 g di maionese - 56 g di aceto di riso

Clean gills from crab. Mix potato starch with togarashi spice. Toss
crab with starch mixture and fry at 400* until crispy. About 3 mins.
Summer Bean Salad: Blanch and shock all beans separately. Mix
beans with sliced radish and add 3 oz of miso vinnaigrette.
Miso Vinaigrette: *In a mixing bowl combine shallot, ginger, thai
chili and garlic. Add miso paste and rice vinegar and a pinch of
sugar, mix together with a whisk. Next add soy sauce, continue to
whisk and slowly add the sesame oil and canola oil.
Yuzu kosho Sauce: Mix all ingredients.

Togliete le branchie dai granchi. Mescolate la fecola di patate con
il Togarashi. Saltate il granchio con la miscela di amido e friggete a
200°C fino a quando diventa croccante, per circa 3 minuti.
Insalata di fagioli estiva: Scottate e raffreddate tutti i fagioli separatamente. Mescolate i fagioli con il ravanello a fette e aggiungete la
vinaigrette di miso.
Vinaigrette di miso: * In una terrina, unite lo scalogno, lo zenzero,
il peperoncino e l'aglio. Aggiungete la pasta di miso, l'aceto di riso
e un pizzico di zucchero, e mescolate con una frusta. Successiva-
mente aggiungete la salsa di soia, continuate a frullare e aggiungete
lentamente l'olio di sesamo e di canola.
Salsa Yuzu kosho: Unite tutti gli ingredienti.

Grilled rack of lamb

INGREDIENTS FOR 4 SERVINGS:
- 1 frenched rack of lamb **Asian Pear Sauce:** - 0,5 lb carots
- 0,5 lb onions - 0,5 lb parsnips - ½ head of garlic - 1 bay leaf
- 2 teaspoons black peppercorns - 1 cup asian pear juice
- 2 quarts chicken stock - 30 each shiso leaves
Shiso Oil: - 4 oz grape seed oil - 20 each shiso leaves
- 1 teaspoon salt **Yuzu Potato Gratin:** - 4 each idaho potatoes
- 2 cups heavy cream - 2 tablespoons yuzu skin - salt and pepper
Garnish: - 1 t micro shiso - sea salt - 4 oz sauteed baby spinach
- 2 caramelized asian pears

Asian Pear Sauce: Cut the vegetables sauteed in large cubes
and caramelize in a pot with oil. Add garlic, bay leaf and peppercorns. Deglaze with Asian pear juice and reduce. Add lamb
stock and reduce by half. Strain and finish with chopped shiso.
Shiso Oil: Quickly blend oil and shiso with a blender to keep
nice green color. Strain and chill.
Yuzu Potato Gratin: Place cream in a medium pot. Add yuzu
skin and season with salt and pepper. Bring to boil and simmer until cream is infused with yuzu flavor, approximately for
20 minutes. Meanwhile, peel and slice potatoes. Use a mandolin to cut thin slices and place into a bowl. Strain yuzu cream
over potatoes. Layer potatoes in baking dish and place into a
325 degree oven for approximately 2 ½ hours or until tender.

brio

BRIO NYC

Owner / Titolare › Massimo Scoditti • **Chef** › Massimo Carbone

786 Lexington Avenue • Ⓜ Lexington Av/63 St • +01 212 980 2300 • **www.brionyc.com**

There are some restaurants that make you really feel at home. Brio is one of them: a very nice owner, a chef that is always available to chat with customers, "very friendly" staff. And maybe this is the secret of the success of this restaurant that since 1990 is part of the most popular Italian restaurants among New Yorkers. The food definitely has its part. Especially because the menu offers a good variety from all the Italian regional cuisines, from Puglia to Emilia, from Tuscany to Lazio. Brio is the best place to catch your breath after shopping in Manhattan, the most dangerous area for your wallet: after visiting Bloomingdale's, H & M, Uniqlo and many other shops located on Lexington Avenue, also think about satisfying your taste.

Ci sono ristoranti che ti fanno davvero sentire a casa. Brio è uno di questi: titolare simpaticissimo, chef sempre disponibile a scambiare quattro chiacchiere con i clienti, personale "very friendly". E forse è proprio questo il segreto del successo di questo locale che dal 1990 è tra i ristoranti italiani più amati dai newyorchesi. Certo, anche il cibo fa la sua parte. Soprattutto perché il menù offre una panoramica completa su tutte le cucine regionali italiane, dalla pugliese alla emiliana, dalla toscana alla laziale. Brio è il posto più adatto per riprendere fiato dopo aver fatto shopping nella zona di Manhattan più pericolosa per il vostro portafogli: dopo aver fatto visita a Bloomingdale's, H&M, Uniqlo e ai mille altri negozi presenti sulla Lexington Avenue, pensate anche a soddisfare il vostro palato.

Wine List › Carta dei Vini	**Cuisine** › Cucina	**Lunch** › Pranzo	**Dinner** › Cena
50 Labels › Etichette	**Italian** › Italiana	$ 40	$ 40

Tuna tartare
Tartare di tonno

INGREDIENTS FOR 4 SERVINGS:
- 1 lb of yellowfin tuna - 1 cup of olive oil - 1 tbsp of mustard - 2 tbsp of kosher salt - 1 cup of minced shallots - 1 tbsp of ground black pepper - 1 diced red pepper

INGREDIENTI PER 4 PERSONE:
- 450 gr di tonno pinna gialla - 236 ml di olio d'oliva - 1 cucchiaio di senape - 2 cucchiai di sale kosher - 100 gr di scalogno tritato - 1 cucchiaio di pepe nero macinato - 1 peperone rosso a dadini

Cut the tuna into ¼ inch dice and place it in a very large bowl. In a separate bowl, combine the olive oil, red pepper, mustard, shallots, salt and pepper and pour the contents over the tuna and mix well. Allow the mixture to sit in the refrigerator for at least on hour for the flavours to blend. Serve with toasted bread with and sliced avocado for decoration.

Tagliate il tonno a dadini da 6mm e ponetelo in una grande ciotola. In una ciotola a parte, unite l'olio d'oliva, il peperoncino, la senape, lo scalogno, il sale e il pepe. Versate il tutto sul tonno e mescolate bene. Lasciate insaporire in frigorifero per almeno un'ora. Servite con pane tostato e fette di avocado per decorare.

Cernia alla mugnaia

INGREDIENTS FOR 4 SERVINGS:
- 4 filet of grouper
- a spoonful of capers
- lemon juice
- 1 bottle of white wine
- 4 tablespoons of butter
- flour

INGREDIENTI PER 4 PERSONE:
- 4 filetti di cernia
- un cucchiaio di capperi
- succo di limone
- 1 bottiglia di vino bianco
- 4 cucchiai di burro
- farina

Coat the filets in flour and shake the excess off. In a large non-stick skillet, heat 2 tablespoons of butter over medium heat. Sautee the fish on both sides until nicely golden brown, remove fish and place on serving platter and keep warm. Return the skillet to the stove and melt 2 tablespoons of butter with lemon juice, capers and white whine, heat untill all ingredients are nicely mixed and then pour over the fish and serve.

Passate i filetti nella farina e togliete quella in eccesso. Scaldate 2 cucchiai di burro a fuoco medio in una grande padella antiaderente. Scottate il pesce su entrambi i lati fino a doratura, poi ponetelo su un piatto da portata e tenete in caldo. Mettete nuovamente la padella sul fuoco e unite 2 cucchiai di burro con il succo di limone, i capperi e il vino bianco. Versate sul pesce e servite!

TALÒ › **Negroamaro Rosato Salento IGP**
CANTINE SAN MARZANO

Colore rosato intenso con riflessi rubino; profumo intenso e persistente, con sentori di ciliegia e lampone. Vino di buon corpo, fresco ed equilibrato al palato.
Abbinamenti: Antipasti all'italiana, zuppe di pesce e brodetti, pesce al cartoccio o al forno, formaggi giovani o leggermente stagionati.

Intensely rosé-coloured with ruby red reflections; complex and persistent aroma, with cherry and raspberry notes. A full-bodied wine, fresh and balanced in the mouth.
Best served with: Italian style starters, fish soups, roasted or foil- baked fish, fresh or slightly aged cheeses.

Tiramisù

INGREDIENTS FOR 4 SERVINGS:
- 2 cups of espresso
- 30 savoiardi biscuits
- 6 egg yolks
- 3 cups of sugar
- 1 cup of mascarpone cheese
- 2 cups of heavy cream
- 1 cup of kahlua liquer
- 2 spoons of cocoa

INGREDIENTI PER 4 PERSONE:
- 2 tazze di espresso
- 30 savoiardi
- 6 tuorli d'uovo
- 675 gr di zucchero
- 225 gr di mascarpone
- 473 ml di panna
- 235 ml di liquore Kahlua
- 2 cucchiai di cacao

A few at a time, dip the first eighteen savoiardi ladyfingers in the espresso and line the bottom of a medium sized pan with them. Combine the yolks and sugar and mix for ten minutes, then add the mascarpone cheese. In a separate bowl mix the cream with one cup of sugar and the Kahlua, add the mascarpone filling and whip again. Spread half the filling in the pan, soak the remaining ladyfingers and make a second layer. Finish by adding the remaining filling and sprinkle with a dusting of cocoa before serving.

Bagnate i primi diciotto savoiardi nel caffè e poneteli sul fondo di una teglia di medie dimensioni. Unite i tuorli e lo zucchero e mescolate per dieci minuti, poi aggiungete il mascarpone. In un'altra ciotola, montate la panna con 225gr di zucchero e il Kahlua, poi aggiungete la crema di mascarpone e sbattete ancora. Stendete metà della crema nella teglia sopra i savoiardi. Bagnate la seconda metà dei savoiardi e fate un secondo strato. Infine coprite con la crema rimanente e prima di servire date una spolverata di cacao.

Bucatini all'amatriciana

INGREDIENTS FOR 4 SERVINGS:
- 320 g di bucatini pasta
- ¼ cup of extra virgin olive oil
- 3 oz of pancetta
- 2 onions
- 1 35 oz can of tomatoes
- basil - salt - pepper

INGREDIENTI PER 4 PERSONE:
- 320 g di bucatini
- 60 ml di olio extra vergine di oliva
- 85 gr di pancetta
- 2 cipolle
- 1 lattina di pomodori da 1kg
- basilico - sale - pepe

In a large saucepan, heat the olive oil and sautée the diced pancetta with the sliced onions until golden brown (for about five minutes). Add the tomato sauce and cook, whilst stirring for 45 minutes. Season to taste with salt, pepper, and add the basil. Cook bucatini in boiling salted water and place them "al dente" in the sauce.

Saltate la pancetta a dadini nell'olio d'oliva in una grande padella, fino a doratura (circa cinque minuti). Aggiungete la salsa di pomodoro e lasciate cuocere, mescolando, per 45 minuti. Condite con sale, pepe e aggiungete il basilico. Cuocete la pasta al dente e aggiungetela al condimento, mantecate e servite.

Hello Mogadorian people,

Start the day

Cafe Mogador

CAFE MOGADOR

Owners / Titolari › Rivika Orlin / Yosi Ohayan / Azul Ohayan • **Chef** › Rivka Orlin

101 Saint Marks Pl • **M** 1 Av [L] • +01 212 677 2226 • **www.cafemogador.com**

Full at breakfast, full at lunch, packed at dinner. Every single day. In my life I have never seen such a trendy place. Yet, from the outside, the Cafe Mogador does nothing to appear or be attractive. The interiors are simple, stark even, and reflect what the place wants to be: a small restaurant where you can taste the Moroccan and Mediterranean cuisine. Clearly the cuisine here plays the main part and it does it so well that since the opening, back in 1983, the Mogador in the East Village has become what today it's called a "landmark": a point of interest. In short, you should go to be able to say that you have been there. But I'll give you some extra reasons to go there: the tagine (especially the lamb one), the chicken, the Mogador burger, the salmon and the cous-cous.

Pieno a colazione, pieno a pranzo, strapieno a cena. Tutti i santi giorni. Nella mia vita non ho mai visto un posto così trendy. Eppure, visto da fuori, il Cafè Mogador non fa nulla per apparire ed essere attraente. Anche gli interni sono semplici, addirittura spartani, e rispecchiano ciò che il locale vuole essere: un ristorantino dove assaporare la cucina marocchina e mediterranea. È evidente che qui la cucina fa la parte da leone. E la fa talmente bene che fin dalla sua apertura, nell'ormai lontano 1983, il Mogador dell'East Village è divenuto subito quel che oggi si chiama "landmark": un punto di riferimento. Insomma, ci dovreste andare anche solo per poter dire di esserci stati. Ma vi offro qualche motivo in più per farlo: le tagine (specie quella d'agnello), il pollo, il Mogador burger, il salmone, il cous-cous.

Wine List › Carta dei Vini	Cuisine › Cucina	Lunch › Pranzo	Dinner › Cena
100 Labels › Etichette	**Maroccan middle eastern** › Marocchina	$ 12	$ 30

Spicy carrots

INGREDIENTS FOR 4 SERVINGS:
- 20 carrots
- 2 tbs salt
- 2 tbs cayenne pepper
- ½ tbs cumin
- 1 ½ tbs icing sugar
- 1 tbs garlic
- 16 oz lemon juice
- 16 oz extra vergin olive oil
- parsley

Cook the carrots al dente and cut in round pieces. Garnish with parsley.

Carote piccanti

INFREDIENTI PER 4 PERSONE
- 20 carote
- 2 cucchiai di sale
- 2 cucchiai di pepe di Caienna
- ½ cucchiaio di cumino
- 1 ½ cucchiaio di zucchero a velo
- 1 cucchiaio di aglio
- 450 g di succo di limone
- 450 g di olio extravergine di oliva
- prezzemolo

Cuocere le carote al dente e tagliarle in pezzi tondi. Guarnire con prezzemolo.

Marinated beets

INGREDIENTS FOR 4 SERVINGS:
- 30 beets
- 2 tbs salt
- 1 tbs black pepper
- 1 ts cumin
- 24 oz lemon juice
- 2 cups extra vergin olive oil
- ½ Red onion chopped fine
- parsley

Cooked the beets "al dente and cut in long pieces. Garnish with parsley.

Barbabietole marinate

INGREDIENTS FOR 4 SERVINGS:
- 30 barbabietole
- 2 cucchiai di sale
- 1 cucchiaio di pepe nero
- 1 cucchiaino di cumino
- 680 g di succo di limone
- 2 tazze di olio extravergine di oliva
- ½ cipolla rossa tritata bene
- prezzemolo

Cuocere le barbabietole al dente e tagliate in pezzi lunghi. Guarnire con prezzemolo.

CATCH

Owner / Titolare › EMM Group • **Chef** › John Beatty

21 Ninth Avenue • Ⓜ 8 Av [L] • +01 212 392 5978 • **www.catchnewyorkcity.com**

If you are looking for happiness, you have to pop in to Catch: beautiful women, attractive men, smiley faces, a lot of talking and cocktails and tempting dishes coming and going. We are at the foot of the High Line, the most fashionable area in New York. A very nice, definitely trendy place with a fascinating roof terrace, that servece up Catch cuisine brunch, lunch and dinner before transitioning to a nightlife destination later on each evening. The dishes of chef John Beatty, will take your attention to the delicious cuisine. The sushi is top-notch, the shrimp scampi is fabulous and the Wagu meat cooked at your table on soapstone is sensational. We also tried the Crispy whole snapper, ugly looking but with a divine taste, and finished off the dinner with delicious desserts. Do not expect a cheap bill, but the place and cuisine are top quality.

Se siete alla ricerca della felicità, dovete fare un salto al Catch: belle donne, uomini attraenti, volti sorridenti, un gran vociare e un via vai di cocktail e piatti invitanti. Siamo ai piedi della High Line, nel quartiere più in di New York. Un locale molto bello, sicuramente alla moda, con una terrazza panoramica affascinante, tanto che ad un certo punto vi chiederete se siete finiti in un ristorante o piuttosto in un nightclub. I piatti dello chef John Beatty, ricondurranno la vostra attenzione sulla cucina, che è ottima. Il sushi è di alto livello, lo shrimp scampi è favoloso e la carne Wagu cotta al tavolo sulla pietra ollare è sensazionale. Abbiamo provato anche il Crispy whole snapper, brutto da vedere ma dal sapore divino, e concluso la cena con dei dolci magnifici. Non vi aspettate un conto abbordabile, ma il posto e la cucina sono di livello superiore.

Wine List › Carta dei Vini	**Cuisine** › Cucina	**Prix-fixe Lunch** › Pranzo a prezzo fisso	**Dinner** › Cena
150 Labels › Etichette	**Globaly-Influenced Seafood**	$ 20 (3 courses) › 3 portate	$ 40-90

INGREDIENTS FOR 4 SERVINGS:
- 4 ea head on prawn - 1 cup of scampi filling - 1 cup of scampi sauce - 3 prawns - 1 cup of chopped marinated Artichokes - 2 oz of fresno chili - 1 cup of chopped roasted tomatoes - 2 cup of white wine - 2 lb of butter - 3 oz of toasted garlic - 1 cup of lemon juice - 1 small potato roll - 1 pinch of alepo chili - 1 oz of chives, chopped - 1 oz of italian parsley, chopped - 2 oz of vegetable oil

INGREDIENTI PER 4 PERSONE:
- 4 gamberi con la testa - 325 g di ripieno di scampi - 225 g di salsa di scampi - 3 gamberoni (per piatto) - 325 g di carciofi marinati tritati - 56 g di Fresno chili - 200 g di pomodori arrostiti tritati - 470 ml di vino bianco - 907 g di burro - 85 g di aglio tostato - 235 ml di succo di limone - 1 piccolo rotolo di patate - 1 pizzico di peperoncino Alepo - 28 g di erba cipollina tritata - 28 g di prezzemolo italiano tritato - 56 g di olio vegetale

Prawns: Cut the shell open from the top of the shrimp down the length along the back. Remove all of the meat from the shell. Save the shell pieces in a separate container because they will be used to plate the dish. Chop all the shrimp meat into bite size pieces. In a hot sautè pan, cook the shrimp in 2 oz of vegetable oil for 1 minute. Remove the shrimp from the saute pan and place in a metal bowl. Place the bowl in the freezer for 3-4 minutes or in an ice bath to stop the cooking process. The shrimp should only be partially cooked at this point. Wash the shrimp shell under cold running water, dry and stuff with aluminum foil to allow the shells to keep their original shape. Bake the shrimp shells on a baking sheet for approximately 45 minutes in a 350° oven until they are bright orange and fully cooked. **Roasted Tomatoes:** Place 1 pint of grape tomatoes in a mixing bowl, season with salt, pepper, and chopped garlic, and roast in the oven at 300° for an hour until all liquid is removed. **Scampi Filling:** In hot saute pan, saute the partially cooked shrimp meat, sliced fresno chilis, tomatos, 2 oz white wine, 4 oz butter, and all scampi sauce. Bring to a boil, season with salt and pepper, and finsh with fresh chopped chives and parsley. **Scampi Sauce:** Combine the remaining white wine, butter, toasted garlic, lemon juice, potato roll and the allepo in a sauce pot and bring to a boil. Add all the indgredients into a blender and puree until smooth. **To Serve:** Place the oven roasted shell in the centre of a plate and scoop 4 oz of hot filling into the shell and pour 2 oz of sauce over the top. Garnish with chopped parsley and chives.

Preparazione gamberi: Pulire i gamberi tagliando il guscio dalla parte superiore scendendo lungo la schiena. Togliete tutta la carne dal guscio. Conservate i pezzi del guscio in un contenitore. Tagliate la carne in bocconcini. Friggeteli in una padella in olio vegetale per 1 minuto, quindi poneteli in una ciotola di metallo. Posizionate la ciotola nel congelatore o in ghiaccio per 3-4 minuti, per arrestare il processo di cottura. I gamberi dovrebbero essere solo parzialmente cotti a questo punto. Lavate i gusci dei gamberi sotto acqua corrente fredda, asciugateli e riempiteli con della carta d'alluminio per non farli deformare. Cuocete in forno i gusci su una teglia per circa 45 minuti a 175°C fino a quando diventano arancioni e sono completamente cotti. **Per i pomodori arrostiti:** Mettete i pomodori in una ciotola e condite con sale, pepe, aglio tritato e arrostite in forno a 150°C per un'ora, fino a quando non ci sarà più la parte liquida.
Preparazione ripieno: Lasciate soffriggere in una padella la carne dei gamberi parzialmente cotti, i peperoncini Fresno a fette, i pomodori, 59ml di vino bianco, 113gr di burro, e tutta la salsa di scampi. Portate ad ebollizione, condite con sale e pepe, e finite con erba cipollina tritata fresca e prezzemolo.
Per la salsa di scampi: Unite la parte restante di vino bianco, il burro, l'aglio tostato, il succo di limone, il rotolo di patate, e l'Alepo in una pentola per salsa e portate ad ebollizione. Mettete tutti gli ingredienti in un frullatore fino ad ottenere una crema liscia.
Per impiattare: Ponete un guscio arrostito nel centro del piatto, aggiungete 113gr di ripieno caldo e versateci sopra 56 gr di salsa. Guarnire con prezzemolo ed erba cipollina tritata.

Shrimp scampi
Gamberoni scampi

Crispy chicken - Pollo croccante

INGREDIENTS FOR 4 SERVINGS:
- 4 ea chicken Breast (boneless) - 1 cup roasted root veg - 1 cup chicken jus - 6 oz chicken breast 4 ea - 2 gal chicken stock - 1 lb butter - 1 cup thai basil chopped - 6 ea eggs - 2 cups all purpose flour - 6 cups panko bread crumb - 10 ea carrots - 2 pc parsnips - 1 ea rutabega - 1 cup carmelized onion - 4 ea spanish onion - 2 cups vegetable oil

Chicken: Let the butter soften to room temperature. In a mixing bowl, put the soft butter, the thai basil, 4 oz of chicken jus and mix thoroughly. Season with salt and pepper to taste. Place the butter mix into a piping bag and cut the tip at 1 inch from the end. Pipe the butter out onto a cookie tray in long, straight rows. Place the tray in the refrigerator to allow the butter to harden. When the butter has firmed up, cut the rows into 3 inch logs and set aside. Take a long thin fillet knife and make small incisions at the top of the breasts and cut to the middle. Set up a standard breading station with flour, eggs, and panko. Bread the chicken. In a skillet, brown 2 breasts at a time in vegetable oil. When golden brown on both sides, finish baking at 350° in an oven until the internal temperature reaches 165°F.

Vegetables: Take half the parsnips, the rutabaga and carrots and cut roughly into half inch squares. Then toss all vegetables in vegetable oil, and roast in a 350° oven until tender. Remove and leave to cool. In large saute pan, heat 2 oz of vegetable oil until pan is very hot. Add roasted vegetables, carmelized onions, and 2 cups of chicken stock, 2 tbsp of butter and cook until vegetables are glazed and all the liquid has evaporated. Season with salt and pepper to taste.

Carmelized Onions: Peel 10 spanish onions and slice them into thin rounds. In a large sauce pot, add 8 oz of butter and leave to melt, add the sliced onions and cook for 2 hours over medium low heat. Contiune to stir, making sure it doesn't stick to the bottom of the pot. The onions will release their liquid. Continue to stir and remove from the heat when the liquid dries up and the onions begin to brown.

Chicken Stock: In large sauce pot, add 10 lbs of chicken bones (backs and necks), 2 large onions cut in quarters, 5 carrots cut into rounds, 10 bayleafs, 2 oz of black pepper corns and cover with cold water. Bring to a boil and then drop down to a simmer. Cook for 2 hours then strain and reserve the liquid. Cool the liquid in an ice bath.

Chicken Jus: Reduce 2 gal of chicken stock with thinly sliced spanish onions and carrots cut into rounds (leave to thicken until it can coat the back of a spoon). Season with salt and pepper. The sauce should be reduced by 3/4 of the amount of the starting liquid. Strain and reserve.

To Serve: Place the sauteed vegetables in the centre of a round plate. Pour 2 oz of chicken jus over the vegetables and let it run onto the plate. Place fully cooked chicken breast on top and finish.

INGREDIENTI PER 4 PERSONE: - 4 petti di pollo (disossati) - 150 g di ortaggi a radice arrostiti - 235 ml di jus di pollo - 170 g di petto di pollo - 7,5 l di brodo di pollo - 453 g di burro - 25 g di basilico tailandese tritato - 6 uova - 280 g di farina - 540 g di pangrattato Panko - 10 carote - 2 pezzi di pastinaca - 1 pezzo di rutabega - 100 g di cipolla caramellata - 4 cipolle rosse - 473 ml di olio vegetale

Preparazione pollo: Lasciate ammorbidire il burro a temperatura ambiente. In una ciotola, unite il burro, il basilico e il jus di pollo e mescolate accuratamente. Condite con sale e pepe quanto basta. Mettete il mix di burro in un sac à poche e tagliate la punta a 2,5cm dalla fine. Formate delle lunghe strisce dritte di burro su di un vassoio. Posizionatelo in frigorifero per consentire al burro di indurire. Quando si sarà raffermato, tagliate le strisce in tronchetti da 7,5cm e mettete da parte. Con un coltello lungo e sottile, fate un'incisione dalla parte superiore del petto di pollo fino a metà. Preparate un'impanatura classica di farina, uova, e pangrattato Panko. Impanate il pollo. In una padella, fate rosolare 2 petti di pollo alla volta in 2,5cm di olio vegetale. Quando entrambi i lati sono dorati, terminate la cottura in forno a 175°C fino a quando la temperatura interna raggiunge 73°C . *Preparazione verdura:* Prendete metà della pastinaca, della rutabaga e delle carote e tagliate grossolanamente a dadini da circa 1cm. Condite con olio vegetale, e mettete in forno a 175°C fino a quando diventano tenere. Togliete dal forno e lasciate raffreddare. Per impiattare, fate riscaldare in una padella 60ml di olio vegetale. Aggiungete le verdure, le cipolle caramellate, 473ml di brodo di pollo e 2 cucchiai di burro, e lasciate cuocere fino a quando le verdure sono glassate e tutto il liquido è evaporato. Condite con sale e pepe a piacere.

Preparazione cipolle caramellate: Sbucciate 10 cipolle spagnole e tagliatele a rondelle sottili. Mettete 225 g di burro in una grande padella, aggiungete le cipolle e lasciatele cuocere per 2 ore a fuoco medio-basso. Continuate a mescolare facendo attenzione a non far attaccare la cipolla al fondo della padella. Le cipolle rilasceranno la loro acqua. Continuate a mescolare e togliete dal fuoco quando tutto il liquido sarà evaporato e le cipolle sono dorate. *Preparazione brodo di pollo:* In una grande pentola, mettete 4.5 kg di ossa di pollo (schiena e collo), 2 grandi cipolle tagliate in quarti, 5 carote tagliate a rondelle, 10 foglie d'alloro, 56 g di pepe nero in grani e ricoprite il tutto con acqua fredda. Portate ad ebollizione e poi abbassate la fiamma. Lasciate cuocere per 2 ore, poi filtrate, mettete da parte il liquido e fatelo raffreddare.

Preparazione jus di pollo: Fate ridurre 7,5 lt di brodo di pollo con la cipolla rossa affettata e le carote a rondelle (lasciate addensare fino a quando rimane coperto il dorso di un cucchiaio). Condite con sale e pepe. Il jus deve essere ridotto per 3/4 della quantità del liquido iniziale. Filtratelo e tenetelo da parte.

Preparazione piatto: Posate le verdure saltate al centro di un piatto da servizio tondo. Versate sopra 60 ml di jus di pollo e lasciatelo cadere sul piatto. Posizionate il petto di pollo cotto sulla parte superiore e terminate il piatto.

SALADS

FARRO SALAD
Pistachio, Parmigiano &
Summer Tomatoes 16

HEIRLOOM TOMATO & BASIL SALAD
Arugula & Strawberries 13

SHEEP'S MILK RICOTTA TOAST
Artichokes, Roman Zucchini and Bacon 14

BLUE CRAB TOAST
Chiles & Cucumber 16

SUMMER LETTUCE SALAD
Snap Peas, Herbs & Creme Fraiche 14

PASTA

GNOCCHI ROSA
Ricotta, Basil, Tomatoes 16

SPAGHETTI NERO
Blue Crab, Chiles & Lemon 22

SPAGHETTI CACIO E PEPE
Black Pepper, Pecorino & Parsley 15

RISOTTO OF SUMMER TOMATOES
Basil & Parmigiano 17

SMALL & LARGE

STICKY FIG BREAD, Housemade Focaccia, Anise Honey & Butter 6

TUSCAN CHICKEN LIVER, Balsamic Raisins, Capers & Walnuts 15

GRILLED SARDINES, Charred Olives & Lemon 15

POACHED EGG, Polenta, Charred Onions, Duck Crackling Crumble 16

OCTOPUS 'SALTIMBOCCA', Ceci Beans, Sage & Prosciutto di Parma 15

GRILLED LONG ISLAND CALAMARI, Borlotti Beans & Red Chiles 15

SOFT SCRAMBLED EGGS Roman Zucchini, Chiles, Toast & Pancetta 16

VEAL PASTRAMI, Pickle Salad, Rye Crisps 17

CRISPLY ROASTED HALF CHICKEN, Herb Salad 23

GRILLED BLACK BASS, Lemon, Fennel Salad & Salsa Verde 24

JUICE & SIDES

GREEN ENVY
Kale, Apple, Cucumber, Pineapple 11

KIDNEY PUNCH
Orange, Tumeric, Beet, Ginger 11

HOT BUTTERED CORN
Jersey's Best with Chives 9

FRENCH FRIED POTATOES
Rosemary & Sea Salt 8

CHARLIE BIRD

Owner / Titolare › Robert Bohr • **Chef** › Ryan Hardy

5 King Street • Ⓜ Houston St • +01 212 235 7133 • **www.charliebirdnyc.com**

At Charlie Bird you are happy, and that's not all. Indeed, it is just what you want from a bar or a restaurant. People feel good and you'll see this on the smiley faces of the people who sit back and relax on the terrace or by the lively atmosphere around the bar counter every evening. You also eat well and can try original dishes, because chef Ryan's American-Italian cuisine is influenced by his travels around the world. Try a Long Island Fluke, or the Grilled Scampi (in pure Mediterranean-style), or the Blue Crab Toast. The Spaghettini Nero is the dish that everyone should try, perhaps followed by the Black Bass (Persian bass). Among the desserts the "Winesap Apple Olive Oil Cake" is a must, it's something that goes beyond the concept of dessert. This place is very nice, as required for a restaurant in Soho, and we heard the best music selection: totally hip hop, but very pleasant.

Al Charlie Bird si sta bene, e non è poco. Anzi, è proprio quello che si chiede ad un locale, bar o ristorante che sia. Si sta bene e lo capisci dai volti sorridenti e rilassati della gente che siede ai tavoli all'aperto, oppure dall'ambiente vivace che si genera ogni sera intorno al bancone bar. E poi si mangia bene e si possono provare piatti originali, perché chef Ryan propone una cucina americana-italiana influenzata dai suoi viaggi in giro per il mondo. Ecco allora un Long Island Fluke, gli scampi grigliati (in puro stile Mediterraneo), oppure il toast al granchio blu. Gli spaghettini nero sono il piatto che tutti dovrebbero provare, magari seguito dal black bass (persico trota). Tra i dolci assolutamente imperdibile il "winesap apple olive oil cake", qualcosa che va oltre il concetto di dessert. Il posto è molto carino, come si richiede ad un locale di Soho, e abbiamo ascoltato la migliore selezione musicale: total hip hop, ma piacevolissima.

Wine List › Carta dei Vini	**Cuisine** › Cucina	**Lunch** › Pranzo	**Dinner** › Cena
150 Labels › Etichette	**American/Italian** › Americana/Italiana	$ 30-45	$ 75

Razor clams with fennel and chiles
Cannolicchi con finocchio e peperoncini

INGREDIENTS FOR 4 SERVINGS:
- 24 ea live razor clams - 2 tbsp extravirgin olive oil
- 3 ea cloves garlic - 1 ea small shallot- 0.5 head fennel, chopped - 8 oz dry white wine - 1 pinch chile flake - 16 ea razor clam shells - 2 tsp razor clam steaming liquid - 4 ea fennel stems, leaves removed, sliced thinl- 1 tbsp lemon juice, fresh squeezed - 2 tsp extravirgin olive oil - pinch maldon salt - 2 tsp calabrian chile paste

INGREDIENTI PER 4 PERSONE:
- 24 cannolicchi vivi - 2 cucchiai di olio extravergine di oliva - 3 spicchi d'aglio - 1 cipollotto piccolo - mezzo finocchio tritato - 236 ml di vino bianco secco - 1 pizzico di fiocchi di peperoncino - 16 gusci di cannolicchi - 2 cucchiaini di liquido di cottura dei cannolicchi - 4 gambi di finocchio senza foglie tagliate a fette sottili - 1 cucchiaio di succo di limone fresco - 2 cucchiaini di olio extravergine di oliva - 1 pizzico di sale di Maldon - 2 cucchiaini di salsa di peperoncino calabrese

Rinse the razor clams to remove all the residual sand. In a large sauté pan over medium heat, add the extravirgin olive oil, garlic, fennel and shallot and cook for 30 seconds. Add the razor clams and chiles, followed by the white wine and cover with a lid. Cook for 2 minutes or until the first wisps of steam escape. Immediately remove from the heat and check that all the razor clams are open and just firm. Strain the liquid and reserve. When the clams are cool enough to handle, remove the straight firm muscle from the surrounding belly. Slice thinly on a bias and reserve in a small mixing bowl. **To serve:** Clean the razor clam shells by separating the halves, rinsing them and reserve them on a towel. In a small bowl, mix the sliced razor clams with the fennel tops, lemon, razor clam steaming liquid, maldon salt and extravirgin olive oil. Place a small portion of the calabrian chile paste on the end of each razor clam shell. Add a spoonful of the razor clam mixture to each shell and serve on ice.

Sciacquate i cannolicchi per rimuovere tutti i residui di sabbia. Mettete l'olio extravergine di oliva, l'aglio, il finocchio e il cipollotto in una grande padella a fuoco medio e fate cuocere per 30 secondi. Aggiungete i cannolicchi e i peperoncini, seguiti dal vino bianco e coprite con un coperchio. Lasciate cuocere per 2 minuti o fino a quando inizia a fuoriuscire un po' di vapore. Togliete immediatamente dal fuoco e controllate che tutti i cannolicchi si siano aperti e raffermati. Filtrate il liquido e mettete da parte. Quando si sono raffreddati al punto da poterli maneggiare, rimuovete il muscolo dritto e sodo da intorno al ventre. Affettate sottilmente in sbieco e conservate in una ciotola piccola. **Per impiattare:** Pulite i gusci dei cannolicchi separando le due metà, sciacquateli e poneteli ad asciugare su un asciugamano. Mescolate i cannolicchi a fette con le cime di finocchio, il limone, il liquido di cottura, il sale Maldon e l'olio extravergine di oliva in una piccola ciotola. Mettete una piccola parte della salsa piccante calabrese all'estremità di ogni guscio. Aggiungete un cucchiaio del composto di cannolicchi ad ogni guscio e servite su ghiaccio.

Charlie Bird farro salad

INGREDIENTS FOR 2-4 SALADAS:
- 1 cup farro, raw (the best is still from Abruzzo, Italy) - 0.5 cup apple cider - 2 cups water, more if necessary - 0.5 tbsp salt, kosher
- 2 each   bay leaves - 1 cup cooked farro - ½ cup parmigiano cheese, shaved with a vegetable peeler - ½ cup cherry tomatoes, fresh from the vine
- ½ cup pistachios, toasted, shelled, whole - ½ cup arugula leaves - 16/20 each basil leaves, whole - 12/16 each mint leaves, whole
- 6 each radish, shaved on the mandolin - 4/5 tbsp extra virgin olive oil - 2 tbsp lemon juice - 2 tsp maldon sea salt

To cook the farro: Cover the farro with the apple cider, water, kosher salt and bay leaves and bring to a simmer.
Cook, adding more water if necessary for 30 minutes or until the farro is tender and the liquid has evaporated.
The end result should be something similar to the consistency of brown rice - but a whole lot easier to cook!
To make the salad: Combine farro, tomatoes, cheese, pistachio together with the lemon and olive oil.
This base can live in the bowl for up to an hour before you wish to plate the salad.
At the last minute add the arugula, basil, mint, radish and maldon sea salt to maximize the crunch and texture of the salad. Eat this salad at room temperature to give the cheese and tomatoes the maximum flavor (but you can serve chilled on a hot summer day).

CHERRY

Owner / Titolare › Jonathan Morr - Eugene Morimoto • **Chef** › Marc Spitzer

355 West 16th Street • Ⓜ 14 St [A,C,E] • +01 212 929 5800 • **www.cherrynyc.com**

I'm not fond of sushi: I find raw fish seasoned "Italian style" (with oil and salt) is a lot tastier. That said, I have eaten in many Japanese restaurants and I think I am able to distinguish quality sushi from production line ones. The experience at the Cherry was shocking. Positively shocking, of course. The place is wonderful, though perhaps a bit too dark. The service was excellent and the waiter suggested fantastic dishes that have earned this trendy restaurant in the Meatpacking District, located just a few steps from the High Line (one of the most beautiful places in New York) our title of Best City Restaurant. The sushi is spectacular, with crab, lobster and salmon that melts in your mouth. The desserts are amazing, especially the apple one. Of course the bill is not cheap, yet not impossible. And I swear that my review on Cherry is not in any way influenced by the presence of two beautiful Naomi Campbell lookalikes in their twenties at the table next to ours.

Non amo il sushi: trovo che il pesce crudo condito "all'italiana" (con olio e sale) sia infinitamente più saporito. Detto questo, ho mangiato in tanti ristoranti giapponesi e penso di essere in grado di saper distinguere la qualità dalla catena di montaggio. L'esperienza al Cherry è stata sconvolgente. Nell'eccezione positiva del termine, ovviamente. Il locale è meraviglioso, per quanto forse un po' troppo buio. Il servizio è stato eccellente ed il cameriere ha saputo suggerirmi piatti fantastici che hanno fatto meritare a questo ristorante alla moda nel Meatpacking District, situato a pochi passi dalla High Line (uno dei luoghi più belli di New York) il nostro titolo di Best City Restaurant. Il sushi era spettacolare, con granchio, aragosta e salmone che si scioglievano in bocca. I dolci si sono rivelati uno spettacolo, specialmente quello alla mela. Certo il conto non è abbordabile, ma nemmeno impossibile. E giuro che i miei giudizi sul Cherry non sono stati in alcun modo influenzati dalla presenza, al tavolo accanto, di due splendide ventenni sosia di Naomi Campbell.

Wine List › Carta dei Vini	Cuisine › Cucina	Lunch › Pranzo	Dinner › Cena
70 Labels › Etichette	Japanese-French	No lunch › Chiuso a pranzo	$ 50-100

Triple chocolate mousse

Tripla mousse al cioccolato

INGREDIENTS FOR 4 SERVINGS:
Milk Chocolate Mousse: - 12 oz milk chocolate - 2 eggs - 5 egg yolks
3 sheets gelatin - 2/3 cup sugar - 3 tbsp water - 2 cups heavy cream
58% Chocolate Mousse: - 10 oz chocolate 58% - 2 eggs - 5 egg yolks
- 2½ sheets gelatin - 2/3 cup sugar - 3 tbsp water - 2 cups heavy cream
66% Chocolate Mousse: - 12 oz Chocolate 66% - 2 eggs - 5 egg yolks
- 2 sheets gelatin - 2/3 cup sugar - 3 tbsp water - 2 cups heavy cream

INGREDIENTI PER 4 PERSONE:
Mousse di cioccolato al latte: - 340 g di cioccolato al latte - 2 uova
- 5 tuorli - 3 fogli di gelatina - 133 g di zucchero - 3 cucchiai di acqua
- 473 ml di panna
Mousse di cioccolato 58%: - 283 g di cioccolato 58% - 2 uova - 5 tuorli
- 2½ fogli di gelatina - 133 g di zucchero - 3 cucchiai di acqua - 473 ml
di panna
Mousse di cioccolato 66%: - 340 g di cioccolato 66% - 2 uova
- 5 tuorli - 2 fogli di gelatina - 133 g di zucchero - 3 cucchiai di acqua
- 473 ml di panna

Milk Chocolate Mousse: Melt the chocolate in a mixing bowl. Place whole eggs and yolks in an electronic mixer. Pour the sugar and water into a sauce pan and heat up to 257°F. Pour the sugar mixture into the eggs slowly while mixing. Once all the sugar is in, turn up the speed to the highest option. When the bottom of the bowl is cold, stop mixing. Melt the gelatin and add it to the mixture. Fold in the melted chocolate.
Whip the heavy cream into stiff peaks and fold into the chocolate.

58% Chocolate Mousse: Melt the chocolate in a mixing bowl. Place whole eggs and yolks in an electronic mixer. Pour the sugar and water into a sauce pan and heat up to 257°F. Pour the sugar mixture into the eggs slowly while mixing. Once all the sugar is in, turn up the speed to the highest option. When the bottom of the bowl is cold, stop mixing. Melt the gelatin and add it to the mixture. Fold in the melted chocolate. Whip the heavy cream into stiff peaks and fold into the chocolate.

66% Chocolate Mousse: Melt the chocolate in a mixing bowl. Place whole eggs and yolks in an electronic mixer. Pour the sugar and water into a sauce pan and heat up to 257°F. Pour the sugar mixture into the eggs slowly while mixing. Once all the sugar is in, turn up the speed to the highest option. When the bottom of the bowl is cold, stop mixing. Melt the gelatin and add it to the mixture. Fold in the melted chocolate.
Whip the heavy cream into stiff peaks and fold into the chocolate

Mousse di cioccolato al latte: Sciogliete il cioccolato in una terrina. Mettete le uova intere e i tuorli in un miscelatore elettronico.
Versate lo zucchero e l'acqua in una casseruola e riscaldate fino a raggiungere 125°C. Versate il composto di zucchero nelle uova mescolando lentamente. Quando è tutto amalgamato, aumentate la velocità al massimo. Quando il fondo del recipiente è freddo, interrompete la miscelazione.
Sciogliete la gelatina e aggiungetela al composto. Incorporate il cioccolato fuso. Montate la panna a neve e incorporatela nel composto di cioccolato.

Mousse di cioccolato 58%: Sciogliete il cioccolato in una terrina. Mettete le uova intere e i tuorli in un miscelatore elettronico.
Versate lo zucchero e l'acqua in una casseruola e riscaldate fino a raggiungere 125° C. Versate il composto di zucchero nelle uova mescolando lentamente. Quando è tutto amalgamato, aumentate la velocità al massimo. Quando il fondo del recipiente è freddo, interrompete la miscelazione.
Sciogliete la gelatina e aggiungetela al composto. Incorporate il cioccolato fuso. Montate la panna a neve e incorporatela nel composto di cioccolato.

Mousse di cioccolato 66%: Sciogliete il cioccolato in una terrina. Mettete le uova intere e i tuorli in un miscelatore elettronico.
Versate lo zucchero e l'acqua in una casseruola e riscaldate fino a raggiungere 125° C. Versate il composto di zucchero nelle uova mescolando lentamente. Quando è tutto amalgamato, aumentate la velocità al massimo. Quando il fondo del recipiente è freddo, interrompete la miscelazione. Sciogliete la gelatina e aggiungetela al composto. Incorporate il cioccolato fuso.
Montate la panna a neve e incorporatela nel composto di cioccolato.

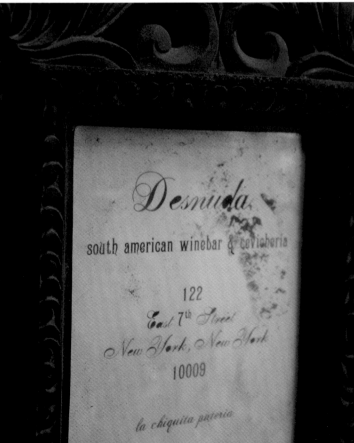

Desnuda

south american winebar & cevicheria

122
East 7th Street
New York, New York
10009

la chiquita pueria

DESNUDA

Owner / Titolare › Peter Gevrekis • **Chef** › Dominic Martinez

122 East 7th St • **M** 2 Av [F] • +01 212 254 3515 • **www.desnudany.com**

The Desnuda is a unique place, for at least two reasons. The first is that this Winebar & Cevicheria has no tables, just a long bar with about fifteen seats in front of the chef and bartender. The second is that the dishes I tasted were sensational. I come from a region where raw fish is a bit like milk: we have it every day, so we know how to appreciate freshness, processing and correct seasonings. That's why I'm not a fan of Japanese style raw fish: olive oil and lemon enhance the fish flavour much more than soy. Desnuda offers a seasoning that is a mix between the Italian and Japanese cuisine, and the result is truly spectacular. The "wild striped bass tiradito" finishes in a second, the "lobster ceviche" is great and regenerates the palate, the dessert made by the strange combination of foie gras and seared tuna, isn't a sweet, but it is exceptional.

Il Desnuda è un posto unico, per almeno due ragioni. La prima è che questo Winebar & Cevicheria non ha tavoli, ma solo un lungo bancone con una quindicina di posti a sedere di fronte allo chef e al barman. La seconda è che i piatti che ho assaggiato erano sensazionali. Vengo da una regione in cui il pesce crudo è un po' come il latte: lo mangiamo ogni giorno e dunque sappiamo apprezzarne freschezza, lavorazione e giusti condimenti. Ecco perché non amo il crudo alla giapponese: olio di oliva e limone esaltano il pesce molto meglio della soia. Al Desnuda propongono un condimento che è una via di mezzo tra la cucina italiana e quella giapponese, ed il risultato è davvero spettacolare. Il "wild stripe bass tiradito" va via in un secondo, il "lobster ceviche" è ottimo e rigenera il palato, il dolce ottenuto dallo strano abbinamento di foie gras e tonno scottato non è un dolce, ma è eccezionale.

Wine List › Carta dei Vini	**Cuisine** › Cucina	**Lunch** › Pranzo	**Average Price** › Prezzo Medio
10 Labels › Etichette	**Ceviche**	**No lunch** › Chiuso a pranzo	$ 60-70

Lobster ceviche

INGREDIENTS FOR 4 SERVINGS:
- 7 lobsters cooked for 7 minutes in boiling water then shocked in an ice bath to stop the cooking process.
Coconut marinade: - 2 cans coconut milk - 4 tbs fish sauce - ¾ cup agave nectar - ¾ cup orange juice - ¾ cup lime juice - 1 jalapeño finely minced with seeds - 1 knob of ginger peeled and finely minced - salt to taste
Mango pico de gallo (a garnish for the lobster ceviche):
- 2 ripe mangos peeled and medium dice - 1 red onion medium dice - 1 jalapeño finely minced - 1 red bell pepper small dice - ½ bunch mint finely chopped - ½ bunch cilantro finely chopped - ½ cup agave nectar - ½ cup lime juice - ½ cup orange juice - salt to taste

Coconut marinade:
Combine all ingredients except the coconut milk. Once everything is mixed, well add the coconut milk this is the marinade for the lobster.

Mango pico de gallo (a garnish for the lobster ceviche):
Combine all ingredients in a large mixing bowl and season to taste.

Take the meat from one lobster tail, claw and knuckle. Roughly chop and place into a small mixing bowl. Next add 5-7 Tbs of the coconut marinade to the lobster meat add a couple pinches of kosher salt and a couple pinches of schimini togorashi to the lobster and a generous drizzle of extra virgin olive oil mix well. Next add a good pinch of cilantro and a good pinch of thinly sliced red onion and mix into lobster meat. Now your ready to serve a place the lobster ceviche in the middle of the plate and then add a couple spoonfuls of the mango pico de gallo next to the lobster ceviche and enjoy.

Wild striped bass tiradito
Tiradito di spigola selvaggia

INGREDIENTS FOR 4 SERVINGS:
- One fillet of wild striped bass cut into loins then sliced sashimi style into 8 slices
Ponzu sauce:
- 1 pint of soy sauce
- 1 pint of yuzu juice
- 1 pint of sudachi juice mixed with rice vinegar

Mix all of the above Ingredients in a large mixing bowl. Then take 3 strips each of konbu (seaweed kelp) and place them inside 2 quart containers. Next add a good handful of bonito flakes into each quart and pour the liquid over the konbu and bonito, place a lid on both and let it set overnight, the longer the better. When the ponzu is rady, take 1 quart of it and strain out the konbu and bonito and place it into a squeeze bottle. This is the sauce for the dish. Then get 1 knob of peeled and thinly julienne sliced ginger and place them into water. Next arrange the fish on a plate with the slices in a straight row, then pour a generous amount of ponzu sauce and a splash of yuzu juice over the fish. Next place a thin slice of ginger on each piece of fish, then put a little pinch of schimini togorashi (Japanese seven spice) on each piece of fish. Then zest the skin of 1 lime over the fish. Combine 3 tablespoons of sesame oil and 3 tablespoons of olive oil in a sauce pot and heat until smoking. When smoking hot, spoon the hot oil over the fish to slightly cook the it.

INGREDIENTI PER 4 PERSONE:
- 1 filetto di persico spigola selvaggio tagliato a filetti e poi in stile sashimi in 8 fettine
Per la salsa Ponzu:
- 1 lt di salsa di soia
- 1 lt di succo di yuzu
- 1 lt di succo Sudachi con aceto di riso

Mescolate gli ingredienti in una ciotola. Prendete 3 strisce a persona di konbu (alghe kelp) e ponetele all'interno di 2 contenitori da quart (946ml), poi aggiungete una manciata abbondante di fiocchi di bonito in entrambi i contenitori e versate il liquido sul konbu e i bonito. Mettete i coperchi e lasciate riposare tutta la notte. Più riposa meglio è. Una volta preparato il ponzu, filtrate il konbu e i bonito e mettetelo in un flacone dispenser per salse. Mettete una noce di zenzero sbucciato e tagliato a julienne in acqua. Ponete il pesce su di un piatto con le fettine in fila, versateci sopra abbondantemente la salsa ponzu e qualche goccia di succo di yuzu. Posizionate una fettina di zenzero su ogni pezzo di pesce e poi aggiungete un pizzico di schimini togorashi (sette spezie giapponesi). Aggiungete infine anche la scorza di 1 lime. Unite in un pentolino 3 cucchiai di olio di sesamo e 3 cucchiai di olio d'oliva e riscaldate fino a far fumare. Quando l'olio è caldo, versatelo sul pesce per cucinarlo leggermente e il piatto è pronto.

DOVETAIL

Owner and Chef / Titolare e Chef › John Fraser

103 West 77th Street • Ⓜ 79 St [1] • +01 212 362 3800 • **www.dovetailnyc.com**

In Upper West Side there's another World Heritage Site, as well as the Natural History Museum. It's called Dovetail, and it's located right behind the museum. Although it appears to be a modern French place, in this American restaurant chef and owner John Fraser serves sensational dishes and the wine cellar holds a "treasure" of 950 references. The place seems perhaps too elegant and for special occasions, but the staff knows how to put customers at ease, and this flattens some grandeur from the air you breathe as soon as you enter. As for the food, we are on the highest levels, and you can tell from the first dishes that come to the table: the Smoked Trout is superb, the Melon Gazpacho is a great alternative to the usual gazpacho, the New York Strip and the Lamb are perfect. The chocolate soufflé is spectacular to admire and eat.

Nell'Upper West Side c'è un altro patrimonio dell'umanità, oltre il Natural History Museum. Si chiama Dovetail, ed è situato giusto alle spalle del museo. Seppure all'apparenza sembri un moderno locale francese, in questo ristorante americano dello chef e proprietario John Fraser si servono piatti sensazionali e la cantina custodisce un "tesoro" di 950 referenze. Il locale appare forse fin troppo elegante e da grandi occasioni, ma il personale sa come mettere i clienti a proprio agio, e questo smorza un po' l'aria da grandeur che si respira non appena varcato l'ingresso. Quanto al cibo, siamo su livelli altissimi e lo si capisce fin dai primi piatti che arrivano a tavola: la trota affumicata è superlativa, il gazpacho al melone una ottima alternativa al solito gazpacho; la New York strip e l'agnello sono perfetti; il soufflé al cioccolato è uno spettacolo: da ammirare e da mangiare.

Wine List › Carta dei Vini	**Cuisine** › Cucina	**Lunch** › Pranzo	**Average Price** › Prezzo Medio
950 Labels › Etichette	**American** › Americana	**No lunch** › Chiuso a pranzo	**$ 75**

Melon gazpacho, cottage cheese, cucumber, basil

Gazpacho di melone con formaggio cottage, cetrioli e basilico

INGREDIENTS FOR 4 SERVINGS:
- ½ ripe honeydew, deseeded and diced
- ½ english cucumber, peeled and diced (reserving peelings)
- 1 ea small leek, diced
- ¼ cup of extra virgin olive oil
- 1 pt of cold water - to taste salt, sugar, and chardonnay vinegar

INGREDIENTI PER 4 PERSONE:
- ½ melone Honeydew maturo senza semi e tagliato a dadini
- ½ cetriolo inglese sbucciato e tagliato a dadini (tenete da parte la buccia)
- 1 porro piccolo tagliato a dadini
- 59 ml di olio extra vergine di oliva
- acqua fredda - sale, zucchero, aceto di chardonnay qb

Gently sweat the leek in extra virgin olive oil until tender. Add the melon and cucumber, cover with water and simmer for 10 minutes. Add the reserved cucumber peels and simmer for 5 more minutes. Puree the mixture with a blender until smooth. Cool quickly over an ice bath.

Serve ice cold. Garnish with diced cucumber, seasoned to taste with salt and sugar, cottage cheese, fresh Italian basil and a good quality finishing olive oil.

Fate sudare delicatamente il porro in olio extra vergine d'oliva fino a quando diventa tenero. Aggiungete il melone e il cetriolo, coprite con acqua, e fate sobbollire per 10 minuti. Aggiungete le bucce di cetriolo messe da parte e lasciate sobbollire ancora per 5 minuti. Poi frullate il tutto fino a quando diventa liscio. Raffreddate rapidamente con un bagnomaria di ghiaccio.
Servite ghiacciato e guarnite con dei cetrioli a dadini conditi a piacere con sale e zucchero, formaggio Cottage, basilico fresco italiano e dell'olio d'oliva di qualità per finire.

TALÒ › Negroamaro Rosato Salento IGP
CANTINE SAN MARZANO

Colore rosato intenso con riflessi rubino; profumo intenso e persistente, con sentori di ciliegia e lampone. Vino di buon corpo, fresco ed equilibrato al palato.
Abbinamenti: Antipasti all'italiana, zuppe di pesce e brodetti, pesce al cartoccio o al forno, formaggi giovani o leggermente stagionati.

Intensely rosé-coloured with ruby red reflections; complex and persistent aroma, with cherry and raspberry notes. A full-bodied wine, fresh and balanced in the mouth.
Best served with: Italian style starters, fish soups, roasted or foil- baked fish, fresh or slightly aged cheeses.

Bittersweet chocolate souffle

Soufflé di cioccolato fondente

INGREDIENTS FOR 4 SERVINGS:
- 125 g 63% chocolate - 32 g butter - 38 g sugar - 140 g egg whites

INGREDIENTI PER 4 PERSONE:
- 125 g di cioccolato 63% - 32 g di burro - 38 gr di zucchero
- 140 g di albumi

Melt the chocolate and butter together over a double boiler. Whip the egg whites to moist stiff peaks. Towards the end, slowly incorporate the sugar. Fold the whites into the warm melted chocolate mixture. Pipe it into buttered, sugared ramekins. Bake at 350°F for 6-8 minutes.

Fate sciogliere il cioccolato e il burro insieme a bagnomaria. Montate gli albumi a neve. Alla fine incorporate lentamente lo zucchero. Aggiungete delicatamente gli albumi alla miscela di cioccolato fuso. Mettete il tutto in stampini o ciotoline imburrate e zuccherate con l'aiuto di un sac à poche. Fate cuocere in forno a 175°C per 6-8 minuti.

Veal ravioli
Ravioli di vitello

INGREDIENTS FOR 4 SERVINGS: Pasta: - 1 ¼ cup all purpose flour - ½ tsp salt - 2 each large egg yolks - 2 tbs water **Braised Veal Breast:** - 2 veal breast - 1 each small onion, diced - 1 each small stalk of celery, diced - 1 each small carrot, diced - 6 each garlic cloves - 1 pt chardonnay - ¼ cup blended oil **To finish:** - ½ cup english peas, shucked and blanched - 2 cups maitake mushrooms - 2 cups mature pea tendrils - 2 tbs extravirgin olive oil - ¼ cup whole butter - 2 tbs shaved chives

Blend the ingredients in a food processor until the dough comes together. Knead on a lightly floured surface until elastic, approximately for 8 minutes. Cover with plastic wrap and let stand for 1 hour. Season the veal with salt and pepper to taste. Sear it in blended oil until brown on all sides. Remove from oil. Sautee the onion, carrot and celery in the remaining oil until tender. Add the garlic and deglaze with the white wine. Add the veal breast, cover with water and bring to a simmer. Remove from heat, cover with foil, and place in a 275°F oven for 2½ hours or until tender. Remove from the oven and let it cool uncovered until it reaches room temperature. Remove the veal from the braising liquid. Separate any unwanted fat or connective tissue and shred with a fork. Season to taste with salt, pepper and lemon zest. Strain the braising liquid and reduce until jus consistency. Cool the braised veal mixture. When completely chilled, roll it into 12 gr spheres. After rolling the pasta, stuff It with the balls of reserved veal breast filling. Reserve the veal braising reduction. Blanch the pasta in boiling selted water until the dough is tender. Sautee the maitake mushrooms in extra virgin olive oil until brown. Add the pea tendrils and cook for 30 seconds until they wilt. Adjust the seasoning with salt, pepper and lemon juice to taste.

INGREDIENTI PER 4 PERSONE: Per la pasta: - 160 g di farina - ½ cucchiaino di sale - 2 tuorli gandi - 2 cucchiai di acqua **Per il petto brasato di vitello:** - 2 petti di vitello - 1 cipolla piccola tagliata a dadini - 1 gambo di sedano tagliato a dadini - 1 carota piccola tagliata a dadini - 6 spicchi d'aglio - Chardonnay - 59 ml di olio misto **Per guarnire:** - 75 g di piselli inglesi sgusciati e scottati - 200 g di funghi Maitake - 50 g di viticci di pisello maturi - 2 cucchiai di olio extravergine di oliva - 57g di burro intero - 2 cucchiai di erba cipollina

Frullate gli ingredienti per la pasta in un robot da cucina fino a quando si impastano bene. Lavorate l'impasto su una superficie leggermente infarinata fino a quando diventa più elastico per circa 8 minuti. Coprite con della pellicola trasparente e lasciate riposare per un'ora. Condite il vitello con sale e pepe a piacere. Scottatelo nell'olio misto fino a quando diventa dorato su tutti i lati. Toglietelo dal fuoco. Saltate la cipolla, la carota, il sedano nell'olio rimanente fino a quando diventano teneri. Aggiungete l'aglio e sfumate con il vino bianco. Aggiungete il petto di vitello, coprite con acqua, e portare lentamente ad ebollizione. Togliete dal fuoco, coprite il tutto con dell'alluminio, e mettete in forno a 135°C per 2 ore e mezza o finché diventa tenero. Togliete dal forno, scoprite e lasciate raffreddare fino a temperatura ambiente. Togliete il vitello dal liquido della brasatura. Togliete il grasso indesiderato e sminuzzate con una forchetta. Condite con sale, pepe e scorza di limone. Filtrate il liquido di brasatura e fate ridurre fino a quando raggiunge la consistenza di un succo. Lasciate raffreddare, quindi create delle palline da 12gr. Dopo aver steso la pasta, farcite con le palline di ripieno di carne. Cuocete i ravioli in acqua salata bollente fino a quando si ammorbidiscono. Saltate i funghi Maitake in olio extra vergine d'oliva fino a quando diventano dorati. Aggiungete i viticci di pisello e lasciate cuocere per altri 30 secondi fino a quando appassiscono. Condite a piacere con sale, pepe e succo di limone.

DUDLEYS

Owner / Titolare › Nick Mathers • **Chef** › Eric Lapkin

85 Orchard Street • **M** Essex St [J,M,Z] • +01 212 925 7355 • **www.dudleysnyc.com**

A nice place, full of lots of young people, with a good Australian cuisine at a good price, which comes almost exclusively from the products of local producers. The Dudleys is one of those places where you gladly return, even two or three times a week, maybe even just for a cocktail accompanied by an appetizer. For example, the lamb meatballs are one of those things you could eat every day, and the Kale salad is among the best in the city. The Bronte Burger is cooked well. The Arctic Char, fish of the salmon family that prefers cold waters, is great. The desserts are simple but well made: the banofee pie was the best we had. Accompanied by a caffe affogato, that here has an extra "t". But we are in the States, and here everything is always exaggerated.

Un posto carino, frequentato da tanti giovani, con una buona cucina australiana a buon prezzo, che nasce quasi esclusivamente dai prodotti di produttori locali. Il Dudleys è uno di quei post dove si torna con piacere, anche due-tre volte la settimana, e magari anche solo per un cocktail accompagnato da un antipastino. Per esempio le polpettine di agnello sono una di quelle cose che mangeresti ogni giorno, e l'insalata di Kale è tra le migliori della città. Il bronte Burger è ben cucinato. L'Arctic Char, pesce delle famiglia dei salmoni che predilige le acque fredde, è ottimo. I dolci sono semplici ma ben fatti: il banofee pie ci è sembrato il migliore. Magari affiancatelo ad un caffè affogato. Che al Dudleys ha una "t" in più e diventa "affogatto". Ma siamo negli States, e qui si esagera sempre.

Wine List › Carta dei Vini	**Cuisine** › Cucina	**Lunch** › Pranzo	**Dinner** › Cena
13 Labels › Etichette	**Australian** › Australiana	$ 15-20	$ 25-35

Artic chair

Salmerino Alpino

INGREDIENTS FOR 4 SERVINGS:
- 4 x5 oz pieces of artic char - 8 oz of farro, cooked - 8 oz of tuscan kale - 8 oz of andalusian tomato sauce - ¼ tsp of cherry pepper relish - 1 tbsp of blended oil - Salt to taste - Pepper to taste
Andalusian sauce: - 1 can of la valle tomatoes - Zest from 1 orange (use peeler) - Zest from 1 lemon (use peeler) - 1 head of fennel (rough chopped) - ¼ cup of olive oil - 1 ½ tbsp of capers - Salt and pepper to taste
Cherry Pepper relish: - 4 cherry peppers, deseeded and minced - 1 tsp of capers, roughly chopped - 2 tbsp of lemon olive oil - 1 pinch of parsley - 1 pinch of chives

INGREDIENTI PER 4 PERSONE:
- 4 pezzi di salmerino alpino da 140 g - 225 g di farro, cotto - 225 g di cavolo riccio toscano - 225 g di salsa andalusa di pomodoro - ¼ cucchiaino di salsa di peperoncino ciliegia - 1 cucchiaio di olio vegetale misto - sale qb - pepe qb. **Per la salsa andalusa:** - 1 lattina di pomodori pelati - scorza di una arancia - scorza di un limone - 1 capo di finocchio (tritato grossolanamente) - 60 ml di olio d'oliva - 1 ½ cucchiaio di capperi - sale e pepe qb. **Per la salsa di peperoncino ciliegia:** - 4 peperoni ciliegia, senza semi e tritati - 1 cucchiaino di capperi, tritati grossolanamente - 2 cucchiai di olio d'oliva al limone - 1 pizzico di prezzemolo - 1 pizzico di erba cipollina

Sweat the fennel in a couple of tablespoons of oil for 3-5 minutes. Next add the can of tomatoes, the orange and lemon zest and simmer on low heat for 10 minutes stirring occasionally. Blend together with the olive oil, salt and pepper until it's smooth. Taste and check seasoning and add 1 ½ tablespoons of capers to every quart of sauce. Cool down properly in an ice bath.

Cherry Pepper relish:
Place your Artic char on a clean surface and make sure the fish is dry. Season it with salt and pepper. Heat up a saute pan that's large enough to fit the amount of fish you would like to cook. Make sure there Is enough oil to coat the bottom of the pan. Once the oil starts smoking, you can add the pieces of fish. Place them skin side down without them touching. Then put the saute pan in the middle of the oven at 350°, 6 minutes for rare, 9 minutes for medium rare and 12 minutes for medium.
While your fish is cooking, heat up a saute pan to medium heat. Place the oil in the pan and allow it to heat up for 30 seconds. Add the farro and Kale to the saute pan, cook for 1 minute and season with salt and pepper.

Assembling the dish:
Place your Andalusian sauce in the centre of the plate and spread it out into a nice size circle. Then add your sautéed farro and kale over half of the sauce and place the fish in the centre of the plate. Half the fish should be on the kale and farro and the other half should be on the sauce. Then add the desired amount of cherry pepper relish on a corner of the fish and enjoy.

(Il salmerino alpino è un salmoide molto simile alla trota).

Saltate il finocchio con un paio di cucchiai di olio per 3-5 minuti. Aggiungete la lattina di pomodori, la scorza di limone e arancia e lasciate cuocere a fuoco basso per 10 minuti mescolando di tanto in tanto. Aggiungete l'olio d'oliva, il sale e il pepe e frullate fino a quando risulta liscio. Controllate il condimento e aggiungete 1 ½ cucchiaio di capperi per ogni 950ml di salsa. Raffreddate bene con un bagnomaria di ghiaccio.

Preparazione salsa di peperoncino ciliegia:
Ponete il salmerino alpino su una superficie pulita e assicuratevi che sia asciutto. Condite con sale e pepe. Riscaldate una padella grande abbastanza da contenere la quantità di pesce che si desidera cucinare. Assicuratevi di mettere abbastanza olio da rivestire il fondo della padella. Quando l'olio inizia a fumare aggiungete il pesce. Posizionatelo con la pelle verso il basso e assicuratevi che non si tocchino l'uno con l'altro. Infine mettete la padella in forno a 175°C, per 6 minuti per cottura al sangue, 9 minuti per cottura media o 12 minuti per cottura normale.
Nel frattempo, mettete a riscaldare una padella a fuoco medio. Fate riscaldare l'olio per 30 secondi. Aggiungete il farro e il cavolo riccio e fate rosolare per un minuto. Condite con sale e pepe.

Preparazione del piatto:
Ponete la salsa andalusa nel centro del piatto da portata e spargetela formando un bel cerchio. Aggiungete il farro e il cavolo riccio su metà della salsa e mettete il pesce al centro del piatto. Metà pesce dovrebbe essere sopra il cavolo e il farro e l'altra metà sulla salsa. Aggiungete la quantità desiderata di salsa di peperoncino ciliegia su un'estremità del pesce.

Lamb meatballs
Polpette di agnello

INGREDIENTS FOR 4 SERVINGS:
-2,5 lbs ground lamb - 238 g milled yukon gold potato
- 12,5 g parmesan cheese, grated - 12,5 g pecorino cheese, grated - 57,5 g milk - 10 g kosher salt (finely ground) -5 g garlic, minced - 2,5 g rosemary leaves (picked and chopped) - 2,5 g black pepper (finely ground) - 2 g cumin, ground - 2 g coriander ground
Turmeric yogurt:
- 1 qt greek yogurt - 1 ¼ tsp turmeric - 1 ¼ tsp black pepper - 1 tsp salt - 3 tbsp olive oil - 2 tsp lemon juice

INGREDIENTI PER 4 PERSONE:
- 1100 g di agnello macinato - 238 gr di patate yukon gold schiacciate - 12,5 g di parmigiano grattugiato
- 12,5 g di formaggio pecorino grattugiato - 57,5 g di latte 10 g di sale kosher (macinato fino) -5 g di aglio tritato
- 2,5 g di foglie di rosmarino (raccolte e tritato)
- 2,5 g di pepe nero (macinato fino)
- 2 g di cumino macinato - 2 g di coriandolo macinato
Per il yogurt curcuma:
- 945 ml di yogurt greco - 1 ¼ cucchiaino di curcuma
- 1 ¼ cucchiaino di pepe nero - 1 cucchiaino di sale
- 3 cucchiai di olio d'oliva
- 2 cucchiaini di succo di limone

Potatoes: Boil enough potato to yield the required amount of milled potato. Cook just until tender, don't overcook. When the potatoes are cool enough to handle, peel and put them through the food mill. Once they have been milled, leave them to cool.
Meatballs: Mix all the ingredients together. Once everything is incorporated well, stop because it's never good to over mix meatballs. Always test a couple of meatballs before making the whole batch. Serve with turmeric yogurt.
Turmeric yogurt: Combine all the ingredients and mix well.

Preparazione patate: Lessate abbastanza patate per produrre la quantità di patate schiacciate necessarie. Cucinatele fino a quando diventano tenere ma non fatele scuocere. Quando si sono raffreddate abbastanza da poterle maneggiare, sbucciatele e passatele attraverso un passaverdure. Poi lasciatele raffreddare.
Preparazione polpette: Mescolate bene tutti gli ingredienti. Quando sono ben incorporati tra loro fermatevi perché non è mai consigliato lavorare troppo l'impasto per le polpette. Provatene sempre un paio prima di cucinarle tutte. Servite con yogurt di curcuma. **Yogurt di curcuma:** Unite tutti gli ingredienti e mescolate bene.

Banofee pie › Tortino Banofee

INGREDIENTS FOR 4 SERVINGS:
- 4 graham pie crust - 2 bananas, large - 3 tbsp dulce de leche - 6 tbsp whipped cream - 20 g coconut, toasted **Yield 8 pie crusts:** - banofee crust - 237 g ap flour - 155 g graham crumbs - 7,5 g baking soda - 232 g butter, room temperature - 100 g brown sugar - 37 g white sugar - 5 g salt

INGREDIENTI PER 4 PERSONE:
- 4 sfoglie per tortino graham - 2 banane grandi - 3 cucchiai di dulce de leche - 6 cucchiai di panna montata - 20 g di cocco tostato **Sfoglia per 8 tortini:** - sfoglia banofee - 237 g di farina - 155 g di Graham sbriciolato - 7,5 g di bicarbonato di sodio - 232 g di burro a temperatura ambiente - 100 g di zucchero di canna - 37 g di zucchero bianco - 5 g di sale

Blend the butter and sugar in a mixer. Once they are blended well add the rest of the ingredients until they are mixed thoroughly. Place into molds and bake until golden brown at 325° for 12-15 minutes. Always check them at the 10 minutes mark.
Assembling the pie: Place individual pies on a cutting board or plate. Spread the dulce de leche over the entire base. Slice the bananas in 1/8" thick rounds on a slight bias. Place the banana slices on top of the dulce de leche starting from the outside and then covering the entire pie. Then add the whipped cream on top of the banana to cover it. Top the pie with the toasted coconut to finish.

Frullate il burro e lo zucchero in un mixer. Quando sono ben amalgamati aggiungete il resto degli ingredienti e frullate bene. Inserite negli stampi e fate cuocere fino a doratura a 160°C per 12-15 minuti. Controllate sempre dopo 10 minuti.
Assemblaggio del tortino: Posizionate il tortino su un tagliere o un piatto. Stendete il dulce de leche su tutta la base. Tagliate la banana a fette da 3mm leggermente in sbieco. Posizionate le fette di banana sul dulce de leche partendo dall'esterno fino a coprire l'intero tortino. Aggiungete la panna montata sopra la banana, fino a coprirla. Infine spolverate il tortino con il cocco tostato.

EATALY

Owner / Titolare › Farinetti Family - Famiglia Farinetti • **Chef** › Alex Pilas / Fitz Tallon

200 Fifth Avenue • Ⓜ E 23 St Broadway [N,R] • +01 212 229 2560 • **www.eataly.com/nyc**

I can't hide my love for this place. Not because it's Italian, but for the simple fact that Eataly, like Chelsea Market or like the Borough Market in London, is a synonymous for good food and good cuisine, quality products obtained with meticulous and nature friendly processes. They are places where it's nice to go to just have a coffee or an ice cream. Yes, I love the confusion and the crowd that assaults Eataly New York everyday (and more generally all the Eatalys in the world) and I love to drink a lager in the terrace-brewery. Good food, nice people and good cookery books to browse through and buy. This, for me, is (almost) paradise.

Non posso nascondere l'amore per questo posto. Non perché sia italiano, ma per il semplice fatto che Eataly, come il Chelsea Market o come il Borough Market a Londra, è sinonimo di buon cibo e buona cucina, di prodotti di qualità ottenuti da lavorazioni meticolose e rispettose della natura. Sono posti in cui è piacevole andare anche solo per sorseggiare un caffè, oppure prendere un gelato. Ebbene sì, amo la confusione e la folla che ogni giorno prende d'assalto Eataly New York (e più in generale tutti gli Eataly del mondo) e adoro bere una bionda sulla terrazza-birreria. Buon cibo, bella gente e buoni libri di cucina da sfogliare e acquistare. Questo per me è (quasi) il paradiso.

Wine List › Carta dei Vini	**Cuisine** › Cucina	**Lunch** › Pranzo	**Dinner** › Cena
900 Labels › Etichette	**Italian** › Italiana	$ 25-30	$ 30-40

Whole flounder with mixed nuts

Piemontese-style crostino with carne cruda

Crostino Piemontese con carne cruda

INGREDIENTS FOR 4 SERVINGS:
For the onions: - 1 firm red onion, about 5 ounces, peeled and thinly sliced - ½ teaspoon of sugar - ½ teaspoon of salt - ¾ cup of rice vinegar, white wine vinegar, or apple cider vinegar - 1 small clove of garlic, peeled and halved - 5 black peppercorns - 5 allspice berries - 3 small sprigs of thyme - 1 small dried chili
For the carne cruda: - ½ pound of beef tenderloin, preferably Razza Piemontese - A baguette, cut into ½-inch slices - ¼ cup of extra virgin olive oil - salt and freshly ground black pepper, to taste

INGREDIENTI PER 4 PERSONE:
Per le cipolle: - 1 cipolla rossa, di circa 140 g, pulita e affettata sottilmente - ½ cucchiaino di zucchero - ½ cucchiaino di sale - 177 ml di aceto di riso, aceto di vino bianco, o aceto di mele - 1 piccolo spicchio d'aglio, sbucciato e tagliato a metà - 5 grani di pepe nero - 5 bacche di pimento - 3 piccoli rametti di timo - 1 piccolo peperoncino secco **Per la carne cruda:** - 226 g di filetto di manzo, preferibilmente piemontese - Una baguette tagliata a fette da circa 1 cm - 59 ml di olio extravergine d'oliva - sale e pepe nero appena macinato qb

To pickle the onions: Boil 2 or 3 cups of water. In a bowl, add the sugar, salt, vinegar, garlic, peppercorns, allspice, thyme and chili. Stir until dissolved. Place the onions in a sieve or colander in the sink. Slowly pour the boiling water over the onions, and let them drain. Add the onions to the bowl with the dissolved mixture, and stir gently to evenly distribute. The onions will be ready in about 30 minutes but taste better after a few hours. Store the covered bowl in the refrigerator. They will be good for several weeks but are best in the first week. **To prepare the carne cruda:** Heat a grill pan over medium-high heat. Drizzle the bread with olive oil and sprinkle with salt and pepper. Toast the bread until it is golden brown, for about 4 minutes per side. Remove from the heat and set it aside. Trim any fat or silver skin from the tenderloin with a sharp knife. Dice the beef into ¼-inch or smaller cubes. Alternatively, pass the tenderloin through the largest die of a meat grinder. Gently spread the meat out on a plate. Dress with the olive oil, salt, and black pepper and mix to evenly incorporate. Top each slice of bread with a spoonful of the beef, add the onions on the side, and serve immediately.

Preparazione cipolle sottaceto: Portate ad ebollizione dell'acqua. Mescolate lo zucchero, il sale, l'aceto, l'aglio, il pepe, il pimento, il timo e il peperoncino in una ciotola. Mettete le cipolle in un colino nel lavandino. Versate lentamente l'acqua bollente sopra le cipolle, e lasciatele scolare. Aggiungete le cipolle alla ciotola con il composto e mescolate delicatamente. Le cipolle saranno pronte in circa 30 minuti, ma è meglio lasciarle riposare per un paio d'ore. Conservatele in frigorifero in un recipiente coperto. Si conservano per diverse settimane, ma sono migliori nella prima settimana. **Preparazione carne cruda:** Scaldate una padella-griglia a fuoco medio-alto. Condite il pane con olio d'oliva, sale e pepe. Tostatelo per circa 4 minuti per lato, toglietelo dal fuoco e mettete da parte. Eliminate il grasso dal filetto con un coltello affilato. Tagliate la carne a dadini piccoli. In alternativa, usate un tritacarne. Spargete delicatamente la carne su un piatto. Condite con l'olio d'oliva, sale e pepe nero e mescolate il tutto per uniformare il sapore. Ponete un cucchiaio di carne su ogni pezzo di pane, aggiungete le cipolle al lato, e servite subito.

INGREDIENTS FOR 4 SERVINGS:
- (1) 1.5 lb whole flounder; top side skinned, bottom side skin on; cleaned and gutted - ½ cup toasted mixed nuts: equal parts shelled and whole - pistachio, hazelnuts, almonds, pecans, walnuts; toasted in a light drizzle of olive oil and seasoned with S&P
- ½ lemon, seeded - olive oil - salt and pepper to taste
- ½ bunch of tarragon or sage

On a hot plancha, pour enough olive oil to surround the fish. Season fish and place top side (flesh side) down. Cook for 4 minutes.
Flip over fish and continue to cook for another 3 minutes; add more olive oil if necessary. Flesh should have a dark brown sear. Warm the mixed nuts. When fish is almost completely cooked, place ½ bunch of herbs onto plancha and cover in olive oil. Flip once, cooking until fried through.
Pick up herbs and brush flesh of fish and garnish with that bunch. With olive oil, sear lemon cut side down until cut side is completely caramelized.
Plate fish on a warm, large oval plate, ½ c mixed nuts below the fish and the charred lemon above the tail.

ED'S LOBSTER BAR

Owner and Chef / Titolare e Chef › Ed McFarland

222 Lafayette Street • Ⓜ Spring St [6] • +01 212 343 3236 • **www.lobsterbarnyc.com**

Ok, I expected to eat an excellent lobster and I had read dozens of positive reviews on the lobster roll, more commonly called lobster sandwich, but I would have never expected to eat some ravioli better than the Italian ones in New York. But it happened: At Ed's Lobster they make unforgettable Ravioli with a unique taste and a sensational sauce. Although the presentation is not at the same level of the flavour, the Ed McFarland's Lobster Ravioli are by far the best dish we tasted in the Big Apple. And the lobster sandwich is just one step below them. In short, this small restaurant that because of its long counter looks a lot like a cocktail bar, knows how to touch your heart and stomach. Without harming your wallets either: eating lobster under $50 is not so simple, not only in New York.

Ok, mi aspettavo di mangiare un'ottima aragosta e avevo letto decine di recensioni positive sul lobster roll, più volgarmente detto panino con l'aragosta, ma non mi sarei mai aspettato di mangiare a New York dei ravioli che nemmeno in Italia. E invece è accaduto: all'Ed's Lobster fanno dei ravioli indimenticabili, dal sapore che non ha paragoni e con un sughetto sensazionale. Malgrado la presentazione non sia dello stesso livello del sapore, i Ravioli Lobster di Ed McFarland sono di gran lunga il miglior piatto che abbiamo assaggiato nella Grande Mela. E il panino con l'aragosta è solo di un gradino inferiore. Insomma, questo ristorantino che a causa del suo lunghissimo bancone assomiglia tanto ad un cocktail-bar, sa come colpirti al cuore e allo stomaco. Senza peraltro far male al portafogli: mangiare aragoste restando sotto i 50 dollari non è poi così semplice. Non solo a New York.

Wine List › Carta dei Vini	Cuisine › Cucina	Lunch › Pranzo	Dinner › Dinner
30 Labels › Etichette	**Seafood** › Pesce	$ 25-45	$ 25-45

Lobster roll
Panino all'aragosta

INGREDIENTS FOR 4 SERVINGS:
For the lobster salad:
- 4 whole 1 ¼ to 1 ½ pound lobsters
- 1 cup of Hellmann's mayonnaise
- ½ stalk of celery, finely minced
- 1 T of freshly squeezed lemon juice
- ½ bunch of chives, finely chopped
- salt and pepper

For the rolls:
- 4 top-split hot dog rolls
- ⅓ cup of butter

INGREDIENTI PER 4 PERSONE:
Per l'insalata di aragosta:
- 560-680 g di aragoste
- 250 g di maionese Hellmann
- ½ gambo di sedano tritato finemente
- 1 cucchiaio di succo di limone appena spremuto
- ½ mazzetto di erba cipollina tritata finemente
- sale e pepe

Per i rotoli:
- 4 panini per hot dog - 76 g di burro

Boil the whole lobsters in a heavy stockpot until they float. Remove from the water and place them in an ice bath. When chilled, shell the meat and clean by removing any cartilage in claw and devein the tail. Chop the lobster into bite-sized chunks. Mix with lobster salad ingredients in large bowl. Melt the butter in a small sauté pan on medium to high heat. Place hot dog buns in the sauté pan and toast them in butter until golden on each side. Stuff each roll with a generous portion of lobster salad and top with a sprinkle of chopped chives.

Fate bollire le aragoste intere in una pentola fino a quando galleggiano. Toglietele dall'acqua e raffreddatele con del ghiaccio. Sgusciate, rimuovete la cartilagine dalla chela e la vena dorsale. Tagliate l'aragosta in bocconcini. Unitela con gli altri ingredienti per l'insalata di aragosta in una ciotola grande. Riscaldate il burro in una piccola padella sul fuoco medio-alto. Posizionate i panini per hot dog nella padella e tostateli nel burro fino a doratura su entrambi i lati. Farcite ogni rotolo con una porzione generosa di insalata di aragosta e finite con una spolverata di erba cipollina tritata.

Cherry pie

INGREDIENTS FOR 4 SERVINGS:
- 2 lbs cherries (pitted) - ½ cup packed light brown sugar - ⅓ cup granulated sugar - ½ teaspoon nutmeg - ¼ cup corn starch - zest from 2 lemons - juice from 1 lemon - 2 table spoon butter
Pie crust: - 2 cups AP flour - 8 ounces cold butter - 1 tablespoon salt - 3 to 6 tablespoon iced water

Mix all ingredients except butter, together. Pour into lightly pre-baked pie crust. Dot with butter. Put pre-made chilled lattice pie crust on top and trim to fit the pie. Brush with egg wash. Bake at 450F for 15 minutes, then lower heat to 375F and bake for 50 to 60 minutes until golden brown. **Pie crust:** In a food processor- pulse flour and salt together- to mix. Cut butter into small pieces. Add to flour mix. Pulse until crumble. Drizzle cold water while pulsing- just enough until dried ingredients all bind together. Knead the dough lightly. Divide into 2- 13 ounces and 9 ounces. Form a ball- then flatten out to about 6 inches round disc size. cover with plastic wrap and chill. use the bigger dough (13 ounces) to make a lattice top- roll out and use a pizza cutter to cut into a 1/2 inch strip and chill again. Roll out the smaller (9 ounces) for the pie crust. it should be big enough to fit a 9 inches round pie pan.

Lobster ravioli

Ravioli di aragosta

INGREDIENTS FOR 4 SERVINGS:
Mushroom cream sauce:
- 2 qts of heavy cream - 2 lbs of silver dollar mushrooms - 3 shallots, chopped finely - Dry sherry (almontillado) - 1 tsp of truffle salt - salt and pepper to taste - 1 qt of lobster stock
Ravioli:
- 2 lbs of cooked lobster meat
- 1 to 2 tbsp of drawn butter
- salt and pepper
- chopped chives

INGREDIENTI PER 4 PERSONE:
Crema di funghi:
- 1.90 lt di panna - 900 g di funghi silver dollar - 3 scalogni tritati finemente - sherry secco (almontillado) - 1 cucchiaino di sale di tartufo - sale e pepe qb - 950 ml di brodo di aragosta
Ravioli:
- 907 g di carne di aragosta cucinata
- 1-2 cucchiai di burro chiarificato
- sale e pepe
- erba cipollina tritata

Mushroom cream sauce:
Heat up the heavy cream in a big pot (enough for all the ingredients) and reduce to about 3/4 on low heat.
Clean the mushroom and cut in quarters. Put a tablespoon of butter in a sauté pan and add the mushrooms. Keep the heat on low, let the mushroom simmer and release all their liquid. Then turn the heat up high and let the water from the mushroom evaporate. When the mushrooms are completely dry, toss them over high heat and splash with dry sherry, about a couple of dashes, but not too much.
Add the teaspoon of truffle salt to the mushrooms and let them caramelize. Then pour them into the pot of heavy cream. In the same sauté pan, pour the lobster stock and reduce to almost a paste (glace) like consistency. Then add to the same pot with heavy cream and mushroom mix.
In a different sauté pan, add a teaspoon of butter and toss the shallot on medium heat until golden brown. Then add a splash of dry sherry. Caramelize and add to the pot. Stir the pot occasionally. Season with salt and pepper to taste.

Ravioli:
Grind cooked lobster meat in a food processor untill it crumbles. Add 1 tablespoon of drawn butter, a pinch of chives, salt and pepper. Mix until it's well kneaded. Bind all the ingredients together with drawn butter. If you need more, add more. Make sure the mixture is not too oily. If the mixture is too soft to shape, chill for 5 to 10 minutes. Roll out about 2 ounces of the mix into little round patties (about 1 1/2 or 2 inch discs). Then chill for 10 minutes, it's easier to handle when making the ravioli.
Use a round shape wonton wrapper and an egg wash/water mix to seal the wonton wrapper together, just the top layer of the wrapper so it's not too wet. Make sure to sprinkle a generous amount of flour on the ravioli so they won't stick together.

Funghi alla panna:
Riscaldate su fuoco basso la panna in una pentola grande (per tutti gli ingredienti) e lasciate che si riduca di circa ¾.
Pulite i funghi, tagliateli in quarti e metteteli con un cucchiaio di burro in una padella. Tenete la fiamma bassa e lasciateli rosolare fin quando rilasciano tutto il liquido. Poi, alzate la fiamma e lasciate che evapori tutta l'acqua. Quando i funghi sono completamente asciutti, saltateli con dello sherry secco (circa un paio di gocce, non troppo). Aggiungete il sale di tartufo e lasciate caramellare. Versate il tutto nella pentola con la panna. Mettete il brodo di aragosta nella padella usata precedentemente per i funghi e riducete fino alla consistenza di una glassa. Versatelo nella pentola con la panna e i funghi. Mettete un cucchiaino di burro in un'altra padella e fate dorare lo scalogno a fuoco medio. Quindi aggiungete una goccia di sherry secco. Lasciate caramellare e aggiungete il tutto alla pentola. Mescolate di tanto in tanto. Aggiustate di sale e pepe.

Ravioli:
Tritate la carne di aragosta con un robot da cucina fino a quando si sbriciola. Aggiungete un cucchiaio di burro chiarificato, un pizzico di erba cipollina, sale e pepe. Impastate bene. Il burro chiarificato serve per legare insieme tutti gli ingredienti. Aggiungete altro burro se necessario. Assicuratevi che la miscela non sia troppo oleosa. Se l'impasto è troppo morbido per dargli una forma, raffreddatelo in freezer per 5 -10 minuti. Formate delle piccole polpette di circa 50gr (dischetti da circa 3-5cm). Poneteli in freezer per 10 minuti per maneggiare più facilmente quando fate i ravioli. Utilizzate dei wonton rotondi per l'involucro e una pastella d'uovo e acqua solo sulla parte superiore per chiuderli senza bagnarli troppo. Assicuratevi di cospargere abbondantemente i ravioli con della farina in modo che non si attacchino l'uno all'altro.

EDI & THE WOLF

Owners / Titolari › Eduard Frauneder - Laura Tribuno • **Chef** › Eduard Frauneder

349 E. 13th Street • Ⓜ 1 Av [L] • +01 212 533 6212 • **www.theredheadnyc.com**

Eduard Frauneder is partners with Wolfgang Ban, the owner of the multi-starry and elegant Seasonal, but his Edi & The Wolf is very different from Seasonal: it's a casual place, decorated in an original way by Philipp Haemmerle (you might not like it, but it certainly has its own personality), full every night, with only a few alternatives on the menu. An unsophisticated restaurant that serves simple Austrian dishes, genuine and good food, accompanied by European not famous but very intriguing wines, that can offer something new and fresh on the palate even to those who have tasted the wines produced in the best cru of the world. The cheese platter is Interesting, excellent mussels and clams cooked with pieces of sausage, and you have to try the free range chicken. Only two desserts, but good.

Eduard Frauneder è partner di Wolfgang Ban, proprietario del pluristellato ed elegante Seasonal, ma il suo Edi & The Wolf è quanto di più lontano si possa immaginare dal Seasonal: un posto informale, arredato in maniera originale da Philipp Haemmerle (non è detto che vi piaccia, ma di certo ha una sua personalità), pieno ogni sera, con poche alternative sul menù. Un "ristorante rustico", che serve piatti austriaci semplici, genuini e buoni, accompagnati da ricercati vini europei poco conosciuti ma davvero intriganti, che sanno offrire qualcosa di nuovo e fresco anche al palato di chi ha degustato i vini prodotti nelle migliori cru del mondo. Interessante il piatto di formaggi, ottime le cozze e le vongole cotte con pezzi di salsiccia, da provare il free range chicken. I dolci sono pochi, solo due, ma buoni.

Wine List › Carta dei Vini	**Cuisine** › Cucina	**Lunch** › Pranzo	**Dinner** › Cena
50 Labels › Etichette	**Austrian** › Austriaca	$ 20	$ 35

Grilled wild octopus

Polpo alla griglia

INGREDIENTS FOR 4 SERVINGS:
Romesco:
- 1 red bell peppers - 1 fresno peppers - ½ cup of toasted almonds
- ½ cup olive oil - ½ cup sherry vinegar - salt and pepper to taste
- xanthan gum as needed

Octopus:
- octopus - salt - olive oil - thyme - garlic -lemon

Confit Potato:
- 2 qts small fingerling potatoes - ½ bunch thyme - ½ cup garlic crushed - ¼ cup black peppercorns - ¼ cup fennel seed - 2 bay leaves
- 1 dried chili - 1 pt olive oil

Grilled Scallion:
- 4 bunches of scallion - salt - olive oil - sherry vinegar

INGREDIENTI PER 4 PERSONE:
Per il romesco:
- 1 peperone rosso - 1 peperoncino Fresno - 85 g di mandorle tostate
- 118 ml di olio d'oliva - 118 ml di aceto di sherry - sale e pepe qb
- Gomma xantana in base alla necessità

Per il polpo:
- Polpo - sale - olio d'oliva - timo - aglio - limone

Per il confit di patate:
- 2 kg di patate fingerling piccole - ½ mazzetto di timo - 70 g di aglio schiacciato - 25 g di pepe nero - 25 g di semi di finocchio - 2 foglie di alloro - 1 peperoncino secco - olio d'oliva

Scalogno grigliato:
- 4 mazzi di scalogno - sale - olio d'oliva - aceto di sherry

Romesco: Char the peppers on the grill and peel them. Toast the almonds in butter, garlic, lemon and thyme and then strain. Blend all the ingredients until smooth. Pass through a chinois.

Octopus: Cure the octopus in enough salt to cover it for 2.5 hours.
Rinse thouroughly and remove the head and separate the tentacles.
Put 4 tentacles per bag with 2 cloves of garlic, 2 sprigs of thyme, 2 slices of lemon and 2 tablespoons of olive oil.
Circulate at 185° for 2.5 hours or 175° for 5 hours.
Cool It down immediately when removing it from the circulator.

Confit Potato: In a rondeau, put all ingredients minus the spices onto a low simmer. Toast the spices then add to the other ingredients.
Cook until barely tender. Cool down immediately.

Grilled Scallion: Trim the roots off the scallions and trim the tops so they are all the same. Grill the scallion until light char marks form on both sides. Place them in the 3rd pan with salt, olive oil and sherry to season.

Preparazione romesco:
Scottate i peperoni sulla griglia e sbucciateli. Tostate le mandorle nel burro, con l'aglio, il timo e il limone e poi scolate. Frullate tutti gli ingredienti fino ad ottenere un impasto liscio e passatelo attraverso un chinois.

Preparazione polpo:
Mettete il polpo sotto sale per 2,5 ore. Sciacquate accuratamente, togliete la testa e separate i tentacoli. Mettete 4 tentacoli per sacchetto con 2 spicchi d'aglio, 2 rametti di timo, 2 fette di limone e 2 cucchiai di olio d'oliva. Fate cuocere in un forno a 85°C per 2,5 ore o 80°C per 5 ore. Raffreddate immediatamente dopo la rimozione dal forno.

Preparazione confit di patate:
Unite tutti gli ingredienti meno le spezie in una casseruola su fuoco basso. Tostate le spezie e poi aggiungetele agli altri ingredienti. Cuocete fino a quando il tutto diventa tenero. Poi, raffreddate immediatamente.

Preparazione scalogno alla griglia:
Tagliate le radici e le cime degli scalogni in modo che siano tutti uniformi. Scottate lo scalogno su entrambi i lati sulla griglia. Ponetelo nella terza padella con olio d'oliva, sale e sherry per condire.

IL PUMO › Sauvignon Malvasia Salento IGP
CANTINE SAN MARZANO

Colore giallo paglierino dai riflessi verdolini; profumo floreale riconducibile alla ginestra e fruttato riconducibile agli agrumi e alla frutta esotica. Vino dalla buona spalla acida, fresco e minerale.
Abbinamenti: Ottimo con antipasti e zuppe di pesce, formaggi giovani a pasta tenera, pasta con sughi leggeri.

Straw yellow colour with green reflections; Scotch broom notes and a hint of citrus and tropical fruits on the nose. Lively in acidity, fresh and mineral.
Best served with: Excellent with starters and fish soup, fresh cheese and pasta with light sauces.

Mixed berry parfait
Parfait di bacche miste

INGREDIENTS FOR 4 SERVINGS:
- 1 cup of vanilla custard - 2 cups of almond, oats, candied brown sugar granola - 1 cup of whipped cream - ½ lb strawberry - ½ lb raspberry - ¼ lb blackberry Vanilla
Custard: - 4 egg yolks - 2 cups of whole milk - ⅓ cup sugar - ⅛ cup cornstarch - 1 spoon softened unsalted butter - 1 teaspoon vanilla extract

INGREDIENTI PER 4 PERSONE:
- 230 g di crema alla vaniglia - 240 g di mandorle, avena, granola muesli con zucchero di canna - 235 ml di panna montata - 225 g di fragole - 225 g di lamponi - 225 g di more
Per la crema alla vaniglia: - 4 tuorli - 470 ml di latte intero - 65 g di zucchero - 12 g di amido di mais - 1 cucchiaio di burro ammorbidito non salato - 1 cucchiaino di estratto di vaniglia

Heat milk over moderate heat until hot but not boiling. While the milk heats, whisk together the yolks, sugar and cornstarch. Add the milk gradually while whisking constantly. Transfer the mixture to moderately low heat, and cook stirring constantly, until It thickened and registers 170°F on a thermometer, for 6 to 10 minutes (do not boil). Add the butter and vanilla extract. Cook the strawberries and raspberries in a double boiler with sugar and cointreau for 10 minutes. Alternate layers, in a clear glass, of vanilla custard, strawberry and raspberry mix, granola and whipped cream. Decorate with fresh blackberries.

Scaldate il latte a fuoco moderato fino a quando diventa caldo, ma non bollente. Intanto, sbattete i tuorli, lo zucchero e l'amido di mais. Aggiungete il latte poco alla volta, mentre continuate a mescolare. Mettete la miscela su fuoco medio-basso e lasciate cuocere mentre continuate a mescolare, fino a quando si addensa e raggiunge 75°C, da 6 a 10 minuti (senza far bollire). Aggiungete il burro e l'estratto di vaniglia. Cucinate le fragole e i lamponi a bagnomaria con lo zucchero e il cointreau per 10 minuti. Create degli strati in un bicchierino di vetro, alternando la crema, le fragole e i lamponi, il muesli e la panna montata. Decorate con more fresche.

Free range chicken

INGREDIENTS FOR 4 SERVINGS:
Broccoli puree: - Blanch some tarragon and mint and 1/2 lb of broccoli stems - 1 shallot - 2 garlic cloves - 1 cup of chicken stock
Kumquat Jam: - shallot - garlic - capers - 1 cup kumquat - 1 chicken stock bouillon - 1/4 cup of picketed Mustard seeds
Pickeling solution: - 1 cup of white vinegar - 1 cup of water - 1/2 cup of sugar for 30 minutes - 20 potatoes - garlic - thyme - 50 g of butter - 4 chicken breasts - canola oil

Broccoli puree: Blanch terragon and mint and 1/2 lb of broccoli stems. Saute 1 shallot and 2 garlic cloves in 1 cup of chicken stock, add blanched broccoli stems and herbs and cook until tender at a high temperature. Blend the mixture with a few ice cubes to keep the color green.
Kumquat jam:
Shallot, garlic, capers and 1 cup of kumquat puréed finely and put to sweat for 30 minutes on a low heat. Add 1 chicken stock buillon. Finish with 1/4 cup of picketed Mustard seeds.
Pickeling solution:
Submerge the mustard seeds in 1 cup of white vinegar, 1 cup of water and 1/2 cup of sugar for 30 minutes.
Fingerling Potatoes:
Saute the potatoes in garlic, tyme and butter.
Sear 4 chicken breasts in canola oil and then roast them for 20 minutes in a high temperature oven with garlic, thyme and butter.
To garnish: Blanch the broccoli heads in hot water, shock them and sautee with sunflower seeds and pepper flakes.

EL ALMACEN

Owner / Titolare › Galarzasuarez LLC. • **Chef** › Matias Romano

557 Driggs Av (Brooklyn) • Ⓜ Bedford Av • +01 718 218 7284 • **www.elalmacennyc.com**

Don't let the entrance to this restaurant with Argentine cuisine, that seems designed more for a pub than for a restaurant, fool you: despite the appearance from the outside, inside the ambiance is really trendy and sociable, and the meat dishes, as well as the fish ones, will surprise you. The food we tasted was fabulous. This Argentinean steak house offers delicious gnocchi and superb pancakes. We also really liked the Costillitas de Cerdo, the Entrena and obviously the Churrasco, the dish of the house. The weekend Brunch has also a very attractive price.

Non lasciatevi spiazzare dall'ingresso di questo locale con cucina argentina che sembra pensato più per un pub che per un ristorante: a dispetto di quel che appare da fuori, all'interno l'ambiente è davvero trendy e socievole, e i piatti, sia quelli di carne che quelli di pesce, vi sorprenderanno. Il cibo che abbiamo degustato è favoloso. Questa steack house argentina propone degli gnocchi gustosissimi e un pancakes ottimo. Ci sono piaciuti tanto anche le Costillitas de Cerdo, la Entrena e ovviamente il Churrasco, il piatto della casa. Il brunch del week-end ha un prezzo davvero interessante.

Wine List › Carta dei Vini	Cuisine › Cucina	Brunch	Dinner › Cena
40 Labels › Etichette	Argentinian-Fusion	$ 16-25	$ 26-50

Grilled cobia with white asparagus, artichokes hearts and aioli

Pesce cobia alla griglia con asparagi bianchi, cuori di carciofo e salsa aioli

INGREDIENTS FOR 4 SERVINGS:
- 2 lb of fresh cobia fillet - 1 bunch of white asparagus - 8 large whole artichokes - 1 lemon (for juice and zest) - 1 tablespoon of chopped italian parsley - 1 tablespoon of choped fresh mint - olive oil - sea salt - black pepper
Aioli: - 2 garlic cloves - 1 large egg yolk - 2 teaspoons of fresh lemon juice - 1 teaspoon of lemon zest - ¼ cup of extra-virgin olive oil - 3 tablespoons of vegetable oil

INGREDIENTI PER 4 PERSONE:
- 907 g di filetto di Cobia fresco - 1 mazzetto di asparagi bianchi - 8 carciofi grandi interi - 1 limone (succo e scorza) - 1 cucchiaio di prezzemolo italiano tritato - 1 cucchiaio di menta fresca tritata - olio d'oliva - sale marino - pepe nero
Per la salsa Aioli:
- 2 spicchi d'aglio - 1 tuorlo d'uovo grande - 2 cucchiaini di succo di limone fresco - 1 cucchiaino di scorza di limone - 59 ml di olio extravergine di oliva - 3 cucchiai di olio vegetale

Boil the artichokes, lower the heat to simmer and make sure the tops of the artichokes are submerged.
Simmer the artichokes until the base can easily be pierced with a knife, for 20 to 40 minutes. Remove the artichokes from the water and place them in a large bowl of ice water to cool completely. Drain artichokes upside down on paper towels. Cut artichokes in half from top through the stem, use a spoon to scoop out the fibrous cores, leaving the hearts and leaves intact. Add lemon juice, parsley, mint, olive oil, sea salt and black pepper. Put aside until use.
Prepare the fish. Once dry, season all sides lightly with salt, pepper and olive oil. When the grill is ready, cook the fish for about 4 minutes, turn over and cook until the flesh is just beginning to separate and the centre is opaque (about 3-4 minutes).
Grill the marinated artichokes and mix them with the raw white asparagus in the same bowl. Put all the vegetables on the grill for about 3 minutes or until grilled.
Serve the grilled vegetables with the fish and the aioli on the side, finish the dish with more parsley, lemon zest and olive oil on top of the fish.
Aioli: Place the garlic, lemon zest and egg in a food processor bowl fitted with a blade attachment. Process until evenly combined, for about 10 seconds.
With the motor still running, slowly add the olive oil, followed by the grapeseed or vegetable oil until completely combined, for about 2 minutes. Stop the processor, add the lemon juice, season with salt, and pulse until thoroughly mixed. Stop and scrape down the sides of the bowl with a rubber spatula, then pulse until all ingredients are evenly incorporated. Let sit for at least 30 minutes before using. Refrigerate in a container with a tightfitting lid for up to 3 days.

Lessate i carciofi, poi fate cuocere a fuoco lento e assicuratevi che le cime dei carciofi siano sommerse. Lasciate cuocere per 20-40 minuti fino a quando la base dei carciofi può essere facilmente perforabile con un coltello. Toglieteli dal fuoco e poneteli in una grande ciotola d'acqua ghiacciata per farli raffreddare completamente. Scolateli a testa in giù su carta assorbente. Tagliate i carciofi a metà dall'alto verso il basso, rimuovete le parti fibrose con un cucchiaio e lasciate intatti il cuore e le foglie. Condite con succo di limone, il prezzemolo, la menta, l'olio d'oliva, il sale marino e il pepe nero. Mettete da parte fino all'uso. Preparate il pesce. Una volta asciutto, condite leggermente entrambi i lati con sale, pepe e olio d'oliva. Grigliate i filetti per circa 4 minuti, poi girateli e lasciateli cuocere fino a quando la carne inizia a separarsi e il centro è opaco (circa 3-4 minuti). Grigliate i carciofi marinati e aggiungete gli asparagi bianchi nella stessa ciotola. Grigliate tutte le verdure per circa 3 minuti. Servite le verdure grigliate con i filetti di pesce e la salsa aioli al lato e finite il piatto con dell'altro prezzemolo, scorza di limone e olio d'oliva sul pesce.
Salsa Aioli: Mettete l'aglio, la scorza di limone e l'uovo nella ciotola di un robot da cucina dotato di supporto con lama. Frullate per circa 10 secondi per far amalgamare tutti gli ingredienti. Con il mixer ancora in funzione, aggiungete lentamente l'olio d'oliva, poi l'olio di vinaccioli o l'olio vegetale, per circa 2 minuti, fino a quando il tutto è amalgamato per bene. Spegnete il mixer, aggiungete il succo di limone, condite con sale, e pulsate fino a miscelazione completa. Usate una spatola di gomma per pulire i lati della ciotola e poi pulsate nuovamente fino al completo incorporamento di tutti gli ingredienti. Lasciate riposare la salsa per almeno 30 minuti prima di utilizzarla. Conservate in frigorifero fino a 3 giorni in un contenitore con coperchio stretto.

Flan with dulce de leche

Churrasco and chimichurri

INGREDIENTS FOR 4 SERVINGS:
- 2 grass fed ribeye lip on steaks (18-20oz each) - 8 idaho potatoes - sea salt - black pepper **Chimichurri sauce:** - 2 cups of chopped fresh parsley - ¼ cup of fresh oregano leaves - 3-6 cloves of garlic - 1 red pepper, chopped - ½ cup of oil (grapeseed oil, canola) - 2 tablespoons of white vineger - Lemon zest - Kosher salt and red pepper flakes to taste

INGREDIENTI PER 4 PERSONE:
- 2 costate di manzo con l'osso (500-560 g ciascuno) - 8 patate Idaho - sale marino - pepe nero **Salsa Chimichurri:** - 50 g di prezzemolo tritato fresco - 6,5 g di origano fresco - 3-6 spicchi d'aglio - 1 peperoncino tritato - 118 ml di olio di vinaccioli o canola - 2 cucchiai di aceto bianco - scorza di limone - sale kosher e fiocchi di peperoncino rosso qb

Get the steaks out of the fridge 30 to 45 minutes before use. Heat a charcoal grill to a high temperature (about 450°F to 550°F). Season the steaks on all sides with sea salt and pepper. When the grill is ready, place the steak onto it and leave to cook undisturbed, until grill marks appear on the bottom and the steak is lightly charred on the edges, for about 4 to 5 minutes. Then flip the steak over and cook for another 6 minutes. The steak will be medium rare in 10-12 minutes total. You can also use an instant-read thermometer, it should register between 125°F and 130°F. Without removing the skin, cut the potatoes into long strips and put them in a large bowl of clean water to remove some starch, prevent them from sticking together and stop the oxidizing process. Heat the oil until it reaches 275 to 300°F. Remove the potatoes from the water and pat dry. Working in small batches, fry the potatoes until they go from shiny to matte, for 3 to 5 minutes. Drain well on paper towels. Re-heat the oil until it reaches 350°F and fry the potatoes again, also in small batches, until they are golden brown and crispy on the outside but soft on the inside. Serve the steak with the fries on a nice wood board or plate and the chimichurri can be on the side or on top of the grilled steak. **Chimichurri sauce:** Chop everything by hand, it should be a chunky texture. Use more or less oil as needed, depending on how much parsley you end up with. Stir all the ingredients together until well blended. Store in the refrigerator until ready to serve.

Uscite le bistecche dal frigo 30-45 minuti prima dell'uso. Scaldate una griglia a carbone a temperatura alta (circa 230-280°C). Condite entrambi i lati delle bistecche con sale e pepe. Quando la griglia è a temperatura, mettetele a cuocere indisturbate per circa 4-5 minuti, fino a quando si vedono i segni della griglia e i bordi sono leggermente abbrustoliti. Capovolgete le bistecche e lasciatele cuocere per altri 6 minuti. Saranno a cottura media in un totale di 10-12 minuti. Potete utilizzare un termometro a lettura istantanea che dovrebbe segnare 50-55°C. Tagliate le patate a strisce lunghe senza sbucciarle e mettetele in una grande ciotola di acqua pulita per rimuovere un po' dell'amido per evitare il processo di ossidazione e che si attacchino l'una all'altra. Scaldate l'olio a 135-150°C. Togliete le patate dall'acqua e tamponatele per asciugarle. Friggete le patate un po' alla volta fino a quando si opacizzano per circa 3-5 minuti. Fatele scolare bene su carta assorbente. Riscaldate nuovamente l'olio a 175°C e friggete ancora le patate fino a quando sono dorate e croccanti all'esterno, ma morbide all'interno. Servite le bistecche con le patatine fritte su di una bella tavola di legno o su di un piatto da portata. Il chimichurri può essere messo al lato o al di sopra delle bistecche. **Salsa Chimichurri:** Tritate tutto a mano grossolanamente. Mettete più o meno olio in base a quanto prezzemolo avete a disposizione. Unite bene tutti gli ingredienti. Conservate in frigorifero fino al momento di servire.

INGREDIENTS FOR 30 SERVINGS:
-5 cups of milk - 2 cups of heavy cream - 3 cans of condensed milk (14oz) - 2 cans of evaporated milk (12oz) - 10 eggs - 8 egg yolks - 3 vanilla beans - 1 cinnamon stick - 2 cups of raw sugar dulce de leche (caramel)
Caramel: - 2 cups of sugar - 2 cups of water

In a medium saucepan over medium-low heat, melt sugar with the water until liquefied and golden in color. Put 3 spoons of this syrup/caramel in each flan's ramekins (4-6oz) **Flan directions:** Preheat oven to 350 degrees. Mix in a medium saucepan the condensed milk, with the evaporated milk, the sugar, vanilla beans and cinnamon stick, put it on the stove. Wisk the eggs with the egg yolks and add this to the previous preparation and mix all together. Run through a drainer and fill the flan containers with this filtered preparation. In preheated oven pour enough hot water into baking pan to come halfway up sides of ramekins. Bake until centers of flans are gently set, about 40 minutes. Transfer flans to rack and cool. Chill until cold, about 2 hours. Cover and chill overnight. (Can be made 2 days ahead). Serve with dulce de leche and some strawberries or blackberries.

El Born
651 Manhattan Ave.
Brooklyn, NY 11222
347-844-9295
elbornNYC.com

NO SMOKING!

el born

TAPAS Y MÁS
PEOPLE PLATILLOS
WINE BEER
DRINKS LIVE MUSIC
JAZZ FLAMENCO
OLÉ LAUGHS BAR
JAMÓN JAMÓN
COCKTAILS FIESTA
AND MORE!

EL BORN
Owner / Titolare › Elena Manich

651 Manhattan Avenue (Brooklyn) • Ⓜ Nassau Av [G] • +01 347 844 9295 • **www.elbornnyc.com**

The "less is more" rule is never wrong, even when talking about restaurants. For example, El Born is a place decorated with taste but without frills. It has a long counter that starts right from the entrance, and a row of tables for two people behind It. And then a simple garden, with red tables and chairs. Everything is simple, but very elegant and pleasant. It seems that Elena, the owner, wanted to create a beautiful restaurant in Brooklyn that gave foreground to the Spanish cuisine. A cuisine that is also simple but perfect, as fast as tasty, with a multitude of tapas that disappear from plates in seconds and still make you want to go on forever. We started with the "croquetas" (goat cheese and apple mixture), and from there it was a crescendo: montadito de bou, cod fish collars, zucchini and blueberries (excellent), squid in aioli sauce, seared tuna with white beans. In the end, Elena sent us into ecstasy with " Chocolate croquetas": if she had brought 100, we would have eaten them all.

La regola del "less is more" non sbaglia mai, anche nel caso dei ristoranti. Prendete El Born: è un locale arredato con molto gusto ma senza tanti fronzoli. Con un lungo bancone che inizia fin dall'ingresso e una fila di tavoli da due posti alle sue spalle. E poi un giardino semplicissimo, con tavoli e sedie rosse. Tutto semplice, ma molto elegante e piacevole. Sembra che Elena, la titolare, abbia voluto creare a Brooklyn un bel locale che lasciasse in primo piano la cucina spagnola. Una cucina anch'essa semplice ma perfetta, veloce quanto saporita, con una moltitudine di tapas che scompaiono dai piatti in pochi secondi e ti fan venire voglia di continuare all'infinito. Abbiamo iniziato con le "croquetas" (formaggio di capra e composto di mele), e da lì è stato un crescendo: montadito de bou, cod fish collars, zucchine e mirtilli (eccellente), calamari in salsa aglioli, tonno scottato con fagioli bianchi. E per finire Elena ci ha mandati in estasi con le "croquetas al cioccolato": ne avesse portate 100, le avremmo mangiate tutte.

Wine List › Carta dei Vini	**Cuisine** › Cucina	**Lunch** › Pranzo	**Dinner** › Cena
35 Labels › Etichette	**Spanish** › Spagnola	**No lunch** › Chiuso a pranzo	$ 25-30

FIVE LEAVES

Owner / Titolare › Justin Mongel - Kathy Mecham • **Chef** › Ken Addington

18 Bedford Ave (Brooklyn) • Ⓜ Nassau Av [G] • +01 718 383 5345 • **www.fiveleavesny.com**

The Five Leaves is "the place you can't miss" in Williamsburg, Brooklyn. You'll gather that before you even get there, when you're about to cross the road and you spot the line of people waiting for a table. It is a place where the clientele is mostly of young people and people in their forties, it's very trendy and is always crowded. But it's the sort of chaos that recharges you with new energy and puts you in a good mood. If you are literally looking for a real restaurant, well, you are in the wrong place. At Five Leaves people socialize, you are together and talking, while drinking a cocktail or eating something simple and different. Ken Addington's cuisine is no frills but it certainly doesn't lack in consistency, and some dishes such as the Steamed Mussels and the Moroccan Scramble are real surprises. We were there for a Sunday brunch, for two wonderful hours, talking to people across the table next to ours. Good food, nice people, affordable prices for all pockets. What else to ask of a restaurant?

The Five Leaves è "the place you can't miss" a Williamsburg, Brooklyn. Lo capisci prima ancora di arrivarci, quando stai per attraversare la strada e scorgi la fila di gente in attesa del suo tavolo. È un posto frequentato per lo più da giovani e quarantenni, è molto trendy ed è perennemente affollato. Ma di quel caos che ti ricarica di energia e ti mette di buon umore. Se cercate un ristorante nel vero senso della parola, beh, avete sbagliato posto. Al Five Leaves si socializza, si sta insieme e si parla bevendo un cocktail o mangiando qualcosa di semplice e di diverso. La cucina di Ken Addington è senza fronzoli ma non certo priva di consistenza, e alcuni piatti come le Cozze al Vapore e lo Scramble Marocchino sono delle vere sorprese. Ci siamo stati per il brunch della domenica, e abbiamo trascorso due ore magnifiche, parlando con i dirimpettai del tavolo accanto al nostro. Buon cibo, bella gente, prezzi accessibili a tutti. Cos'altro chiedere ad un ristorante?

Wine List › Carta dei Vini	**Cuisine** › Cucina	**Lunch** › Pranzo	**Dinner** › Cena
80 Labels › Etichette	Australian/American	$ 30	$ 50

Steamed mussels

INGREDIENTS FOR 4/6 SERVINGS:
- 2 kg fresh mussels, cleaned thoroughly - 1tbs unsalted butter -
5 shallots sliced thin - 4 cloves of garlic sliced thin
- large pinch saffron - 1 tsp turmeric - 1 thinly sliced head of
fennel - 1 tbs minced ginger.

Sachet:
- ¼ c coriander seeds
- 2 tbs fennel seed - 2 tbs black pepper - thyme - bay leaf
- 1 c white wine - 2 tbs pernod - 4 c canned coconut milk
- 2 tbs seasoned rice wine vinegar - 2 thick slices of sourdough
- 1 peeled garlic clove - 1c loosely packed cilantro leaves
- ½ c thinly sliced scallions - ½ c thinly sliced hot red chilies
- 1 tsp lemon juice - 1tbs extra virgin olive oil.

Place sachet ingredients into cheese cloth and wrap
thoroughly and tie with a bit of wine.
Warm Butter in an 8qt sauce pot. Sweat out shallots,
fennel, ginger and garlic with sachet, saffron
and turmeric till soft.
Add wine and pernod, reduce till almost dry.
Add coconut milk and reduce slowly by half
to a rich consistency.
Remove Sachet and bring to simmer, add mussels to
coconut sauce, cover with a heavy lid and allow to steam
until all mussels have opened.
Season with salt and rice vinegar, salt and white pepper
to taste.
Brush sourdough with olive oil and lightly grill or toast,
rub with garlic clove and cut into large chunks.
Toss bread with fresh cilantro, scallion, chilies,
olive oil and lemon juice. Season with salt to taste
and top mussels with the mixture

Ricotta pancakes

INGREDIENTS FOR 4 SERVINGS:
- 7 eggs separated - 2.75 c ricotta - 2c flour - 1 tbs baking powder
- 1.5 c milk - 1.5 tsp salt - 2 tsp sugar - zest of one lemon
Honeycomb Butter: - 8 # butter-diced and brought up to room temp
- ¼ c honey - 2t salt - 1c sugar - ½ c maple syrup - 1 t baking soda

Whip whites to stiff peaks. Combine Ricotta, milk, yolks and zest. Sift
together flour, baking powder, salt and sugar. Combine wet and dry
ingredients then fold in whites. Set the batter onto a buttered griddle
until bubbling, partially set and golden. Flip and continue cooking
until fully set. Set a stack of 3 pancakes per serving and garnish with
whole sliced banana, strawberries, Blueberries and a scoop of honeycomb butter. Serve with maple syrup.
Honeycomb Butter: Honeycomb is a crunchy toffee candy that is
aerated with baking soda. We crumble it and fold it into softened
butter to for extra texture and depth on the dish. Heat Sugar and
Golden Syrup together on low heat until sugar has dissolved. Whisk
in Baking Soda. Pour out onto Silpat and let cool. Crack Honeycomb
into manageable pieces and pulse in robotcoup into course graduals.
Fold all ingredients together.

FLINDERS LANE

Owners / Titolari › Chris Mc Pherson - Chris Rendell • **Chef** › Chris Rendell

162 Avenue A • **M** 1 Av [L] • +01 212 228 6900 • **www.flinderslane-nyc.com**

The Flinders Lane is undoubtedly one of the nicest surprises in New York: a nice little trendy place in East Village (a few steps away from Tompkins Square Park), it's always full, and this made me discover a cuisine that I still don't know, the modern Australian one: I admit I had been to Sydney, but I only had a feast with fresh fish. In this place, named after a street in Melbourne, and where you can admire one of the most beautiful murals I've ever seen, you can enjoy an incredible variety of dishes and fusion flavors and at some point you risk "con-fusion". In Chris Rendell's kitchen, there is a bit of everything: oysters, Great Britain, fish, noodles, Indonesia and Malaysia, meat, New York and China. An explosion of aromas and textures that, judging from the line to get a table, is very successful.

Il Flinders Lane è senza dubbio una delle più belle sorprese di New York: un bel localino alla moda nell'East Village (a pochi passi dal Tompkins Square Park), sempre pieno, che mi ha fatto scoprire una cucina che ancora non conoscevo, quella australiana moderna: ammetto di essere stato a Sydney e di essermi fermato alle scorpacciate di pesce freschissimo. In questo locale che prende il nome da una strada di Melbourne ed in cui ammirerete uno dei più bei murales che abbia mai visto, potrete assaporare una incredibile varietà di piatti e sapori fusion e ad un certo punto rischierete di andare in con-fusion. Nella cucina di Chris Rendell infatti, c'è un po' di tutto: ostriche, Gran Bretagna, pesce, noodles, Indonesia e Malesia, carne, New York e la Cina. Una esplosione di profumi e consistenze che a giudicare dalle file per accaparrarsi un tavolo riscuote un buon successo.

Wine List › Carta dei Vini	**Cuisine** › Cucina	**Lunch** › Pranzo	**Dinner** › Cena
120 Labels › Etichette	**Modern Australian**	$ 15	$ 45

Diver caught scallops

Capesante in salsa piccante

INGREDIENTS FOR 4 SERVINGS:
- 16 larger scallops

For the macadamia/chili relish:
- 5 red pepper-finely diced - 5 red onions-finely diced
- 2 cups cashews-roasted roughly chopped
- 5 pc dried red chili, deseeded, deep-fried until black, broken into small pieces - 300 gms chili/garlic sauce* - 300 mls water
- 200 mls veg oil - 5 tsp salt - 2 tsp ground white pepper
- 250 gms sugar - 60 mls sesame oil - 125 mls rice wine vinegar
- 250 mls white wine

For the braised hijiki:
- 125 g hijiki - 2 l water - 2 c soy sauce - 1 c mirin - 1 c rice vinegar

INGREDIENTI PER 4 PERSONE:
- 16 capesante medio-grandi

Per la salsa di macadamia/peperoncino:
- 5 peperoni rossi a dadini - 5 cipolle rosse a dadini - 300gr di anacardi tostati e tritati grossolanamente - 5 pezzi di peperoncino rosso essiccato, senza semi, fritto fino a diventare nero e sbriciolato in piccoli pezzi - 300 g di salsa peperoncino/aglio* - 300ml di acqua
- 200 ml di olio vegetale - 5 cucchiaini di sale - 2 cucchiaini di pepe bianco macinato - 250 g di zucchero - 60 ml di olio di sesamo
- 125 ml di aceto di riso - 250 ml di vino bianco

Per il brasato di alga hijiki:
- 125 g di alga hijiki - 2 lt d'acqua - 470 ml di salsa di soia
- 235 ml di mirin - 235 ml di aceto di riso

For the Macadamia/Chili Relish:
Heat a heavy base pot and add oil. Once smoking add the red peppers and onion and fry until fragrant. Add the chili sauce, sugar and allow colour to darken. Add sea salt, white pepper, vinegar, sesame oil and water. Bring to the boil and reduce by about a quarter. Stir in cashews and dried chilies. Remove from the heat. Set aside.
Chili garlic sauce can be found in Asian grocery stores.

For the Braised Hijiki:
Rinse the dry Hijiki under running water in a fine strainer for 10 minutes. Combine all liquids in a pot and bring to a boil. Add the Hijiki and low simmer for 45minutes-1 hour. Allow to cool in the liquid.

For the Scallops:
Heat a heavy base sauté pan. Add a little oil to coat the pan. Season the scallops with salt and pepper. Let the scallops brown on one side for 1 -2 minutes, then turn them and allow to cook for another minute. Remove them from the pan and place on kitchen paper.

To serve:
Warm the relish and place 1 tablespoon or relish on each plate. Place the scallops in the centre of the relish. Dress micro pea shoots (if not available baby arugula is a good substitute) with the braised Hijiki and olive oil and place it on top of the scallops.

Preparazione della salsa di macadamia/peperoncino:
Riscaldate una casseruola dal fondo pesante e aggiungete l'olio. Quando fuma, aggiungete i peperoni rossi e la cipolla e fate friggere fino a quando diventano fragranti. Aggiungete la salsa di peperoncino e lo zucchero e lasciate scurire. Aggiungete il sale, il pepe bianco, l'aceto, l'olio di sesamo e l'acqua. Portate ad ebollizione e lasciate ridurre di circa un quarto. Aggiungete gli anacardi e i peperoncini secchi. Togliete dal fuoco e mettete da parte.
La salsa di peperoncino con aglio si può trovare nei negozi alimentari asiatici.

Preparazione Hijiki brasato:
Sciacquate l'Hijiki sotto acqua corrente in un colino fine per 10 minuti e poi asciugatelo. Unite tutti i liquidi in una pentola e portate ad ebollizione. Aggiungete l'Hijiki e fate cucinare a fuoco lento per 45 minuti-1 ora. Lasciatelo raffreddare nel liquido.

Preparazione capesante:
Scaldate una padella dalla base pesante e aggiungete un filo d'olio per rivestire il fondo. Condite le capesante con sale e pepe e mettetele in padella a scurire per 1 -2 minuti per lato. Toglietele dalla padella e mettetele su carta da cucina.

Preparazione del piatto:
Scaldate la salsa di macadamia e mettetene 1 cucchiaio per piatto. Ponete le capesante sopra la salsa. Condite dei micro germogli di piselli (se non sono disponibili, la rucola baby è una buona alternativa) con l'Hijiki brasato e olio d'oliva, e metteteli sopra le capesante.

Pan roasted squid
Calamari arrosto (con anguria)

INGREDIENTS FOR 4 SERVINGS:
- 4 large tubes of Squid, Cleaned and sluiced in ¼ inch rings - 1 red chili-finely sliced - 2 cloves garlic finely sliced - 1 lemon - ¼ cup picked Parsley - ¼ cup picked Thai Bail - Olive oil - -1 small watermelon cut into rectangle 4 pieces 3 inches x 5 inches

INGREDIENTI PER 4 PERSONE:
- 4 grandi tubi di calamari puliti e tagliati ad anelli da 6 mm - 1 peperoncino rosso tritato finemente - 2 spicchi d'aglio tritati - 1 limone - 5 g di prezzemolo raccolto - 5 g di Thai Bail raccolto - olio d'oliva - 1 anguria piccola tagliata in 4 pezzi rettangolari da 7.5 cm x 12.5 cm

Pre heat a grill. When hot, lightly oil the watermelon and place It on the hot grill until there are nice grill marks on both sides. Pre heat a large sauté pan and add olive oil to coat it. Add the squid tubes, allow to cook for 1 minute, then add the chili and garlic. Sauté for a further minute. Squeeze lemon over the squid and season with salt and pepper. In a mixing bowl, place the picked herbs, add the cooked squid and toss. Place the grilled watermelon on 4 plates. Divide the squid salad evenly on top of the watermelon. Finish with a drizzle of olive oil.

Riscaldate una griglia. Quando è calda, cospargete l'anguria di olio, mettetela sulla griglia calda e lasciatela fino a quando si vedono i segni di cottura su entrambi i lati. Riscaldate una grande padella e aggiungete olio d'oliva per rivestire il fondo. Aggiungete i calamari e lasciate cuocere per un minuto, poi, aggiungete il peperoncino e l'aglio. Lasciate soffriggere per un altro minuto e condite con succo di limone, sale e pepe. Mettete le erbe in una terrina, aggiungete i calamari cotti e saltate il tutto. Mettete l'anguria grigliata su 4 piatti da portata. Aggiungeteci sopra l'insalata di calamari. Terminate con un filo d'olio d'oliva.

Hamachi, chinese salted black beanse
Hamachi e fagioli neri cinesi salati

INGREDIENTS FOR 4 SERVINGS:
For the Dressing*: - 1 cup of vegetable oil - ¾ cup of lemon juice - ½ cup of light soy - ¼ cup of black beans (coverd with cold water) - 1 red pepper, peeled and finely diced - 1 clove of garlic, minced - 1 cup of red onion, diced and rinsed under running water for 10 minutes - 1 knob of ginger, julienned finely - ½ cup of scallion, finely chopped in rounds
For the Hamachi*: 1 piece of Hamachi (around ½ pound)

INGREDIENTI PER 4 PERSONE:
Per il condimento*: - 235 ml di olio vegetale - 177 ml di succo di limone - 118 ml di soia leggera - 60 ml di fagioli neri in acqua fredda - 1 peperone rosso sbucciato e tagliato a dadini - 1 spicchio d'aglio tritato - 150 g di cipolla rossa a dadini, sciacquata sotto acqua corrente per 10 minuti - 1 noce di zenzero tagliato a julienne - 115 g di scalogno tritato finemente
Per il Hamachi*: 1 pezzo di Hamachi (circa 225 g)

This is a great simple dish. The dressing can be made in advance and most ingredients can be found in high-end Asian grocery stores. **For the Dressing*:** Rinse the red onion under water for 10 minutes and allow it to drain. Combine the remaining ingredients in a large bowl, mix and set aside. *This dressing can be made a few days in advance. Before using it, remove it from the refrigerator to allow the oils to reach room temperature.
To serve: Finely slice the Hamachi so each plate has 6-7 pieces. Mix the dressing with a spoon and lightly coat each piece of fish with it. Garnish the dish with pieces of Lily Bulb, cilantro and Shiso leaf.

Questo è un piatto semplice e grandioso. Il condimento può essere preparato in anticipo e la maggior parte degli ingredienti possono essere trovati in negozi di specialità alimentari asiatiche. **Preparazione del condimento*:** Sciacquate la cipolla rossa sotto l'acqua per 10 minuti e lasciate scolare. Unite gli altri ingredienti in una grande ciotola, mescolate e mettete da parte.
* Questo condimento può essere preparato con qualche giorno di anticipo. Prima di utilizzarlo toglietelo dal frigorifero per consentire agli oli di tornare a temperatura ambiente. **Preparazione del piatto:** Affettate finemente l'Hamachi in modo da ottenere 6-7 pezzi per piatto. Mescolate il condimento con un cucchiaio e cospargete ogni pezzo di pesce con questo condimento di fagioli neri. Guarnite il piatto con pezzi di Lily Bulb, coriandolo e foglie di Shiso.

GNOCCO

Owners / Titolari › Gian Luca Giovanetti - Pierluigi Palazzo • **Chef** › Gian Luca Giovanetti

337 East 10th Street • **M** 1 Av [L] • +01 212 677 1913 • **www.gnocco.com**

It is true that New York is the centre of the world and you can find everything, but the gnocco Emiliano is one of the things we would have never expected to find here. But we found Gnocco, a great little Italian restaurant in the East Village that makes amazing pizza (above all, the Tartufata). This place is really cute. Wood predominates in the hall and in the garden, and this makes the place even more cozy and intimate. Gian Luca and Pierluigi's (the two owners) friendliness and chef Claudio's dishes, do the rest. The gnocco fritto with crudo ham and other cold cuts is obviously the best way to start a dinner, which continues with tastes of fresh pasta. Also excellent, and not at all too heavy, the spaghetti with clams and pesto. We finished off with desserts that matched the quality of what had preceded them. What else to say: Gnocco is a classic Italian restaurant which is easy to fall in love with and where you'd always happily go back, even if you are not Italian.

È verò che New York è il centro del mondo e vi si può trovare tutto, ma lo gnocco emiliano, quello proprio no, non ce lo saremmo mai aspettati. E invece c'è, da Gnocco, un ottimo ristorantino italiano nell'East Village che fa delle pizze strepitose (su tutte, la Tartufata). Il posto è davvero carino. Nelle sala e nel giardino predomina il legno, e questo rende il locale ancora più accogliente e intimo. La simpatia di Gian Luca e Pierluigi (i due proprietari) i piatti di Claudio, lo chef, fanno il resto. Lo gnocco fritto con prosciutto crudo e salumi è ovviamente il modo migliore per aprire la cena, che prosegue con degli assaggi di pasta fresca. Ottimi, e per nulla pesanti, anche gli spaghetti alle vongole e pesto. Abbiamo concluso con dei dolci all'altezza di ciò che li aveva preceduti. Che dire: Gnocco è il classico ristorante italiano di cui è facile innamorarsi. E dove si torna sempre volentieri. Anche se non si è italiani.

Wine List › Carta dei Vini	**Cuisine** › Cucina	**Brunch**	**Average Price** › Prezzo Medio
60 Labels › Etichette	**Italian Traditional** › Italiana tradizionale	$ 18	$ 30

Fried gnocco

INGREDIENTS FOR 4 SERVINGS:
- 1 kg of flour type 0 - 25 g of salt - 70 g of olive oil
- 18 cl of sparkling water - 40 cl of milk

Mix all the ingredients. When the mixture is homogeneous, cover and leave it to rest for 30 minutes, then roll it out with a rolling pin until it's about 1,5mm thick. Cut the dough into rhomboid shapes. Fry them in hot sunflower oil (or lard) until golden brown. Drain the oil, and serve the gnocco with salami, crudo ham or other ingredients to your liking.

Gnocco fritto

INGREDIENTI PER 4 PERSONE:
- 1 kg di farina tipo 0 - 25 g di sale - 70 g di olio d'oliva
- 18 cl di acqua frizzante - 40 cl di latte

Impastate il tutto. Quando l'impasto è omogeneo copritelo e lasciatelo riposare per 30 minuti, quindi stendetelo con il mattarello fino ad un'altezza di circa 1 millimetro e mezzo. Tagliate l'impasto ricavandone delle forme romboidali. Friggete in olio di girasole bollente (o strutto suino) fino a doratura. Fate scolare l'olio, quindi servite gli gnocchi accompagnandoli con salame, prosciutto crudo o altri ingredienti a piacere.

Spaghetti alla chitarra

INGREDIENTS FOR 4 SERVINGS:
Spaghetti ingredients: - 1 kg of semola flour - 60cl of water
Dressing ingredients: - 400 g of clams - 200 g of green beans
- garlic, olive oil, salt and pepper to taste

Knead the semola thoroughly with water, then stretch the dough with a rolling pin and cut the spaghetti approximately 2mm thick. Cook them in boiling salted water.
Clean the basil and blanch it in boiling water for 30 seconds. Then cool it with ice and blend it with an immersion blender, add extra virgin olive oil, Parmesan cheese, salt and pepper.
Clean the clams and remove any sand that remains. Heat some olive oil in a frying pan, add the garlic, salt and pepper, and then the clams and cook for a few minutes. Add the green beans and blanch slightly. Stir in the pasta cooked al dente, then serve.

INGREDIENTI PER 4 PERSONE:
Per gli spaghetti: - 1 Kg di semola - 60 cl di acqua
Condimento: - 400 g di vongole - 200 g di fagiolini - aglio, olio di oliva, sale e pepe qb

Impastate la semola con l'acqua, fate amalgamare bene, quindi stendete il composto con il mattarello e ritagliate degli spaghetti di circa 2 mm di spessore. Fateli cuocere in acqua bollente salata. Mondate il basilico. Scottatelo in acqua bollente per 30 secondi. Raffreddatelo con del ghiaccio, quindi emulsionate con il frullatore ad immersione, aggiungendo olio extra vergine, parmigiano reggiano, sale e pepe. Pulite le vongole evitando che rimanga della sabbia al loro interno. Scaldate in una padella un filo di olio d'oliva, aglio, sale e pepe, quindi versateci le vongole e fatele cuocerle per qualche minuto. Aggiungete i fagiolini e scottateli leggermente. Mantecate il tutto con la pasta cotta al dente, quindi servire in tavola.

Pizza tartufata
Truffled Pizza

Chocolate cake
Dessert al cioccolato

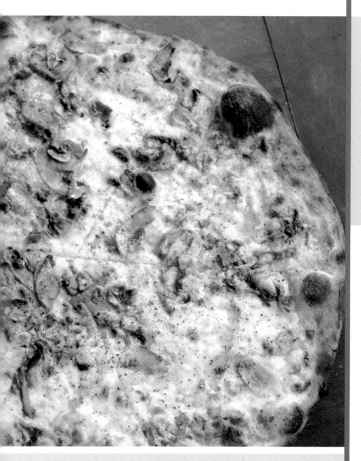

INGREDIENTS FOR 4 SERVINGS:
Chocolate mousse ingredients: - 15 cl of milk - 300 g of chocolate - 300 g of whipped cream
Coffee mousse ingredients: - 40 g of sugar - 30 cl of cream - 7 g of Nescafé
Frosting ingredients: - 9 cl of cream - 10 cl of water - 130 g of sugar - 25 g of powdered milk - 30 g of cocoa - 20 almonds - 7 g of gelatin - 10 berries - mint leaves - 10 savoiardi (ladyfingers) - coffee

INGREDIENTI PER 4 PERSONE:
Per la mousse al cioccolato: - 15 cl di latte - 300 g di cioccolato - 300 g di panna montata
Per la mousse al caffè: - 40 g di zucchero - 30 cl di panna - 7 g di Nescafé
Per la glassa: 9 cl di panna - 10 cl di acqua - 130 g di zucchero - 25 g di latte in polvere - 30 g di cacao - 20 mandorle tritate - 7 g di colla di pesce - 10 frutti di bosco - foglioline di menta - 10 savoiardi - caffè

Chocolate mousse: Melt the chocolate in the milk, then add the cream and continue stirring over low heat, then leave to cool.
Coffee mousse: Heat the cream over low heat and add the sugar, the powdered milk, the Nescafé and the chopped almonds. Then leave to cool.
Frosting: Heat the cream over low heat, add the water and the sugar, the powdered milk, some cocoa and the gelatin at the end. Then leave to cool.
Put a Savoiardo biscuit soaked in coffee at the base of a cutter, cover it with a layer of the chocolate mousse, then add a layer of the coffee mousse and chopped almonds, then add another layer of the chocolate mousse and then add a thin layer of the frosting. Leave to set in the refrigerator for 3 hours before serving and decorate with berries and mint leaves on top.

INGREDIENTS FOR 4 SERVINGS:
Dough for 10 pizzas: -1 l of water - 1.7 kg of flour - 7 g of dry yeast - 50 g of salt - 50 g of extra virgin olive oil
Pizza topping: -30 g of truffle sauce - ½l of liquid cream - 10 champignons mushrooms - 150 g of chopped Speck - ½ kg of Mozzarella cheese - 2 tbsp of truffle oil (to finish off)

Whipped truffle cream:
Pour the cream into a container or a mixing bowl, add a tablespoon of truffle sauce, 5gr of salt, a sprinkle of pepper and whisk.

After stretching out the pizza dough, add the truffle cream sauce with a spoon on the base of the pizza, then add the mushrooms, the speck and the mozzarella. You decide the amount of the ingredients to your liking, but don't overdo with the truffle sauce to prevent that its flavour covers the others. Bake and then finish off with a drizzle of truffle oil and some truffle flakes if available.

Mousse al cioccolato: Sciogliete il cioccolato nel latte, quindi aggiungete la panna e continuate a mescolare a fuoco basso. Poi lasciate raffreddare.
Mousse al caffè: Scaldate a fuoco basso la panna e aggiungete lo zucchero, il latte in polvere e il Nescafé, le mandorle tritate, e poi lasciate raffreddare.
Glassa: Scaldate a fuoco lento la panna, aggiungendo acqua e zucchero, latte in polvere, un po' di cacao e infine la colla di pesce, poi lasciate raffreddare.
Posizionate alla base del coppa-pasta il biscotto savoiardo bagnato nel caffè, coprite con uno strato di mousse al cioccolato, poi uno strato di mousse al caffè e le mandorle tritate, un altro strato di mousse al cioccolato e infine un leggero strato di glassa al cioccolato. Lasciate raffreddare in frigo per 3 ore e prima di servirlo, decorate al vertice con frutti di bosco e foglioline di menta.

JACOB'S PICKLES

Owner / Titolare › Jacob Hadjigeorgis

509 Amsterdam Avenue • Ⓜ 86 St [1] • +01 212 470 5566 • **www.jacobspickles.com**

I admit, this review is impartial, because in my opinion Jacob's Pickles is a wonderful place. It is the place that I dream of opening but I never will: friendly, lively, welcoming, casual. The kind of place where you feel good no matter what you eat or drink. Yes, I admit it, I love this restaurant and I gladly come back to it whenever I'm in New York. I hope that Jacob and Michelle open other JP around Manhattan, maybe in the East Village. As for the cuisine, it's all simple dishes, zero kilometers produce, that often uses ingredients grown in the property. The fried pickles are what it takes to open up your stomach and down the first of many great American craft beers. The Maccheroni with Cheese are good. The mussels with beer and pork pieces fly down, taking lots of bread with them. The "Pickles Cheeseburger" is juicy and tasty (and requires a second beer). Finish off with the Fried Oreo (only the Americans could think of frying chocolate cookies...) and the vanilla ice cream-dessert: a time bomb, which allows you to extend your stay in this great place. God bless Jacob's Pickles.

Lo ammetto, questa recensione è imparziale, perché a mio avviso il Jacob's Pickles è un posto meraviglioso. È il locale che sogno di aprire e che non avrò mai: friendly, vivace, accogliente, casual. Il genere di posto dove stai bene a prescindere da ciò che mangi o bevi. Sì, lo ammetto, adoro questo ristorante e ci torno volentieri ogni volta che sono a New York. Anzi, spero che Jacob e Michelle aprano altri JP in giro per Manhattan, magari nell'East Village. Quanto alla cucina, si tratta di piatti semplici, a chilometro zero, che spesso propongono ingredienti coltivati nell'orto di proprietà. I fried pickles sono quello che ci vuole per aprirsi lo stomaco e buttar giù la prima delle tante ottime birre artigianali americane. I maccheroni col formaggio sono buoni. Le cozze con birra e pezzi di maiale richiedono tanto pane. Il "Pickles Cheeseburger" è succoso e saporito (e richiede la seconda birra). Infine gli Oreo fritti (solo gli americani potevano pensare di friggere dei biscotti al cioccolato...) e il dolce-gelato alla vaniglia: una bomba ad orologeria, che ti consente di allungare la permanenza in un posto fantastico. God bless Jacob's Pickles!

Beer List › Carta delle birre	Cuisine › Cucina	Brunch	Dinner › Cena
25 Labels › Etichette	Southern Comfort Food	$ 20	$ 25

Mussels and beer

Cozze e birra

INGREDIENTS FOR 4 SERVINGS:
Braised Bacon: - 2 lbs nitrite free slab bacon - 1 lb onion, large dice - 6 oz celery, medium dice - 6 oz carrots, medium dice - 2 thyme sprig - 2 rosemary sprig - 16 fl oz chardonnay white wine -32 fl oz chicken stock
Mussels: 2 lbs Prince Edward island mussels debearded and cleaned - 4 oz of finely chopped shallots - 2 jalapenos thinly sliced - 8 fl oz of Allagash beer - 12 fl oz of chicken broth from the braised pork belly - 4 oz of sweet unsalted butter large dice

INGREDIENTI PER 4 PERSONE:
Per la pancetta brasata: - 900 g di pancetta a fette senza nitriti - 450 g di cipolla tagliata a cubetti grandi - 170 g di sedano tagliato a cubetti medi - 170 g di carote tagliate a cubetti medi - 2 rametti di timo - 2 rametti di rosmarino - 473 ml di vino bianco chardonnay - 946 ml di brodo di pollo
Per le cozze: - 907 g di cozze nere pulite - 113 g di scalogno tritato finemente - 2 jalapenos a fette sottili - 236 ml di birra chiara - 354 ml di brodo di pollo dalla pancia di maiale brasato - 113 g di burro non salato tagliato a dadi grandi

Braised Bacon:
Take the slab bacon and cut it into ½" pieces. Use a large stainless steel rondeau and place it on medium heat. Slowly render the scored side in the rondeau. Add the 3 fl.oz of canola oil and add the diced bacon. Develop a deep brown sear on all of the pieces of bacon. Remove the pieces of bacon from the pan and reserve for later use.
Use the excess grease in the pan. Add the diced onions and allow them to soften for 5 minutes. Then add the celery and carrots. Allow the vegetables to get caramelized in the pot which will take 15 minutes. Add the thyme and rosemary sprigs. Add the white wine. Reduce the wine by ½ and add the chicken stock. Reduce the heat to a low flame and cover the pot with aluminum foil. Allow the bacon to cook for 20 minutes. Remove the bacon from the liquid and reserve for later. Take the remaining liquid and strain it so all that remains is a clear broth. Discard the vegetables and herbs. Reserve the braised bacon for later use.
Mussels:
Place a stainless steel rondeau on high heat, add the 2 fl. oz of canola oil and the finely chopped shallots. Add the braised bacon and gently move it around using a wooden spoon. Add the mussels and allow to cook for a 1 minute. Add the allagash beer and allow to cook for another minute. Add the thinly sliced jalapenos to the beer. Add the chicken broth, cover the pan with aluminum foil and allow to steam open for 5 minutes. Add the diced butter and move it around the liquid with a wooden spoon so that it becomes thick. Cover and allow to cook for 1 more minute. Portion into 4 soup bowls, ladle in the sauce and enjoy.

Preparazione della pancetta brasata:
Prendete la pancetta a fette e tagliatela in pezzi da 1,3cm. Utilizzate una grande casseruola in acciaio inox su fuoco medio. Mettete 88 ml di olio di canola e aggiungete la pancetta a dadi. Lasciate cuocere fino a quando tutti i pezzi si scuriscono.
Togliete i pezzi di pancetta dalla casseruola e mettete da parte. Utilizzate il grasso rimasto nella casseruola e aggiungete le cipolle e lasciatele ammorbidire per 5 minuti. Aggiungete il sedano e le carote. Lasciate caramellare le verdure per circa 15 minuti. Aggiungete i rametti di timo e rosmarino, poi il vino bianco. Lasciate ridurre il vino per metà e aggiungete il brodo di pollo. Abbassate la fiamma e coprite la casseruola con della carta alluminio. Lasciate cuocere la pancetta per 20 minuti, poi toglietela dal liquido e mettetela da parte. Drenate il liquido rimanente in modo da ottenere un brodo chiaro. Scartate le verdure e le erbe e conservate la pancetta.
Preparazione delle cozze:
Utilizzate una casseruola in acciaio inox a fuoco vivo e aggiungete 59 ml di olio di canola. Aggiungete lo scalogno tritato finemente e poi la pancetta brasata e mescolate delicatamente con un cucchiaio di legno.
Aggiungete le cozze e lasciatele cuocere per un minuto, poi versate la birra e lasciate cuocere ancora per un minuto. Aggiungete i jalapenos a fette sottili e poi aggiungete il brodo di pollo e coprite la casseruola con della carta di alluminio e lasciate cuocere a vapore per 5 minuti. Aggiungete il burro a dadi e mescolate con un cucchiaio di legno per fare inspessire. Coprite e lasciate cuocere per un minuto ancora. Dividete in 4 ciotole. Buon appetito.

TALÒ › Verdeca Puglia IGP
CANTINE SAN MARZANO

Colore giallo paglierino con riflessi dorati; al naso rivela sorprendenti profumi di fiori bianchi e vaniglia; al palato è fresco e giustamente minerale con una buona persistenza sapida.

Straw yellow colour with green reflections; scotch broom notes and a hint of citrus and tropical fruits on the nose. Lively in acidity, fresh and mineral.

Abbinamenti: Frutti di mare, crostacei e pesci lessi con salse leggere.

Best served with: Excellent with starters and fish soup, fresh cheese and pasta with light sauces.

Fried Pickles
Cetrioli fritti

INGREDIENTS FOR 4 SERVINGS:

For the Batter: - 1 lb unbleached all purpose flour - 32 fl. oz. of seltzer water - ⅛ oz of ground white pepper - ¼ oz of paprika, sweet

For Spicy Red Mayo: - 4 egg yolks - ¼ fl. oz kosher salt - ½ fl. oz lemon juice, fresh - 2 oz sriracha - 0.05 oz coleman's mustard powder - 0.05 oz ground white pepper **For Frying the Pickles:** - 64 oz canola oil - 1 lb of Jacob's special sour pickle

INGREDIENTI PER 4 PERSONE:

Per la pastella: - 453 g di farina non sbiancata - 946 ml di acqua frizzante - 3,5 g di pepe bianco macinato - 7 g di paprika dolce

Per la maionese rossa piccante: - 4 tuorli - 7 g di sale kosher - 14 ml di succo di limone fresco - 56 g di salsa Sriracha - 1,4 g di senape in polvere di Coleman - 1,4 g di pepe bianco

Per la frittura: - 1,8 kg di olio di canola - 453 g di cetrioli sour pickle

To prepare the batter: In a stainless steel bowl, combine the flour, paprika and white pepper. Use a whisk to combine the seltzer and reserve for later use.

To preparing the Spicy Red Mayo: In a kitchen aid mixer bowl, combine the dry mustard, kosher salt, egg yolks, Sriracha and lemon juice. While the mixer is on medium speed, slowly add the canola oil in steady stream. As the egg yolk mixture and oil begin to emulsify, slowly increase the speed of the mixer. Once all of the oil has been added, reserve the sauce for later use.

To prepare the pickles: Heat the canola oil in a stainless steel rondeau set on medium heat. Allow the oil to reach 335°F. Take a pickle at a time, gently pat it dry from the brine, dip into the batter, gently brush the side of it against the bowl and place it in the fryer. Keep repeating step number 4 and allow the pickles to cook for 4 minutes. Place the fried pickles In a bowl and serve with pickle brine and sriracha sauce in ramekins.

Preparazione della pastella: Unite la farina, la paprica e il pepe bianco in una ciotola in acciaio inox. Aggiungete l'acqua frizzante utilizzando una frusta e mettete da parte per dopo.

Preparazione della maionese rossa piccante: Unite la senape secca, il sale kosher, i tuorli, la Sriracha e il succo di limone in un mixer da cucina. Mentre il mixer è a velocità media, aggiungete lentamente l'olio di canola a filo continuo. Quando la miscela inizia ad emulsionare, aumentate lentamente la velocità del mixer. Quando avete aggiunto tutto l'olio mettete la salsa da parte per dopo.

Preparazione dei cetrioli: Mettete l'olio di canola in una casseruola di acciaio a fuoco medio. Lasciate riscaldare l'olio a 170°C. Prendete ogni cetriolo sottaceto e asciugate delicatamente il liquido dalla salamoia. Passate ogni cetriolo nella pastella e scuotete delicatamente prima di friggerli. Lasciateli cuocere per 4 minuti. Mettete i cetrioli fritti in una ciotola e servite con la salamoia e la salsa Sriracha in ciotoline.

Fried Oreos

INGREDIENTS FOR 4 SERVINGS:

For the Oreo Batter: - 1 lb king arthur unbleached all purpose - flour - ¼ oz light brown sugar - 14 fl oz of seltzer water - 4 oz of panko bread crumbs - 24 fl oz of hudson valley whole milk

For the Home Made Cream: - 16 fl oz hudson valley heavy cream 40% - 3 oz of 10x confectionery sugar

For Frying the Oreos: - 64 oz canola oil - Oreo cookies

Preparing the batter:

In the stainless steel bowl combine the flour, and brown sugar. Using a whisk combine the seltzer and milk and reserve for later use.

Preparing the oreos and cooking them:

In the stainless steel rondeau set on medium heat add the canola oil.

Place the fryer thermometer in the oil and allow the oil to be heated until 335°f.

Take each Oreo cookie and dip into the batter and place in the bowl with the panko bread crumbs. Keep repeating step number 3 and allow the battered and breaded Oreo cookies to fry for 30 seconds. In the small dessert plate place the fried Oreos with the ramekins of the lightly sweetened whipped cream. Serve and enjoy

KAFANA

Owner and Chef / *Titolare e Chef* › Vladimir Ocokoljic

116 Ave C • 🚇 Av C/E 8 St M9 • +01 212 353 8000 • **www.kafananyc.com**

Kafana is located in the quieter part of the East Village, on Avenue C, a stone's throw from the East River Park. You are in New York, but once seated at the table, especially if you dine inside, you feel like you have stepped back in time and space. You are in a bistro of Mediterranean-Balkan Europe in the 60s and 70s, more precisely in the disappeared Yugoslavia, and will eat just like a Serb, an Italian or a Greek would eat: very well! Chef Vladimir, a stubborn and nostalgic fan of the Red Star Belgrade, does not care much about the details and the presentation of his dishes, but goes straight to the matter only by making sure that they contain good food. In our opinion, he succeeds perfectly, given that he prefers to use simple ingredients: vegetables, cheese and greens. The lamb with vegetables and yogurt may seem a gamble, but It has a fresh and revitalizing taste that will leave you surprised. The sausages, marinated for a whole night, are spectacular. Sardines cooked lightly on the grill, let out the scent of the sea, and seem freshly caught (pity that only a few restaurants in New York have them in their menus). Great food and exceptional prices. I will come back to Kafana every time I'm in New York. Also because, I love to tease fans of teams that have disappeared or that no longer win anything.

Kafana si trova nella parte più tranquilla dell'East Village, sulla Avenue C, a due passi dall'East River Park. Siete a New York ma una volta seduti al tavolo, specie se cenate all'interno, vi sembrerà di aver fatto un salto indietro nel tempo e nello spazio. Vi ritroverete così in un bistrot dell'Europa Mediterranea-Balcanica anni '60-'70, più esattamente nella scomparsa Jugoslavia, e mangerete come mangia un serbo, un italiano, un greco. Cioè bene. Chef Vladimir, ostinato e nostalgico tifoso della Stella Rossa di Belgrado, non si cura molto dei dettagli e della presentazione dei suoi piatti, ma va al sodo e si preoccupa che contengano cose buone. A nostro giudizio ci riesce alla perfezione, considerato il fatto che predilige usare ingredienti poveri: verdure, formaggi, ortaggi. L'agnello con le verdure e lo yogurt potrà sembrare un azzardo, e invece ha un sapore fresco e rivitalizzanti che vi lascerà di stucco. Le salsicce, lasciate a marinare una intera notte, sono spettacolari. Le sardine appena scottate sulla griglia sprigionano profumo di mare e sembrano appena pescate (peccato che a New York solo pochi ristoranti le propongano nel loro menù). Cucina ottima, prezzo eccezionale. Tornerò al Kafana ogni volta che sarò a New York. Anche perché adoro sfottere i tifosi di squadre scomparse o che non vincono più nulla.

Wine List › Carta dei Vini	Cuisine › Cucina	Lunch › Pranzo	Dinner › Cena
100 Labels › Etichette	**Serbian** › Serba	$ 20	$ 30

Lamb Stew

INGREDIENTS FOR 4 SERVINGS:
- 2 lb lamb necks (you can use different lamb cuts)
- 2 bundles of scallions if in not sure more is better
- 2 lb baby spinach - 4 garlic cloves sliced - 2 cups of stock
or water - 1 cup of white wine - flour - frying oil (blend
or sunflower) - salt and pepper - yogurt

Roll the lamb necks in flour, add salt and pepper and
deep fry quickly for a minute or pen fry to seal them.
Preheat the oven to 400°F. Move the meat to a casserole,
add the chopped scallions, white wine and stock. Cover
the casserole and cook in the oven until the meat starts
falling off the bone (approximately for 1 1/2 hours). Take
the casserole out of the oven, allow some time to cool and
then remove the bones. Move the casserole to the stove,
uncover it, add the baby spinach and sliced garlic and
cook until the spinach is ready. Serve it with a scoop of
yogurt.

Stufato di agnello

INGREDIENTI PER 4 PERSONE:
- 905 g di collo di agnello (è possibile utilizzare anche altri
tagli di agnello) - 2 fasci di scalogno - 905 g di spinaci baby
- 4 spicchi d'aglio affettati- 470 ml di brodo o acqua - 235 ml
di vino bianco - farina - olio per friggere (misto o di girasole)
- sale e pepe - yogurt

Infarinate l'agnello, conditelo con sale e pepe e frigge-
telo velocemente per un minuto. Riscaldate il forno a
200°C. Mettete la carne in una casseruola e aggiungete
lo scalogno tritato, il vino bianco e il brodo. Coprite la
casseruola e fate cuocere in forno finché la carne inizia a
cadere dell'osso (ci vorrà circa un'ora e mezza). Uscite la
casseruola dal forno, lasciatela raffreddare e poi rimuovete le ossa. Mettete la casseruola sui fornelli, aggiungete gli
spinaci e l'aglio a fette e lasciate cuocere fino a quando gli
spinaci saranno cotti. Servite con un cucchiaio di yogurt.

Cheese pie

INGREDIENTS FOR 4 SERVINGS:
- 1 lb of thick fillo dough
- 10 oz Feta cheese
- 10 oz cottage cheese
- 12 oz kefir
- 2 eggs
- salt
- blend oil

Mix feta, cottage cheese, 2 eggs and kefir in a big bowl. Use a fork to crumble feta. Depending how salty the feta cheese is, add approx 1/2 tea spoon of salt. Set aside.
Preheat oven to 400F. At Kafana we use 8" round 3" tall baking pan. Grease the baking pan and cover the bottom and sides with a layer of fillo and extend it slightly over the sides (cut one fillo sheet into 3 pieces that way it will be easier to do so).
Take the next fillo sheet dip it into the mix in the bowl then wrinkle, squeeze and place it inside the baking pan. Repeat until the baking pan is 2/3 full. Take another sheet of fillo, it should be your last one, cover the pan and then roll the extensions forming little crown around the edges. Brush it with oil and put it in the oven.
Bake it for 45 minutes or until gold and brown. Cool it on a rack for about 15 minutes.
We cut it into 4 large pcs but you can cut it into 8 or even more pieces.
Enjoy.

Sour cherry pie

INGREDIENTS FOR 4 SERVINGS:
- 4 cups of fresh pitted sour cherries it can be substituted with jar of pitted sour cherries.
- 1 lb of thin fillo dough
- chopped walnuts
- bread crumbs
- butter
- baking paper
- vanilla sugar

Preheat the oven at 400°F. Place some baking paper into a baking pan. Spread the fillo sheet on top of it and brush lightly with melted butter and sprinkle with about one 1/2 tablespoon of sugar. Repeat with two more sheets, placing them on top of each other. About 2 1/2" from the edge of the long side of the fillo sheets, sprinkle 1 tablespoon of chopped walnuts, 1 tablespoon of sugar, 1 tablespoon of bread crumbs and place approximately 1 cup of drained sour cherries in a row on top. Fold the edges over the cherries and then roll the fillo. Repeat this with the remaining fillo. You should have enough for 4-6 rolls depending on fillo thickness.
Bake in a preheated oven for 25-35 minutes or until gold and brown. Cool on a rack for about 15minutes and then cut into 3-4" pieces. Dust with vanilla sugar and arrange on a serving plate.

Torta di visciole

INGREDIENTI PER 4 PERSONE:
- 900 g di visciole fresche snocciolate (possono essere sostituite con le amarene)
- 450 g di fogli di pasta fillo sottile
- noci tritate
- pangrattato
- burro
- carta da forno
- zucchero vanigliato

Riscaldate il forno a 200°C e posizionate della carta da forno in una teglia. Stendete la pasta fillo nella teglia, spennellatela leggermente con del burro fuso e cospargetela con circa un 1/2 cucchiaio di zucchero. Ripetete questo procedimento con altri due fogli di pasta fillo posizionandoli uno sopra l'altro.
Cospargete, a 6 cm dal bordo lungo, un cucchiaio di noci tritate, poi un cucchiaio di zucchero, poi un cucchiaio di pangrattato ed infine circa 225gr di visciole in fila. Piegate il bordo sopra le visciole e poi arrotolate la pasta fillo. Ripetete questo procedimento con la pasta fillo rimanente. Dovreste avere abbastanza pasta per 4-6 rotoli a seconda dello spessore.
Fate cuocere in forno per 25-35 minuti o fino a quando diventa dorato. Lasciate raffreddare su una griglia per circa 15 minuti, poi tagliate in 3-4 pezzi, spolverateli con lo zucchero vanigliato e poneteli su un piatto da portata.

LIATICO › Aleatico di Puglia Dolce Naturale DOP
CANTINE SAN MARZANO

Questo vino di colore rosso rubino molto intenso, al naso mostra un carattere straordinario, offre una fragranza che ricorda l'uva matura, insieme a profumi più tenui ed eleganti di fiori. Al palato la sua dolcezza si accosta in fitta armonia a una buona acidità e a tannini di nobile spessore organolettico. Vino di grande piacevolezza e di spiccata personalità, pronto per essere apprezzato subito e che non smette di evolvere per un lungo invecchiamento.
Abbinamenti: Dolci a pasta secca e crostate agli agrumi, torte alle mele e alla crema. Vino da meditazione.

This ruby red coloured wine has an extraordinary scent which recalls ripe grapes, together with softer and more elegant notes of flowers. Its sweetness fits in with a good acid structure and noble tannins. A wine of great pleasantness and strong personality, ready to drink, which continues to evolve for a long ageing.
Best served with: Perfect with dry biscuits and citrus tarts, apple and cream pies. Meditation wine.

LA MASSERIA

Owner / Titolare › Pino Coladonato - Enzo Ruggiero - Peppe Iuele • **Chef** › Pino Coladonato

235 West 48th Street • Ⓜ 49 St [N,Q,R] • +01 212 582 2111 • **www.lamasserianyc.com**

When you are being biased it's better to immediately put the record straight. I was born in Puglia: the most beautiful region in Italy and the one that currently expresses the best cuisine in the country. That said, I have eaten in so many bad Puglia style restaurants, in Italy and abroad, and for nothing in the world I would put in my book a place that does not represent Puglia in the best way possible. So now you'll understand that I ate really well at La Masseria, not only because the food is excellent and authentically Italian (from Southern Italy, very different from food from Milan or Venice), but also because in this restaurant you can feel the main feature of Puglia: treating guests better than you would with family. Try the Scallops with Artichokes, the Octopus with Fava Beans, the Spaghettini with Green Beans and the Lobster Risotto. Continue with grilled fish and finish the meal with tiramisu or apple pie. Welcome to Puglia, in New York.

Quando si è di parte è meglio mettere subito le cose in chiaro. Sono nato in Puglia: la regione più bella d'Italia e quella che al momento esprime la migliore cucina del Paese. Detto questo, ho mangiato in tanti pessimi ristoranti pugliesi, sia in Italia che all'estero, e per nulla al mondo metterei sul mio libro un locale che non rappresenti al meglio la Puglia. Fatta questa premessa, avrete capito che alla Masseria ho mangiato benissimo, non solo perché la cucina è ottima e autenticamente italiana (del Sud Italia, cosa ben diversa da quella di Milano o Venezia), ma anche perché in questo ristorante si tocca con mano la principale caratteristica dei pugliesi: quella di trattare l'ospite meglio di un parente. Provate le capesante con i carciofi, il polpo con le fave, gli spaghettini con i fagiolini e il risotto all'aragosta. Proseguite con la grigliata di pesce. Finite la cena con il tiramisù o la torta di mele. Benvenuti in Puglia, New York.

Wine List › Carta dei Vini	**Cuisine** › Cucina	**Lunch** › Pranzo	**Dinner** › Cena
300 Labels › Etichette	**Italian Regional** › Italiana Regionale	$ 35	$ 50

Spaghetti con fagiolini

INGREDIENTS FOR 4 SERVING:
- 12 oz of large spaghetti (80 grams per person) - 1 lbs sweet cherry tomato (pomodoro pachino) - 1 lbs italian string beans - fresh basil - 2 oz of pecorino - 4 oz cacio ricotta - 4 oz extra virgin olive oil - 5 clove of garlic

Cut the cherry tomatoes and marinated with basil, salt, pepper and 1 oz of oil. Place in sauce pan 4 pieces of garlic with 2oz of oil, when the garlic turns golden color combine the marinated tomato. Keep at very low temperature. Place large pot of water salt to taste, place the already clean string beans with spaghetti at the same time. When still of dente strain it and incorporated into the cherry tomato. Mix and add the pecorino cheese, basil and remaining oil. Plate the spaghetti and finish with cacio ricotta.

INGREDIENTI PER 4 PERSONE:
- 320 g spaghetti - 450 g pomodoro ciliegia (pachino) - 450 g fagiolini italiani - Foglie di basilico fresco - 60 g di pecorino - 120 oz cacio ricotta - 4 cucchiai olio extravergine di oliva - 5 spicchi d'aglio

Tagliare i pomodorini e marinarli con basilico, sale, pepe e due cucchiai di olio. Far dorare in casseruola 4 pezzi di aglio in due cucchiai di olio, quindi unire il pomodoro marinato e cuocere a temperatura bassa. In acqua (salata) cuocete insieme i fagiolini già puliti e gli spaghetti. Scolate al dente e versate nel sugo. Mescolare e aggiungere il pecorino, il basilico e un filo di olio. Impiattare e finire con una bella spruzzata di cacio ricotta.

Apple pie

INGREDIENTS FOR 4 SERVINGS:
- 4 golden delicious apple
- 3 ½ oz of sugar
- 3 oz of orange juice
- 3 oz of white wine
- 2 oz of butter
- 6 oz of puff pastry sheet
- 1 egg

Peel and slice the apples.
Combine in a pan apples, sugar,
orange, butter and wine.
Cook the apples (not to soft),
until the liquid evaporates.
Roll out the puff pastry
and cut it into four equal parts,
egg wash them, add
the apple, filling and close
it with the sides of the
dough up. Brush with
egg wash
and sugar.
Cook at
400 degrees
until golden
brown
(10 min).

UKGEAI ALMUND, FRESH LIME

- ZOMBIE - RUM, GINGER SYRUP, OJ, FRESH LIME

- BEACH BUM - BOURBON, RASPBERRY LIQEUR,
                    PINEAPPLE

- BLUE HAWAIIAN - VODKA, BLUE CURACAO, AGAVE,
                        PINEAPPLE, FRESH LIME

- ALL TIKI DRINKS $10

FRESH LEMON, SODA

$10 - TITO'S MULE - TITO'S VODKA, GINGER SYRUP, FRESH

$7 PICKLEBACK SHOT!!
$5 FIREBALL SHOT!!

- CASH ONLY -

T BE:R
T ACTION
ISLAND IPA
SUNSHINE PILS
LING LAGER
CIDER 10 OZ
MOON
ESPECIAL
OINT SUMMER

BOS
FE + WHISKEY
E + TEQUILA
TULLAMORE DE

NO SMOKING

CASH ONLY

HAPPY
M-F
$3 WELL
$1 OFF E

CPR Kit Is Located
Behind The Bar

TULLAMORE
DEW

TULLAMORE
DEW

TULLAMORE
DEW

LANDHAUS AT THE WOODS

Owners and Chef / Titolari e Chef › Matthew Lief - Michael Felix - Maria De La Cruz

48 South 4th Street (Brooklyn) • +01 718 710 5020 • **www.thelandhaus.com**

I love the slogan of this place "Farm to sandwich", from the breeding to the sandwich. It makes you want to re-evaluate fast and practical food, that in some parts of the world is so frowned upon, but is now destined to get more and more importance on the market. The Landhaus At The Woods is a simple, night-time place, crowded and alive, youthful, and missing it would be a shame, because it can offer something interesting and tasty. Like the traditional Fried Chicken Wings, or the Shrimp Burger and the Lamb Burger. If you are fond of bacon, then you can't miss the Landhaus BLT and the Maple Bacon On a Stick (according to "The Village Voice" it's the best in New York). And also rivers of beer.

Amo lo slogan di questo locale: "farm to sandwich", dall'allevamento al sandwich. Dà la sensazione di voler restituire importanza al cibo veloce e pratico, che in alcune parti del mondo è così mal visto, ma è destinato ad occupare sempre più importanti fette di mercato. Il Landhaus è un posto semplice, notturno, affollato e vivo, molto giovanile, e perderselo è un peccato, perché sa offrire qualcosa di interessante e gustoso. Come le tradizionali Chicken Wings (ali di pollo) fritte, oppure lo Shrimp Burger (hamburger ai gamberi) e il Lamb Burger (d'agnello). Se siete appassionati del bacon, allora non potete non ordinare il Landhaus BLT e il Maple Bacon on a stick (secondo "The Village Voice" il migliore di New York). E poi birra a fiumi.

Wine List › Carta dei Vini	**Cuisine** › Cucina	**Lunch** › Pranzo	**Dinner** › Cena
Only Beers and Cocktails	**Creative American**	**No lunch** › Chiuso a pranzo	$ 15

Shrimp Burger

INGREDIENTS FOR 6/8 SERVINGS:
For the Shrimp Burger: - 2 lbs good quality raw, peeled and deveined shrimp
- 3 tbsp shallots, finely minced - 2 tsp cayenne pepper - 2 tbsp worcestershire
sauce - 1 tbsp salt - 1 cup panko bread crumbs - Peanut or Canola oil for frying
- 1 head iceberg lettuce finely shredded- 8 hamburger buns - 1 tbsp butter
For the spicy tartar: - 1 cup mayonnaise - ¼ cup chopped dill pickles
- 2 tbsp chopped red onion - 1 tbsp chopped jalapeño - 1 tbsp smoked paprika
- 1 tsp cayenne pepper - 1 tbsp salt

Place half of the shrimp in a food processor and blend to a paste.
Coarsely chop the remainder of the shrimp and combine in a bowl
with shallots, cayenne pepper, worcestershire and salt.
Mix well. Form the mixture into approximately 8 thin hamburger
shaped patties and roll the patties in panko breadcrumbs until they
are thoroughly coated. Patties can be kept in fridge for up to two days
or frozen for up to 3 months. Combine all the tartar sauce ingredients
in a bowl and mix well. Check for seasoning and add salt and pepper
as needed.
To Cook Patties: Heat 1/4 inch of oil in a heavy bottomed pan. When
oil is hot fry the patties until golden brown. Meanwhile butter the
buns and toast them in the oven until lightly golden brown.
Serve patties on buns with iceberg lettuce, spicy tartar and an ice cold
american lager.

Crispy duck wings
Ali di anatra croccanti

INGREDIENTS FOR 6/8 SERVINGS:
- 2 lbs of duck drumettes or duck drumsticks - 1 knob of ginger the
size of your thumb, peeled and chopped into small pieces - 1 pint
of white wine - ½ cup of soy sauce - 1 bunch of scallions, roughly
chopped - 1 tbsp of salt - ¼ cup of Korean gochujang fermented chili
paste - ½ cup of sweet chili sauce - Peanut or canola oil for shallow fat
frying - 1 bunch of Thai basil leaves, removed from the stem

INGREDIENTI PER 6/8 PERSONE:
- 900 g di ali o cosce di anatra - 1 noce di zenzero delle dimensioni del
vostro pollice, sbucciato e tagliato a pezzetti - 470 ml di vino bianco
- 118 ml di salsa di soia - 1 mazzetto di scalogno tritato gossolanamente - 1 cucchiaio di sale - 59 ml di pasta di peperoncino fermentato
- 118 ml di salsa di peperoncino dolce - olio di arachidi o canola per
friggere - 1 mazzetto di foglie di basilico tailandese

Preheat the oven to 300° and clean the duck of any hairs.
Place the duck in a deep casserole with ginger, white wine,
soy sauce, scallions and salt. Cover the duck with a piece of
parchment paper and then tightly cover the pan with aluminum foil. Bake for 3 hours. Take it out of the oven, uncover
the pan and allow the liquid to come down to room temperature before removing the duck. When the liquid is at room
temperature, move the duck to a rack and allow to dry. At this
point the duck can be stored in the refrigerator for up to 5
days. When ready to fry, whisk together the gochujang and
sweet chili sauce in a bowl. Heat 1 inch of oil in a heavy sauté
pan until it reaches approximately 325°F. Fry the basil leaves
just until they are crispy and set aside. Working in batches, fry
the duck until crispy on all sides. Keep turning the duck in the
oil to crisp evenly. Remove the duck and glaze with the chili
mixture. Garnish with basil leaves and serve.

Riscaldate il forno a 150°C e pulite l'anatra. Mettetela in una
casseruola profonda con lo zenzero, il vino bianco, la salsa
di soia, lo scalogno e il sale. Coprite con carta da forno e poi
ricoprite ermeticamente la casseruola con carta alluminio.
Lasciate cuocere per 3 ore. Togliete dal forno, scoprite la
casseruola e lasciate che il liquido si raffreddi a temperatura
ambiente prima di spostare l'anatra. Ponetela su di una griglia
e lasciatela asciugare. A questo punto potete conservare la
carne in frigorifero fino a 5 giorni. Quando volete fare la
frittura, sbattete insieme il gochujang e la salsa di peperoncino dolce in una ciotola. Scaldate 2,5cm di olio in una padella
dal fondo pesante, fino a quando raggiunge circa 160°C.
Friggete appena le foglie di basilico fino a quando diventano
croccanti e mettete da parte. Poi friggete l'anatra un po' alla
volta fino a quando diventa croccante. Continuate a ruotare
l'anatra nell'olio per assicurarvi che sia croccante su tutti i lati.
Rimuovete l'anatra dall'olio e spennellatela con la miscela di
peperoncino. Guarnite con le foglie di basilico e servite.

LAUT
Owner / Titolare › Salil Mehta

15 East 17 Street • **M** Union Square • +01 212 206 8989 • **www.lautnyc.com**

Conveniently located at Union Square, Laut was one of the first Malaysian restaurants to receive a Michelin Star in NY. The restaurant it's focused on bringing the best recipes, dishes and flavors from South East Asia. Laut, in Bahasa Melayu (Malay Language), translates to Sea. These straits or seas of these coastal cities played a crucial role in the region's history, navigating traders and travelers from all over the world. At Laut, you'll navigate through an adventurous journey of flavors through an amazing cuisine. The menu ranges from local favorites, street foods, different curries, spicy & sour broths, satays, noodles, bread (roti), and rice dishes, all generously portioned and spiced. Laut is well worth a visit.

Questo posto l'ho scoperto grazie ad un articolo del "Corriere della Sera", che parlava di Laut non solo come del primo ristorante malese premiato con la stella Michelin, ma anche come uno dei ristoranti stellati meno cari al mondo. Ho voluto provarlo, e posso confermare che è così: cucina ottima e prezzi incredibili, intorno ai 25-30 dollari per un buon pasto. Il locale è esattamente come uno se lo immagina, asian-style, senza fronzoli, focalizzato sui sapori, quasi sempre speziati e corposi. Iniziate con un "Rendang" accompagnato da un Teh Tarik, magari freddo, che malgrado il colore non proprio invitante rinfresca il palato che ancora ricorda il curry. Il "Roti Canai", un altro piatto tipico a base di carne di manzo tenerissima, riso e cetrioli, è buonissimo. Lo "Young coconut pudding" è il degno finale di un pranzo sorprendente. Laut merita una visita.

Wine List › Carta dei Vini	Cuisine › Cucina	Lunch › Pranzo	Dinner › Cena
9 Labels › Etichette	**Malaysian-Singaporean-Thai**	**$ 10-12 (1 course)** › 1 portata	**$ 25-30**

LEXINGTON BRASS

Owner / Titolare › EMM GROUP • **Chef** › Cesar Gutierrez

517 Lexington Avenue • Ⓜ 51 St [6] • +01 212 392 5976 • **www.lexingtonbrass.com**

A refreshing alternative to the traditional midtown dining mélange, Lexington Brass abandons the old school model of formal white tablecloths for a bustling, bistro-like experience better suited for the new wave of modern Manhattan diners. Stripped of pomp and circumstance, the Lexington Brass design is spacious but edgy, emoting an air of casual refinement with top-notch service and a simple menu of bistro favorites that, for the weary traveler or overworked Manhattanite, will feel reminiscent of home. You can taste at any hous the lobster Mac'n'Cheese, Parmesan Truffle Fries, French Onion Soup, Short Rib Cannelloni and platters of oysters and shrimp cocktail. As warm and hospitable as the hotel within which it resides, this airy American bistro ensures that locals and visitors alike will find solace and satisfaction within its walls.

Una bella alternativa alla tradizionale cena molto in voga midtown, Lexington Brass ha messo da parte le tovaglie bianche per proporre una vivace esperienza bistro, sicuramente più adatto per il popolo di Manhattan. Spogliato di pomposità e formalità, Lexington Brass è spazioso, raffinato ma informale, con un servizio di prim'ordine e un menù semplice che propone l'aragosta al formaggio, patatine fritte al parmigiano e tartufo, zuppa di cipolle Francese, cannelloni, ostriche e cocktail di gamberi. Caldo e ospitale come l'hotel in cui si trova, questo American Bistro assicura conforto e soddisfazione per il palato. Ci siamo stati per il brunch domenicale, e vi abbiamo mangiato tante cose interessanti.

Wine List › Carta dei Vini	Cuisine › Cucina	Lunch › Pranzo	Dinner › Cena
70 Labels › Etichette	**American Brasserie**	$ 25	$ 35

Brass ale beer waffles

Waffle alla birra

INGREDIENTS FOR 4 SERVINGS:
- ¾ cup whole milk
- 2 tbsp amber beer
- 1 egg
- ¼ tsp vanilla extract
- 1 cup cake flour
- 1 ¼ tbsp granulated sugar
- ¾ tsp malt powder
- 1 ½ tsp baking powder
- 1 oz melted butter, unsalted

Cinnamon butter:
- 1 stick or 8 tbsp unsalted butter
- 1½ tbsp cinnamon powder

Garnish:
- ½ cup quartered strawberry
- ½ cup blueberry
- ½ cup blackberry
- 2 pcs sliced banana

INGREDIENTI PER 4 PERSONE:
- 177 ml di latte intero
- 2 cucchiai di birra ambrata
- 1 uovo
- ¼ cucchiaino di estratto di vaniglia
- 128 g di farina per dolci
- 1 ¼ cucchiaio di zucchero semolato
- ¾ cucchiaino di malto in polvere
- 1 ½ cucchiaino di lievito in polvere
- 28 g di burro non salato fuso

Per il burro di cannella:
- 1 panetto di burro o 8 cucchiai di burro non salato
- 1½ cucchiaini di cannella in polvere

Per guarnire:
- 63 g di fragole tagliate in quarti
- 63 g di mirtilli
- 63 g di more
- 2 pezzi di banana a fette

In a mixing bowl, sift together the cake flour, sugar, malt powder and baking powder. In a large bowl, combine the milk, beer, egg, and vanilla extract. Slowly pour the liquid and melted butter into the dry ingredients and combine well.
Keep 1 stick of butter at room temperature and when soft, mix with the cinnamon until incorporated well. Pre-heat a waffle maker on medium heat, spray it with pam and bake until golden brown.

Garnish:
Place the mixture of berries, bananas and cinnamon butter on top of golden waffles and sprinkle powdered sugar on top.

Setacciate la farina per dolci, lo zucchero, il malto in polvere e il lievito, e unite il tutto in una ciotola. Unite il latte, la birra, l'uovo e l'estratto di vaniglia in una ciotola grande. Aggiungete lentamente i liquidi e il burro fuso agli ingredienti secchi ed amalgamate bene. Lasciate 1 panetto di burro a temperatura ambiente. Quando si è ammorbidito, mischiatelo con la cannella fino ad incorporarli bene. Riscaldate una piastra per waffle a temperatura media, spruzzate con dello spray alimentare antiaderente e fate cuocere dei waffle, con l'impasto preparato, fino a doratura.

Per guarnire:
Ponete il mix di frutti di bosco, le banane e delle gocce di burro di cannella sopra i waffle dorati ed infine date una spolverata di zucchero a velo.

Ricotta cheesecake

INGREDIENTS FOR 4 SERVINGS:
- 105 g butter - 52 g sugar - 1 ½ vanilla beans
- 350 g cream cheese - 135 g ricotta - 130 g yuzu juice
- 100 g egg yolks - 110 g egg whites - 40 g sugar - 13 g corn starch

Preheat an oven to 275°F. In the bowl of an electric mixer with a paddle attachment, cream the butter, sugar and vanilla beans until extremely light and fluffy. Next add the cream cheese and ricotta and continue creaming until the mixture is smooth. Scrape down the sides of the mixing bowl and add the yuzu juice and mix until incorporated. Scrape down the sides of the bowl again and add the egg yolks. Mix until completely emulsified. Remove the mixture from the bowl and set aside in a larger bowl. Clean the bowl of the mixture and add the heavy cream. With the whisk attachment, whisk until it is medium stiffness then remove from bowl and set aside. Clean the bowl to the mixer and add the egg whites. With the whisk, whip the egg whites until they are shiny and add the sugar. Keep whisking for another 5 minutes and add the cornstarch, mix just until incorporated. Fold the meringue into the cream cheese mixture, then fold in the whipped cream. Place the batter in molds or a lined baking pan and bake at 275°F for 1 hour or until it springs back when gently touched. Cool and keep in the refrigerator until use.

Benedict royale

INGREDIENTS FOR 4 SERVINGS:
- 4 each english muffin, sliced in half, open face
- 8 each egg
- 16 g trout roe
Hollandaise:
- 1 each egg yolk 1each
- 2 ½ oz. clarified butter
- 2 tsp tabasco
- 2 tsp lemon juice
- to taste salt

INGREDIENTI PER 4 PERSONE:
- 4 muffin inglesi, tagliati a metà
- 8 uova
- 16 g di uova di trota
Per la salsa hollandaise:
- 1 tuorlo
- 70 g di burro chiarificato
- 2 cucchiaini di Tabasco
- 2 cucchiaini di succo di limone
- sale qb

Heat a pot of water, when boiling place a bowl on top and whisk the egg yolk until foamy. Remove the bowl from top of the pot and slowly whisk in the clarified butter. Season with lemon juice, tabasco and salt. Keep in a warm area.
Toast the english muffin lightly in a pan. Poach the eggs in barely simmering water with a few drops of white wine vinegar. Stir the water around clock wise and drop the eggs until the whites are set and the yolks are barely cooked. Place the poached eggs on top of the muffins and spoon some hollandaise on top. Garnish with caviar of your choice.

Mettete a bollire una pentola d'acqua e quando bolle adagiateci sopra una ciotola con i tuorli d'uovo e montateli fino a quando hanno una consistenza spumosa. Spostate la ciotola dal calore e aggiungete lentamente il burro chiarificato mescolando con una frusta. Condite con il succo di limone, il tabasco e il sale e tenete al caldo. Tostate leggermente i muffin inglesi in una padella. Appena l'acqua (con qualche goccia di aceto di vino bianco) inizia a bollire, cuocete le uova in camicia. Mescolate l'acqua in senso orario e fate cuocere le uova fino a quando i bianchi sono sodi e i tuorli appena cotti. Mettete le uova in camicia sopra i muffin tostati e un cucchiaio di salsa hollandaise al di sopra. Guarnite con caviale di vostra scelta.

LUZZO'S

Owner / Titolare › Michele Iuliano • **Chef** › Michele Iuliano

213 First Avenue • **M** 1 Av [L] • +01 212 473 7447 • **www.luzzosgroup.com**

Michele Iuliano is the man behind the ovens at Luzzo's Group - a family of Southern Italian restaurants designed around each of their unique neighborhoods including its iconic East Village flagship Luzzo's. Trained in Naples, Italy, Iuliano has created an ever-expanding empire of southern Italian restaurants that lean heavily on sincere Neapolitan techniques in order to cater to the market's growing demand for undiluted, true-to-form regional cooking.

Michele Iuliano è il fondatore del Gruppo Luzzo, azienda a gestione famigliare nata dalla pizzeria (oggi divenuta un'icona) situata nell'East Village. Cresciuto a Napoli, col passare degli anni Iuliano è riuscito a creare un piccolo impero in costante espansione, che ancora oggi si basa sulla eccezionale qualità della pizza servita nei vari locali. Pizza ovviamente napoletana, col classico bordo rinforzato e dai sapori genuini. Ma da Luzzo's è possibile mangiare anche gli antipasti della tradizione italiana e ottimi piatti di pasta. Ne sono certo: quello di Michele Iuliano è un successo che non conoscerà soste.

Wine List › Carta dei Vini	**Cuisine** › Cucina	**Lunch** › Pranzo	**Dinner** › Cena
50 Labels › Etichette	Pizzeria	$ 20	$ 30

Gnocchi alla sorrentina

INGREDIENTS FOR 4 SERVINGS:
- 800 gr of potato gnocchi
- 800 gr of tomato passata sauce
- 200 gr of mozzarella
- half an onion
- basil
- parmesan cheese
- extra virgin olive oil
- salt and pepper

INGREDIENTI PER 4 PERSONE:
- 800 g gnocchi di patate
- 800 g passata di pomodoro
- 200 g di mozzarella
- metà cipolla
- basilico
- parmigiano
- olio extra vergine
- sale e pepe

Cut the mozzarella into cubes and set aside.
Finely chop the onion and sauté it in extra-virgin olive oil. When the onion is golden, add the tomato passata sauce and some salt and leave to cook for 20 minutes, stirring with a wooden spoon.
Turn the heat off the sauce so it doesn't become too thick. After you have removed it from the heat, add some whole fresh basil leaves.
Meanwhile, boil the gnocchi in salted water for a few minutes and drain them as soon as they come up to surface. Then put the gnocchi in a baking dish, cover them with the tomato sauce, the diced mozzarella and a sprinkle of Parmesan cheese.
Bake at 200°C for 10-15 minutes.
The gnocchi are ready when the Parmesan has turned to a golden colour and the mozzarella has melted.

Tagliate la mozzarella a cubetti e mettetela da parte.
Tritate finemente la cipolla e fatela soffriggere in olio extra-vergine d'oliva; quando la cipolla assume il caratteristico colore biondo, aggiungete la passata di pomodoro ed il sale e fate cuocere il sugo per 20 minuti, girandolo con un cucchiaio di legno.
Spegnete il sugo prima che la salsa si inspessisca troppo e, solo dopo che il fuoco è spento, aggiungete il basilico fresco conservando intere le foglie.
Nel frattempo lessate gli gnocchi in acqua salata per pochi minuti: scolateli non appena risalgono a galla.
Disponete ora gli gnocchi in una pirofila da forno, cospargendoli con il sugo di pomodoro, i cubetti di mozzarella e spolverando infine con il parmigiano.
Infornate la pirofila a 200°C e per 10/15 minuti circa: gli gnocchi saranno pronti quando il parmigiano assumerà un colore dorato e la mozzarella sarà fusa.

TALÒ › Malvasia Nera Salento IGP
CANTINE SAN MARZANO

Colore rosso rubino intenso; profumo complesso riconducibile a frutti rossi maturi e spezie. Vino di corpo assai robusto, dall'attacco piacevolmente morbido e di lunga persistenza.
Abbinamenti: Carni rosse, arrosti con salse elaborate, formaggi mediamente stagionati.

Thick ruby red; intense and complex bouquet with notes of red fruits and spices. A full-bodied wine with a pleasantly smooth impact and a long ending.
Best served with: Red meat, roasted meat with rich sauces, average mature cheese.

MASSERIA DEI VINI

Owner / Titolare › Pino Coladonato - Enzo Ruggiero - Peppe Iuele • **Chef** › Pino Coladonato

887 9th Avenue • **M** 59 St Columbus Circle [1] • +01 212 315 2888 • **www.masseriadeivini.com**

Masseria dei Vini (Masseria of Wines) is the new venture brought to you from the La Masseria team. Restaurateurs Pino Coladonato, Peppe Iuele and Enzo Ruggiero have collaborated again with interior design expert Libby Langdon to bring you a modern and updated version of a "Masseria". In the region of Puglia, in Southern Italy, masserias are fortified farmhouses, and many of them have now been transformed into restaurants or hotels. Executive chef Pino Coladonato, native of Rutigliano (Bari), has created a menu that blends traditional with modern without overpowering one or the other. The menu features beautiful dishes from Puglia, a lot of which incorporate fish, shellfish and a plethora of fresh homemade pastas. The menu offers gourmet pizza Neapolitan style from a Ferrara wood-burning pizza oven and also offered is an extensive wine by the glass program and a large selection of bottles, mainly from Italy, but without ignoring the rest of the world.

Masseria dei Vini è la nuova avventura dei tre ristoratori italiani Pino Coladonato, Peppe Iuele e Enzo Ruggiero, che anche in questo caso si sono avvalsi della collaborazione dell'interior design Libby Langdon, che ha elaborato una versione più moderna del ristorante "La Masseria", uno dei più apprezzati ristoranti italiani di New York. L'Executive chef Pino Coladonato ha creato un menù che unisce tradizione e modernità, dando vita a piatti ricchi di sapore e colore. Assolutamente da provare la pizza, cotta "alla napoletana". La lista dei vini è davvero ben fatta ed offre buona parte dei vitigni italiani, senza però ignorare il resto del mondo.

Wine List › Carta dei Vini	**Cuisine** › Cucina	**Lunch** › Pranzo	**Dinner** › Cena
300 Labels › Etichette	**Italian Regional** › Italiana Regionale	$ 35	$ 50

Terra Mare

INGREDIENTS FOR 4 SERVINGS:
- 4 small octopus (or cuttlefish, or both)
- 4 small cuttlefish
- 12 oz of fava pure
- 12 oz broccoli di rapa
- extra virgin olive oil
- 1 lemon
- salt and pepper

INGREDIENTI PER 4 PERSONE:
- 4 polpi piccoli
- 4 seppioline
- 500 g puree di fave
- 500 g broccoli
- olio extra vergine di oliva
- 1 limone
- sale e pepe

Prepare the fava beans pure cooking with one piece of bay leaves and one clove garlic.
Boil the tender part of the broccoli di rapa (keep them ready).
Season octopus (or cuttlefish) with salt, pepper olive oil and grill it.
When ready lay on the plate fava pure, in the center place broccoli di rapa drizzle with extra virgin oil.
And top place the octopus and cuttlefish.
Dressing with olive oil and lemon mixed.

Preparare il puree di fave cuocendole con una foglia di alloro e uno spicchio d'aglio.
Lessare la parte tenera dei broccoli di rapa (e tenerli a parte).
Marinare i polpi con sale, olio d'oliva e pepe, quindi scottarli sulla griglia.
Quando saranno giunti a cottura, impiattare adagiando il puree di fave sul fondo del piatto, a seguire i broccoli di rapa e il polpo (o le seppioline).
Aggiungere un filo d'olio extravergine e una spruzzata di limone.

ESTELLA › Moscato Salento IGP
CANTINE SAN MARZANO

Colore giallo paglierino tenue con riflessi verde brillante; si apre all'olfatto con fragranti note floreali e mielate unite a sentori di frutta esotica fresca. Avvolge il palato con una decisa spalla acida, supportata quest'ultima da un'armonica morbidezza.
Abbinamenti: Ideale per la cucina di mare: antipasti misti, crostacei crudi, primi piatti con sughi rosa di pesce.

Light straw yellow colour with bright green reflections; it reveals some fragrant flower and honey notes, together with fresh exotic fruit scents. Its taste is definitely acid and supported by a balanced softness.
Best served with: Ideal with sea food: mixed starters, raw shellfish, first courses with light fish sauces.

MIRA SUSHI & IZAKAYA

Owner / Titolare › Andrew Lee • **Chef** › Brian Tsao

46 West 22nd Street • Ⓜ 23rd Street • +01 212 989 7889 • **www.mirasushi.com**

We are bonded to Mira Sushi & Izakaya in a particular way, because it was the first restaurant we visited during our "tour of New York." We expected the usual sushi restaurant, but we found a "sushi-newyor-ker-restaurant", with a very American atmosphere, attended by groups of young people. A great chatty, lively atmosphere, a very helpful general manager and so many interesting dishes that go well beyond the usual sushi and sashimi. For example, the "Spicy Tuna Pizza", a good aperitif to accompany a cocktail. Taste the chicken wings, the "Salmon Pokè" and the meat tacos are great and very beautiful to see. The best comes with the "Kyoto Crunchy Sloppy Joe" and the "Teriyaki Chicken." Finish off with the "Honeycomb Dream". The Mira Sushi & Izakaya passed the test with top marks.

Al Mira Sushi & Izakaya siamo legati in maniera particolare, perché è stato il primo ristorante visitato durante il nostro "tour newyorkese". Ci aspettavamo il solito sushi-restaurant, e invece siamo entrati in un "sushi-newyorker-restaurant", dall'atmosfera molto americana, frequentato da tanti comitive di giovani. Un gran bel vociare, atmosfera vivace, un general manager molto disponibile e tanti piatti interessanti che vanno ben oltre il solito sushi e sashimi. Per esempio la "spicy tuna pizza", un buon aperitivo, ottima accompagnatrice di un cocktail. Saporite le ali di pollo, ottimi e molto belli da vedere il "salmon pokè" e i tacos di carne. Il meglio arriva con il "Kyoto crunchy sloppy Joe" e il "teriyaki chicken". Gran chiusura con "l'honeycomb dream". Il Mira Sushi & Izakaya è promosso a pieni voti.

Wine List › Carta dei Vini	Cuisine › Cucina	Lunch › Pranzo	Dinner › Cena
15 Labels › Etichette	Japanese › Giapponese	$ 15	$ 35

Kyoto crunchy sloppy joes

INGREDIENTS FOR 4 SERVINGS:
- 1 lb shallots, peeled and thinly sliced - 2 quarts vegetable oil
For the Korubuta Ground Pork Sauce:
- 3 lbs korubuta pork (if not available, any high quality pork will work) - 2 tbsp chinese fermented bean paste (lee kum brand or other) - 2 tbsp soy sauce - 1 tbsp sugar - ½ can coca cola
- 1 tbsp mushroom dark soy sauce - 4 tbsp butter - 1 cup panko
- 4 hawaiian buns (any type of slider bun will do)
sharp cheddar cheese, as much as your heart desires!, sliced
- 1 thai sour mustard green, finely minced

INGREDIENTI PER 4 PERSONE:
- 453 g di scalogno pelato e tagliato a fette sottili - 1,8 lt di olio vegetale **Per la salsa Korubuta di suino macinato:** - 1,3 kg di suino korubuta (se non disponibile, qualsiasi altra carne suina di alta qualità) - 2 cucchiai di pasta di fagioli fermentati cinese (marca Lee Kum o altra) - 2 cucchiai di salsa di soia - 1 cucchiaio di zucchero - ½ lattina di coca cola - 1 cucchiaio di salsa di fungo scuro di soia - 4 cucchiai di burro - 63 g di pangrattato - 4 panini hawaiani (o qualsiasi altro tipo di panino rotondo) - formaggio Cheddar forte a piacere, tagliato a fette - 1 verde di senape aspro tailandese, tritato finemente

In a heavy sauce pot, place the vegetable oil and sliced shallots at room temperature. This is very important, if the shallots are placed into hot oil they will easily burn. Place onto the stove and cook over medium heat. Allow the oil and shallots to slowly heat up until the oil starts bubbling, this takes quite some time, but you need to keep your eye on it. Once the oil bubbles, take a wooden spoon and keep the shallots in motion. Once they turn golden brown, immediately remove them and place them into a large bowl lined with paper towels. It is normal for the shallots to turn a shade darker even out of the oil. Reserve overnight.

The next day, in a large heavy sauce pot, cook the pork with about three tablespoons of the shallot infused vegetable oil. When the pork is about half cooked and most of the moisture has rendered out of the meat, leaving you with a good amount of natural juices, add the bean paste, soy sauce, sugar and Coca Cola. When all the ingredients have incorporated, turn the heat to low and allow the sauce to reduce by 15-20%, for about 20 to 25 minutes. Once the sauce has reduced, add in all of the crispy shallots you cooked the day before. The shallots will absorb any leftover liquid from the sauce. The sauce is done!
In another sauce pot, melt the butter, add the panko bread crumbs and stir until they turn golden brown. Toast the slider bun with a piece of cheddar cheese. Top with pork sauce, Thai mustard and panko! Enjoy!

Mettete l'olio vegetale e lo scalogno a fette a temperatura ambiente in una pentola da salsa con fondo pesante. Questo passaggio è molto importante, perchè se immergete gli scalogni in olio bollente si bruceranno facilmente. Mettete la pentola sul fuoco e fate cuocere a fuoco medio. Lasciate riscaldare l'olio e lo scalogno lentamente fino a quando l'olio inizia a bollire. Prendete un cucchiaio di legno e muovete lo scalogno di continuo fino a quando diventa dorato. Toglietelo immediatamente dal fuoco e mettetelo in una ciotola capiente rivestita con carta da cucina. È normale che lo scalogno diventi di una tonalità più scura anche a cottura terminata. Tenete da parte tutta la notte.

Il giorno dopo, cucinate il suino con circa tre cucchiai di olio vegetale di scalogno in una grande pentola da salsa con fondo pesante. Quando la carne è a circa metà cottura, e la maggior parte del grasso si è sciolto lasciando una buona quantità di fondo di cottura, aggiungete la pasta di fagioli, la salsa di soia, lo zucchero e la Coca Cola. Quando tutti gli ingredienti si sono incorporati, abbassate il fuoco al minimo e fate ridurre la salsa del 15-20% per circa 20-25 minuti. Quando la salsa si è ridotta, aggiungete lo scalogno croccante che avete cotto il giorno prima. Gli scalogni assorbiranno i liquidi residui nella salsa. La salsa è pronta!
In un'altra pentola, fate sciogliere il burro, aggiungete il pangrattato Panko e mescolate fino a quando diventa dorato. Tostate il pane da panino con un pezzo di formaggio Cheddar. Aggiungete la salsa di carne di suino, la senape tailandese e il pangrattato. Buon appetito!

Spicy sashimi salad

INGREDIENTS FOR 4 SERVINGS:
- 1lb spring lettuce mix - ½ cup soy mustard dressing (found in most Asian Supermarkets) - 3 tbsp sriracha - 4 pieces kani (imitation crab) - 6 pieces jumbo shrimp (boiled and peeled) - 4 oz tuna - 4 oz salmon - 4 oz octopus - 2 navel oranges, cut into wedges

Wash spring lettuce mix and dry well on paper towels. Once spring mix is dried, keep in a cool place.
In a bowl combine soy mustard dressing and sriracha and reserve.
Cut kani, shrimp, tuna, salmon and octopus into 1/4" to 1/2" cubes.
Place spring mix, orange wedges and seafood into a large bowl with approximately half of the prepared sriracha-soy mustard sauce and mix well.
Portion the salad mixture onto four plates and drizzle more sauce over the top and around the salad in a decorative manner. Enjoy!

INGREDIENTS FOR 4 SERVINGS:
- 1 pack Vietnamese rice paper, round **For the Bulgogi Marinade:** - 1 lb beef rib eye, thinly sliced - 3 cups tamari soy sauce - 2 cups light brown sugar - 1 cup sherry wine - 1 cup garlic, ground - 1 cup onion, ground in a food processor - 2 cups water - ½ cup sesame oil - 2 tbsp black pepper - 2 cups fresh pineapple juice (substitute canned if not available) **For the Scallion Slaw:** - 1 cup scallions, rinsed in cold water and fine julienne - ½ cup rice vinegar or mirn - ¼ cup sugar - 2 tbsp Korean chili flakes - 3 tbsp tamari soy sauce - 2 tbsp sesame oil **For the Garnish:** - 1 large asian pear, peeled and shaved with a cheese grater just before use - 1 cup kimchee, drained well and minced

INGREDIENTI PER 4 PERSONE:
- 1 confezione di carta di riso vietnamita rotonda **Per la marinatura del Bulgogi:** - 453 g di costata di manzo tagliato a fette sottili - 710 ml di salsa di soia Tamari - 450 g di zucchero di canna chiaro - 236 ml di sherry - 140 g di aglio tritato - 150 g di cipolla tritata in un robot da cucina - 473 ml di acqua - 118 ml di olio di sesamo - 2 cucchiai di pepe nero - 473 ml di succo di ananas fresco (sostituibile con quello in scatola se non è disponibile) **Per l'insalata di cipolline:** - 100 g di cipolline sciacquate in acqua fredda e tagliate sottilmente a julienne - 118 ml di aceto di riso o di Mirin - 56 g di zucchero - 2 cucchiai di fiocchi di peperoncino coreano - 3 cucchiai di salsa di soia Tamari - 2 cucchiai di olio di sesamo **Per guarnire:** - 1 pera asiatica gande, pelata e gattugiata appena prima dell'uso - 224 g di kimchee, drenato e tritato

Bulgogi Marinade: Combine all the ingredients in a bowl and allow the beef to marinate overnight in the refrigerator. The next day, cook the marinated beef in a hot pan until well done, for about 5-10 minutes. Don't overcrowd the beef in the pan. This is very important to get optimal flavor from the marinade. **Scallion slaw:** Combine all the ingredients in a bowl and let them marinate for 20 minutes. **Taco:** Slowly place rice paper into a 375° high smoke point oil (soy bean, vegetable or corn). The rice paper will immediately begin to puff up. When the skin has lightened in colour (which will be very fast), use a wooden spoon to push down the centre of the rice paper to create the shape of a taco shell. Hold the rice paper in this position until it begins to firm up. Once the paper has firmed, it is ready to be removed from the hot oil. Place it onto a tray lined with paper towels to remove excess oil and let it cool. **To assemble:** Make sure the kimchee is drained well otherwise the taco shell will absorb the liquid and become soft. Place a layer of minced kimchee on the bottom of the taco shell followed by the cooked beef. Garnish with scallion slaw and shaved Asian pear.

Preparazione della marinatura del Bulgogi: Unite tutti gli ingredienti in una ciotola e lasciate marinare il manzo per una notte intera in frigorifero. Il giorno dopo, fate cuocere il manzo marinato in una padella bollente fino a quando è ben cotta, per circa 5-10 minuti. Evitate di sovraccaricare di carne la padella. Questo è molto importante per ottenere il sapore ottimale dalla marinata. **Preparazione dell'insalata di cipolline:** Unite tutti gli ingredienti in una ciotola e lasciate marinare per 20 minuti.
Preparazione del tacos: Mettete lentamente la carta di riso in olio fumante a 190°C (di soia, vegetale o di mais). La carta di riso inizierà subito a gonfiarsi. Quando il colore sarà diventato più chiaro (avverrà molto velocemente), usate un cucchiaio di legno per spingere al centro della carta di riso per creare la forma a guscio dei tacos. Tenete la carta di riso in questa posizione fino a quando inizia a raffermarsi. Quando diventa solido, toglietelo dall'olio. Mettetelo su un vassoio rivestito con carta da cucina assorbente per eliminare l'olio in eccesso e lasciate raffreddare. **Per assemblare il piatto:** Assicuratevi di drenare bene il kimchee, altrimenti il guscio del tacos assorbirà il liquido e diventerà morbido. Adagiate uno strato di kimchee (carne) tritato sul fondo del tacos, poi aggiungete la carne. Guarnite con l'insalata di cipolline e la pera asiatica grattugiata.

Appetizer › Antipasto

Beef bulgogi tacos
Tacos di manzo bulgogi

MOLYVOS

Owner / Titolare › The Livanos Family • **Chef** › Carlos Carreto • **Collaborating Chef** › Diane Kochilas

871 Seventh Avenue • Ⓜ 57 St-7 Av [N,Q,R] • +01 212 582 7500 • **www.molyvos.com**

As well as the Oceana, the other Livanos group restaurant we visited during our stay in New York, the Molyvos, seems designed to impress clients. It's huge, beautiful, with care in each detail. New York style in size and for the "showiness" of the halls, yet so incredibly Greek and Mediterranean, that it just seems to be having dinner at a restaurant in Corfu, Santorini, or Molyvos, the village located on the island of Lesvos. The owner Nick Livanos explained to us that his goal "is to bring philoxenia - Greek style hospitality - in the heart of New York, the city where in 1997, the year that Molyvos opened, the only known Greek dishes were the Greek salad and the Baklava cookies." Judging by the success of his restaurant, I would say that his goal was largely achieved. The restaurant has the largest all-Greek wines-list in the U.S. with over 500 bottles.

Come l'Oceana, l'altro ristorante del gruppo Livanos che abbiamo visitato durante il nostro soggiorno a New York, anche il Molyvos sembra pensato per stupire i clienti. È enorme, bellissimo, curato in ogni dettaglio, newyorchese nelle dimensioni e nella "spettacolarizzazione" delle sale, eppure così incredibilmente greco e mediterraneo che appunto sembra di cenare in un ristorantino di Corfù, Santorini, oppure di Molyvos, il villaggio situato sull'isola di Lesvos. Il proprietario Nick Livanos ci ha spiegato che il suo obiettivo «è quello di portare la filoxenia - l'ospitalità in stile greco - nel cuore di New York, città in cui nel 1997, anno di apertura del Molyvos, gli unici piatti greci conosciuti erano l'insalata greca e i biscotti Baklava». A giudicare dal successo che il suo ristorante continua a mietere, direi che il risultato è stato ampiamente raggiunto. Il locale offre una incredibile lista-vini composta da oltre 500 vini greci.

Wine List › Carta dei Vini	**Cuisine** › Cucina	**Lunch** › Pranzo	**Dinner** › Cena
520 Labels › Etichette	**Greek** › Greca	$ 30-50	$ 30-50

Sympetherio salad

Insalata Sympetherio

INGREDIENTS FOR 6/8 SERVINGS:
- ½ cup dried baby fava beans - ½ cup dried chickpeas
- ½ cup navy beans - ½ cup coarse bulgur
- ½ cup large lentils, rinsed - salt
- ½ cup extra virgin olive oil, or more, if desired
- 2 cups chopped scallions (whites and greens)
- 1 cup finely chopped dill or flat-leaf parsley
- strained juice of 2 large lemons, or more if desired
- 12 cherry tomatoes, halved

INGREDIENTI PER 6/8 PERSONE:
- 100 g di fave secche - 100 g di ceci secchi
- 100 g di fagioli navy - 115 g di bulgur grosso
- 100 g di lenticchie grandi sciacquate - sale
- 118 ml di olio extra vergine di oliva o di più se lo si desidera
- 200 g di scalogno tritato (parte bianca e verde)
- 20 g di aneto tritato o di prezzemolo a foglia piatta
- succo filtrato di 2 limoni grandi o di più se lo si desidera
- 12 pomodori ciliegini tagliati a metà

Soak the fava beans, chickpeas and navy beans separately, overnight, in ample water. Drain when ready to use.
With a small sharp knife, remove the small black "eye" and husks from the fava beans and discard.
Bring the fava beans to a boil in a medium pot of unsalted water. Simmer for 10 minutes, then drain the beans, discarding the water, which will be brown.
Place the bulgur in a bowl with ½ cup of water and let it soak until all the water is absorbed, for about two hours.
Place the blanched favas, chickpeas and navy beans in a large pot with fresh water. Bring to a boil, reduce heat and simmer for 1 ½ hours, skimming any foam off the surface of the water.
Add the lentils to the pot, season lightly with salt, and continue to simmer for another 35 minutes or until tender but al dente.
Heat 3 tablespoons of olive oil in a skillet and sauté the scallions for 5 to 7 minutes, until wilted. Mix into the beans. Add the soaked bulgur, dill or parsley and lemon juice and continue to simmer a few more minutes, until the herbs are wilted.
Remove from heat, adjust seasoning with additional salt and lemon juice if desired and a drizzle of the remaining olive oil.
Let stand for at least 30 minutes before serving.
To serve, garnish with the halved cherry tomatoes.

Mettete a bagno le fave, i ceci e i fagioli separatamente in abbondante acqua per tutta la notte. Scolate prima dell'uso. Rimuovete l'occhio nero e il guscio delle fave con un coltellino affilato e scartate.
Portate le fave ad ebollizione in una pentola media con acqua non salata. Fate bollire per 10 minuti, poi scolate le fave e scartate l'acqua che sarà diventata marrone.
Mettete il bulgur in una ciotola con 118ml di acqua e lasciate fino a quando avrà assorbito tutta l'acqua, per circa due ore.
Mettete le fave sbucciate, i ceci e i fagioli in una pentola con acqua fresca. Portate ad ebollizione, poi abbassate la fiamma e fate sobbollire per un ora e mezza, togliendo la schiuma che si forma sulla superficie dell'acqua.
Aggiungete le lenticchie, condite leggermente con sale e continuate a cuocere per altri 35 minuti o fino a quando diventano tenere, ma al dente.
Scaldate 3 cucchiai di olio d'oliva in una padella e fate soffriggere lo scalogno per 5-7 minuti, fino a quando si sarà appassito.
Poi aggiungetelo nella pentola con i fagioli. Aggiungete il bulgur, l'aneto o il prezzemolo e il succo di limone e continuate a cuocere per qualche minuto, fino a quando si sono appassite anche le erbe. Togliete dal fuoco, condite con altro sale e succo di limone se lo si desidera, e aggiungete un filo di olio d'oliva da quello avanzato.
Lasciate riposare per almeno 30 minuti prima di servire guarnite con i pomodorini tagliati a metà.

MP TAVERNA

Owner / Titolare › Michael Psilakis • **Chef** › Michael Psilakis

31-29 Ditmars Boulevard Astoria • **M** Astoria - Ditmars Blvd [N,Q] • +01 718 777 2187

One Bridge Street Irvington • **R** Irvington • +01 914 231 7854

1363 Old Northern Blvd. Roslyn • +01 516 686 6486

www.michaelpsilakis.com

Taking a walk through the streets of Astoria, a neighborhood in Queens, I wondered why a New Yorker would come here, given the shortage of attractions. I found a valid reason in this restaurant, opened by chef Michael Psilakis, a place that for its beauty and its Greek cuisine, is worth the 20-30 minutes by subway you need to get here from Manhattan. MP Taverna is the modern interpretation of a Greek taverna: great looking contemporary design, with a long bar counter and many outdoor seats. We were here for brunch, and, thanks to the beautiful sunny day, we spent two really nice hours, accompanied by exciting food: a great octopus with chickpeas, fantastic scallops with cauliflower, a Greek paella made with barley instead of rice, then an excellent sea bass and a very tender lamb. To end the meal we couldn't miss the yogurt with fresh fruit, confirming that good things don't always have to be complicated. Our final verdict: a really great place. I have a good reason to come back to Astoria.

Passeggiando per le vie di Astoria, un quartiere del Queens, mi sono chiesto perché un newyorchese dovrebbe venire da queste parti, vista la penuria di attrazioni. Un motivo valido l'ho trovato in questo ristorante aperto dallo chef Michael Psilakis: un locale che, per la sua bellezza e la sua cucina greca, vale i circa 20-30 minuti di metropolitana che servono per arrivare fin qui da Manhattan. MP Taverna è l'interpretazione in chiave moderna della taverna greca: design molto ben curato, contemporaneo, con un lungo bancone bar e tanti posti all'aperto. Ci siamo stati per il brunch e, complice la bella giornata di sole, abbiamo trascorso due ore davvero piacevoli, accompagnate da cibo entusiasmante: un ottimo polpo con i ceci, delle fantastiche capesante con cavolfiore, una paella greca fatta con l'orzo al posto del riso, e poi un eccellente branzino e un tenerissimo agnello. Per concludere, non poteva mancare lo yogurt con frutta fresca, a conferma che le cose buone non devono necessariamente essere complicate. Giudizio finale: davvero un gran bel posto. Ho un buon motivo per tornare ad Astoria.

Wine List › Carta dei Vini	**Cuisine** › Cucina	**Lunch** › Pranzo	**Dinner** › Cena
30 Labels › Etichette	**Greek** › Greca	$ 30-40	$ 30-40

Octopus and chickpea salad

Polpo e insalata di ceci

INGREDIENTS FOR 6 TO 8 SERVINGS:
- 1 (4-6 pound) octopus, cleaned, whole legs only - kosher salt and cracked black pepper - blended oil (50% canola, 50% extra-virgin olive) as needed - 6 whole cloves garlic, peeled - 2 fresh bay leaves or 4 dried leaves - ¼ tsp red chile flakes - 1 ¾ cups chickpea confit (recipe follows) - 2 cups cooked black-eyed peas - ½ small red onion, roughly chopped- 8 scallions, green part only, thinly sliced - 10 large, plump sun-dried tomatoes cut into strips - 1 tbsp finely chopped parsley- 1 tbsp finely chopped dill - 3 tbsp extra-virgin olive oil plus 1 ½ tbsp fresh lemon juice - ladolemono (recipe follows) - small handful torn fresh herbs, such as dill, mint, and/or parsley. **Chickpea Confit:**
- Makes about 3 Cups - Cloves from 1 head of garlic, separated and peeled - 1 tsp cumin seeds - 1 tsp mustard seeds - 2 ½ cups cooked chickpeas (such as Goya) well rinsed and well drained - Kosher salt and whole black peppercorns - Blended oil (50% canola and 50% extra-virgin olive oil). **Ladolemondo:** - ¼ cup fresh lemon juice - 1 tbsp dijon mustard - 1 tbsp dry greek oregano - kosher salt and cracked black pepper - ½ cup extra-virgin olive oil.

INGREDIENTI PER 6/8 PERSONE:
- 1 polpo (da 1800 g-2700g) pulito, solo tentacoli interi - sale kosher e pepe nero incrinato - olio misto (50% di canola 50% di extra vergine d'oliva) qb - 6 spicchi d'aglio interi sbucciati - 2 foglie di alloro fresco o 4 foglie di alloro secche - ¼ di cucchiaino di fiocchi di peperoncino rosso - 290 g di confit di ceci (segue ricetta) - 300 g di fagioli dagli occhi neri cotti - ½ cipolla rossa piccola tritata grossolanamente - 8 scalogni, solo la parte verde, tagliata a fette sottili - 10 pomodori secchi grandi tagliati a listarelle - 1 cucchiaio di prezzemolo tritato finemente - 1 cucchiaio di aneto tritato finemente - 3 cucchiai di olio extravergine di oliva e 1 ½ cucchiaio di succo di limone fresco - ladolemono (segue ricetta) - piccola manciata di erbe fresche: aneto, menta, e/o prezzemolo. **Per il confit di ceci:** - Per circa 700 ml - spicchi di un'intera testa aglio, separati e sbucciati - 1 cucchiaino di semi di cumino - 1 cucchiaino di semi di senape - 500 g di ceci cotti (come Goya) sciacquati e scolati bene - sale kosher e pepe nero in grani - olio misto (50% olio di canola e 50% di olio extra vergine d'oliva). **Ladolemondo:** - 60 ml di succo di limone fresco - 1 cucchiaio di senape di Digione - 1 cucchiaio di origano greco secco - sale kosher e pepe nero incrinato - 118 ml di olio extravergine di oliva

Octopus is perhaps one of the most recognized of all the Greek dishes, but many people are afraid of it because they think it's difficult to cook. The technique in this recipe solves that problem - the result is beautifully tender. Once you learn this technique, you can add diced octopus to a cold seafood salad, a bowl of pasta with tomato sauce, or a risotto. Sear the legs in batches of two to avoid overcrowding the pan. Season the legs with kosher salt and pepper to taste. Place a large skillet over the highest heat and let it get smoking hot. Film the pan with a little blended oil and add two of the legs, tentacle side down. Sear, turning to a reddish brown, for 1-2 minutes. Transfer to a Dutch oven or a roasting pan and sear the remaining legs, returning the pan to super hot each time.
Chickpea Confit: In a Dutch oven or a heavy pot, combine the garlic, cumin, mustard seeds and chickpeas. Season to taste with kosher salt and pepper, and barely cover with blended oil. Cover the pot and cook at 325°F until aromatic but not browned, for about 45 minutes. When the mixture is cool, transfer it, with all the oil, to a sterilized glass container and use as you like. If the chickpeas are covered with oil, the confit could last up to 3 weeks in the refrigerator. Always save the oil for another use, for example, in a cumin vinaigrette for sautéing.
Ladolemondo: In a bowl, combine the lemon juice, mustard, oregano, ½ teaspoon of kosher salt and a generous grinding of pepper. Whisk to blend the mixture completely and, while whisking, drizzle the olive oil. This sauce will separate, so you must whisk or shake it in a jar before using it.

Il polpo è forse uno dei piatti greci più conosciuti, ma molte persone lo evitano perché pensano che sia difficile da cucinare. In questa ricetta, è la ricetta stessa che risolve il problema: il polpo risulta molto tenero. Una volta che avete imparato questa tecnica, potrete aggiungere il polpo a dadini ad una insalata di mare fredda, ad un piatto di pasta al pomodoro o ad un risotto. Scottate due tentacoli alla volta, per evitare di riempire eccessivamente la padella. Condite con sale kosher e pepe a piacere. Riscaldate una padella grande su fiamma alta. Rivestite la padella con un filo d'olio misto e aggiungete due tentacoli, con le ventose verso il basso. Scottate per 1-2 minuti fino a quando diventa di un marrone rossiccio. Trasferite poi in una casseruola di ghisa o in una teglia da forno e scottate i tentacoli restanti, riscaldando nuovamente ogni volta la padella.
Preparazione confit di ceci: Mettete l'aglio, il cumino, i semi di senape e i ceci in una casseruola di ghisa o in una pentola pesante. Condite a piacere con sale kosher e pepe, e coprite appena con l'olio misto. Coprite la pentola e lasciate cuocere a 160°C fino a quando è fragrante ma non rosolato (per 45 minuti circa). Quando si è raffreddato, mettete il confit con il suo olio in un contenitore di vetro sterilizzato, e utilizzate a piacere. Se i ceci sono ricoperti di olio, il confit può durare fino a 3 settimane in frigorifero. Conservate sempre l'olio per un altro uso, ad esempio, per una vinaigrette di cumino.
Preparazione ladolemondo: In una ciotola, unite il succo di limone, la senape, l'origano, ½ cucchiaino di sale kosher, e pepe macinato abbondante. Frullate bene il composto mentre aggiungete l'olio d'oliva. Questa salsa si separerà, quindi usate una frusta o sbattete in un vasetto prima dell'utilizzo.

Grilled branzino
Branzino alla griglia

INGREDIENTS FOR 4 SERVINGS:
- 4 branzino's 1-2 lbs each, scaled and gutted - 24 cherry tomatoes, halved- 24 kalamata olives, pitted - 24 green olives, pitted - 2 sweet onions sliced into rings, grilled, and reserved - 10 fingerling potatoes, par cooked and reserved - 3 cloves of garlic, sliced thin - ½ cup feta cheese
- 2 lemons - extravirgin olive oil - salt and pepper - 1 tb dry oregano
- 1 tb each of fresh chopped parsley, basil, and dil

INGREDIENTI PER 4 PERSONE:
- 4 branzini da 450-900 g squamati ed eviscerati - 24 pomodorini tagliati a metà - 24 olive kalamata snocciolate - 24 olive verdi snocciolate - 2 cipolle dolci tagliate ad anelli, grigliati e messi da parte - 10 patate fingerling, cotte e messe da parte - 3 spicchi d'aglio tagliate a fette sottili
- 70 g di feta - 2 limoni - olio extravergine di oliva - sale e pepe - 1 cucchiaio di origano secco
- 1 cucchiaio di prezzemolo fresco tritato - 1 cucchiaio di basilico fresco tritato - 1 cucchiaio di aneto fresco tritato

Pre-heat a grill to med-high. Paint fish with extravirgin olive oil season with salt and pepper, and place on the grill. Char on each side for approx 8 min. For warm salad, in a large heavy-bottomed pan add 2 tb extravirgin olive oil and heat through. Brown garlic and potatoes. Then, add tomatoes, olives, onion rings, dry oregano, and feta cheese. Transfer to a serving platter and place the fish on top of the warm salad. Squeeze fresh lemon juice on top, then drizzle with extravirgin olive oil, and sprinkle with fresh herbs.

Riscaldate una griglia a temperatura medio-alta. Spennellate il pesce con olio extravergine di oliva, condite con sale e pepe e mettetelo sulla griglia. Scottate entrambi i lati per circa 8 minuti. Per preparare l'insalata tiepida, mettete sul fuoco 2 cucchiai di olio extravergine di oliva in una grande padella dal fondo pesante. Fate dorare l'aglio e le patate, aggiungete i pomodori, le olive, gli anelli di cipolla, l'origano secco e la feta. Mettete in un piatto da portata e adagiate il pesce in cima all'insalata tiepida. Condite con succo di limone fresco, un filo d'olio extravergine di oliva e una spolverata di erbe fresche.

Homemade greek yogurt
Yogurt "greco"

INGREDIENTS FOR 4 SERVINGS:
- 1 quart whole goat's, sheep's or cow's milk
- 2 tbsp plan full-fat yogurt (live active cultures)

INGREDIENTI PER 4 PERSONE:
- 945 ml di latte intero di capra, pecora o mucca
- 2 cucchiai yogurt intero (fermenti lattici vivi)

Spoon 2 tablespoons of milk into a bowl and stir in the yogurt. In a saucepan, bring the remaining milk to a boil. Let it stand off the heat without stirring for about 15 minutes. A skin will form on the surface. Using a table knife, make a small opening in the skin and carefully pour the yogurt mixture into the milk in the saucepan. Cover the pot with a kitchen towel and transfer it to an oven. Turn the light on and close the oven door. Let it stand for 16 hours. Using a skimmer or a slotted spoon, lift off the skin and discard it. Carefully ladle the yogurt into a sieve lined with a double layer of cheesecloth and refrigerate until lots of the whey has drained and the yogurt is thick, for at least 4 hours. Transfer the yogurt to a bowl and serve.

Mettete 2 cucchiai di latte in una ciotola e aggiungete lo yogurt. Portate il resto del latte ad ebollizione in una casseruola. Togliete dal fuoco e lasciate riposare senza mescolare per 15 minuti circa, fino a quando si forma una pelle sulla superficie. Con un coltello da tavola fate una piccola apertura nella pelle e versateci dentro, con attenzione, la miscela di yogurt. Coprite la casseruola con un canovaccio e mettetela in forno. Accendete la luce e chiudete lo sportello del forno. Lasciate riposare per 16 ore. Utilizzando una schiumaiola o un mestolo forato, rimuovete la pelle e scartatela. Mettete con attenzione lo yogurt in un setaccio rivestito con un doppio strato di garza e conservate in frigorifero per almeno 4 ore, fino a quando la maggior parte del siero è stato drenato e lo yogurt è corposo. Mettete lo yogurt in una ciotola e servite.

OCEANA

Owner / Titolare › The Livanos Family • **Chef** › Ben Pollinger and Colleen Grapes

120 West 49th Street • Ⓜ 47-50 Sts Rockefeller • +01 212 759 5941 • **www.oceanarestaurant.com**

Oceana, the flagship of the Livanos Restaurant Group for over two decades, is located on 49th Street, just west of Rockefeller Center, and steps away from Radio City Music Hall and Broadway's famed theaters. A pure and natural ethos characterizes the cooking style of Executive Chef Ben Pollinger. Bold flavors emerge from his innovative compositions, while simple preparations of whole fish and other offerings subtly tease the palate. With a focus on seasonal products and the finest seafood, Chef Pollinger ensures a dining experience unlike any other.

Vantando quasi due decenni di successi nella sua location precedente, Oceana offre dei piatti audaci di pesce americani in uno spazio moderno ed elegante, ad ovest sulla 49esima strada, a ovest del Rockefeller Center. La celebrata cucina di questo locale è caratterizzata da ingredienti freschi e di stagione provenienti da tutto il mondo. Un ethos puro e naturale caratterizza lo stile di cucina dello chef Ben Pollinger. Sapori audaci emergono dalle sue innovative composizioni, mentre le semplici preparazioni di pesce intero ed altri piatti stuzzicano sottilmente il palato. Concentrandosi sui prodotti di stagione ed i migliori frutti di mare, chef Pollinger assicura un'esperienza gastronomica diversa da qualsiasi altra.

Wine List › Carta dei Vini	Cuisine › Cucina	Prix-fixe Lunch › Pranzo a prezzo fisso	Dinner › Cena
550 Labels › Etichette	**Innovative American seafood**	**$ 35 (3 courses)** › 3 portate	**$ 35-80**

General tsao's lobster
L'aragosta del Generale Tsao

INGREDIENTS FOR 4 SERVINGS:
Lobster:
- 1½ lbs of cleaned Maine lobster meat, diced into 1½ inch pieces
Batter: - ½ cup of egg whites - 1 tbsp of soy sauce - 1 tbsp of fish sauce
- 1 cup of cornstarch
Sauce: - 4 cloves of garlic, sliced - 1 inch of ginger, julienned - 2½ cups of lobster broth - 2 tbsp of sugar - ¾ cup of soy sauce - ½ cup of sweet chili sauce - 1 tbsp of sesame oil - 1 tsp of rice wine vinegar - 4 tbsp of cornstarch
To serve: - 1 bunch of scallions thinly sliced - 1 cup of cashews, toasted - 4 tbsp of chopped cilantro

INGREDIENTI PER 4 PERSONE:
Per l'aragosta: - 680 g di polpa d'aragosta del Maine pulito e tagliato a dadini da circa 3-4 cm
Per la pastella: - 118 ml di albumi - 1 cucchiaio di salsa di soia
- 1 cucchiaio di salsa di pesce - 125 g di amido di mais
Per la salsa: - 4 spicchi d'aglio tagliato a fette - 2,50 cm di zenzero tagliato a julienne - 590 ml di brodo d'aragosta - 2 cucchiai di zucchero - 177 ml di salsa di soia - 118 ml di salsa di peperoncino dolce - 1 cucchiaio di olio di sesamo - 1 cucchiaino di aceto di riso - 4 cucchiai di amido di mais
Per servire: - 1 mazzetto di cipolline tagliate sottilmente - 150 g di anacardi tostati - 4 cucchiai di coriandolo tritato

Batter: Whisk the whites with the soy and fish sauces. Whisk in the cornstarch. Toss the lobster in batter, deep fry it in batches at 375° until golden and cooked, for about four minutes. **Sauce:** Sauté the garlic and ginger in a drop of canola oil. Add broth, sugar, soy sauce, chili sauce, sesame oil and vinegar. Bring to a simmer. Thicken with cornstarch according to instuctions on box. **To serve:** Sauté the scallions in a drop of canola oil until wilted. Add the sauce, cashews and cilantro. Toss in lobster to coat. Serve over steamed black sticky rice.

Preparazione pastella: Sbattete i bianchi con la salsa di soia e di pesce. Aggiungete l'amido di mais. Passate l'aragosta nella pastella e friggete un poco alla volta a 190°C fino a doratura e cottura completa per quattro minuti circa. **Preparazione salsa:** Saltate l'aglio e lo zenzero in poco olio di canola. Aggiungete il brodo, lo zucchero, la salsa di soia, la salsa di peperoncino, l'olio di sesamo e l'aceto. Portate lentamente a ebollizione. Addensate con l'amido di mais in base alle indicazioni sulla confezione. **Per servire:** Saltate le cipolline in poco olio di canola fino a farle appassire. Aggiungete la salsa, gli anacardi e il coriandolo. Aggiungete l'aragosta per farla insaporire. Servite sopra del riso nero cotto a vapore.

Scallop ceviche with peaches, ginger and thai basil

INGREDIENTS FOR 4 SERVINGS:
- 1 pound scallops, diced ¼ inch - 1 tsp fine sea salt - Juice of 1 each lemon, lime and orange - 2 peaches, diced ¼ inch - 2 tbs ginger, minced - ½ fresh green chili, halved, seeded and sliced - 2 tbs cilantro chiffonade - 2 tbs chives minced - 2 tbs Thai basil chiffonade - 2 leaves shiso chiffonade - 2 tsp dhana dal - 1 tsp coarse sea salt - 3 tbs extra-virgin olive oil

Season the scallops with fine sea salt and freshly ground black pepper. Marinate in citrus juices for one hour. Drain scallops well, reserving juices. Add peaches, ginger, chili, herbs, dhana dal, coarse sea salt and extra virgin olive oil to the scallops. Mix gently with a spatula. Taste and add salt and pepper if needed. If it needs a little more acidity then add some of the reserved citrus juices. If not, discard reserved juice. Serve in a glass.

SUCK MY
★
⚡ OFICINA LATINA ⚡
NEW YORK CITY
COCKTAILS
HAPPY HOUR ←

OFICINA LATINA

Owners / Titolari › Maurizio Max Busato e Paolo Votano

24 Prince Street • Ⓜ Blecker [6] • +01 646 381 2555 • **www.oficinalatinanyc.com**

Can I be honest? When I arrived at the Oficina Latina I was hesitant: it looked more like a bar for alcohol lovers than a restaurant. But the liveliness and the voices of the bar counter placed right at the entrance of the restaurant and the smiley faces of the customers were like a magnet. Once you have passed the crowded entrance you can sit in the very original and colorful but dark dining room, and the waiters will introduce Max and Paolo's Pan-American bistro menu and a fantastic world of tastes and flavors will open up: guacamole, bocadillos, ceviche, tacos, paella and a lot of good meat. The Oficina is a melting-pot of dishes from Argentina, Mexico, Peru, Uruguay, Venezuela, Chile and Cuba, with lots of theme music and a young clientele (25-50 years) in age and spirit. After the meal, don't miss the "passion & love": two shots of good rum, accompanied by slices of orange to suck with streaks of cinnamon, coffee and brown sugar. In conclusion, the Oficina Latina was a nice discovery, an original place, full of life, that next time I'll rush in to without any hesitation.

Devo essere sincero? Quando sono arrivato dinanzi all'Oficina Latina ho avuto qualche remora: sembrava più un bar per amanti dell'alcol che un ristorante. Però la vivacità e il vociare di quel bancone bar posto proprio all'ingresso del locale e i volti sorridenti dei clienti sono stati come una calamita. Superato l'affollato ingresso ci si accomoda nella sala, molto originale e colorata, seppur buia, e i camerieri ti introducono al menù del bistrot panamericano di Max e Paolo, e si apre un mondo fantastico di gusti e sapori: guacamole, bocadillos, ceviche, tacos, paella e tanta buona carne. L'Oficina è un melting-pot di piatti argentini, messicani, peruviani, uruguayani, venezuelani, cileni e cubani, con tanta musica a tema e una clientela giovane (25-50 anni) nell'età e nello spirito. A fine pasto non perdetevi il "passion & love": due cicchetti di buon rum accompagnati da spicchi di arancia da succhiare con le strisciate di cannella, caffè e zucchero di canna. Concludendo, l'Oficina Latina è stata una bella scoperta, un posto originale e pieno di vita, in cui la prossima volta mi fionderò senza esitazioni.

Wine List › Carta dei Vini	**Cuisine** › Cucina	**Lunch** › Pranzo	**Dinner** › Cena
20 Labels › Etichette	**South American** › Sud Americana	$ 15-25	$ 25-40

Chivito

INGREDIENTS FOR 4 SERVINGS:
- 1 boneless rib steak, 1 pound, sliced horizontally into 4 thin steaks (you can ask the butcher to do this) - coarse salt
- 4 sandwich rolls - ½ cup aioli - four 1/8-inch-thick slices pancetta - 2 tablespoons olive oil - 4 large eggs
- 4 slices boiled ham (about 4 ounces)
- 4 ounces queso blanco or monterey jack, sliced 1/4 inch thick
- 4 boston lettuce leaves - 2 tomatoes, sliced
- 2 roasted peppers

Pound the steaks lightly with a meat mallet until they are evenly about 1/4 inch thick. Sprinkle with salt to taste. Split the rolls and spread aioli on both halves; set aside. Heat a chapa or a two-burner cast-iron griddle over medium-high heat. As it is heating, crisp the pancetta on it, turning once; set aside. When the chapa is hot enough that a drop of water sizzles on the surface, add the steaks and cook, without moving, for 2 minutes. Turn and cook for another minute, or until done to taste. Meanwhile heat the olive oil until it shimmers, then fry the eggs until the whites are cooked but the yolks are still runny. Place a steak on the bottom half of each of the rolls and top with a slice each of ham, cheese, and crisp pancetta and a fried egg. Cover the other halves with the lettuce, tomatoes, and roasted pepper, and close the sandwiches. Slice in half and serve.

Arepa

Braised short ribs for filling arepas: Sprinkle the ribs with coarse salt and pepper. Place them in an even layer in a slow cooker. Add the next 7 ingredients, cover, and cook on low heat until the meat is tender, for about 8 hours. Using a slotted spoon, transfer the ribs to a serving bowl. Discard thev parsley and bay leaves. Spoon the fat off the top of the sauce and pour the sauce over the ribs. Adjust the oven rack to the middle position and preheat the oven to 325°F. Combine 1 cup of water, and 1 teaspoon of vegetable oil in a medium bowl and knead with hands until a dough is formed. Take a small amount and flatten it between your palms. If the edges crack, knead in more water, a tablespoon at a time until dough is supple and smooth but not sticky. Season the dough to taste with salt, then cover and set aside for 5 minutes. Divide dough into four even pieces and roll into balls. Working on a wooden cutting board or a regular cutting board with a sheet of plastic wrap or parchment paper on top of it, flatten each ball down to a disk with a diameter of about 4-inches and ½-inch thick. Melt the butter in a 12-inch cast iron or non-stick skillet over medium-low heat. Add the arepas and cook, moving them around the pan and rotating them occasionally, until the first side is charred in spots and a dry crust has formed, for about five minutes. Flip the arepas and cook them on the second side until a dry crust has formed, for about five more minutes. Transfer to a baking sheet and bake until cooked through, for about 10 minutes. Remove from the oven, leave to rest for 5 minutes, split, fill, and serve.

Preparazione delle costolette brasate per la farcitura delle arepas:
Condite le costolette con sale grosso e pepe. Ponetele in modo uniforme in uno slow cooker. Aggiungete gli altri 7 ingredienti, coprite e lasciate cuocere a fuoco lento finché la carne diventa tenera, per circa 8 ore. Spostate le costolette e ponetele nel piatto di portata. Togliete il prezzemolo e l'alloro. Rimuovete il grasso dalla parte superiore dei succhi di cottura e versateli sulle costolette.
Mettete il vassoio del forno nella posizione centrale e riscaldatelo a 160°C. Impastate con le mani la farina di masarepa, 235 ml di acqua e un cucchiaino di olio vegetale in una ciotola di medie dimensioni. Prendete una piccola quantità dell'impasto e schiacciatelo tra i palmi delle mani. Se i bordi si rompono, aggiungete più acqua, un cucchiaio alla volta, fino ad ottenere un impasto morbido e liscio, ma non appiccicoso. Condite con sale, coprite e lasciate riposare per 5 minuti. Dividete l'impasto in quattro pezzi uguali e formate delle palline. Lavorate su un tagliere di legno o un tagliere regolare con sopra della pellicola trasparente o carta da forno. Stendete ogni palla fino a formare un disco con diametro di circa 10 cm e spesso 12 mm. Fate sciogliere il burro in una padella di ghisa o antiaderente da 30 cm a fuoco medio-basso. Aggiungete le arepas e lasciatele cuocere, spostandole intorno alla padella e ruotandole di tanto in tanto, per circa 5 minuti, fino a quando un lato è leggermente abbrustolito e si sta formando una piccola crosta secca. Capovolgete e lasciate cuocere sul secondo lato allo stesso modo per circa altri 5 minuti. Poneteli su di un vassoio in forno per circa 10 minuti. Toglieteli dal forno, lasciateli riposare 5 minuti, dividete, farcite e servite.

INGREDIENTS FOR 4 SERVINGS:
- 1 ½ cups masarepa - 1 ½ cups water, plus more as necessary - 1 teaspoon vegetable oil - kosher salt
- 2 teaspoons butter
Braised short ribs for filling arepas: - 4 ½ pounds 3 inch long beef short ribs - coarse kosher salt - 2 cups dry red wine - 1 14.5 ounce can diced tomatoes in juice - 1 6 ounce package sliced button mushrooms - ½ cup finely chopped onion - 6 garlic cloves, peeled - 6 fresh italian parsley sprigs - 2 bay leaves

INGREDIENTI PER 4 PERSONE:
- 225 g di farina di mais masarepa - 350 ml d'acqua, più altra se necessaria - 1 cucchiaino di olio vegetale - sale kosher - 2 cucchiaini di burro
Per le costole brasate per la farcitura delle arepas:
- 2 kg di costatine di manzo da 7,5cm - sale grosso kosher - 470 ml di vino rosso secco - 1 lattina da 410 g di pomodori in succo a dadini - 1 pacchetto da 170 g di funghi champignon a fette - 75 g di cipolla tritata finemente - 6 spicchi d'aglio pelati - 6 rametti di prezzemolo italiano fresco - 2 foglie di alloro

PERIYALI

Owners / Titolari › Steve Tzolis - Nicola Kotsoni • **Chef ›** Charles Bowman

35 West 20th Street • Ⓜ E 23 St - Broadway • +01 212 463 7890 • **www.periyali.com**

If you've been on holiday on a Greek island, you will find amazing how the Periyali is able to reproduce the same environment and the same atmosphere as in Santorini, Mykonos and Kefalonia. Once you have stepped through the front door, you'll feel like being in a restaurant in the Mediterranean: inspired by the white, green, and blue of the sky and the sea. A very nice and always crowded place, because the chef Charles Bowman (already at "La Cote Basque" and "River Café") offers everything you would expect from a Greek restaurant: excellent tapas-style appetizers, a good moussaka and fresh fish. Authentic flavors and sincere fragrances, that ensure long life to this restaurant opened back in 1987 by Nicola Kotsoni and Steve Tzolis, owners of other popular places In New York city (The Cantinori, The Bar Room, Bar Six, Amali).

Se siete stati in vacanza in un'isola greca, troverete incredibile come il Periyali riesca a riprodurre lo stesso ambiente e la stessa atmosfera che si respira a Santorini, Mykonos o Cefalonia. Varcata la porta d'ingresso, vi sembrerà di stare in un ristorantino del Mediterraneo: tutto all'insegna del bianco, del verde e del blu del cielo e del mare. Un locale molto bello e sempre affollato, perché la cucina dello chef Charles Bowman (già al "La cote Basque" e al "River Cafè") propone tutto ciò che ci si aspetta da un ristorante greco: degli ottimi antipasti in stile tapas, una buona moussaka e del pesce freschissimo. Sapori autentici e profumi sinceri, che assicurano lunga vita ad un ristorante aperto nell'ormai lontano 1987 da Nicola Kotsoni e Steve Tzolis, proprietari di altri apprezzati locali newyorchesi in città (Il Cantinori, The Bar Room, Bar Six, Amali).

Wine List › Carta dei Vini	Cuisine › Cucina	Lunch › Pranzo	Dinner › Cena
140 Labels › Etichette	**Greek** › Greca	$ 26	$ 42

Horiatiki (Greek salad)

INGREDIENTS FOR 4/6 SERVINGS:
- 1 lb feta cheese - 1.5 English cucumbers or 3 regular cucumbers (1.5lb approx) - 2 medium size ripe tomatoes cut into wedges 1 medium size red onion, thinly sliced and the slices separated into rings (0.5 cup) - 1 cup Periyali's Salad dressing - see below - 12 large romaine lettuce leaves - 16 Kalamata olives - 12 green olives
Periyali's Salad Dressing:
- ¼ cup chicken broth - see below - 1 tbsp red-wine vinegar - 1 tsp balsamic vinegar - 1 tbsp lemon juice - ½ cup plus - 2 tbsp regular (non extra-virgin) olive oil - ¾ tsp minced fresh thyme or ⅛ tsp dried thyme leaves, crumbled - ¾ tsp minced fresh oregano or ⅛ tsp dried oregano leaves, crumbled - ½ tsp minced flat-leaf parsley - ½ tsp minced chives - ¾ tsp salt- pinch white pepper

Bring the chicken broth to a boil in a small saucepan. Reduce the heat and simmer until it's reduced by half to about 2 tablespoons. Remove from the heat, pour into a medium-size bowl and set aside until just warm. Stir in the vinegars and lemon juice. Begin adding a mixture of the oils, drop by drop at first, and then in a thin, steady stream, beating constantly with a wire whisk until the mixture thickens. Beat in the herbs, salt and pepper. Cover and store in the refrigerator. Bring to room temperature and beat lightly to remix before using.
Salad mix: Cut feta cheese into small cubes and place them in a large bowl. Peel the cucumbers and slice them thinly. Add the cucumbers, tomato wedges and onion rings to the cheese. Pour the dressing over the cheese mixture and toss gently until well mixed. Arrange the lettuce leaves on a small platter. Spoon the cheese mixture over the lettuce and garnish with olives.
Note: The lettuce can be torn into bite-size pieces if you prefer. In this case, you will need about 6 cups of torn lettuce.

Horiatiki (insalata greca)

INGREDIENTI PER 4/6 PERSONE:
- 453 g di feta - 680 g di cetrioli inglesi o 3 cetrioli regolari (circa 680g) - 2 pomodori maturi di medie dimensioni tagliati a spicchi - 1 cipolla rossa di medie dimensioni tagliata a fette sottili e le fette separate ad anelli (80g) - 236 ml di condimento per insalata Periyali (vedi sotto) - 12 grandi foglie di lattuga romana - 16 olive Kalamata - 12 olive verdi
Condimento per insalata Periyali: - 59 ml di brodo di pollo (vedi sotto) - 1 cucchiaio di aceto di vino rosso - 1 cucchiaino di aceto balsamico - 1 cucchiaio di succo di limone - 118 ml più 2 cucchiai di olio di oliva (non extravergine) - ¾ di cucchiaino di timo fresco tritato o ⅛ di cucchiaino di foglie di timo essiccato e sbriciolato - ¾ di cucchiaino di origano fresco tritato o ⅛ di cucchiaino di foglie di origano essiccato e sbriciolato - ½ cucchiaino di prezzemolo a foglia piatta tritato - ½ di cucchiaino di erba cipollina tritata - ¾ di cucchiaino di sale - un pizzico di pepe bianco

Portate ad ebollizione il brodo di pollo in un pentolino. Abbassate il fuoco e fate sobbollire fino a fare ridurre della metà, quindi circa 2 cucchiai. Toglietelo dal fuoco, versatelo in una ciotola di medie dimensioni e mettete da parte fino a quando è tiepido. Aggiungete i due aceti e il succo di limone. Poi iniziate ad aggiungere la miscela di oli, prima goccia a goccia e poi a filo, mischiando di continuo con una frusta fino a quando il tutto si addensa. Aggiungete le erbe aromatiche, il sale e il pepe. Coprite e conservate in frigorifero. Prima dell'utilizzo, portate a temperatura ambiente e mischiate leggermente.
Preparazione insalata:
Tagliate il formaggio feta a dadini e ponetelo in una grande ciotola. Sbucciate i cetrioli e tagliateli a fette sottili. Aggiungete i cetrioli, le fette di pomodoro e gli anelli di cipolla nella ciotola con la feta. Aggiungete il condimento e mescolate delicatamente fino a quando i sapori sono ben miscelati. Ponete le foglie di lattuga su un piccolo piatto da portata. Aggiungete il composto di formaggio sopra la lattuga. Guarnite con le olive.
Nota: La lattuga può essere strappata in pezzi piccoli se si preferisce. In questo caso avrete bisogno di circa 450 gr di lattuga strappata.

ESTELLA › Moscato Salento IGP
CANTINE SAN MARZANO

Colore giallo paglierino tenue con riflessi verde brillante; si apre all'olfatto con fragranti note floreali e mielate unite a sentori di frutta esotica fresca. Avvolge il palato con una decisa spalla acida, supportata quest'ultima da un'armonica morbidezza.
Abbinamenti: Ideale per la cucina di mare: antipasti misti, crostacei crudi, primi piatti con sughi rosa di pesce.

Light straw yellow colour with bright green reflections; it reveals some fragrant flower and honey notes, together with fresh exotic fruit scents. Its taste is definitely acid and supported by a balanced softness.
Best served with: Ideal with sea food: mixed starters, raw shellfish, first courses with light fish sauces.

INGREDIENTS FOR 8/10 SERVINGS:

- 1 slender egg plant (1.5lbs approx) - salt - all purpose flour, for dredging eggplant slices - regular (not extra-virgin) olive oil - 2.5 lbs lean ground lamb - 1 medium sized onion, finely chopped (0.5 cup) - 2 large garlic cloves, minced - 2 bay leaves - 3-inch cinnamon stick - 4 whole allspice - 1 cup whole, peeled canned tomatoes, chopped - 1 cup dry white wine - 2 tbsp tomato paste - freshly ground black pepper, to taste - 0.5 cup grated graviera or parmesan cheese - 2 tbsp chopped flat-leaf parsley - ¼ tsp ground nutmeg. **Bechamel Sauce:** - 6 tbsp butter - 6 tbsp all-purpose flour - 1 quart milk - 1 tsp salt - ½ tsp ground nutmeg - 2 eggs - ⅛ tsp white pepper

INGREDIENTI PER 8/10 PERSONE:

- 1 melanzana piccola (680 g circa) - sale - farina per infarinare le fette di melanzana - Olio d'oliva (non extravergine) - 1.1 kg di carne magra macinata di agnello - 1 cipolla di medie dimensioni tritata finemente (75 g) - 2 grandi spicchi d'aglio tritati - 2 foglie di alloro - 1 bastoncino di cannella da 7,60cm - 4 bacche di pimento intere - 225 g di pomodori pelati in scatola tritati - 235 ml di vino bianco secco - 2 cucchiai di concentrato di pomodoro - pepe nero macinato fresco a piacere - 45 g di formaggio groviera o parmigiano grattugiato - 2 cucchiai di prezzemolo a foglia piatta tritato - ¼ cucchiaino di noce moscata grattugiata. **Besciamella:** - 6 cucchiai di burro - 6 cucchiai di farina - 946 ml di latte - 1 cucchiaino di sale - ½ cucchiaino di noce moscata - 2 uova - ⅛ di cucchiaino di pepe bianco.

This is Periyali's rendition of quite probably the best-known of all the Greek dishes. Like most old and popular recipes, it will almost always change slightly from region to region and from cook to cook. One thing that never varies is the topping of thick, creamy béchamel sauce sprinkled with cheese, that everybody loves, and kids (of all ages) scrape off and eat first.

Trim and peel the eggplant and cut it into 1/3-inch slices. Lightly sprinkle the slices with salt and set aside on paper towels to drain for about 30 minutes. Grease a 13x9-inch baking dish and set aside. Preheat the oven to 400°F. Sprinkle the flour on a sheet of waxed paper. Lightly coat the eggplant slices with flour, shaking off the excess. Pour just enough olive oil into a jelly-roll pan or another shallow roasting pan to lightly coat the bottom. Place the pan in the oven to heat the oil. When it's hot, add the eggplant slices in one layer, sprinkling each slice with a few drops of oil. Bake, turning once to brown lightly on both sides, for 10-15 minutes per side. Remove from the oven and set aside. Reduce the oven heat to 375°F.

Heat a large, heavy skillet over medium-high heat. When it's hot, add the ground lamb and cook, stirring, over medium heat until it has browned and most of the fat has cooked out. With a slotted spoon, move the lamb to a large plate lined with several sheets of paper towels. Discard the fat remaining in the skillet and wipe the skillet with paper towels. Return the lamb to the skillet. Stir in the onion, garlic, bay leaves, cinnamon stick, allspice, tomatoes, wine and tomato paste. Simmer the meat sauce, uncovered, for about 35 minutes or until most of the liquid has been absorbed. Remove the bay leaves, cinnamon stick and allspice. Season to taste with salt and pepper. Arrange the eggplant slices in one layer in the prepared baking dish. Sprinkle evenly with ¼ cup of the graviera and parsley. Spoon the meat sauce evenly over the eggplant and set aside. To make the béchamel sauce, in a heavy 3-quart saucepan, melt the butter over medium heat. Stir in the flour. Cook, stirring, until the mixture bubbles. Off the heat, with a whisk, briskly stir the milk into the flour mixture all at once. Return to medium heat and cook, stirring constantly with the whisk, until the mixture bubbles. Reduce the heat slightly, and continue to cook for about 10 minutes, stirring constantly. The sauce should be quite thick. Remove from the heat and stir in the salt, nutmeg and pepper until well blended. Beat the eggs in a small bowl. Stir a big spoonful of the hot sauce into the eggs to temper them, then whisk the egg mixture into the sauce. Pour the sauce over the eggplant, smoothing the top. Sprinkle with ground nutmeg and then the remaining ¼ cup of cheese.

Bake for about 25 minutes, or until hot enough. Set aside for 10-15 minutes before cutting. Serve the moussaka with a green salad.

Tagliate e sbucciate le melanzane e tagliatele a fette da 8mm. Conditele leggermente con sale e mettetele da parte su carta assorbente a drenare per circa 30 minuti. Imburrate una teglia da 33x22cm e mettetela da parte. Riscaldate il forno a 200°C. Mettete la farina su un foglio di carta da forno. Infarinate le fette di melanzana, lasciando cadere l'eccesso. Versate la quantità necessaria di olio d'oliva in una padella jelly-roll o in un'altra teglia poco profonda per rivestire leggermente il fondo. Ponete la teglia in forno per riscaldare l'olio. Quando è caldo, aggiungete le fette di melanzana in un unico strato, bagnando ogni fetta con qualche goccia di olio. Lasciate cuocere, girando una volta per far dorare entrambi i lati, per 10-15 minuti per lato. Togliete la teglia dal forno e mettetela da parte. Abbassate il calore del forno a 190°C.

Scaldate una padella grande e pesante a fuoco medio-alto. Quando è calda, aggiungete l'agnello macinato e fate cuocere, mentre mescolate, a fuoco medio fino a quando si è scurito e la maggior parte del grasso si è sciolto. Togliete l'agnello dalla pentola con un mestolo forato e ponetelo in un grande piatto foderato con più fogli di carta assorbente. Eliminate il grasso rimanente nella padella e pulitela con carta assorbente.

Mettete nuovamente l'agnello nella padella. Aggiungete la cipolla, l'aglio, le foglie di alloro, la cannella, le bacche di pimento, i pomodori, il vino e il concentrato di pomodoro. Lasciate cuocere il ragù coperto, per circa 35 minuti, o fino a quando la maggior parte del liquido è stato assorbito. Togliete le foglie di alloro, la cannella e le bacche di pimento e aggiustate di sale e pepe.

Formate uno strato di fette di melanzana nella teglia preparata precedentemente. Cospargetele uniformemente con metà del formaggio e il prezzemolo. Aggiungete la salsa di carne sopra le melanzane in modo uniforme e mettete da parte. Per fare la besciamella, fate sciogliere il burro a fuoco medio in una casseruola da 3 litri. Aggiungete la farina e lasciate cuocere, mescolando continuamente con la frusta, fino a quando bolle. Togliete dal fuoco e aggiungete velocemente il latte tutto in una volta mentre continuate a mescolare con la frusta. Mettete nuovamente la casseruola a fuoco medio e fate cuocere, mentre continuate a mescolare con la frusta, fino ad ebollizione. Abbassate leggermente la fiamma e continuate la cottura per circa 10 minuti, mescolando continuamente. La besciamella deve essere molto densa. Toglietela dal fuoco e mantecate con il sale, la noce moscata e il pepe, fino a quando è tutto ben amalgamato. Sbattete le uova in una piccola ciotola. Aggiungete un grosso cucchiaio di besciamella alle uova per temperarle, poi frullate le uova nella besciamella. Versate la besciamella sopra le melanzane e lisciate la parte superiore. Spolverate con noce moscata e la parte restante del formaggio. Fate cuocere in forno per circa 25 minuti, o fino a quando è abbastanza caldo.

Lasciate riposare per 10-15 minuti prima di tagliare. Servite la moussaka con insalata verde.

PIG AND KHAO

PIG AND KHAO

Owner / Titolare › Leah Coen • **Chef** › Leah Coen

68 Clinton Street • Ⓜ Delancey St [F] • +01 212 920 4458 • **www.pigandkhao.com**

Philippine cuisine has little to do with the Chinese one and even less with the Japanese one. Bit it has something in common with the Thai, and in fact the Pig and Khao cuisine of chef Leah Coen is presented as Filipino-Thai. This is a trendy place with a young clientele surching for different dishes, often quite simple, with affordable prices. The best thing we tried is the Khao Soi, a soup with curry, coconut milk, chicken, eggs, noodles, scallions and vegetables, but unfortunately the recipe is secret, so if you want to try it you'll have to go to the Pig & Khao. It will certainly not be a shame, order a cocktail, sit at the bar overlooking the kitchen and enjoy the chefs at work first, and then their dishes after.

La cucina filippina ha poco a che fare con quella cinese e ancor meno con quella giapponese. Ha invece qualcosa in comune con la thailandese, ed infatti al Pig and Khao la cucina della chef Leah Coen viene presentata come filippino-thai. Il suo è un locale trendy con clientela giovane in cerca di piatti diversi, spesso abbastanza semplici, con prezzi accessibili. La cosa più buona che abbiamo provato è il Khao Soi, una zuppa con curry, latte di cocco, pollo, uova, noodles, scalogno e verdure, ma purtroppo la ricetta è segreta, e dunque se volete provarla vi tocca andare al Pig&Khao. E non sarà certo un sacrificio: ordinate un cocktail, sedetevi al bancone che si affaccia sulla cucina a vista e gustatevi prima gli chef al lavoro e poi i loro piatti.

Wine List › Carta dei Vini	Cuisine › Cucina	Brunch	Dinner › Cena
6 Labels › Etichette	Thai/Philippines	$ 15-20	$ 15-40

Turon

INGREDIENTS FOR 4 SERVINGS:
- 2 ea banana cut into quarters - 4 tbs light brown sugar
- ½ tsp ground cinnamon - 8 ea spring roll wrappers (wei chan brand)

Salted Caramel:
- 2 cups whole milk - 300 g sugar - 60 g butter
- 1 tbs kosher salt - 3 cups heavy cream - 5 ea egg yolks
- ½ tbs vanilla extract

INGREDIENTI PER 4 PERSONE:
- 2 banane tagliate in quarti - 4 cucchiai di zucchero di canna chiaro
- ½ cucchiaino di cannella in polvere - 8 involucri per involtini primavera

Per il caramello salato:
- 473 ml di latte intero - 300 g di zucchero - 60 g di burro
- 1 cucchiaio di sale kosher - 709 ml di panna da montare
- 5 tuorli - ½ cucchiaino di estratto di vaniglia

To roll the turon: Place ½ tbs of brown sugar on the bottom corner of the spring roll wrapper (note the wrapper should be face down in a diamond shape with one of the points pointing towards you).

Place a pinch of cinnamon on top of the brown sugar and then place a piece of banana on top, cut side down.

Roll the bottom of the wrapper once, until it covers the banana then fold in the edges and continue to roll the wrapper. Seal with water.

To cook the turon: Fry the turon in oil at 350° until the outside is golden brown and the banana inside has warmed through. Serve with salted caramel ice cream.

Salted caramel: Place the milk in a large bowl over another bowl with ice and water. Put to the side with a fine strainer. In a saucepot, add the sugar and cook until it makes a dark caramel (don't let it burn). Turn off the heat and add the butter to the caramel with the salt. Slowly add the cream to the caramel mixture (be careful because it will bubble up). Turn the heat back onto medium heat and let the caramel melt back into the cream. Slowly temper the egg yolks into the cream mixture and cook until it thickens and coats the back of a spoon. Pour the cream mixture through a fine strainer into the milk. Once ice cream base is cold, spin it in an ice cream machine and keep in the freezer.

Preparazione del turon: Mettete ½ cucchiaio di zucchero di canna sull'angolo in basso dell'involucro per involtini primavera (l'involucro deve essere rivolto verso il basso, a forma di diamante, con uno degli angoli che punta verso di voi). Mettete un pizzico di cannella sopra lo zucchero di canna e poi la banana con il lato tagliato verso il basso. Rotolate l'involucro una volta fino a coprire la banana, piegate i bordi e continuate a rotolare. Sigillate con acqua.

Cuocere il turon: Friggete il turon in olio a 175°C fino a quando diventa dorato e la banana all'interno si è riscaldata. Servite con gelato al caramello salato.

Preparazione del caramello salato: Mettete il latte in una grande ciotola appoggiata su un'altra ciotola con acqua e ghiaccio. Mettete da parte con un colino fine. Mettete a cuocere lo zucchero fino a quando diventa un caramello scuro (assicurandovi di non farlo bruciare). Spegnete il fuoco e aggiungete il burro e il sale. Aggiungete poi lentamente la panna (fate attenzione perché farà schiuma). Accendete nuovamente la fiamma a fuoco medio e lasciate fondere il caramello con gli ingredienti fino a diventare una crema. Aggiungete lentamente i tuorli al composto per temperarli e fatelo cuocere fino a quando si addensa e riveste un cucchiaio. Versate la crema attraverso il colino fine nel latte. Quando l'impasto per gelato si è raffreddato, mettetelo nella gelatiera e poi conservatelo in freezer.

11 FILARI › Primitivo di Manduria Dolce Naturale DOP
CANTINE SAN MARZANO

Colore rosso rubino intenso con sfumature granate; profumo persistente e complesso, con sentori di frutti surmaturi che ricordano la confettura di ciliegie e i fichi secchi; leggere note speziate. Il corpo, di tutto rispetto, avvolge piacevolmente il palato con sensazioni mielate mitigate da una giusta acidità.

Abbinamenti: Vino da meditazione. Trova un ottimo equilibrio con pasticceria secca a base di mandorle, crostate di frutta, formaggi dal gusto deciso e stagionati.

Intense ruby red, with garnet reflections; persistent and complex to the nose, with notes of mature fruits which recall cherry jam and dry figs; slightly spicy. The full body gives the mouth some pleasant honeyed sensations, supported by a good acid structure.

Best served with: Meditation wine. Excellent with dry almond cakes, fruit tarts, savoury and matured cheeses.

Spinach Pizza
Served on whole wheat
spinach, guanciale, fontina

Teas Pizza
Burrata Cheese,
Cherry Tomatoes, Gorgonzol

AMALFITANA
Imported smoked bufala mo

PIZZETTERIA BRUNETTI

PIZZETTERIA BRUNETTI

PIZZETTERIA BRUNETTI

PIZZETTERIA BRUNETTI

PIZZETTERIA BRUNETTI

PIZZETTERIA
BRUNETTI
PIZZA WINE BAR · ESTABLISHED 2009

Come join us
for Lunch
OUR GARDEN IS
OPEN!
Try our NEW**
WHOLE WHEAT
GLUTE

GOOD FRIENDS,
GOOD WINE, GOOD TIMES

PIZZETTERIA
BRUNETTI
PIZZA WINE BAR · ESTABLISHED 2009

Dolci

Ricotta Zeppole
Served with Nutella sauce
9
Nutella Pizza
12
Dollops of ricotta/Sprinkled with powd

Tiramisu
9

Pannacotta
Served with Berries

PIZZETTERIA BRUNETTI

Owners and Chef / Titolari e Chef › Jason and Michael Brunetti

› 626 Hudson Street • Ⓜ 8 Av [L] • +01 212 255 5699 • **www.pizzetteriabrunetti.com**
› 103 Main Street (Westhampton Beach) • +01 631 288 3003

Usually in my books I don't review pizzerias, but my friend's insistence was fatal. "You have to go to that place, it is much more than a normal pizzeria." I got carried away, because (I know this will make someone smile) it isn't easy to put up with restaurants for lunch and dinner, every day. My friend was right: Pizzetteria Brunetti is a place that has to be seen because, despite the retrò name, it offers a good Neapolitan pizza in a modern and cozy place, and also, it offers original specialties, such as Mozzarella in Carrozza, pizza with clams or the Zeppole, a typical Italian dessert. There are also the Meatballs (a dish that I have always hated, because It's an example of the old Italian 60s cuisine) and I must admit that I liked these too. I have to thank my friend for suggesting this little place, and I'm willing to bet that Jason and Michael Brunetti will open other pizzerias soon.

Solitamente non recensisco nei miei libri le pizzerie, ma l'insistenza di un amico è stata fatale. «Devi andare in quel posto, è molto più della solita pizzeria». Mi sono lasciato trasportare, anche perché (so che la cosa potrà far sorridere) non è facile reggere a lungo i ristoranti sia a pranzo che a cena, ogni benedetto giorno. Il mio amico aveva ragione: la Pizzetteria Brunetti è un posto da vedere perché, a dispetto del nome retrò, offre una buona pizza napoletana in un locale moderno e accogliente, e propone anche qualche specialità "fuori dal coro", come la mozzarella in carrozza, la pizza alle vongole o le zeppole, un tipico dolce italiano. Ci sono anche le meatballs (un piatto che ho sempre odiato, perché esempio della vecchia cucina italiana anni '60) e devo ammettere che mi sono piaciute anche quelle. Devo ringraziare il mio amico per avermi suggerito questo localino, e sono pronto a scommettere che Jason e Michael Brunetti apriranno presto altre pizzerie.

Wine List › Carta dei Vini	**Cuisine** › Cucina	**Lunch** › Pranzo	**Dinner** › Cena
30 Labels › Etichette	**Italian Pizzeria**	$ 10	$ 25

Mozzarella in carrozza

INGREDIENTS FOR 1 SERVING:
- 1 sandwich - beat 2 whole eggs in a bowl - 1 cup of milk
- 1 tsp of fresh pepper - ½ tsp of sea salt - bread crumbs
- flour - sliced ham

Deep fried mozzarella sandwich stuffed with ham.
Place a piece of cow milk mozzarella and a slice of ham
between two slices of sandwich bread. Cut the sandwich in
half from one corner to the corner. Dip into flour and bread
crumbs. Deep fry until colour gets brownish. Dry the excess
oil with bounty paper. Sprinkle with a pinch of fresh parsley.
Serve with some marinara sauce at the side. Enjoy!

INGREDIENTI PER 1 PERSONA:
- 1 tramezzino - battete 2 uova intere in una ciotola - 236 ml
di latte - 1 cucchiaino di pepe fresco - ½ cucchiaino di sale
marino - pangrattato - farina - fette di prosciutto

Tramezzino di mozzarella fritto e farcito con prosciutto.
Posizionate un pezzo di mozzarella di latte vaccino e una fetta di prosciutto tra due fette di pane da tramezzino. Tagliate il
tramezzino a metà da un angolo all'altro. Passateli nella farina
e nel pangrattato. Metteteli a friggere fino a quando si scuriscono. Tamponate l'olio in eccesso con della carta da cucina
e spolverate con un pizzico di prezzemolo fresco. Servite con
della salsa marinara al lato. Buon appetito!

Zeppole alla Nutella

INGREDIENTS FOR 4 SERVING:
- 1 ricotta - 3 orange zest - 3 eggs - 22 oz of flour
- 1 vanilla bean - 6 table spoon of sugar
Nutella sauce: - 3 teaspoon of Nutella
- ½ cup of heavy cream - ½ cup of black chocolate

Mix all the ingredients in a bowl and let them dry. Fry and finish off with powder sugar. Serve with Nutella sauce on the side. Buon Appetito!

INGREDIENTI PER 4 PERSONE:
- 1 ricotta - 3 scorze d'arancia - 3 uova - 623 g di farina
- 1 baccello di vaniglia - 6 cucchiai di zucchero
Crema alla nutella: - 3 cucchiaini di Nutella
- 118 ml di panna - ½ tazza di cioccolato fondente

Mescolate tutti gli ingredienti in una ciotola e lasciateli asciugare. Friggete ed infine spolverate con lo zucchero a velo. Servite con la crema di Nutella al lato. Buon Appetito!

pure food and w

Organic ingredients and
handcrafted flavors

LUNCH MENU
2014

pure food and wine

A

PURE FOOD AND WINE

Owner / Titolare › Sarma Melngailis • **Executive Chef** › David Kupperberg

54 Irving Place • Ⓜ 14 St-Union Sq [4,5,6] • +01 212 477 1010 • **www.oneluckyduck.com**

It is difficult to convince an omnivore to eat in a vegetarian restaurant, but curiosity, the positive reviews of "Pure Food and Wine" and, I admit it, the desire to get to know Sarma Melngailis, made me overcome my reluctance. My review: half a disappointment (because Sarma wasn't there) and a very good impression of the cuisine, which without using meat or fish, offers original and tasty dishes, that can still be amazing and evoke authentic and lost flavors to which unfortunately our palate has gotten unaccustomed to, because biological courgettes and fruit without pesticides are really different from what we usually buy in supermarkets. You can especially tell by tasting the "raw" dishes in this restaurant, which reveal the exceptional quality and purity of the ingredients. This restaurant offers an experience not comparable to any other one, it's attended by many young people, mostly women. The wines are all organic or biodynamic, and the cocktails are made with sake Momokawa produced in Oregon which is obviously organic too. I would happily go back again.

È difficile convincere un onnivoro a mangiare in un ristorante vegetariano, ma la curiosità, le recensioni positive del "Pure Food and Wine" e - lo ammetto - la voglia di conoscere Sarma Melngailis hanno fatto vincere la mia ritrosia. Bilancio finale: una mezza delusione (perché Sarma non c'era) e un'ottima impressione dalla cucina, che pur senza usare carne e pesce riesce a proporre piatti originali e saporiti, che riescono a stupire e rievocano sapori autentici e perduti ai quali purtroppo il nostro palato si è disabituato, perché le zucchine biologiche e la frutta senza pesticidi sono davvero diverse da quello che solitamente acquistiamo al supermercato. Te ne accorgi soprattutto assaggiando i piatti "crudi" di questo ristorante, che rivelano l'eccezionale qualità e la purezza degli ingredienti. Il ristorante, che offre una esperienza non paragonabile ad altri locali "normali", è frequentato da tanti giovani, in maggioranza donne. I vini sono tutti biologici o biodinamici, e i cocktails sono a base di sake Momokawa prodotto in Oregon. Ovviamente è bio anch'esso. Valutazione finale: ci tornerei volentieri.

Wine List › Carta dei Vini	**Cuisine** › Cucina	**Lunch** › Pranzo	**Average Price** › Prezzo Medio
50 Labels › Etichette	Raw Vegan › Vegano	$ 25-30	$ 40-50

Zucchini and heirloom tomato lasagna

Lasagne di zucchine e pomodori Heirloom

INGREDIENTS FOR 6 SERVINGS:
For the Pine Nut Ricotta: - 2 cups of pine nuts (soaked for 1 hour or more in water and drained) - 2 tbsp of freshly squeezed lemon juice - 2 tbsp of nutritional yeast - 1 tsp of sea salt - 6 tbsp of water
For the tomato sauce: - 2 cups of sun-dried tomatoes (soaked in water for 2 hours or more and drained) - ½ cup of diced fresh tomatoes - ¼ cup of onion, chopped - 2 tbsp of lemon juice - ¼ cup of cold pressed extra virgin olive oil - 1 tbsp plus 1 teaspoon of agave nectar - 2 tsp of sea salt - a pinch of hot pepper flakes - 2 tsp of chopped thyme - 2 tsp of chopped oregano
For the basil-pistachio pesto: - 2 cups of packed basil leaves - ½ cup of raw pistachios - ¼ cup +2 tbsp of cold pressed extra virgin olive oil - 1 tsp of sea salt - A pinch of freshly ground black pepper
For the lasagna: - 2 to 3 medium zucchini, with the ends trimmed - 2 tbsp of cold pressed extra virgin olive oil - 3 medium heirloom tomatoes, sliced about 1/4" thick - 1 tbsp of finely chopped fresh oregano - 1 tbsp of fresh thyme leaves - whole basil leaves for garnish

INGREDIENTI PER 6 PERSONE:
Per la ricotta di pinoli: - 270 g di pinoli (a bagno per un'ora o più in acqua e poi lasciati drenare) - 2 cucchiai di succo di limone appena spremuto - 2 cucchiai di lievito alimentare - 1 cucchiaino di sale marino - 6 cucchiai di acqua **Per la salsa di pomodoro:** - 110 g di pomodori secchi (a bagno in acqua per 2 ore o più e scolati) - 100 g di pomodori freschi tagliati a dadini - 40 g di cipolla tritata - 2 cucchiai di succo di limone - 59 ml di olio extra vergine di oliva pressato a freddo - 1 cucchiaio e 1 cucchiaino di nettare di agave - 2 cucchiaini di sale marino - 1 pizzico di fiocchi di peperoncino piccante - 2 cucchiaini di timo tritato - 2 cucchiaini di origano tritato **Per il pesto al basilico-pistacchio:** - 30 g di foglie di basilico - 50 g di pistacchi crudi - 59 ml + 2 cucchiai di olio extra vergine di oliva spremuto a freddo - 1 cucchiaino di sale marino - 1 pizzico di pepe nero appena macinato **Per le lasagne:** - 2 o 3 zucchine medie con le punte tagliate - 2 cucchiai di olio extra vergine di oliva spremuto a freddo - 3 pomodori hairloom medi tagliati a fette da circa 6 mm - 1 cucchiaio di origano fresco tritato - 1 cucchiaio di timo fresco - foglie intere di basilico per guarnire

Pine Nut Ricotta: Place the pine nuts with the lemon juice, nutritional yeast and salt in a food processor and pulse a few times until thoroughly combined. Add the water gradually and process until the texture becomes fluffy, like ricotta.
Tomato sauce: Squeeze all the liquid out of the tomatoes. Place all of the above ingredients except for the herbs in a high-power blender and blend, but not too much, keeping the texture slightly chunky. Taste for seasoning, add herbs and pulse.
Basil-pistachio pesto: Place the above ingredients in a high-power blender and blend until smooth but still chunky.
Lasagna: Cut the ends off the zucchini and cut into 2 to 3" lengths. Slice each piece into very thin slices using a mandoline or a vegetable peeler. Just before assembling, toss in bowl with olive oil and the oregano, thyme and a pinch of salt and pepper. Line the bottom of a 9x13" baking dish with a layer of zucchini slices, each one slightly overlapping the other. Spread about 1/3 of the tomato sauce over it and top with dollops of ricotta and pesto, using about 1/3 of each. Layer on top about 1/3 of the tomato slices. Add another layer of zucchini slices and repeat twice more with the tomato sauce, ricotta, pesto and tomato slices. Serve immediately, or cover with plastic and let it sit at room temperature for a few hours. Garnish with fresh basil leaves. Alternatively, make individual servings, by placing about 3 zucchini slices, slightly overlapping each other, in the centre of each serving plate, to make a square shape. Spread the tomato sauce over the zucchini, top with small dollops of ricotta and pesto and a few tomato slices. Repeat twice more and garnish with fresh basil leaves.

Preparazione della ricotta di pinoli: Unite i pinoli con il succo di limone, il lievito alimentare e il sale in un robot da cucina e pulsate un paio di volte fino a quando sono completamente combinati. Aggiungete gradualmente l'acqua e continuate a frullare fino a quando la consistenza diventa soffice, come quella della ricotta.
Preparazione della salsa di pomodoro: Spremete bene tutto il liquido dai pomodori. Mettete tutti gli ingredienti elencati sopra (tranne le erbe) in un frullatore ad alta potenza e frullate fino ad ottenere una consistenza grossolana. Condite quanto basta, aggiungete le erbe e pulsate per unire il tutto.
Preparazione del pesto al basilico-pistacchio: Unite gli ingredienti elencati sopra in un frullatore ad alta potenza ma non troppo, in modo da avere una consistenza grossolana.
Preparazione delle lasagne: Tagliate le punte delle zucchine e poi a pezzi lunghi da 5-7cm. Tagliate ogni pezzo a fette molto sottili con un mandolino o un pelapatate. Appena prima dell'uso, saltatele in una ciotola con l'olio d'oliva e l'origano, il timo e un pizzico di sale e pepe. Foderate il fondo di una teglia da 22x33cm con uno strato di fette di zucchine, posizionandole ognuna leggermente sovrapposta all'altra. Stendete sopra circa 1/3 della salsa di pomodoro e poi aggiungete mucchietti di ricotta e di pesto, usando circa 1/3 di ciascuno. Poi fate uno strato con circa 1/3 delle fette di pomodoro. Aggiungete un altro strato di fette di zucchine e ripetete il procedimento altre due volte con la salsa di pomodoro, la ricotta, il pesto e il pomodoro. Servite immediatamente, o coprite con della pellicola e lasciate riposare a temperatura ambiente per qualche ora. Guarnite con foglie di basilico fresco. In alternativa, per fare porzioni singole, posizionate circa 3 fette di zucchine leggermente sovrapposte, al centro di ogni piatto di portata, per creare una forma quadrata. Stendete la salsa di pomodoro sopra le zucchine, aggiungete un po' di ricotta e di pesto e qualche fetta di pomodoro e ripetete questo procedimento altre due volte. Guarnite con foglie di basilico fresco.

SALINAS

Owners / Titolari › Luis Bollo - Nicolas Matar - Mary Catherine Mikula - Donald Mikula • **Chef** › Luis Bollo

136 9th Avenue • 🅼 14 St [A,C,E] • +01 212 776 1990 • **www.salinasnyc.com**

I can only think of one word to describe this restaurant: unbelievable! I'll explain why in a few words. This place is: friendly, romantic, refined in every detail. The food: everything is good, from the appetizers to the desserts. The service: excellent, practically perfect. For all these reasons, Salinas is at the top of our list of restaurants in New York. The start is sparkling, obviously with lots of tapas: the Mojo Picon Boquerones go down in three seconds, the squid croquets are delicious and the Gazpacho de Pepino is fantastic, the best gazpacho I've ever tasted. The Salmoreno Fideos is not to be missed, as well as the Paella. And the desserts finish off beautifully a fantastic dinner. In short, you understand that you will not find the Spanish molecular and experimental cuisine that was in fashion until a few years ago. Here you will eat very well.

Per descrivere questo ristorante mi viene in mente una sola parola: unbelievable! Vi spiego perché in poche parole. Locale: accogliente, romantico, curatissimo in ogni dettaglio. Cibo: tutto ottimo, dall'antipasto ai dolci. Servizio: eccellente, praticamente perfetto. Ecco, per tutti questi motivi, Salinas è al top della nostra classifica dei ristoranti di New York. La partenza è frizzante, ovviamente con una sfilza di tapas: i Boquerones al Mojo picon vanno giù in tre secondi, le croquetas ai calamari sono gustosissime e il gazpacho de pepino è fantastico, il miglior gazpacho che abbia mai assaggiato. Il Fideos al salmoreno è da non perdere, così come la Paella. E i dolci chiudono in bellezza una cena con i fiocchi. Insomma, avrete capito che qui non troverete la cucina spagnola molecolare e sperimentale andata di moda fino a qualche anno fa. Qui si mangia. Benissimo.

Wine List › Carta dei Vini	**Cuisine** › Cucina	**Lunch** › Pranzo	**Average Price** › Prezzo Medio
75 Labels › Etichette	**Spanish** › Spagnola	**No lunch** › Chiuso a pranzo	$ 55

Nuestra paella

INGREDIENTS FOR 4 SERVINGS:
- 1 tbsp extra virgin olive oil - 1,5 lb chicken (cut into 2 oz. pieces)
- 6 oz chorizo curado (small dices) - 1 green pepper (small dices)
- 1 red pepper (small dices) - 0,5 onion (small dices)
- 1 tsp garlic (minced) - 2 tbsp sepia (small dices)
- 4 scallops - 8 manila clams
- 4 red shrimp - 3 tbsp sofrito
- 1 pinch saffron - 4 cups bomba rice
- 28 oz chicken stock - to taste salt

Sofrito:
- 3 onion (sliced thin) - 3 tomato (peeled)
- 3 garlic (whole) - 1 tbsp extra virgin olive oil
- 1 tsp salt

Garnish:
- 1 lemon (cut into 4 wedges)

INGREDIENTI PER 4 PERSONE:
- 1 cucchiaio di olio extra vergine di oliva - 680 g di pollo (tagliato in pezzi da 56gr) - 170 g di chorizo curado (tagliato a dadini)
- 1 peperone verde (tagliato a dadini) - 1 peperone rosso (tagliato a dadini) - ½ cipolla (tagliata a dadini) - 1 cucchiaino di aglio (tritato)
- 2 cucchiai di seppia (tagliata a dadini) - 4 capesante
- 8 vongole di manila - 4 gamberoni rossi
- 3 cucchiai di sofrito - 1 pizzico di zafferano
- 840 g di riso Bomba - 795 g di pollo - sale qb

Per il sofrito:
- 3 cipolle (tagliate a fette sottili) - 3 pomodori (pelati)
- 3 spicchi di aglio (interi) - 1 cucchiaio di olio extra vergine di oliva
- 1 cucchiaino di sale

Per guarnire:
- 1 limone (tagliato in 4 spicchi)

Sofrito: Place the onions, garlic, olive oil and salt into a large skillet and cook on a low/medium flame (onions will start to sweat). Cook slowly until the onions juices evaporate and caramelize. Add the tomatoes and cook until the juices evaporate. Remove from the stove and blend in a food processor until smooth. Place in a bowl and cool in the refrigerator until needed.

Paella: Place a paella pan (about 38 cm wide) over a low/medium flame. When hot, drizzle olive oil around the pan, add the chicken and let it brown. Once the chicken is brown, move it to the outer edges of the pan. Add the onions, peppers and chorizo. Cook for about one minute until the vegetables start to soften, then move to the outer edges of the pan. Add garlic until it browns and then add the sepia and cook for about 30 seconds. Add the sofrito, saffron, and the bomba rice and mix all the ingredients well. Cover with chicken stock, add salt to taste and bring to a boil. When boiling, place in a 400°F oven and bake for 15 minutes. After 15 minutes add the clams, scallops and shrimp in the paella and return It to the oven for about 5 more minutes. Remove it and let it stand for about 5 minutes, then serve. Equally divide rice, scallops, mussels and shrimp in each plate, garnish with a lemon wedge. Enjoy!

Sofritto: Mettete le cipolle, l'aglio, l'olio d'oliva e il sale in una grande padella e fate soffriggere a fuoco medio-basso. Lasciate cuocere lentamente fino a quando i succhi delle cipolle evaporano e iniziano a caramellare. Aggiungete i pomodori e lasciate cuocere finché evaporano tutti i liquidi. Togliete dal fuoco e frullate con un robot da cucina fino a quando risulta liscio. Ponetelo in una ciotola a raffreddare in frigorifero fino al bisogno.

Preparazione della paella: Mettete una padella da paella (larga circa 38cm) su fiamma media-bassa. Quando è calda, aggiungete un filo di olio d'oliva e fate dorare il pollo. Una volta cotto, spostatelo ai bordi della padella. Aggiungete le cipolle, i peperoni, e il chorizo. Fate cuocere per circa un minuto fino a quando le verdure cominciano ad ammorbidirsi e spostate il tutto verso i bordi della padella. Aggiungete l'aglio fino a farlo dorare, poi aggiungete la seppia, e lasciate cuocere per circa 30 secondi. Aggiungete poi il sofrito, lo zafferano, e il riso bomba, e mescolate bene tutti gli ingredienti. Ricoprite il tutto con il brodo di pollo, condite con sale quanto basta e portate ad ebollizione. Quando inizia a bollire mettete la padella in forno a 200°C per 15 minuti. Passati i 15 minuti, aggiungete le vongole, le capesante e i gamberi, e rimettete la padella in forno per altri 5 minuti circa. Togliete dal forno, lasciate riposare per circa 5 minuti e servite. Dividete equamente il riso, le capesante, le vongole, e i gamberi per ogni piatto, e guarnite con una fetta di limone. Buon appetito!

TALÒ › Verdeca Puglia IGP
CANTINE SAN MARZANO

Colore giallo paglierino con riflessi dorati; al naso rivela sorprendenti profumi di fiori bianchi e vaniglia; al palato è fresco e giustamente minerale con una buona persistenza sapida.

Abbinamenti: Frutti di mare, crostacei e pesci lessi con salse leggere.

Straw yellow colour with green reflections; scotch broom notes and a hint of citrus and tropical fruits on the nose. Lively in acidity, fresh and mineral.

Best served with: Excellent with starters and fish soup, fresh cheese and pasta with light sauces.

Mango flan
Flan di mango

INGREDIENTS FOR 4 SERVINGS:
Flan: - 4 oz cream cheese - 2 oz condensed milk - 32 oz evaporated milk - 8 oz mango puree - 8 oz heavy cream - 1 eggs - 1/8 oz vanilla extract
Mango and passion fruit granitta:
- mango puree - 4 oz passion fruit puree - 2 oz water
- salt to taste - 8 oz Agar Agar
Garnish: - 2 unit local summer berries - 8 unit golden kiwi (diced)

INGREDIENTI PER 4 PERSONE:
Per il flan: - 113 g di crema di formaggio - 56 g di latte condensato - 907 g di latte evaporato - 225 g di purea di mango - 225 g di panna da montare - 1 uovo - 3,5 g di estratto di vaniglia
Per la granita di mango e frutto della passione: - Purea di mango - 113 g di purea di frutto della passione - 56 gr d'acqua - sale qb - 226 g di Agar Agar
Per guarnire: - 2 unità di bacche estive - 8 unità di kiwi golden (a dadini)

Direction for the flan: Preheat oven to 350°F. Add the eggs to a mixer with a whisk attachment and mix until smooth, for about one minute. Add the rest of the ingredients and mix until smooth, for about 3 minutes. Place 4 4oz ramekins in a 2" deep baking pan. Fill the ramekins almost to the top. Fill the baking pan with hot water, about half way up the ramekins, to create a water bath. Cover with aluminum foil and carefully place in the oven. Bake for about one hour (to test doneness, place the tip of a small paring knife into the centre of the flan, when removed it should be clean). When ready, carefully remove from the water bath and place in the refrigerator until cold (preferably overnight). **For the Mango Granitta:** Add the purees, water and salt to a sauce pot and bring up to 90°C. Remove from the stove top and add the Agar Agar and whisk until well incorporated. Pass through a chinois into a bowl and place it in the freezer until frozen (preferably overnight).

Preparazione del flan: Riscaldate il forno a 175°C. Sbattete le uova in un mixer fino a quando risultano lisce per un minuto circa. Aggiungete il resto degli ingredienti e frullate per circa 3 minuti fino a quando l'impasto risulta liscio. Ponete 4 ciotoline da 100gr in una teglia da forno profonda 5cm. Riempite le ciotoline quasi fino al margine. Riempite la teglia d'acqua calda fino a metà per fare una cottura a bagnomaria. Coprite la teglia con carta di alluminio e posizionatela con cura in forno. Lasciate cuocere per circa un'ora (per verificare la cottura, posizionate la punta di un piccolo coltello da cucina al centro di un flan, quando lo uscite dovrebbe essere pulito). A cottura terminata, rimuovete con attenzione le ciotoline dal bagnomaria e ponetele in frigorifero a raffreddare (preferibilmente per tutta la notte). **Preparazione della granita di mango:** Mettete le puree, l'acqua ed il sale in una pentola e portate a 90°C. Togliete dal fuoco e aggiungete l'Agar Agar e frullate fino a quando risulta ben incorporato. Passate attraverso un colino in una ciotola e mettete in freezer a congelare (preferibilmente per tutta la notte).

Tosta de Boquerón

INGREDIENTS FOR 4 SERVINGS:
- 16 chardonnay vinegar marinated anchovies
- 8 tbsp canarian guacamole - 4 tsp truffle caviar - 4 slices sliced multi-grain bread - escama sea salt (similar to maldon) - fresh chives
Canarian Guacamole: - 1 avocado - 0,5 small red onion (minced)
- 0,3 bunch cilantro (minced) - 0,5 canarian hot pepper - 1 tsp cumin
- 1 tbsp lemon juice - 2 tbsp olive oil - 1 tbsp green pepper parsley puree
- (1 green pepper, 1/2 bunch of parsley, 1 0z. of olive oil = blanch and blend all together) - salt and pepper - escama sea salt (spanish maldo sea salt)

Directions for the Toasted Multigrain Bread: Remove crust from the bread and cut lengthwise into 4 pieces about 1"x4". Drizzle the bread with olive oil and toast at 350 degrees for 4 minutes.
Directions for the Canarian Guacamole: Place all ingredients into a bowl and mix them well together. Season with salt and pepper.
Final presentation: Reheat the bread into the oven for 30 seconds at 350 degrees. Place some Canarian guacamole on top of toasted bread. Place a marinated anchovies on top of each toasted bread and Canarian guacamole. Put a little dollop of truffle caviar on top of each anchovy. Season with escama sea salt and fresh chives.

SEASONAL
Owner and Chef / Titolare e Chef › Wolfgang Ban

132 West 58th Street • Ⓜ 57 St [F] • +01 212 957 5550 • **www.seasonalnyc.com**

It's hard to say something new or not already said about a restaurant that for years has collected stars and still makes new successes. Certainly it won't be me to say that the kitchen of Wolfgang Ban, which starts from the Austrian tradition but goes very far, far away, has some defects, simply because, it doesn't have any. You just have to know that you will eat and admire masterpieces, but the portions are certainly not generous. The bill is generous, considering that eating in a starred restaurant for only 29$ (for a three-course lunch) and about 68$ (for dinner) is a good deal. The smoked salmon looks like it has been drawn. The vegetables and greens accompanying the sea bass are a sculpture worthy of the best museums. The chef's origins are perceived more clearly In the desserts. As for the wine, you can choose among about 275 labels. In short, if you want to impress someone, a woman or a customer, Seasonal is really the ideal place.

Difficile dire qualcosa di nuovo e o di non già detto su un ristorante che da anni raccoglie stelle e registra continui successi. Di certo non sarò io a dire che la cucina di Wolfgang Ban - che parte dalle tradizioni austriache ma va molto, molto lontano - abbia qualche difetto, semplicemente perché non ne ha. Sappiate solo che ammirerete e mangerete dei capolavori, ma le porzioni non saranno generose. Generoso è invece il conto, perché mangiare in un ristorante stellato con soli 29 dollari a pranzo (tre portate) e circa 68 (a cena) lo si può considerare un buon affare. Il salmone affumicato sembra disegnato. Le verdure e gli ortaggi che accompagnano il branzino sono una scultura degna del miglior museo. Nei dolci si percepiscono più nettamente le origini dello chef. Quanto ai vini, potrete scegliere tra circa 275 etichette. Insomma, avrete capito che se volete far colpo su qualcuno, una donna o un cliente, Seasonal è davvero il posto ideale.

Wine List › Carta dei Vini	**Cuisine** › Cucina	**Prix-fixe Lunch** › Pranzo a prezzo fisso	**Dinner** › Cena
275 Labels › Etichette	**Modern Austrian**	$ 29 (3 courses) › 3 portate	$ 68

Branzino

INGREDIENTS FOR 4 SERVINGS:
Pickling Liquid:
- 180 g sugar - 300 g champagne vinegar
- 600g water - 1 carrot - 1 onion - 5 g black pepper corn
- 2 bay leaf - 2 all spiceberries - 3 g fennel seed
Parsley Water:
- 200 g blanched wet parsley - 4 g garlic
- 6 g vegetable base - 60 g ice cubes - 100 g cold water
- salt, pepper, sugar - blend and strain through chinois
Parsley Root Stock:
- 100 g shallot - 30 g garlic - 30 g chardonnay vinegar
- 10 g white peppercorn - 450 g parsley root juice

INGREDIENTI PER 4 PERSONE:
Per il liquido per sottaceto:
- 180 g di zucchero - 300 g di aceto di champagne - 600 g d'acqua
- 1 carota - 1 cipolla - 5 g di pepe nero in grani - 2 foglie di alloro
- 2 bacche di pimento - 3 g di semi di finocchio
Per l'acqua al prezzemolo:
- 200 g di prezzemolo sbollentato bagnato - 4 g di aglio - 6 g di base vegetale - 60 g di cubetti di ghiaccio - 100 g di acqua fredda
- sale, pepe, zucchero - frullate e filtrare attraverso un chinois.
Per il brodo di radice di prezzemolo:
- 100 g di scalogno - 30 g di aglio - 30 g di aceto chardonnay
- 10 g di pepe bianco in grani - 450 g di succo di radice di prezzemolo

Pickling liquid for vegetables:
Place the sugar, vinegar, water, carrot, onion, peppercorn, bay leaf, allspice and fennel seeds into a pot. Bring it to a boil. Set aside and let it rest for 30 minutes. Strain it through a fine mesh. The pickling liquid is for the following items: fiddlehead, breakfast radish, watermelon radish and white pearl onions.

Salt baked golden baby beets:
Cover the bottom of a baking dish with salt, add a little champagne vinegar and place beets on to it. Cover with tin foil and bake until tender.
Oven roasted baby carrots: Place carrots on a baking dish and toss with olive oil. Add a couple of sprigs of thyme and bake until tender.

Yellow cherry tomatoes:
Bring a pot of water to a boil. Fill a bowl with ice and water. Once the water is boiling, drop the tomatoes into it and when cooked, transfer them into the ice water bath. Peel when cool.

Slow roasted cherry tomatoes:
Split the cherry tomatoes in half and arrange them on a parchment lined baking dish. Drizzle with olive oil, sprinkle with rosemary, thyme and garlic, add a dash of salt and pepper to season and bake in oven.

Parsley water:
Place the blanched parsley, garlic, water and ice cubes in a mixing cup and blend finely. Season with salt and pepper. Strain through a fine mesh.

Parsley root stock:
Juice the parsley root, bring to a boil, strain and cool. Sweat the garlic, onion and peppercorn in a sauce pan and deglaze with vinegar and then add parsley juice. Reduce to taste and strain.

To finish the parsley root sauce:
Bring the stock and parsley water to a simmer and mount with butter.

Branzino:
Pan seared, skin on, with olive oil, garlic and thyme for flavor.

Preparazione del liquido sottaceto per le verdure: Mettete lo zucchero, l'aceto, l'acqua, la carota, la cipolla, il pepe, l'alloro, le bacche di pimento e i semi di finocchio in una pentola. Portate ad ebollizione e lasciate da parte a riposare per 30 minuti. Filtrate attraverso un colino a maglia fine. Il liquido per sottaceto è per i seguenti alimenti: i fiddlehead (germogli di felce), i ravanelli, i ravanelli anguria e le cipolline bianche.

Preparazione barbabietole baby in sale: Ricoprite il fondo di una teglia con del sale, aggiungete un po' di aceto di champagne ed adagiateci le barbabietole. Coprite con carta stagnola e fate cuocere fino a quando diventano tenere.

Preparazione carote baby al forno: Mettete le carote in una teglia e conditele con olio d'oliva. Aggiungete un paio di rametti di timo e fate cuocere fino a quando diventano tenere.

Preparazione pomodorini gialli: Portate una pentola di acqua ad ebollizione. Intanto, riempite una ciotola con acqua e ghiaccio. Quando l'acqua nella pentola è bollente mettete a cuocere i pomodori, poi, una volta cotti, metteteli a bagno nell'acqua ghiacciata. Quando si sono raffreddati, togliete la buccia.

Preparazione pomodori arrostiti: Dividete i pomodorini a metà e poneteli su una teglia foderata con carta da forno. Condite con l'olio di oliva, rosmarino, timo, aglio, un pizzico di sale e pepe e fate cuocere in forno.

Preparazione acqua al prezzemolo: Frullate il prezzemolo sbollentato con l'aglio, l'acqua e i cubetti di ghiaccio. Condite con sale e pepe e filtrate facendo passare attraverso un colino a maglia fine.

Preparazione del brodo di radice di prezzemolo: Estraete il succo dalla radice del prezzemolo, portatelo ad ebollizione, filtratelo e lasciatelo raffreddare. Rosolate l'aglio, la cipolla e i grani di pepe in una casseruola e sfumate con l'aceto, poi aggiungete il succo di prezzemolo. Fate ridurre a piacere e poi filtrate.

Per finire la salsa di radice di prezzemolo: Portate il brodo e l'acqua del prezzemolo lentamente ad ebollizione e poi mantecate con il burro.

Preparazione del branzino: Scottate il branzino con la pelle, in olio d'oliva, con aglio e timo per insaporire.

SOMTUM DER

Owner / Titolare › Supanee Kitmahawong • **Ex. Chef** › Kornthanut Thongnum • **Chef** › Kridsanai Nenthanunt

85 Avenue A • **M** 2 Av [F] • +01 212 260 8570 • **www.somtumdernyc.com**

I love Asian restaurants furnished with simplicity and good taste. The Somtum Der, in the East Village, is one of these. An inconspicuous little place, characterized by its fishing pot chandeliers (traps used to catch fish and lobsters), where you will feel well and can appreciate Thai cuisine from the Isan region (located in the Northeast of the country). The papaya salad is good, the fried chicken is very interesting and don't miss the beef marinated in coconut. The green tea panna cotta adds a touch of originality to the desserts too. Pleasant ambience, great prices. And the big tables give an opportunity to make friends with other customers.

Adoro i ristoranti asiatici arredati con semplicità e buongusto. Il Somtum Der, nell'East Village, è uno di questi. Un localino poco appariscente, caratterizzato dai lampadari ottenuti usando le nasse (le trappole per pesci e aragoste), in cui si sta bene e si può apprezzare la cucina thailandese della regione dell'I-san (situata a Nord-Est del paese). Buona l'insalata di papaya, molto interessante il pollo fritto, da non perdere la carne di manzo marinata nel cocco. La panna cotta al the verde dà un tocco di originalità anche ai dessert. Ambiente molto alla mano, prezzi ottimi. E i grandi tavoli danno l'occasione per fare amicizia con gli altri clienti.

Wine List › Carta dei Vini	**Cuisine** › Cucina	**Lunch** › Pranzo	**Dinner** › Cena
10 Labels › Etichette	**Authentic Thai-Isan**	$ 12	$ 25

Tum Kor Moo Yang
Spicy papaya salad mixed with grilled pork

Tum Kor Moo Yang
Insalata di papaya piccante con maiale grigliato

INGREDIENTS FOR 4 SERVINGS:
Grilled Pork Butt:
- 120 g pork butt (boston butt) - ¾ tbs fish sauce
- ½ tsp pork broth powder - ½ tbs vegetable oil
- 1 tbs oyster soy sauce - ½ tbs palm sugar
- ½ tbs roasted rice grain - ½ tbs dried chili peppers

Somtum (papaya salad):
- 2-3 pieces bird's eye chili (red) - 2-3 cloves garlic
- 1.5 tbs palm sugar - 2 tbs fish sauce
- ½ tbs lime juice - 1 tbs tamarind juice
- 2-3 wedges lime (cut into wedges) - 2-4 piecescherry tomatoes
- 4-5 pieces long bean (cut into 2 inches long each)
- 100 g green papaya, julienned

Grilled Pork Butt:
Grilled Pork Butt: Cut pork butt into 1 cm pieces and put them into a bowl. Put the rest of the ingredients in the bowl and mix well by hand. Marinate for 10-15 minutes. Transfer to the grill until cooked, then cut the pork into smaller pieces.

Somtum (papaya salad):
Put the chili and garlic into a mortar and use the pestle to crush them together. Add flavour by adding palm sugar, fish sauce, lime juice, tamarind juice and use a spoon and pestle to mix the ingredients well. Add the lime wedges, long beans and cherry tomatoes (cut the tomatoes into smaller pieces right before putting them into the mortar). Mix well again. Add the green papaya and continue to mix. Add the grilled pork butt and mix with the rest. Transfer to a plate.

INGREDIENTI PER 4 PERSONE:
Per il maiale gigliato:
- 120 g di culatello (Boston butt) - ¾ di cucchiaio di salsa di pesce
- ½ cucchiaino di brodo di carne di maiale in polvere - ½ cucchiaio di olio vegetale - 1 cucchiaio di salsa di soia di ostriche - ½ cucchiaio di zucchero di palma - ½ cucchiaio di grano di riso scottato - ½ cucchiaio di peperoncini essiccati
Per il Somtum (insalata di papaya): - 2-3 pezzi di peperoncino piri piri (rosso) - 2-3 spicchi d'aglio - 1,5 cucchiai di zucchero di palma - 2 cucchiai di salsa di pesce - ½ cucchiaio di succo di lime - 1 cucchiaio di succo di tamarindo - 2-3 spicchi di lime (tagliati a spicchi) - 2-4 pomodori ciliegini - 4-5 fagiolini lunghi (tagliati in pezzi da 2cm) - 100 g di papaya verde tagliata a julienne

Preparazione del culatello grigliato:
Tagliate la carne di suino in pezzi da 1cm e metteteli in una ciotola. Mettete il resto degli ingredienti nella ciotola e mescolate bene a mano. Lasciate marinare per 10-15 minuti. Cucinate alla griglia fino a cottura completa e poi tagliate la carne in pezzi più piccoli.

Preparazione del Somtum (insalata di papaya):
Pestate il peperoncino e l'aglio in un mortaio. Condite aggiungendo lo zucchero di palma, la salsa di pesce, il succo di lime, il succo di tamarindo e utilizzate un cucchiaio e il pestello per amalgamare bene. Aggiungete il lime in spicchi, i fagiolini lunghi e i pomodori (tagliate i pomodori in pezzi più piccoli prima di metterli nel mortaio). Mescolate bene di nuovo. Aggiungete la papaya verde e continuate a mescolare. Aggiungete la carne grigliata e mescolate con gli altri ingredienti. Mettete in un piatto da portata.

F › Negroamaro Salento IGP
CANTINE SAN MARZANO

Colore rosso porpora molto carico e profondo, profumo ricco e complesso, con note di spezie, frutti di bosco, e confettura di ciliegia. Vino di grande corpo, morbido e armonico, ricco di tannini nobili, con un finale piacevolmente persistente.
Abbinamenti: Primi piatti robusti, carni rosse, selvaggina, formaggi pecorini stagionati. Vino da meditazione.

Very deep purple red, wide and complex to the nose, with notes of spices, soft fruit, and cherry jam. A full-bodied wine, soft and balanced, rich in fine tannins, with a pleasantly long lasting finish.
Best served with: Savoury first courses, red meat, game, pecorino cheese. Meditation wine.

Sa Poak Gai Tod Der
Der styled deep fried chicken thigh

INGREDIENTS FOR 4 SERVINGS:
- 200 g each chicken thigh 2 pieces - ½ tsp salt - ½ tbs chicken broth powder
- ¼ tsp white pepper (grounded) - ½ tbs red curry paste - ¼ cup tempura powder
- ¼ cup water - ¼ cup ice (crushed) 2-3 cloves garlic - 2-3 pieces coriander's root -
1 piece (julienned) lemongrass
Dipping Sauce for Fried Chicken Thigh: - 2 tbs fish sauce - 1 tbs palm sugar - 1 tbs
ground dried chili - 2 tbs tamarind juice - 1 tbs lime juice - ½ tbs roasted rice grain

Put garlic, cilantro root, julienned lemongrass in a mortar and crush ingredients with the pestle. Transfer to a bowl. Add the rest of the
ingredients into the bowl including water and ice. Mix well. Take the
bone out of the chicken thigh. Put the thigh into the bowl and massa-
ge the ingredients into it. Do not squeeze the chicken or it will break.
Cover the bowl with a lid and transfer to refrigerator for 1 hour.
To deep fry the chicken thigh: Boil 4 cups of vegetable oil in a frying
pan and heat on a high temperature until boiled. Then turn the fire
into medium. Put the skin side of the chicken thigh to the heated oil
until golden brown. Flip the thigh and continue to fry until the thigh
floats. Continue for 5 minutes and turn the fire to high before removing the chicken. Cut the thigh into pieces and serve with the dipping
sauce. **Dipping Sauce for Fried Chicken Thigh:** Mix all ingredients
together well and serve. *Optional:* Add a bit of sliced Kaffir lime leave
or sliced cilantro to enhance flavor and aroma.

Panna Cotta Thai Tea
Panna Cotta al tè tailandese

INGREDIENTS FOR 4 SERVINGS:
- 0.6 oz Thai tea powder - 8 oz Heavy cream - 16 oz Milk
- 2 egg yolk - 2 oz sugar - ¼ oz gelatin **Topping milk:**
- 3.5 oz sweetened condensed milk - 6 oz evaporated milk

INGREDIENTI PER 4 PERSONE:
- 17 g di tè Tailandese in polvere - 226 g di panna da montare
- 453 g di latte - 2 tuorli d'uovo - 56 g di zucchero - 7 g di gelatina
Topping al latte: - 100 g di latte condensato zuccherato
- 170 g di latte evaporato

Gelatin: Gelatin: Mix 6 oz of milk with gelatin and set
aside.
Thai tea milk: Put 10 oz of milk with the Thai tea powder together and heat on low fire until very hot. Do not
boil. Filter out the powder and set aside.
Pana cotta: Mix the egg yolks with the sugar. Beat
together until light and fluffy and set aside. Heat the
Thai tea milk, add the heavy cream slowly and stir. Add
the egg yolks and stir until the eggs are cooked and
the sugar has melted. Slowly add the gelatin and mix.
Be careful not to add the gelatin too quickly, otherwise
there will be a lot of bubbles. Stir well until the mixture is
blended. Transfer to a mold and set aside to cool down.
Keep it in the freezer until the panna cotta is hard and
then transfer it to the refrigerator before serving.
Topping: Mix both types of milk together. Transfer to
small cup and serve with the panna cotta.

Preparazione della gelatina: Mescolate 170gr di latte
con la gelatina e mettete da parte.
Preparazione del latte al tè tailandese: Riscaldate 283gr
di latte con il tè in polvere a fuoco basso fino a quando
diventa molto caldo, ma senza farlo bollire. Filtrate il tè e
mettete da parte.
Preparazione della panna cotta: Sbattete i tuorli con lo
zucchero fino ad ottenere un impasto chiaro e spumoso
e mettete da parte. Scaldate il latte al tè tailandese,
aggiungete lentamente la panna e mescolate. Aggiungete i tuorli e mescolate fino a quando le uova sono
cotte e lo zucchero si è sciolto. Aggiungete lentamente
la gelatina. Fate attenzione a non aggiungerla troppo
velocemente altrimenti farà molte bolle. Mescolate fino
a quando il composto è miscelato bene. Mettetelo in
uno stampo e lasciatelo da parte a raffreddare. Tenete in
freezer fino a quando la panna cotta si è indurita e poi
lasciatela in frigorifero fino a prima di servire.
Preparazione del topping al latte: Mescolate entrambi
i tipi di latte insieme. Mettete il composto in una ciotoli-
na e servite con la panna cotta.

SUPPER

Owner / Titolare › Frank Prisinzano • **Chef** › Nacho Netzahuat

156 East 2nd Street • Ⓜ 2 Av [F] • +01 212 477 7600 • **www.supperrestaurant.com**

Supper Is presented, online, as the classic northern Italian tavern. But nothing in this restaurant reminds you of Italy, except for the food, which serves generous portions of main Italian dishes. Everything else is New York style, actually, pure East Village style: the queue at the entrance, the halls, the wooden furniture, the open kitchen where you can see the chefs always busy on the grill. After the initial surprise, we tried the excellent Veal Meatballs, the Spaghetti Pomodoro with Stracciatella and Basil, the Pappardelle with Asparagus Peas and Tomatoes, the Roasted Chicken, the Tiramisù and the Chocolate Valrhona. Everything in huge portions as only Italian grandmothers and mothers give you.

Il Supper si presenta, online, come la classica osteria del Nord Italia. In realtà nulla in questo ristorante fa pensare all'Italia, eccezion fatta per il cibo, che propone generose porzioni di piatti della cucina di base italiana. Tutto il resto è newyorchese, anzi, puro stile East Village: la fila all'ingresso, le sale, gli arredamenti in legno, la cucina a vista con i cuochi sempre indaffarati alla griglia. Superata la sorpresa iniziale, abbiamo provato delle ottime polpettine di vitello, gli spaghetti al pomodoro con la stracciatella e il basilico, le pappardelle agli asparagi con piselli e pomodori, il pollo arrosto, il tiramisu e la Valrhona al cioccolato. Tutto in quantità industriali come solo le nonne e le mamme italiane sanno fare.

Wine List › Carta dei Vini	**Cuisine** › Cucina	**Brunch**	**Dinner** › Cena
50 Labels › Etichette	**Italian** › Italiana	$ 15-25	$ 40

Polpettine di vitello

INGREDIENTS FOR 4 SERVING:
- ½ pound of ground veal - 5 cloves of smash garlic
- ½ chopped onions - 10 leaves of sage - 1 full hand parsley
- 1 full hand of parmigiano cheese - 1 egg - black pepper
- pullman bread (no crust) and a little milk

Mix all the ingredients together in a mixing bowl then roll the meatballs by hand. Place them in a pan and bake for 20 minutes in the oven at 300 degrees.
While those are cooking, add some broth and reduce it by cooking it.

INGREDIENTI PER 4 PERSONE:
- ½ kg di macinato di vitello - 5 spicchi d'aglio schiacciati
- ½ cipolla tritata - 10 foglie di salvia - 1 mazzetto di prezze-molo - 1 pugno di formaggio parmigiano - 1 uovo
- pepe nero - pan grattato e un po' di latte

Mischiate tutti gli ingredienti in una coppa, quindi, una volta ottenuta la consistenza desiderata, realizzate le polpette usando le mani. Infornatele in forno caldo a 300° per 20 minuti, bagnando di tanto in tanto con del brodo per non far seccare troppo la carne.

Spaghetti al pomodoro

INGREDIENTS FOR 4 SERVING:
-300 g of spaghetti - 1 can of "La Carmela" Tomatoes
- ½ chopped onion - 5 teeth smash garlic
- ½ cup of extra virgin olive oil - parmesan and stracciatella cheese - fresh basil

First we cook the onion and the garlic. When the onion and garlic getting brown in pan we add the tomatoes. When the spaghetti are cooked put them in the tomato sauce, then add fresh basil, parmesan cheese and stracciatella cheese on top.

INGREDIENTI PER 4 PERSONE:
- 320 g di spaghetti- 1 lattina di pomodori pelati
- ½ cipolla tritata - 5 spicchi d'aglio schiacciati - ½ bicchiere di olio extra vergine di oliva - parmigiano e stracciatella
- basilico fresco

Far dorare in una padella con olio caldo la cipolla e l'aglio, quindi aggiungere i pomodori. Cuocere a parte in abbondante acqua salata, gli spaghetti: quando sono al dente versarli nel sugo di pomodoro e aggiungere il basilico fresco e il parmigiano. Impiattare e guarnire con la stracciatella e una foglia di basilico.

THE CECIL

Owner / Titolare › Richard Parson • **Chef** › Alexander Smalls

210 West 118th Street • Ⓜ 116 St [B,C] • +01 212 866 1262 • **www.thececilharlem.com**

 If you still have doubts or fears about going to Harlem and moving from the usual tourist districts in New York, put aside any doubt and run to the Cecil: you'll find a very nice place and sensational dishes, the result of a cuisine that defines itself as African-Asian-American. A cuisine that's inspired by travels and studies of the African diaspora by chef Alexander Smalls, who gives shape to an incredible mix of flavours, styles, and perfumes that will leave you stunned. The "Oxtail Dumpligs" are very delicate, the freshly grilled watermelon salad, with Cheese, Mango and Shiso is exceptional and fresh, the "Gumbo" is a bomb ready to explode for the delight of your taste buds, the "Malva Pudding Cake" and the "Milk Chocolate Peanut Tart" will take you to heaven. The coffee from Tanzania recommended to us by the waitress was unforgettable, just like this place created by businessman Richard Parson and his multifaceted chef.

Se avete ancora delle riserve o dei timori sull'andare ad Harlem e uscire dai soliti quartieri turistici di New York, mettete da parte ogni dubbio e correte al Cecil: vi attendono un locale molto bello e dei piatti sensazionali, frutto di una cucina che si definisce Afro-Asiatica-American. Una cucina ispirata dai viaggi e dagli studi della diaspora africana effettuati dallo chef Alexander Smalls, che si sostanzia in un incredibile mix di sapori, stili, profumi che vi lascerà a bocca aperta. Gli "oxtail dumpligs" sono delicatissimi; l'insalata con anguria appena grigliata, formaggio, shiso e mango è eccezionale e freschissima; il "gumbo" è una bomba pronta ad esplodere per la gioia delle vostre papille gustative; il "Malva pudding cake" e il "Milk chocolate peanut tart" vi condurranno in Paradiso. Il caffè della Tanzania consigliatoci dalla cameriera era indimenticabile, proprio come questo posto creato dall'uomo d'affari Richard Parson e dal suo poliedrico chef.

Wine List › Carta dei Vini	Cuisine › Cucina	Brunch	Dinner › Cena
35 Labels › Etichette	Afro/Asian/American	$ 25-30	$ 40-50

Afro asian american gumbo

Gumbo afro asiatico americano

INGREDIENTS FOR 4 SERVINGS:
- 2 cups chinese chicken sausage
- 1 cup vegetable oil
- ½ cup flour
- ½ cup of dried shrimp
- 2 cups minced onion
- 1 stalks minced celery
- 2 cups minced red bell pepper
- 2 cups fresh okra (sliced in rings)
- juice from 1 lemons
- 2 tablespoons of worcestershire sauce
- 6 ½ cups chicken stock
- 1 tablespoon minced fresh thyme
- 4 cloves minced garlic
- 2 tablespoons ground bay leaf
- ¼ teaspoon cayenne pepper
- 1 ½ cups chopped grape tomatoes
- 2 tablespoons tomato paste
- 1 ½ cups lump crabmeat
- 2 cups gulf shrimp

INGREDIENTI PER 4 PERSONE:
- 450 g di salsiccia di pollo cinese
- 236 ml di olio vegetale
- 64 g di farina
- 50 g di gamberetti essiccati
- 300 g di cipolla tritata
- 1 gambo di sedano tritato
- 350 g di peperoni rossi tritati
- 200 g di gombo fresco (tagliato ad anelli)
- succo di un limone
- 2 cucchiai di salsa worcestershire
- 1,5 lt di brodo di pollo
- 1 cucchiaio di timo fresco tritato
- 4 spicchi d'aglio tritato
- 2 cucchiai di foglie di alloro tritati
- ¼ di cucchiaino di pepe di Caienna
- 250 g di pomodori grappolo tritati
- 2 cucchiai di concentrato di pomodoro
- 675 g di polpa di granchio
- 650 g di gamberetti

In a pot, melt the butter with the oil and cook the all purpose flour continuously stirring until you get a dark chocolate roux (not burnt!).

Once your roux is as desired, add all of the chopped vegetables (except the okra). This will stop the roux from over cooking and burning.

Continue to cook the vegetables on moderately high heat for ten minutes, then add the dried shrimp and gumbo spice mixture and the tomatoe paste. After about 5 minutes, pour in all of the stocks.

Stir vigorously, add the remaining ingredients and let them simmer for about an hour on very low heat. Remember to continue to stir.

Sciogliete il burro con l'olio in una padella e fate cuocere la farina, mescolando continuamente, fino ad ottenere un colore cioccolato scuro (non bruciato!).

Aggiungete tutte le verdure tritate (tranne il gombo), per non fare bruciare la salsina appena ottenuta.

Lasciate cuocere a fuoco medio-alto per dieci minuti, poi aggiungete i gamberetti essiccati, le spezie per il gumbo e il concentrato di pomodoro.

Dopo circa 5 minuti, aggiungete tutti i liquidi e mescolate vigorosamente. Aggiungete gli ingredienti rimanenti e lasciate cuocere a fuoco lento per circa un'ora.
Non dimenticate di continuare a mescolare.

Watermelon salad

INGREDIENTS FOR 6/8 SERVINGS:
- ½ seedless watermelon cubed - ½ c pumpkin seeds - 2 cups syranno corn bread
- 10 shisho leaves shredded - 1c mango dressing - ½ c dates - 1 cup cloumage cheese (goat curd)
Lime Mango Dressing: - ¼ c lime juice - 1 whole sweet ripe mango chopped coarsely
- 1c sake wine - 1 qt watermelon trim - 1pc bird's eye chili - salt to taste - 2c oil
Toasted Pumpkin Seeds: - 1c pumpkin seeds - ½ tsp cayenne pepper - oil- just enough to lightly coat seeds - 1 tsp sugar - salt to taste

Lime Mango Dressing:
Add all the ingredients in the vita mix, blend on high slowly adding oil until mixture is smooth.
Toast seed with all ingredients and place on a half sheet tray and roast for 6-10 minutes at 350 degrees F.
Combine all ingredients except the cloumage cheese, croutons and pumpkin seeds in a large mixing bowl season with salt and pepper as needed. Smear a table spoon of the cloumage cheese on the base of the desired plate before topping with the tossed watermelon salad. Garnish with the corn bread croutons and pumpkins seeds.

Black rice salad
Insalata di riso nero

INGREDIENTS FOR 6/8 SERVINGS:
- 6 cups of black rice - 2 cups of bok choy - 2 cups of roasted papaya medium dice - 2 ears of grilled corn - 1 qt of baby heirloom tomatoes, sliced in half - 2 cups of charred tomato vinaigrette - Fried lotus root as needed
Cook Black Rice with: - 2cups of veg stock - 2 or 3 lime leaves - 2 cups of orange juice - 1 onion, in chunks - 1 bay leaf - Salt and pepper to taste
Charred Tomato Vin.: - 2 tomatoes - 1 bunch of scallions - 2 pc of garlic - 1 small pc of ginger - 1 red onion sliced - 2 cups of oil - Salt & pepper to taste - 1 pc of bird's eye chili - 1 cup of japanese rice vinegar

INGREDIENTI PER 6/8 PERSONE:
- 1,2 kg di riso nero - 140 g di bok choy - 280 g di papaia arrostita a cubetti - 2 pannocchie di mais alla giglia - 1 kg di pomodori heirloom tagliati a metà - 473 ml di vinaigrette di pomodoro scottato - Radice di loto fritta a piacere
Per il riso nero: - 473 ml di brodo vegetale - 2 o 3 foglie di lime - 473 ml di succo d'arancia - 1 cipolla tagliata gossolanamente - 1 foglia di alloro - sale e pepe qb.
Per la vinaigrette di pomodoro scottato: - 2 pomodori - 1 mazzetto di scalogno - 2 spicchi d'aglio - 1 pezzo piccolo di zenzero - 1 cipolla rossa tagliata a fette - 473 ml di olio - sale e pepe qb - un pezzo di peperoncino piri piri - 236 ml di aceto di riso giapponese

Steam rice for 45 minutes/1 hour or until tender.

Cook the vegetables until they are heavily charred in an over or on a grill, after seasoning lightly with salt and oil. Then put everything in a vita mix and blend until semi-smooth.

Cuocete il riso a vapore per 45 minuti-1 ora fino a quando diventa tenero.

Condite le verdure con olio e sale e poi scottatele in forno o su una griglia.
Poi mettete tutto in un mixer e frullate fino a quando diventa semi-liscio.

THE RED CAT

Owner / Titolare › Jimmy Bradley • **Chef** › Michael Cooperman

227 10th Avenue • **M** 23 St [C,E] • +01 212 242 1122 • **www.theredcat.com**

There are many places in New York where you have the feeling that everyone is happy: The Red Cat is one of them. Always busy, always noisy and attended by nice people. Among the numerous places to see in the High Street area, you cannot miss Jimmi Bradley's restaurant: it is as suitable for business lunches as it is for romantic dinners or friend gatherings. In short, it's a place for everyone, with a contemporary American cuisine, that offers many specialties worth mentioning, such as the spicy lamb tartare, or the Atlantik Hake, the tacos with shrimp and the pistachio parfait.

Ci sono tantissimi posti a New York dove hai la sensazione che tutti siano felici: The Red Cat è uno di questi. Sempre affollato, sempre rumoroso e ben frequentato. Tra i numerosi locali da vedere in zona High Street, il ristorante di Jimmi Bradley non potete perdervelo: è indicato per pranzi di lavoro come per cene romantiche o serate tra amici. Insomma un locale per tutti i gusti, con una cucina americana contemporanea che propone tante specialità degne di rilievo, come la tartare piccante di agnello, o l'Atlantik Hake, i tacos ai gamberi e il semifreddo al pistacchio.

Wine List › Carta dei Vini	**Cuisine** › Cucina	**Lunch** › Pranzo	**Dinner** › Cena
225 Labels › Etichette	**Seasonal American**	$ 25	$ 55

Pistachio semifreddo with warm chocolate sauce

Diver scallops, avocado salad
Capesante e insalata di avocado

INGREDIENTS FOR 4 SERVINGS:
For bacon vinaigrette: - 2 slices of bacon (lardons) - 1 tbsp shallots minced - 1 sprig of thyme (picked) - 1 tbsp unsalted butter -1 tbsp sherry vinegar - 1 tsp Dijon mustard. **Avocado salad:** - 1 to 2 limes - a splash sherry vinegar - 1 tbsp soft butter - 1 ripe avocado - to taste kosher salt - to taste freshly ground black pepper - to taste piment d espelette **To finish the dish:** - 2 dozen cherry tomatoes - 3 sprigs basil - 16 large diver scallops

INGREDIENTI PER 4 PERSONE:
Per la vinaigrette di pancetta: - 2 fette di pancetta - 1 cucchiaio di scalogno tritato - 1 rametto di timo - 1 cucchiaio di burro non salato - 1 cucchiaio di aceto di sherry - 1 cucchiaino di senape di Digione
Per l'insalata di avocado: - 1-2 lime - aceto di sherry - 1 cucchiaio di burro morbido - 1 avocado maturo - sale kosher qb - pepe nero appena macinato qb - peperoncino d'espelette qb **Per completare il piatto:** - 2 dozzine di pomodorini - 3 rametti di basilico - 16 capesante grandi

Bacon vinaigrette: Cook the bacon on low heat until crispy and the fat has rendered out, then add the shallot and cook until translucent. In a separate pot, brown the butter on low heat stirring with a whisk the whole time. When it becomes a golden brown color, add the sherry vinegar and mustard. Then combine with the bacon mixture and season with salt and black pepper. **Avocado salad:** Split the avocado, remove the seed, scoop it from the skin and cut it into small dice. In a mixing bowl, gently toss the avocado with the remaining ingredients, but do not over mix as you want the avocado to still be chunky for the dish.
To finish the dish: Put a 12inch cast iron pan (or sautee pan) on medium high heat, season the scallops with salt, piment d'Espelette and freshly ground black pepper. When the cast iron pan is hot add the canola oil, then the scallops and let them cook for about two minutes on each side. On a large plate, make a layer of avocado and then the scallops. Gently toss the tomatoes in the warm bacon vinaigrette, season with salt and pepper and place the tomato mixture on top of the scallops. Garnish with small basil leaves

Preparazione della vinaigrette di pancetta: Cucinate la pancetta a fuoco basso fino a quando diventa croccante e il grasso si è sciolto, poi aggiungete lo scalogno e fate cuocere fino a quando diventa traslucido. In una pentola a parte imbrunire il burro a fuoco basso mescolando costantemente con una frusta. Quando risulta dorato, aggiungete l'aceto di sherry e la senape. Unite con la pancetta e condite con sale e pepe nero. **Preparazione insalata di avocado:** Aprite l'avocado, rimuovete il nocciolo con una paletta e tagliatelo a dadini. In una terrina mischiatelo con il resto degli ingredienti, ma non troppo perché deve rimanere compatto. **Preparazione del piatto:** Mettete una padella in ghisa da 30cm a riscaldare su fuoco medio-alto, condite le capesante con sale, peperoncino d'espelette e pepe nero appena macinato. Quando la padella è bollente aggiungete l'olio di canola, poi le capesante, e fate cuocere per circa due minuti per lato. Adagiate uno strato di avocado su un grande piatto da portata, poi aggiungete le capesante. Saltate delicatamente i pomodori nella vinaigrette di pancetta calda, condite con sale e pepe e mettete il composto sopra le capesante. Infine guarnite con delle piccole foglie di basilico.

INGREDIENTS FOR 4 SERVINGS:
The brittle: - 1½ cups whole pistachio - 8 ounces superfine sugar - 1 tsp fresh lemon juice - 4 ounces cold water
The semifreddo: - 7 ounces egg whites - 5 ounces superfine sugar - 1 ½ cups heavy cream, whipped to medium peaks

The brittle: Pre heat the oven to 325 degrees. Toast nuts and keep warm. Over medium high heat combine water, sugar and lemon juice in a non-reactive saucepan. Simmer for about 10 minutes or until the caramel is light amber. Mix nuts with the caramel, spread on a non-stick baking pan and cool in a dry place. Once cool pulse in a food processor until there are pieces no larger than a whole pistachio nut and some praline dust.

The semifreddo: Place whites in a mixer with a whisk and beat until frothy then slowly add the sugar. Continue to beat until thick and fluffy approximately 10 minutes. Fold in the whipped heavy cream then fold in the pistachio brittle. Place in parchment lined molds then freeze overnight. Un mold, place on plates and drizzle warm chocolate sauce over.

THE REDHEAD

Owners / Titolari › Gregg Nelson - Rob Larcom - Meg Grace Larcom • **Chef** › Ben Chiu Maes

349 E. 13th Street • Ⓜ 1 Av [L] • +01 212 533 6212 • **www.theredheadnyc.com**

I liked The Redhead primarily because it offers a cuisine that dares strange combinations and invites you to try unpredictable dishes. And because it's a pleasant place, with an English pub style, attended by nice people and lively, like only the places in the East Village can be. The first surprise was the "bread carbonara", a soft flatbread stuffed American style, with the inevitable egg and, of course, the bacon in addition to vegetables in season. The Jersey tomatoes with squid are also interesting, and the soft homemade Pretzels (with beer cheese). Very light and full of scents and flavours, the shrimp soup with milk, sausage and mascarpone. Also the combination of fried chicken and watermelon has scored top marks. To finish off, a nice sundae and, above all, an incredible "Elvis it's it", cookie ice cream with peanut butter, banana ice cream and crispy bacon peanuts. In conclusion, you will understand that if you are a conservative for tastes, you have to stay away from the Redhead. But you must know that you are missing out on something great.

Il Redhead mi è piaciuto innanzitutto perché propone una cucina che azzarda strani abbinamenti e invita a provare piatti mai scontati. E poi perché è un posto piacevole, in stile pub inglese, molto ben frequentato e vivace, come lo sono solo i locali dell'East Village. La prima sorpresa è stato il "pane alla carbonara", una piadina sofficissima farcita all'americana, con l'immancabile uovo e, ovviamente, il bacon in aggiunta a verdure di stagione. Interessanti anche i pomodori Jersey con calamari e il Pretzels soffice fatto in casa (con formaggio alla birra). Leggerissima e carica di profumi e sapori la zuppa di gamberi con latte, salsiccia e mascarpone. Promosso a pieni voti anche l'abbinamento tra pollo fritto e anguria. Per chiudere un bel Sundae e, soprattutto, un incredibile "Elvis it's it", gelato a biscotto con burro di arachidi, gelato alla banana e arachidi croccanti alla pancetta. Insomma, avrete capito che, se in fatto di cucina siete dei conservatori, dovete stare alla larga dal Redhead. Ma sappiate che vi perdete qualcosa di grande.

Wine List › Carta dei Vini	**Cuisine** › Cucina	**Lunch** › Pranzo	**Dinner** › Cena
60 Labels › Etichette	**Southern American Comfort Food**	**No lunch** › Chiuso a pranzo	$ 25-50

Fried chicken
Pollo Fritto

INGREDIENTS FOR 4 SERVINGS:
- 1 quart water - ⅓ cup plus 1 teaspoon kosher salt - ¼ cup packed light brown sugar - 4 large garlic cloves, smashed - 4 thyme sprigs - 1 tbsp cracked black peppercorns - One 3½ pound chicken, cut into 8 pieces - Vegetable oil, for frying - 2 cups all-purpose flour - 1½ tsp baking powder - 1½ tsp cornstarch - ½ tsp freshly ground black pepper - ¼ tsp cayenne pepper

INGREDIENTI PER 4 PERSONE:
- 945 ml di acqua - 90 g più un cucchiaino di sale kosher - 50 g di zucchero di canna - 4 spicchi d'aglio grandi schiacciati - 4 rametti di timo - 1 cucchiaio di pepe nero incrinato - 1 pollo da 1580 g tagliato in 8 pezzi - olio vegetale per friggere - 256 g di farina - 1½ cucchiaino di lievito in polvere - 1½ cucchiaino di amido di mais - ½ cucchiaino di pepe nero appena macinato - ¼ cucchiaino di pepe di Caienna

In a large, deep bowl, combine the water with ⅓ cup of the salt, the brown sugar, garlic, thyme sprigs and black peppercorns and stir to dissolve the salt. Add the chicken pieces, submerging them in the brine. Refrigerate the chicken overnight. Preheat the oven to 300°. In a large, heavy pot, heat 2 inches of oil to 325°. Drain the chicken and pat dry with paper towels. In a large bowl, combine the flour, baking powder, cornstarch, black pepper, cayenne and the remaining 1 teaspoon of salt. Set a rack over a large rimmed baking sheet near the stove. Dredge half of the chicken pieces in the spiced flour, then shake off the excess. Fry the chicken pieces for about 10 minutes. Reduce the heat if the chicken browns too quickly. Transfer the chicken pieces to the rack and keep them warm in the preheated oven while you coat and fry the remaining chicken pieces. Serve the fried chicken hot. Accompany with sliced watermelon, pickled red onions, mint, smoked almonds and a drizzle of olive oil.

In una grande ciotola profonda, unite l'acqua, 90 g di sale, lo zucchero di canna, l'aglio, i rametti di timo e i grani di pepe nero e mescolate fino a far sciogliere il sale. Aggiungete i pezzi di pollo, sommergendoli nella salamoia e mettete in frigorifero per una notte. Riscaldate il forno a 150°C. In una grande pentola dal fondo pesante, scaldate 5cm di olio a 160°C. Scolate il pollo e asciugatelo con carta assorbente. In una grande ciotola, unite la farina, il lievito, l'amido di mais, il pepe nero, il pepe di Caienna e il restante cucchiaino di sale. Mettete una griglia su una grande teglia vicino ai fornelli. Cospargete metà dei pezzi di pollo di farina speziata, e scrollate l'eccesso. Friggete i pezzi di pollo per circa 10 minuti. Se il pollo si cucina troppo in fretta abbassate la fiamma. Mettete i pezzi di pollo sulla griglia e teneteli in caldo nel forno mentre preparate e friggete i rimanenti pezzi. Servite il pollo fritto caldo, con fette di anguria, cipolle rosse sottaceto, menta, mandorle affumicate e un filo di olio d'oliva.

Carbonara flatbread

INGREDIENTS FOR 4 SERVINGS:
- ½ cup grated parm
- ½ cup marscarpone
- salt and pepper to taste
- 8 slices of bacon - one cup of english peas
- 4 farm fresh eggs
- flatbread (your favorite middle eastern style flatbread)
- salt and pepper

For the spread: mix the grated Parm with the Mascarpone, combine and season to taste with salt and pepper. Finely slice the bacon. Blanch one cup of english peas. Chop and season with 2 T grated parm, salt and pepper.
Preheat oven to 450 degrees F.
Equally divide the spread between four 4 inch flatbreads. Top with sliced bacon. Place in oven to melt cheese and crisp bottom of flatbread.
Fry 4 sunny side up eggs until white is set and yolk is still runny. Season with salt and pepper.
When flatbreads are ready, remove from oven. Garnish with English pea relish, slice to your liking and top with sunny side up egg.

Low country shrimp

INGREDIENTS FOR 4 SERVINGS:
- 3 cups of water - 3 cups of milk - 1 cup of anson mills antebellum white grits - salt to taste - ¼ marscapone - 2 dozen medium size shrimp - 2 celery ribs - 1 medium size onion - 1 green bell pepper - 3 cloves of garlic - 2 medium size andouille sausage - 2 t of herbs (chives, parsley and thyme) - 1 cup of whole, peeled tomatoes, deseeded and chopped - 1 t brandy - 3 t butter

Bring water and milk to a boil. Whisk in grits and turn down to a simmer, continue to whisk until grits thicken, approximately for 10 minutes. Once thickened, turn heat down to low and cook for three hours, whisking every 10-15 minutes to prevent bottom from burning. Once grits are fully cooked, season with salt and pepper and mount with marscapone. While grits are cooking. Prepare the remaining ingredients. Clean the shrimps and save the shells for stock. Saute the shells in a small pot with the diced onions, carrot, celery and garlic. Add 4 cups of water and bring to a simmer. Simmer for one hour, strain and cool. This should yield approximately 3 cups of full flavored shrimp stock.
Dice 1 green bell pepper, a medium size onion and 2 celery ribs. Mince the garlic.
Slice 1/4" coins of 2 medium size Andouille sausage (or alternatively a spicy sausage from your region). Mince the herbs.
Once grits are cooked, cover and keep warm in a bain marie.
Once all ingredients are ready you can prepare the dish. In a large saute pan, sear the seasoned shrimp until it's just pink on the edges (not cooked thru). Set the shrimp aside. In the same pan, sear the sausage coins until crispy on both sides. Add the diced vegetables and garlic to the pan and saute until tender. Deglaze the pan with brandy and then add the tomato and enough stock to barely cover the vegetables. Reduce for 2-3 minutes, add butter and stir to emulsify. Season with salt and pepper and add the shrimp to the pan and poach to finish cooking in the sauce. Taste and adjust the flavor accordingly.
Portion the creamy grits into 4 soup or entree bowls. Evenly distribute the shrimp and sausage among the bowls. Spoon the vegetables and sauce over the shrimp and sausage. Finish the plate with freshly chopped herbs.

Gamberetti low country

INGREDIENTI PER 4 PERSONE:
- 710 ml di acqua - 710 ml di latte - 160 g di formaggio bianco cremoso - sale qb - 56 g di mascarpone - 2 dozzine di gamberetti di medie dimensioni - 2 gambi di sedano - 1 cipolla di medie dimensioni - 1 peperone verde - 3 spicchi d'aglio - 2 salsicce piccanti di medie dimensioni - 2 cucchiaini di erbe (erba cipollina, prezzemolo e timo) - 200 g di pomodori pelati, senza semi e tritati - 1 cucchiaino di brandy - 3 cucchiaini di burro

Portate l'acqua e il latte ad ebollizione. Aggiungete il formaggio mescolando con una frusta e abbassate la fiamma. Lasciate cuocere a fiamma bassa mentre continuate a mescolare per circa 10 minuti, fino a quando si addensa. Quando si è addensato, abbassate la fiamma al minimo e lasciate cuocere per tre ore, frullando ogni 10-15 minuti per evitare che si attacchi al fondo. Condite con sale e pepe e sbattete con il mascarpone.
Pulite i gamberi e conservate i gusci per il brodo. Saltate i gusci in una piccola padella con delle cipolle a dadini, della carota, del sedano e dell'aglio. Aggiungete 1 lt di acqua e portate ad ebollizione. Fate bollire per un'ora, poi scolate e lasciate raffreddare. Dovrebbe produrre circa 700 ml di brodo di gamberetti dal gusto forte.
Tagliate a dadini un peperone verde, una cipolla di medie dimensioni e 2 gambi di sedano. Tritate l'aglio.
Tagliate a rondelle da 6 mm due salsicce. Tritate le erbe.
Quando la crema di formaggio è pronta, copritela e tenetela in caldo a bagnomaria.
In una padella grande, scottate i gamberi conditi fino a farli colorare di rosa sui bordi (non interamente cotti) e poi metteteli da parte. Nella stessa padella, scottate la salsiccia fino a quando diventa croccante su entrambi i lati. Aggiungete le verdure a dadini e l'aglio e soffriggete fino a quando diventano teneri. Sfumate con il brandy e poi aggiungete il pomodoro e abbastanza brodo per coprire tutta la verdura. Fate ridurre per 2-3 minuti, aggiungete il burro e mescolate per emulsionare. Condite con sale e pepe e aggiungete i gamberetti per terminare la loro cottura nella salsa. Assaggiate e condite se necessario. Dividete la crema di formaggio in 4 ciotole da zuppa. Distribuite i gamberi e la salsiccia tra le ciotole. Aggiungete le verdure e la salsa sopra i gamberi e la salsiccia. Infine spolverate con le erbe fresche tritate.

WALLFLOWER

Owners / Titolari › Xavier Herit - Jason Soloway • **Chef ›** Michael Gutowski - Regis Wong

235 West 12th St. • Ⓜ 14 St [1,2,3] • **www.wallflowernyc.com**

A small place that isn't very conspicuous in a very nice area of New York, at a corner on Greenwich Avenue: if you don't know the address, it's hard to notice the Wallflower. But if you happen to be inside, the size of the kitchen and miniature dining room (only 15 seats) are secondary compared to the goodness of the food and cocktails. You'll discover that the Wallflower is a little gem, where you can enjoy unique things such as an Adam & Eve or a Betty Draper (cocktails are prepared by Wavier Herit, bartender for seven years in the Daniel) or taste sublime and highly refined dishes.

Un posticino poco evidente in una zona molto bella di New York, ad angolo con Greenwich Avenue: se non si conosce l'indirizzo si fa fatica ad accorgersi del Wallflower. Ma se ci capiti dentro, le dimensioni mignòn della cucina e della sala (appena 15 posti) passano in secondo piano rispetto alla bontà del cibo e dei cocktail. Scoprirete così che il Wallflower è una piccola gemma, dove potrete sorseggiare cose uniche come l'Adam & Eve o il Betty Draper (i cocktail sono preparati da Wavier Herit, sette anni da bartender al Daniel) oppure gustare piatti dal sapore sublime e molto ricercato.

Wine List › Carta dei Vini	**Cuisine** › Cucina	**Prix-fixe Lunch** › Pranzo a prezzo fisso	**Average Price** › Prezzo Medio
80 Labels › Etichette	French › Francese	No lunch › No lunch	$ 50-60

Sea scallops, corn cobs and maitake mushrooms

Capesante, funghi e granturco

INGREDIENTS FOR 4 SERVINGS:
- 1 lb of diver sea scallops
- 5 ea corn cobs (remove kernals from cob)
- 0.5 lb of Maitake mushrooms
- 1 bunch of purslane
- 1 bunch of thyme
- 1 head of garlic
- 1 cup of butter (whole)

Beurre Blanc:
- 0.5 lb of whole unsalted butter, in cubes
- 2 cups of white wine
- 1 shallot, sliced
- 1 tbsp of black peppercorns
- 1 lemon wedge

INGREDIENTI PER 4 PERSONE:
- 450 g di capesante di mare
- 5 Pannocchie di granturco (rimuovere i chicchi dalla pannocchia)
- 225 g di funghi Maitake (o altro tipo)
- 1 mazzetto di porcellana di mare
- 1 mazzetto di timo
- 1 testa di aglio
- 226 g di burro (intero)

Per il beurre Blanc:
- 225 g di burro intero non salato a dadini
- 470 ml di vino bianco
- 1 scalogno affettato
- 1 cucchiaio di pepe nero in grani
- 1 spicchio di limone

Make the buerre blanc: Reduce the white wine with the shallots and peppercorns by half, then whisk in the butter over very low heat until the butter is emulsified into the shallot reduction. Add a few drops of lemon and salt to taste. Keep this at room temperature.

Make the corn puree: Remove corn from cobs and juice half the corn, reserve the rest for searing. Reduce this liquid by half over low heat until it thickens into a puree. Strain through a chinois.

Cook the mushrooms and scallops: Remove the scallops from the fridge and pat dry with a towel, then season lightly with salt. Get a hot cast iron pan very hot with blended oil and sear the corn kernels. Remove the corn from pan, then sear the Maitake mushrooms. Cook the mushrooms for 60 senconds then add butter, thyme, and garlic. Baste the liquid over the mushrooms for 2-3 minutes until cooked and then drain them with a towel on a tray. Follow the same procedure with the scallops. When searing the scallops, do not move them around in the pan. Watch closely until the outside begins to caramelize and when the scallop no longer sticks to the pan, flip them over and baste with butter, thyme, and garlic.

To assemble the dish: Place 1 tablespoon of the corn puree on each plate, then add 3-4 scallops, and top with the corn kernels and mushrooms. Toss the picked purslane in olive oil and salt and use to garnish the plate. Drizzle with the buerre blanc before serving.

Preparazione del buerre blanc: Fate ridurre a metà il vino bianco con lo scalogno e i grani di pepe, poi mantecate con il burro a fuoco molto basso fino a quando è emulsionato nella riduzione di scalogno. Condite a piacere con qualche goccia di limone e sale. Tenete a temperatura ambiente.

Preparazione della purea di mais: Togliete il mais dalle pannocchie e metà del succo. Conservate il resto per fare la scottatura. Fate ridurre a metà questo liquido su fuoco basso fino a quando non si addensa e diventa una purea. Passate attraverso un chinois.

Preparazione funghi e capesante: Uscite le capesante dal frigo, asciugatele con uno strofinaccio e conditele leggermente con sale. Riscaldate dell'olio misto in una padella in ghisa e scottate i chicchi di mais. Togliete il mais dalla padella e scottate i funghi Maitake. Fate cuocere i funghi per 60 secondi, poi aggiungete il burro, il timo e l'aglio. Bagnateli con il liquido fino a cottura per altri 2-3 minuti e poi scolate e asciugate i fughi con uno strofinaccio su di un vassoio. Seguite la stessa procedura per le capesante. Quando le scottate, non muovetele in padella. Guardate attentamente quando iniziano a caramellare e non aderiscono più alla padella, capovolgetele e bagnatele con burro, timo e aglio.

Preparazione del piatto: Ponete un cucchiaio di purea di mais sul piatto da portata, adagiateci sopra 3-4 capesante per piatto, poi aggiungete il mais e i funghi. Saltate la porcellana in olio d'oliva e sale e usatela per guarnire. Aggiungete una spruzzata di blanc buerre prima di servire.

ph › D. Fitch

Bobby Seeger
Motorcycle Manufacturer

(www.indianlarry.com)

What do you like about NYC and Newyorkers?
I love the old New York, the grime, the people.
NYC is now Disney NYC.
What do you dislike about NYC and Newyorkers?
I used to love all New Yorkers, When neighborhoods were neighborhoods and characters wandered the streets.. Now a days most people don't speak much to one another in the streets, the phone is what every person holds and looks at all day long.
What is your favourite restaurant?
The best restaurants are Oficina Latina on Prince st. also Peasant on elizabeth st. Then into Brooklyn i eat Jimmy's Diner on Union ave. then i goto Sweet Chick on bedford ave some late nights i chow down at Talde on 7th ave in Brooklyn.
The best place for shopping?
I enjoy shopping at Genuine Motorworks in Brooklyn, i know they have most of my needs & i enjoy Made in America goods.
Where is your favourite place in the city?
I enjoy riding one of my Indian Larry Motorcycles through the city streets late at night, just hopping bridge to bridge then east to west. I truly haven't been in another city and enjoyed roaming around like NYC. I like wrapping the night up with a double shot of espresso under the Brooklyn Bridge on the Brooklyn side.
A place or thing that tourists can't miss?
You can't miss sitting in between the Bridges on the Brooklyn side watching the ships head north in the east river.
What is your next project/dream?
My next dream project is to open a school that offers kids a shot at learning a trade. It's in the works right now and i believe The Aidan Jack High School will help and guide many into some trades that are lost..

(italian text at page 363)

CHIC & CHEAP!
A collection of
charming boutique hotels
with affordable prices

Where to
STAY

CHIC E POCO COSTOSI!
Una collezione di
boutique hotel di charme
e design con prezzi accessibili

70 PARK AVENUE
70 Park Avenue
www.70parkave.com

This New York boutique hotel in Midtown Manhattan on Park Avenue is a favorite with guests the world over. First class amenities, personalized service, a friendly atmosphere and exceptional comfort combine with an ideal location just steps from Grand Central Station, making 70 Park Avenue Hotel a distinctive choice for business and play.

ACE HOTEL
20 West 29th Street
www.acehotel.com/newyork

A central hub for New Yorkers, Brooklynites and international travelers, and a hotbed of startups, freelancers and people who just want to kick it. However bustling the lobby gets, the hotel is a respite from New York's mayhem - full of local art, thoughtful details and the best beds in the universe.

AKWAABA
347 MacDonough Street, Brooklyn
akwaaba.com

Make yourself at home in a glorious 1860s landmark mansion. The meticulously restored Italianate villa features exquisite architectural details, including 14-foot ceilings and ornate fireplaces, while the décor is a blend of antiques and Afrocentric elegance. Located in historic Stuyvesant Heights.

BEST WESTERN PLUS PRESIDENT
book.bestwestern.com

The Best Western Plus President Hotel at Times Square is a 334 room lifestyle hotel property offering chic guest rooms. Each room comes complete with upgraded bedding and linens, 37-inch or 42-inch flat panel televisions, free Wi-Fi Internet access, and iHome iPod® docking station.

BRYANT PARK HOTEL
40 West 40th Street
www.bryantparkhotel.com

The Bryant Park Hotel has emerged since opening in 2001 as a "Designer Luxury Hotel" receiving countless awards for service and accommodations. The hotel caters to the fashion culturati, Hollywood and Film Industry, as well as cosmopolitans, both native and transient.

CARLTON
88 Madison Avenue
www.carltonhotelny.com

A luxury 4 star hotel with 317 generously sized guest rooms and remarkable suites that were designed by renowned architect, David Rockwell. Distressed mirrored furnishings, polished nickel, tall leather headboards, and dark walnut trimmings all combine beautifully to create a unique aesthetic that stands apart from other luxury hotels in New York City.

AMERITANIA
230 West 54th Street
www.ameritanianyc.com

Located in the vivacious heart of the New York City Theater District. Housed in a gorgeous Beaux Arts building, the lobby of The Ameritania is decorated in rich mahogany, illuminated by sleek chandeliers of floating translucent discs. The innovative aesthetic continues in the 219 luxurious guest rooms.

BELLECLAIRE
250 West 77th Street
www.hotelbelleclaire.com

Surrounded by an eclectic array of cultural offerings, Belleclaire combines classic charm with modern conveniences in a landmark building designed by Emery Roth in 1903. Hotel Belleclaire has been considered a "fascinating stylistic anomaly" worthy of landmark status.

BENTLEY HOTEL
500 East 62nd Street
bentleyhotelnyc.com

The Bentley Hotel transcends the average midtown hotel experience - gridlocked traffic, blaring horns, pedestrians packed like sardines - by offering an oasis of comfort and convenience: 197 richly appointed guest rooms infused with European elegance and sophistication.

CROSBY STREET HOTEL
79 Crosby Street
www.firmdalehotels.com/hotels/new-york/crosby-street-hotel

Situated on a quiet cobbled street in the heart of New York's vibrant SoHo neighbourhood. There are 86 bedrooms and suites over 11 floors. Each has high ceilings and full length windows. Interior design by Kit Kemp reflects a fresh, contemporary style. There is The Crosby Bar, a private leafy garden, guest drawing room, several stylish private event and meeting rooms and a fully equipped gym.

DISTRIKT HOTEL
342 West 40th Street
www.distrikthotel.com

Four star amenities and service with a refreshing design located close to everything New York has to offer. Located on West 40th Street between 8th and 9th Avenues, and steps away from Times Square, Bryant Park, Broadway, the Theater District and Madison Square Garden.

DUANE STREET HOTEL
130 Duane Street
duanestreethotel.com

A modern yet classic Tribeca hotel for the urban sophisticate. Nowhere else in New York will you find a neighborhood where old industrial warehouses conceal lavish penthouse lofts, where haute couture and haute cuisine are hidden away on quiet side streets, where celebrities walk around unnoticed on a sunny day. Stylish design and refined amenities along with intimate, personalized service.

EMPIRE HOTEL
44 West 63rd Street
www.empirehotelnyc.com

The 426 richly appointed guest rooms at The Empire Hotel represent a new standard in New York City boutique hotel accommodations. Each room combines the earth tones from Central Park and the dignified modernism of Lincoln Center to provide effortlessly sophisticated comfort.

EUROSTARS WALL STREET
129 Front Street
www.hoteleurostarswallstreet.com

Technology, design and a sophisticated atmosphere in the heart of the Financial District. The Wall Street Hotel New York is what most resembles the essence of a boutique hotel: small, modern and stylish. The best way to participate in the rebirth of Lower Manhattan is experiencing in the way of design and fashion.

FLATIRON
9 West 26th Street
www.flatironhotel.com

Located in the heart of Manhattan, the Flatiron Hotel is a sophisticated, exciting way to experience New York. With modern, luxurious rooms and amenities, and live music every night, the Flatiron Hotel is a destination in and of itself in the center of New York's most vibrant area.

GRAN TRIBECA
2 Ave of Americas
www.tribecagrand.com

The Tribeca Grand Hotel's 201 guest rooms and suites are meticulously designed to reflect the residential luxury of downtown New York and provide the ideal retreat from city pursuits.
With intimate neighborhood views and exacting standards, the sleek, mid-century modern accommodations are fitted with the latest technology and offer maximum comfort.

HOTEL AMERICANO
518 West 27th Street
www.hotel-americano.com

Located in the heart of the Chelsea Riviera between the High Line and the Hudson River, Hôtel Americano keeps life's choices simple. Three room types offered, all with the feel of an urban ryokan with wooden platform beds, warm lighting, and luxurious natural materials, some with soaking tubs and fireplaces.

HOTEL CHANDLER
12 East 31st Street
www.hotelchandler.com

Discover a secret gem at the intersection of the Flatiron District and Murray Hill. Hotel Chandler, member of Small Luxury Hotels of the World, is located between the Empire State Building, Madison Square Park, Penn Station and Times Square. This NYC boutique hotel provides an air of stately elegance that contrasts favorably with the over-the-top hip style of other Flatiron District hotels.

GILD HALL
15 Gold Street
www.thompsonhotels.com/hotels/gild-hall

New York meets New Amsterdam. Set among Lower Manhattan's curving colonial-era streets, Gild Hall is a unique Financial District hotel brings the hidden side of Wall Street to life. Richly designed by the ever eclectic Jim Walrod, Gild Hall is your home to a truly essential New York experience.

GRAMERCY PARK HOTEL
2 Lexington Avenue
www.gramercyparkhotel.com

A modern take on a traditional grand New York Hotel, with its custom-designed, handcrafted furnishings and rotating collection of 20th century artwork, including masterpieces from Warhol and Basquiat. Every room features unique luxury amenities, Italian linens, exquisite artwork, luxurious beauty products.

GRAND SOHO
310 West Broadway
www.sohogrand.com

353 custom hotel rooms and suites and 2 sprawling Penthouse Lofts that reflect the history and character of the neighborhood. The Hotel stands 17-stories offering stunning views of downtown Manhattan. Each room is equipped with flat-screen plasma televisions and iPod dock and speakers. Original artwork is provided by the Howard Greenberg Gallery.

HOTEL LE BLEU
370 4th Avenue., Brooklyn
www.hotellebleu.com

There's a quiet synergy that exists between Brooklyn and hotel le bleu - a mutual respect for the importance of individual style, and a deep appreciation for our unique borough. Situated in the chic Park Slope neighborhood, hotel le bleu guests are fully immersed in all things Brooklyn. Discover graceful brownstones, cutting-edge restaurants and cafés, trend-setting shopping, renowned musical venues and much more.

HOTEL ON RIVINGTON
107 Rivington Street
www.hotelonrivington.com

In the epicenter of the hip and historic Lower East Side, "on Rivington" is an urban oasis with sleek, modern design and breathtaking Manhattan views. Enjoy modern rooms and suites that feature unique appointments such as balconies, soaking tubs, exterior-facing steam showers or floor-to-ceiling glass walls designed by Grzywinski + Pons.

HUDSON
356 West 58th Street
www.morganshotelgroup.com

Urban adventure, daredevil design, and energetic social hub, Hudson takes convention and turns it on its head. Hudson is stylish, democratic, young at heart and utterly cool. Born from the innovative vision of design impresario Philippe Starck, this luxury New York boutique hotel is exuberantly energetic, breathtakingly beautiful and architecturally unpredictable.

INK 48
653 11th Avenue
www.ink48.com

A Midtown Manhattan hotel that makes an impression with more than its stunning city views. Kimpton lends its indelible mark on the Manhattan landscape with a sweeping Midtown hotel that pays homage to the city's literary scene, while treating guests to chic amenities worth penning a poem about.

KIMPTON EVENTI
222 Kearny St
www.kimptonhotels.com

This skyrise boutique hotel is a destination in itself, one that will completely transform your New York experience. Located in Manhattan's historic Chelsea neighborhood, Eventi puts you close to everything: the theater district, Madison Square Garden, all the museums, shopping, dining and nightlife.

MODERNE
243 West 55th Street
www.modernehotelnyc.com

The Moderne combines the essence of an intimate European hotel with the glamour and style of a chic New York City townhouse. The hotel's thirty-seven sleek and sophisticated guestrooms provide an ultramodern interior, and each richly appointed guest room reflects the whimsical spirit of the 1950's Color Field art movement.

NIGHT HOTEL
157 West 47th Street
www.nighthoteltimessquare.com

Not just a hotel, but rather a place to spend the night. That's the mantra of this fashionable midtown Manhattan hotel. Located on West 47th Street, only steps from the Theater District, Central Park, Rockefeller Center, and Fifth Avenue. Overnight in fully modern guest accommodations, exquisitely appointed with designer artwork and luxury.

THE NOLITAN
30 Kenmare Street
www.nolitanhotel.com

Nolita ("North of Little Italy") is a neighborhood in New York and The Nolitan Hotel is your home when you're here. At the corner of Kenmare and Elizabeth Streets, The Nolitan Hotel combines luxurious downtown living with luxury boutique hotel services and amenities to create a distinct New York City experience.

NU HOTEL BROOKLYN
85 Smith Street Brooklyn
nuhotelbrooklyn.com

Few Brooklyn hotels can boast the same spirit and moxie of NU Hotel, downtown Brooklyn's original boutique hotel. Offering the luxury amenities and exceptional service of other boutique hotels in NYC while channeling Brooklyn's distinct personality, NU Hotel draws inspiration from the creative energy of the borough's thriving art scene and the urban dynamism that defines the neighborhood.

MONDRIAN SOHO
9 Crosby Street
www.morganshotelgroup.com

Situated downtown in lower Manhattan, Mondrian SoHo is shaped by Benjamin Noriega Ortiz' provocative design, inspired by Jean Cocteau's 1946 French film "La Belle et la Bête", and features 270 rooms, an indoor-outdoor bar, Isola Trattoria & Crudo Bar restaurant with lush garden seating, and Mister H, a discreet nightlife space.

MORGANS
237 Madison Avenue
www.morganshotelgroup.com

From the moment it opened its doors on Madison Avenue in New York City, Morgans startled the world with a convention-shattering attitude and distinctive design sensibility, concocted by legendary designer Andree Putman. Conveniently located in midtown Manhattan.

NEW YORKER
481 8th Avenue & 34th Street
www.newyorkerhotel.com

Located on 8th avenue, Wyndham New Yorker is a premier hotel with the unique blend of stylish Art deco design and urban flair. Designed with the business traveler in mind, the hotel offers thoughtful amenities and comfortable rooms - ideal for work, play and relaxation. In its rooms have once slept Muhammad Ali, JFK, Jennifer Hudson.

NYLO
2178 Broadway at W 77th Street
www.nylohotels.com/nyc

NYLO New York City blends NYLO's signature urban, industrial design with the energy, color and fashions of New York's Jazz Era, creating a comfortable, social and stylish hotel experience. Guests will appreciate the location's convenient access to Manhattan's business and leisure destinations, access to the residential amenities of one of New York's best neighborhoods, and three highly fashionable bar and restaurant venues.

ONE UN
One United Nations Plaza
www.millenniumhotels.com/usa/oneunnewyork

Formerly Millennium UN Plaza Hotel, ONE UN New York is the United Nations' new fashionable neighbor. The hotel's re-branding as ONE UN with the launch of the hotel's new luxury West Tower will mark not only the completion of a more than $30-million phase I renovation, but also a new era for both the hotel and its neighborhood, historically underserved by the luxury hotel market.

RAVEL
8-08 Queens Plaza South
www.ravelhotel.com

An exciting choice for visitors to New York City, the Ravel Hotel in Long Island City welcomes the discerning traveler who appreciates sophistication, style, and value.
Setting the standard for a Long Island City boutique hotel, the Ravel invites guests to enjoy an environment where superior service and distinctive surroundings create a unique experience.

RENAISSANCE NEW YORK HOTEL 57
130 East 57th Street
www.marriott.com/hotels/travel/nycbr-renais-sance-new-york-hotel-57

A chic boutique hotel in Manhattan where modern design meets classic elegance. This midtown Manhattan hotel showca-ses a completed couture masterpiece by award-winning designer Jordan Mozer, creating the perfect complement to 57th Street and Lexington Avenue's prestigious galleries and upscale shops.

ROOM MATE GRACE
125 West 45th Street
grace.room-matehotels.com

Room Mate Grace has 139 avant-garde design rooms in New York, all equipped with free wifi, flat screen TV, Ihome, etc.. Room Mate Grace features an indoor pool with bar to order drinks there, sauna and steam room.

ROYALTON
44 West 44th Street
morganshotelgroup.com

Royalton has been brilliantly reinvented by Roman and Williams, reinstating its place as the stylish living room of Manhattan, and cros-sroads for international travelers and the New York elite. Designer Charlotte Macaux brings a unique vision to the classic minimalist charm of Royalton's Guestrooms and suites, retaining Philippe Starck's original bold features.

THE PEARL
233 West 49th Street
www.pearlhotelnyc.com

The lobby's exquisite terrazzo floor is a clear indication of the attention to detail and artistry that went into the design of this hotel. Pearl's sophisticated and elegant décor was inspired by the highly valued gem of the same name: the pearl, a symbol of perfect beauty. The Pearl intends to achieve that same flawless effect through the servi-ce and accommodations it provides.

THE POD HOTEL
The Pod Hotel 51 › 230 East 51st Street
The Pod Hotel 39 › 145 East 39th Street
www.thepodhotel.com

A new generation of affordable hotels out with the excessive and the unne-cessary. Surprising details, intelligent design, all on a budget. The Pod Hotel are created for savvy travelers: people who want to seek and explore.

THE STRAND HOTEL NYC
33 West 37th Street
www.thestrandnyc.com

With accommodations like these, it's nearly impossible to tell where form gives way and function begins. Designer Lisa Knight has decked out the Strand's 177 hotel rooms and suites in distinctive upholstered pieces, neutral shades and light textures. Warm mahoganies and rich walnuts complement softly palleted walls displaying vintage prints culled from the Condé Nast archives.

THE GEM HOTELS
(HUDSON YARDS AND CHELSEA)
200 Park Avenue South
www.thegemhotel.com

Excellent hospitality service in an unpretentious, accessible and sustainable manner. The Gem Hotel Midtown West is located two blocks from the Jacob Javits Convention Center. They are both urban oasis, where you'll getaway and rejuvenate in a chic, intimate setting perfect for couples.

THE JAMES
27 Grand Street
www.jameshotels.com/new-york

The James New York is one of the 25 top hotels in New York City according to Conde Nast Traveler, Reader's Choice Award-Best in the World - bringing luxury liberated from tradition to Soho. Outdoor spaces throughout the hotel include a seasonal Urban Garden and rooftop pool deck and bar.

THE MARCEL AT GRAMERCY
201 East 24th Street
www.themarcelatgramercy.com

Located at 24th street and Third Avenue-hidden within the calm oasis of the historic Gramercy District. The contemporary lobby with cozy seating offer a perfect start to any stay. The Marcel at Gramercy holds 136 guest rooms, each one blending elements of the chic mod lobby.

TRYP
345 West 35th Street
www.tryphotels.com

Located in the heart of Midtown Manhattan at 345 West 35th Street; between 8th and 9th Avenues. The hotel's décor is a whimsical blend featuring the Mediterranean origins of Wyndham Group and New York City chic with some of the largest rooms found in NYC (up to 455 square feet) accommodating up to 8 persons, reclaimed wood floors and fantastic New York City views.

YOTEL
570 Tenth Avenue
yotelnewyork.com

Cabins are perfectly formed and intuitively designed to place an array of amenities at your fingertips. Super-strength WiFi is completely free to use. The expansive terrace and all the cabins showcase stunning views of the city skyline, looking uptown at the skyscrapers of Times Square or downtown toward Hudson and Financial District.

Z HOTEL
11-01 43rd Avenue
www.zhotelny.com

This vibrant boutique hotel located in Long Island City features a sleek, Jazz Age theme combined with modernist industrial chic in a slender yet stunning 14-story tower. You'll immediately be transported back to the golden age of travel as you enter the transportation-hub themed lobby. All the 100 stylish and comfortable guest rooms feature luxurious amenities.

Chiemi Nakai
Pianist, composer, arranger

(www.chieminakainy.com)

What do you like of New York and New Yorkers?
I like NY because here is the center of world music which I love. I like New Yorkers because they have independent spirit and concentrating their own purpose to make their dreams come true.
What do you dislike about NYC and New Yorkers?
I dislike the cold and long winter.
Your favourite restaurants?
Oficina Latina in Manhattan and Geido, Flatbush in Brooklyn.
A place for shopping?
Union Square area, China Town.
Your favourite place in the city?
Meatpacking district, West Village, Soho.
A place that tourists can't miss?
Meatpacking district, downtown Brooklyn, live music.
Your next project/dream?
Recording the rest of my compositions and Releasing the second CD in 2015. Performing with my trio project at Blue Note, Zinc bar, Dizzy's Jazz Club, Standard, SOB's and Jazz Festivals in the world.
Touring with my trio project to go to Japan, Europe, South America and in US. Composing more songs which are fusions of Latin, R&B and Pop-Rock. Playing at big stages collaborating with musicians of different genre like R&B and Rock.

(italian text at page 363)

Cheap EATS

Tutti amiamo mangiare a buon
prezzo. Giusto, ma dove?
In un sacco di posti, anche
per strada. Non ci credete?
Voltate pagina...

We all love cheap eats.
Ok, but where? In a lot of places.
Yes, in New York.
Also in the streets of New York.
Don't you believe us? Turn the page...

EL ARIPO CAFE
Venezuelan
172 Delancey Street
www.elaripocafe.com

AMMA
Indian
246 East 51st Street (between 2nd and 3rd Avenues)
www.ammanyc.com

A SALT AND BATTERY
Fish and Chips
112 Greenwich Avenue (bewteen 12th and 13th Streets)
www.asaltandbattery.com

A family restaurant located in the Lower East Side of Manhattan, owned and operated by the Sanchez Family who also live in Manhattan's Lower East Side for over 30 years. The cafè offer a variety of authentic Venezuelan and Puerto Rican dishes. All the dishes are freshly prepared with the love and care of the family environment. The specialty here are the Arepas, grilled corn-dough patties, lightly crispy on the outside soft and moist on the inside accompanied with grandmas secret Caribbean sauce, and carefully stuffed with your filling of choice. You have to try also "El Pabellon", the Venezuelan traditional plate (white rice with shredded beef accompanied with black beans topped with white powdered cheese, maduros, avocado and an arepa, $ 12.75), and the "Chupetas con Tostones" (Venezuelan style fried chicken wing lollipops accompanied with tostones and grandmas secret garlic sauce, $ 10.95).

Ristorante a conduzione familiare ubicato nell'East Side di Manhattan. Offre specialità venezuelane e portoricane preparate con prodotti freschi di giornata. Le specialità della casa sono le Arepas, che potete farcire a vostro piacimento. Provate anche "El Pabellon" e le "Chuopetas copn tostones".

A culinary journey through the Indian Sub Continent. Though the menu is largely familiar, Amma, taking a cue from Indian-fusion restaurants like Tamarind, serves main courses on individual plates, with nan, rice and vegetables, rather than family style. The service is genial, and the rosewater lassi actually tastes and smells of rosewater... Lunch special: 3 courses for $ 17, 2 courses for $ 12.

Un viaggio culinario attraverso il sub continente indiano: da Amma potrete assaporare tante specialità della cucina asiatica preparate come se stesse mangiando a casa vostra. Prezzi ottimi a pranzo: 3 portate per 17 dollari, due portate per soli 12 dollari.

If you are a fan of fish and chips, you can't miss this place in the West Village neighborhood of Manhattan, that serves pub food and english cuisine using only the freshest and finest quality fish and ingredients fried in the best vegetable oil. The menu is very simple: just choose your fish and order chips with a side of curry. You will be happy.

Se siete fan del fish&chips, non potete perdervi questo posto nel West Village. Al "Salt and battery" si serve autentica cucina da pub inglese, con patatine fritte rigorosamente in olio vegetale. Menu semplice: basta scegliere il vostro pesce e ordinare le patate con il curry. E sarete felici.

SHAKE SHACK
Burger
Everywhere in New York
www.shakeshack.com

CALEXICO
Tacos
www.calexico.net

CLINTON STREET BAKING
Pancakes
4 Clinton Street (bewteen East Houston & Stanton)
www.clintonstreetbaking.com

The new bible for burger lovers: an incredible success-story started with a hot dog cart. In this restaurant-chain the burgers are incredible juicy, cheesy and delicious. The menu is pretty simple, with just some different type of burgers, hot dog, fries and frozen custards. Hamburger from 3.95 $, hot dog from 3 $.

La nuova Bibbia per i fanatici del burger: Shake Shack è una incredibile storia di successo imprenditoriale nata da un carretto che vendeva hot-dog. In quella che oggi è divenuta una catena di ristoranti potrete gustare succosi e deliziosi burger al formaggio (a partire da 3.95 dollari) e ovviamente gli hot-dog (da 3 dollari). Attenti però: creano dipendenza.

«What about a taco cart? After all, there is no better street food than a taco», said one day the Calexico brothers. In their second year in business, they won the Vendy Award for Best Street Food in New York City. The Vendys are like the Oscars for street food. And it changed everything. Today they're still out there slinging tacos and burritos on the streets of New York, but instead of one cart they are owners of a small fleet. Nobody is more surprised by this development than they are.

"Che ne dite di un carretto di tacos? IN fin dei conti non c'è cibo di strada migliore dei tacos", dissero un giorno i fratelli Calexico. Due anni dopo vinsero il Vendys, il premio riservato ai migliori venditori di street-food a New York. Se vogliamo fare un paragone con il cinema, dire Vendys è come dire Oscar. Da allora tutto è cambiato, ma i fratelli Calexico li trovate ancora per le strade di New York. Non più nei carretti ma all'interno di comodi locali.

This are the "Best pancakes in the city" (New York Magazine): the popular little bakery-café opened in 2001 by chef Neil Kleinberg and DeDe Lahamn is located in the Lower East Side. The 32 seat spot is comfortable and lived in, humble and well worn; in the morning it smells like blueberry muffins and fresh ground coffee; in the evening, buttermilk fried chicken and waffles. All day and night it sounds like latin-southern-blue note jazz.

Secondo il New York Magazine, quelli del Clinton Street Baking sono i migliori pancakes della città. Il bakery-cafè di Neil Kleinberg e DeDe Lahamn aprì nel Lower East Side nel 2001. La saletta con soli 32 posti a sedere è comfortevole e vissuta. Al mattino potrete sentire il profumo dei muffins caldi e del caffè appena fatto. La sera invece quello del pollo fritto e dei waffles. I profumi sono accompagnati, tutto il giorno, dalle note di buon latin-southern jazz.

LOS TACOS n. 1
Tacos
75 9th Avenue (Chelsea Market)
www.lostacos1.com

Los Tacos No. 1 was created after three close friends from Tijuana, Mexico, and Brawley, California, decided to bring the authentic Mexican taco to the east coast. The authentic taste comes from family recipes and from fresh, simple and tasteful ingredients straight from home.

Los Tacos No. 1 è stato creato da tre amici di Tijuana (Messico) e Brawley (California) che decisero di portare gli autenticxi tacos messicani sulla east coast. Il sapore originale arriva direttamente dalle ricette di famiglia e dagli ingredienti freschi utilizzati in cucina.

JG MELON
Burger
1291 3rd Avenue

One of those places where you have to enter, even at the cost of having to do a queue. It is located in front of Central Park and it's usually attended only by New Yorkers. Excellent fries, nice the cheesecakes and the warm chocolate cake.

In fatto di hamburger è una istituzione. Uno di quei posti in cui dovete entrare se capitate a Manhattan, anche a costo di dover fare un po' di fila. È situato di fronte a Central Park e solitamente è frequentato solo da newyorchesi. Ottime le patatine, ma anche il cheesecake e il tortino al cioccolato caldo.

JOE'S PIZZA
Pizza
Two locations: 7 Carmine Street; 150 East 14th Street
www.joespizzanyc.com

They still are what they're always been: a classic NY slice joint. No glossy corporate backing, no fancy pants pies, no pretentious nonsense and no gimmicky budget pizza either. Established in 1975 by Joe Pozzuoli, Joe's Pizza is a Greenwich Village institution and a perennial Top 10 in restaurant guides and publications. In 2009 GQ listed Joe's Pizza as one of the "Best 25 Pizzas on Earth".

Ancora oggi questo posto è quello che è sempre stato: un rivenditore di pizza al trancio. Nessuna pretenziosità, nessun extra, niente sconti fasulli: solo buona pizza a prezzi onesti. Creato da Joe Pozzuoli nel 1975, Joe's Pizza è oggi una istituzione del Greenwinch Village ed è sempre nelle classifiche dei migliori ristoranti. Nel 2009 il magazine GQ lo ha inserito in quella deille migliori 25 pizze della Terra. Scusate se è poco.

LA LUCHA
Tacos
147 Avenue A (between 9th and 10th)
www.laluchanyc.com

A classic Taqueria, full of smells, flavors and colors, where people gather to eat tacos. And that's what La Lucha want to bring to NY, the opportunity for New Yorkers to get a taste of real Mexican street food. Once inside La Lucha you´ll be in Mexico´s City Downtown, a few blocks from Arena Coliseo, eating tacos, listening to mambo, and drinking rice water.

Un locale nato dall'amore per il wrestling e per i tacos. Se volete assaporare il vero cibo da strada messicano, siete finiti nel posto giusto. Dateci dentro con le quesadillas e i tacos, le tortillas e il formaggio fritto.

LA MAISON
THE CROQUE MONSIEUR
Sandwiches
17 East 13th Street
www.croquemr.com

The Croque Monsieur, a seemingly simple sandwich with a fantastically fancy name. It's a rustic - yet utterly sophisticated- treat. At once salty, smokey, creamy, cheesy, crunchy. La Maison du Croque Monsieur in Greenwich Village is the world's first eatery dedicated solely to the culinary classic. On the menu are savory, breakfast and sweet variations of the sandwiches.

Il nome trae in inganno: si tratta di un posto dove mangiare dei sandwich, ma che sandwich! Croccanti, cremosi, pieni di formaggio. Le parole non bastano: dovete provarli.

NOM WAH
Dim Sum
13 Doyers Street
www.nomwah.com

The oldest Dim Sum restaurant in NYC, dating back to the 1920's. Where? In Chinatown, of course. All dishes are shown as pictures. We suggest to order the Fried dim sum sampler: 8 pieces of assorted fried dim sum (for $ 9.95). This Tea Parlor offers also fried rice and noodles, ice cream and almond cookie.

Il più antico ristorante di Dim Sum a New York risale al 1920 e fu aperto ovviamente in Chinatown, dove ancora oggi si trova e riscuote successo. Vi consigliamo di partire con i quelli fritti: 8 pezzi a meno di 10 dollari sono "a good deal". Il Mom Wah non offre solo Dim Sum ma anche riso fritto, noodles, gelati e biscotti alle mandorle.

NUM PANG
Cambodian Sandwich
6 Locations in NYC: Union Square, Nomad, Times Square, Grand Central, Chelsea Market, Battery Park - **www.numpangnyc.com**

Bon Appetit named their sandwiches "one of the top 25 things to eat in 2012", The Village Voice awarded them "Best Sandwich of 2013", and they have been one of the highest rated sandwich shops in Zagat since opening. Ratha Chaupoly and Ben Daitz met on the Clark University Campus in 1994. The pair decided to open up the first Num Pang Sandwich shop near Union Square in March of 2009 and soon after a location in Midtown East. With graffiti art on the walls and 80s/90s hip hop blasting from the speakers, crowds extend all the way down the block to order these creative Asian sandwiches and sides that combine the flavors from Ratha's childhood in Cambodia with Ben's culinary technique.

Bon Appetit ha descritto i sandwich del Num Pang come "una delle 25 cose migliori da mangiare nel 2012". Il Village Voice li ha eletti "Best Sandwich del 2013". Zagat dà ogni anno al Num Pang un rating ottimo. Insomma, dovete andare in una delle sei locations disseminate per Manhattan: graffiti sui muri, musica hip hop nelle sale e, ovviamente, un buon sandwich di ispirazione asiatico-americana della premiata ditta Chaupoly-Daltz.

OM RESTAURANT
Indian
1593 Second Avenue
www.omrestaurantnyc.com

Amazing food with unbelievable flavors and surprising costs if you order "OM Special": one appetizer and one entrée for just $ 14.95. The menu offer a lot of lamb dishes, vegetarian and non vegetarian specialties. If you want fish: salmon tikka, tandoori shrimp, kochin crab curry. It's really difficult to find a negative review about this place.

Cibo incredibile con un costo sorprendente: un antipasto e un piatto principale per soli 15 dollari. Il menù offre tanti piatti a base di agnello, ma anche specialità per vegetariani, e tanto pesce, dal salmon tikka ai gamberi in tandori fino al granchio al curry. Trovare qualcosa di negativo in questo posto è davvero difficile.

THE HALAL GUYS
Halal
W. 53rd Street & 6th Avenue - W. 53rd Street & 7th Avenue - E. 14th Street & 2nd Avenue - LaGuardia - Community College - **www.thehalalguysny.com**

Recognized as the pioneer in quick-service street food cart service. The Halal Guys still consider street food cart an integral part of its business. It all started in 1990, when the founding partners opened a hot dog cart on West 53rd & 6th Avenue. They saw a huge demand among the Muslim cab drivers needing to have a halal Muslim meal... Today the quick-service halal street cart company is going national, creating a chain that keeps the core values and provides opportunities to new partners who want to share The Halal Guys experience.

In alcuni casi le recensioni e le parole sono superflue: per gli Halal Guys parla la fila di clienti che ogni giorno attendono pazientemente il loro piatto a base di pollo, riso, agnello, pane conditi con la magica salsa bianca (il tutto a soli 6 dollari). L'attività fu avviata da un emigrante egiziano nel 1990, e oggi questo carretto è divenuto una istituzione.

SALTIE
Sandwich and Sweets
378 Metropolitan Ave, Brooklyn
www.saltieny.com

Saltie is an eatery in Williamsburg, Brooklyn, that was created and is run by three pioneers of the Brooklyn food scene. The shop boasts a devoted following of diners who love their magnificent sandwiches, soups, egg bowls, drinks, and sweets.

Lo chiamano "sandwich shop", ma è molto più di un sandwich shop. Ve ne renderete conto dopo aver assaggiato il Captains Daughter (focaccia ripiena di sardine, uova, capperi, finocchio, prezzemolo e salsa verde: una delizia!) o lo Scuttlebutt sandwich (uova, cavoli, feta, olive, capperi). Biscotti e dolci non sono da meno.

SOUVLAKI
Greek Cuisine
116 Stanton Street
www.souvlakigr.com

A little "Taste of Mykonos" in the heart of New York City's Lower East Side. Often lovingly referred to as "the hamburger of Greece", souvlaki is undeniably the signature street food item in the country. With references of its preparation dating back to Ancient Greece, this perfect little sandwich has remained a constant in Greek food culture. A traditional combination of charcoal grilled meat, wrapped in a warm pita with the must-have accompaniment of tzatziki sauce, tomato, onion and french fries - just simple, fresh ingredients.

Sapori di Mykonos, una delle più famose isole greche, nel cuore di New York, nel Lower East Side. La specialità della casa sono ovviamente i souvlaki, lo spiedino di carne che dà il nome al locale e che può essere gustato nella classica pita, acocmpagnato da insalata, pomodori, salsa tzatziki, cipolle e patatine fritte.

THE PENROSE
American Bar
1590 Second Avenue
www.penrosebar.com

The Penrose, in the Upper East Side, is a bar for all times. From its crisp porcelain tile flooring, to its reclaimed wooden interiors and exposed brick walls, "The Penrose" is a place without pretense. Food, drinks, service and space are inspired by old American and Cork traditions.

Il Penrose, nell'Upper East Side, è un bar buono e bello a tutte le ore. L'ambiente creato dai mattoncini e dalle mattonelle in porcellana è davvero originale e accogliente. Un posto senza grandi pretese ma con un'unica promessa: farvi stare bene e farvi assaporare i sapori della cucina americana tradizionale.

SWEET GREEN
Vegeterian
NoMad: 1164 Broadway - Tribeca: 413 Greenwich St
www.sweetgreen.com

Founded in 2007, sweetgreen is a destination for delicious food that's both healthy for you and aligned with your values. They source local and organic ingredients from farmers. The food is delicious, healthy and transparent.

Se siete vegetariani, o volete semplicemente un pasto veloce a base di ingredienti freschi e salubri, Sweet Green è un'ottima scelta. Sul menù ogni pietanza è accompagnata dalle calorie che contiene. Le insalate sono ottime e originali, ma se volete potete comporle a vostro piacere. Lo yogurt è eccellente.

TACOMBI
Tacos
267 Elizabeth Street
www.tacombi.com

Born on the balmy beaches of the Yucatan, began selling tacos out of converted VW bus in Playa del Carmen. Now, comfortably parked in Nueva York, Tacombi on Elizabeth street transports people from the streets of Nolita to the streets of Mexico, offers a piece of the Mexican beachside lifestyle and shares with them the diversity of Mexican street food culture.

La storia del Tacombi iniziò vendendo tacos a bordo dello storico furgone della Volkswagen sulle spiagge di Playa del Carmen. Oggi il furgone è parcheggiato nel locale di Elizabeth Street, a New York (Nolita) e tutto intorno ci sono tavolini sempre pieni di bella gente. Non c'è la spiaggia, ma restano i tacos.

TAIM
Falafel & Smoothie Bar
222 Waverly Place, West Village
45 Spring Street, Nolita
www.taimfalafel.com

Taïm is the love child of husband and wife team, chef Einat Admony (search Balaboosta in this book) and Stefan Nafziger. In 2005, homesick for the favorite street food of Tel Aviv, they heard of a tiny store front available on quiet Waverly place and decided to open their own falafel shop. Relying on her years of international cooking experience as well as her roots, Einat created a menu centered around street food with a gourmet twist. The freshness and quality of the ingredients coupled with Taïm's spin on traditional falafel flavors give new meaning to the concept of fast food.

Taim è il nome del figlio della chef Einat Admony (proprietaria del Balaboosta, che trovate nella sezione Ristoranti di questo libro) e del marito Stefan Nafziger. E' anche il nome di questo locale che serve ottimi falafel e che nacque nel 2005 dalla voglia di servire lo street-food di Tel Aviv a New York. Einat ha creato un menù a base di cibo di strada impreziosito da trovate gourmet, dando vita ad un nuovo concetto di fast food.

SHOPPING
in New York

New York è la capitale dello shopping. Nessun'altra città al mondo vi offre così tante alternative: dai mega shopping centre ai mercatini, dai negozi di lusso a quelli vintage. Ce n'è per tutti i gusti. E per tutte le tasche

No other city in the world offers so many alternatives: mega shopping centers, street-markets, luxury shops, vintage stores... There's really something for everyone. And for all budgets

ATRIUM
644 Broadway
www.atriumnyc.com

SUPREME
274 Lafayette Street
www.supremenewyork.com

THE MARKET
159 Bleecker Street
www.themarketnyc.com

Since 1994, Atrium has been known for its extensive selection of fashion-forward merchandise and has become the ultimate destination for risk-taking style. With a 7,500 square foot flagship in Manhattan, and locations in Brooklyn and Miami Beach, Atrium provides a personalized shopping experience that draws everyone from industry insiders and celebrities, to the everyday shopper. The company's mission is simple - to provide customers with today's best fashion brands and tomorrow's top trends.

Atrium è un negozio incredibile dove potrete trovare capi costosissimi accanto a pezzi a buon mercato. In entrambi i casi si tratta comunque di capi unici, spesso di grandi marche. Tenetelo d'occhio soprattutto in periodo di saldi.

In April 1994, Supreme opened its doors on Lafayette Street in downtown Manhattan and became the home of New York City skate culture. At its core was the gang of rebellious young New York skaters and artists who became the store's staff, crew and customers. Supreme grew to be the embodiment of the downtown culture, playing an integral part in its constant regeneration. Skaters, punks, hip-hop heads - the young counter culture at large - all gravitated towards Supreme.
While it grew into a downtown institution, Supreme established itself as a brand known for its quality, style and authenticity.
Over its eighteen year history, Supreme has worked with some of our generation's most groundbreaking designers, artists, photographers and musicians - all who have helped continue to define its unique identity and attitude.

Se avete figli adolescenti, non uscirete da qui senza aver comprato almeno un cappellino. Perché Supreme è uno dei brand più di tendenza tra i giovanissimi.

The Market NYC is located in the heart of trendsetting Greenwich Village at 159 Bleecker Street, between Sullivan and Thompson Streets. It's one of the largest indoor markets in New York City and the biggest retail store on historic Bleecker Street. From designer clothes and jewelry to vintage, art books, lamps, hand-made soap, artifacts, paintings, eyewear and collectibles, The Market pulsates with creativity. On any day, visitors can buy the most original designs and watch artisans at work, from designers sewing garments to silversmiths crafting rings.

Una collettiva di artigianato locale, artisti vari, creatori di abbigliamento. The Market riunisce una trentina di stand in cui potrete trovare tante idee regalo. E per di più si trova in una zona molto bella, soprattutto se siete in vena di spendere soldi.

UNIQLO
666 5th Avenue at 53rd Street
www.uniqlo.com

In 1984, Fast Retailing, headed by Tadashi Yanai, opened the first UNIQLO store in Hiroshima, Japan. Since then, the brand has evolved from a chain of roadside stores to an international leader in style, quality, and fun. It doesn't matter who you are or where you live, UNIQLO makes clothes that transcend all categories and social groups.

UNIQLO è una creazione del giapponese Tadshi Yanal e attrae masse di giovani e di genitori quarantenni che amano vestirsi in maniera unica, senza fare sconti alla qualità e al divertimento.

THE CHALCK BOARD
341 Lafayette St., between Bleecker + Bond

A chalck board on your t-shirt. A nice idea. An original gift for children.

Il modo più originale per personalizzare la propria T-Shirt e averne una diversa ogni giorno: le magliette con la lavagna e i gessetti sono un must che non potete perdervi. Faranno contenti i bambini, ma anche i più grandi.

TOWN HOUSE SHOPS
504 West Broadway (on Laguardia Place)
www.townhouseshops.com

Imagine a place where you can shop comfortably for the latest fashion trends or timeless accessories... with friendly and helpful customer service, never pushy... all at a reasonable price! This is Town House Shops... Welcome home to trends, friends, and timeless treasures...

Immaginate un posto dove poter comprare in tutta serenità e comodità le ultime novità o accessori senza tempo... con un servizio amichevole e professionale, e sempre a prezzi ragionevoli. Bene, Town House è tutto questo. Benvenuti.

SHOPPING

UNITED NUDE
25 Bond Street
www.unitednude.com

UN has positioned itself at the intersection of design and fashion and has gained international recognition for the brand's creative work. Known for clarity, elegance and innovation, United Nude shoes are sold in over 40 countries, with flagship stores in Amsterdam, London and New York.

Questo posto colpisce le donne (ma anche gli uomini) per il design del punto vendita, per le sue luci, per l'originalità dei modelli di scarpe in vendita, e per la possibilità di farsi stampare il proprio modello con la stampante 3D. Assolutamente da vedere.

BOND No9
9 Bond St/ Lafayette Street
www.bondno9.com

For the first time in fragrance history, a major, full-blown fragrance collection was launched as an homage to a great city. The name of this fragrance collection is Bond No. 9 (which is also the address of its headquarters boutique at 9 Bond Street, in NoHo). The city, of course, is New York. The Bond No. 9 collection of women's, men's, and unisex eaux de parfum, has a dual mission: restore artistry to perfumery, and mark every New York neighborhood with a scent of its own. Each fragrance represents a specific downtown, midtown, or uptown locale, or a city-wide sensibility. With new introductions every season, Bond No. 9 infuses the island of Manhattan with scents. Bond No. 9 was created and founded by Laurice Rahme in 2003.

Un profumo? Qui ne troverete a volontà: unici, floreali, leggeri o forti, unisex, per uomo e per donna. Avrete solo una difficoltà: riuscire a sceglierne solo uno.

MACY'S
151 West 34th Street
www.macys.com

No one would have guessed that the small, fancy dry goods store that opened on the corner of 14th Street and 6th Avenue in New York City in 1858 would grow to be one of the largest retailers in the world. Tioday Macy's, Inc. is one of the nation's premier omnichannel retailers, with 2014 sales of $28 billion. The company operates the Macy's and Bloomingdale's brands with about 825 stores in 45 states.

Si può andare a New York senza fare un salto da Macy'S? No, non si può. Perché in tema di shopping questo mega-store è una istituzione, e malgrado il passare degli anni, resta una tappa obbligata per acquisti a prezzi scontatissimi nel settore abbigliamento, casa, elettronica.

MARIMEKKO
200 5th Ave
www.marimekko.com

The name Marimekko is a play on words, yet completely descriptive. 'Mari' is an anagram of the first name of the company's founder, Armi Ratia, while 'mekko' means 'dress' in Finnish. And it was indeed Mari's dresses that started it all in 1951.

Il nome Marimekko nasce da un gioco di parole: Mari è l'anagramma del nome del fondatore dell'azienda, Armi Ratia, mentre Mekko in finlandese significa "vestito" . E fu così che nel 1951 nacque questo marchio di abbigliamento che negli Usa riscuote grande successo.

FOXY & WINSTON
392 Van Brunt Street, Red Hook, Brooklyn
www.fozyandwinston.com

Jane Buck established Foxy & Winston (named after her parents who live in Norfolk, England) in 2005. Her charming shop and studio (opened in 2009) is in Red Hook, Brooklyn, just a few short blocks from the water and nestled in amongst a row of wonderfully unique stores. Here she creates playful and vibrant designs on stationery and textiles, using screen printing and letterpress techniques. Over the years she has built a reputation from her whimsical line of paper goods, organic screen-printed textiles and custom letterpress stationery.

Foxy & Winston fu creato da Jane Buck nel 2005. Il suo incantevole negozio-studio si trova a Red Hook, Brooklyn, non lontano dal mare e in una zona ricca di negozietti carini. Qui potrete trovare strani oggetti di design che vi lasceranno a bocca aperta: tessuti, capi d'abbigliamento, lettere d'auguri, accessori, articoli per la casa.

BAKED
359 Van Brunt Street, red Hook, Brooklyn
www.bakednyc.com

Matt Lewis and Renato Poliafito started Baked in January 2005 in the neighborly neighborhood of Red Hook, Brooklyn. They really like dessert. Perhaps, a little too much. They tend to think of themselves as dessert archeologists - digging and researching and eating their way through the regional desserts of America. They spend a disproportionate amount of their vacation time in bakeries, chocolate shops, coffee houses and used book stores and they spend almost all of their discretionary income on cake and coffee and cookies and wine. They still own and operate the bakery (with a lot of help) in addition to writing best-selling cookbooks creating cool new products and building empires (or something like that).

Matt Lewis e Renato Poliafito avviarono Baked nel gennaio 2005 nel quartiere di Red Hook, a Brooklyn. Amavano e amano i dolci, forse anche troppo, e amano descriversi come gli archeologi del dessert, perché trascorrono quasi tutto il loro tempo e i loro guadagni tra pasticcerie, libri dedicati ai dolci, panetterie, vini e biscotti. Le loro creazioni sono una gioia per gli occhi e per il palato.

URBAN OUTFITTERS
www.urbanoutfitters.com

ANTHROPOLOGIE
85 Fifth Avenue / 16th Street
www.anthropologie.com

M&M's World
Times Square, 1600 Broadway
www.mmsworld.com

Founded in 1970, Urban Outfitters operates more than 130 stores in the United States, Canada and Europe, all offering an eclectic mix of merchandise. Stores thinked for persons with interest in contemporary art, music and fashion. From men's & women's apparel and accessories to items for the apartment, UO offer a lifestyle-specific shopping experience for the educated, urban-minded individual in the 18 to 30 year-old range.

Fondato nel 1970, oggi Urban Outfitters è negli States un marchio di successo con più di 130 stores, ognuno dei quali offre un mix eclettico di articoli che vanno dall'abbigliamento agli accessori (anche per la casa), fino ai dischi e ai libri. Negozi davvero belli, moderni, ben curati, con tante chicche di cui è facile innamorarsi.

Founded in 1992 in Wayne, Pennsylvania, Anthropologie has grown into a one-of-a-kind destination for those seeking a curated mix of clothing, accessories, gifts and home décor to reflect their personal style and fuel their lives' passions.

Nato nel 1992 in Pennsylvania, il brand Anthropologie si è subito imposto come destinazione obbligata per quanti cercano un mix di vestiti, accessori, idee regalo e home decòr di qualità.

Opened in 2006 and positioned in the heart of Times Square, M&M'S® World features 25,000 square feet on three levels that are packed with a huge range of exclusive M&M'S® chocolates and merchandise, including clothing, kitchenware, bedding, jewelry, and glassware, as well as seasonal items and specially-designed New York-themed M&M'S branded products.
In 2012 M&M'S® World New York launched the Personalized Printer, which will allow guests to create customized M&M'S® right in the store. Store visitors can select from a variety of images, as well as create customized messages that will be printed on M&M'S® Brand Milk Chocolate Candies in about two minutes.

Aperto nel 2006, M&M'S World è divenuto una piccola destinazione turistica per le famiglie in viaggio con i figli. Il flagship store di Times Squares offre l'opportunità di divertirsi e di creare i propri M&M'S personalizzati.

ALDO (Shoes)
10 stores in Manhattan
www.aldoshoes.com

PIQ
8 Grand Central Terminal
www.piqproducts.com

DEWEY'S CANDY
141 Front Street, Brooklyn
www.deweyscandy.com

Guided by a strong set of values, Aldo Bensadoun set out to build a "different" kind of modern company, one founded on compassion and ethics, aiming to influence society in both fashion and social responsibility. Simply put, Mr. Bensadoun created a brand with a conscience; a brand that cares. Specializing in the design and production of quality, stylish and accessible footwear and accessories, the ALDO Group has an unsurpassed knowledge of the shoe retail business.

Uno dei marchi di scarpe più diffusi e amati in America: nei tanti negozi di Manhattan troeverete sempre nuovi interessanti modelli ma anche il corner con i saldi del momento.

PIQ's clever and colorful brand serves as a one stop shopping destination, seamlessly integrating an assortment of globally curated products that is sure to induce smiles on faces of all ages. The New York Times describes PIQ's diversity as, "There's a new aspect in retail that's a mix of day-to-day with designer toys. So the grandmother can come in and find something for the grandchildren, and at the same time find something for herself." The brand is constantly adapting to the ever-changing marketplace as well as taking on the unique personality of each new city it resides in.

Se cercate una idea regalo o qualcosa di curioso e innovativo, non eprdetevi questo negozietto situato nella galleria di Gran Central Terminal. Tanti oggetti di design a prezzi abbordabili.

A store that exude happines, fun, and is inviting for people of all ages. Young and old loves candies, and you'll love this store owned by Allison "Dewey" Oblonsky and located in Brooklyn. This is, without doubt, the sweetest spot in Dumbo.

Un negozio sinonimo di divertimento, felicità, colore. Interessante per gente di ogni età, perché tutti amiamo i dolci e le caramelle. Questo è senza dubbio il negozio più dolce di Dumbo.

LIK (Gallery)
419 West Broadway
www.lik.com

A true survivor of Manhattan's competitive art world, LIK SOHO is one of the proud and few prominent galleries remaining in the hip and trendy downtown neighborhood. Since opening in 2008, this fine art gallery from Peter Lik has become a fixture among premiere shopping, popular bars, and top restaurants. The clean interior aesthetic of white and gray walls, allow the magical landscape images to immediately engage the viewer. The theme of classic NYC icons is proudly emphasized here, including the awe-inspiring vision, "Empire." A true New York experience awaits you at LIK SOHO.

Se siete alla ricerca di quadri interessanti, pezzi unici, stampe d'autore.la galleria Lik a Soho troverà quel che fa per voi.

APPLE
767 Fifth Avenue - 45 Grand Central Terminal
www.apple.com

Think different. Be different. Each Apple store in Manhattan is unique and amazing.

Pensa differente. Sii differente. Come i vari Apple Store di Manhattan: ognuno diverso dall'altro. Ognuno unico e stupendo.

MC NALLY JACKSON STORE
234 Mulberry Street
www.mcnallyjacksonstore.com

If you are a nostalgic of the pre-digital age, you'll love this store that sells notebooks and desk accesories, gift-cards, pens and pencils, lights, chairs.

Se siete dei nostalgici dell'era pre-digitale, o se siete allergici a computer e iPad, amerete questo negozio che vende accessori da scrivania, lettere, penne e matite, lampade e sedie da lettura.

THE MEADOW (Food)
523 Hudson Street
www.atthemeadow.com

MAST BROTHERS
111 North 3rd Street, Brooklyn
www.mastbrothers.com

BELLOCQ (Tea)
104 West Street, Brooklyn
www.bellocq.com

The Meadow is a place where the beautiful, the delicious, and the unexpected are brought together for your pleasure. It is specialized in artisan salt, great chocolate bars, bitters and other gourmet items for the bar and kitchen, and in Portland, carry a close selection of Oregon and European wines and vermouths. The Meadow also offers full service floristry, and the air is suffused in the aromas and colors of fresh cut flowers arranged with imagination and a love of nature. With a close selection of books on food and culture, curated works of art, and a few comfortable chairs set by the window, The Meadow is a place where you can step outside of time for a moment, linger, and let your mind wander.

The Meadow è un posto in cui bellezza, bontà e sorpresa si fondono per il vostro piacere. Specializzato in sale, cioccolato, vermouth e vini, offre anche una selezione di libri dedicati al cibo e alla cultura del buon vivere. Da vedere.

An amazing artisanal chocolate factory in Brooklyn. Sourcing cocoa with unique flavor profiles, Michael and Rick Mast roast the beans in small batches and then hand wrap each bar with custom-designed papers. Their many varietals make ideal gifts for bakers and chocolate lovers.

Una fantastica fabbrica del cioccolato. Si trova a Brooklyn ed è la creatura dei fratelli Michael e Rick Mast, che vendono le loro barrette in carta pregiata di design. Così la cioccolata diventa una idea-regalo.

The award-winning tea company and purveyor of evocative artisan blends, has relocated their 'tea atelier' to Greenpoint, New York following the success of their Kings Road, London shop, Bellocq Tea Atelier. The business, which offers a unique and evocative line of handcrafted blends, with seductive names such as 'Kikuya', 'Le Hammeau' and 'Noble Savage', also curates an inspiring selection of the organic full leaf teas. Bellocq is refining the luxury tea business to suit the evolving and sophisticated taste of the modern client.

Se siete appassionati di tea, allora non potete perdervi una visita in questo negozio di Greenpoint, da sempre pluripremiato per le sue selezioni di blend artigianali.

Jeryl Brunner
Journalist, Author

(www.jerylbrunner.com)

Jeryl is a reporter, writer, people wrangler, explorer and thrill seeker. And she is the author of the books "My City, My Los Angeles" and "My City, My New York".

What do you like about NYC and Newyorkers?
New Yorkers are a passionate bunch and we sacrifice and put up with a lot to live here. The lack of space. Tiny apartments. The noise. The constant intensity. But we know it's all worth it!

What do you dislike about NYC and Newyorkers?
The lack of space. Tiny apartments. The noise. The cost of things.

What's your best restaurants?
Fred's at Barneys. Rotisserie Georgette. Luigi's.

A place for shopping?
The Sunday flea market on Columbus Avenue (at 76th Street).

Your favourite place/area in the city?
Central Park and the bike path along the Hudson River.

A place or a thing that tourists can't miss?
Don't miss the opportunity to see live theater.

Your next project/dream?
Performing and more performing.

(italian text at page 363)

PLEASE DO NOT LEAN ON GLASS RAIL

*There are a lots
of things you can do
with your kids
in New York...*

Ci sono tante cose che
potete fare e vedere a
New York con i vostri figli...

FAMILY
attractions

AMERICAN MUSEUM OF NATURAL HISTORY

Central Park West at 79th Street
www.amnh.org

The American Museum of Natural History is one of the world's preeminent scientific and cultural institutions. Since its founding in 1869, the Museum has advanced its global mission to discover, interpret, and disseminate information about human cultures, the natural world, and the universe through a wide-ranging program of scientific research, education, and exhibition. The Museum is open daily from 10 am to 5:45 pm except on Thanksgiving and Christmas.

Una delle istituzioni scientifiche e culturali più importanti e popolari al mondo. Fin dalla sua fondazione, che risale al 1869, il museo è stato sempre un pioniere nelle attività di scoperta, interpretazione e diffusione dei fenomeni naturali, scientifica e culturali. E' aperto ogni giorno dalle 10 alle 5.45.

CENTRAL PARK

www.centralparknyc.org

Central Park is the 843-acre masterpiece of landscape architecture designed in the 19th century by Frederick Law Olmsted and Calvert Vaux and designated New York City's first scenic landmark in 1974. As one of America's greatest works of art and the nation's first public park, Central Park has become the most famous and beloved urban park in the world. The Park covers the land from 59th Street to 110th Street between Fifth Avenue and Central Park West (Eighth Avenue).
Central Park is open daily from 6:00 am until 1:00 am. FREE entry for everyone since 1858.

Non c'è nulla che più e meglio di Central Park incarni lo spirito di New York: gigantesco, bellissimo, sorprendente, sempre animato e pieno di vita ed eventi. È il parco più bello del mondo: stupendo in primavera, rinfrescante d'estate

BROOKLYN BRIDGE

The Brooklyn Bridge opened in 1883. At the time, it was the longest suspension bridge. It has been designated a National Historic Landmark by the National Park Service, and a New York City Landmark by the Landmarks Preservation Commission. More than 120,000 vehicles, 4,000 pedestrians and 3,100 bicyclists cross the Brooklyn Bridge every day.

Aperto nel 1883, su progetto del tedesco John Augustus Robeling, è stato il primo ponte costruito con l'acciaio e a lungo è rimasto il ponte sospeso più lungo al mondo. Collega Manhattan a Brooklyn: la passeggiata di circa due chilometri è una esperienza indimenticabile, perché permette di godere di viste panoramiche sensazionali. La corsia per pedoni e biciclette è stata realizzata sopra le carreggiate riservate alle auto. A metà ponte, immancabili, ci sono i lucchetti dell'amore.

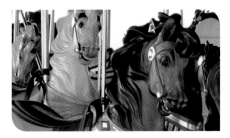

JANE'S CAROUSEL
East River, Brooklyn Bridge Park
www.janescarousel.com

A classic 3-row machine with 48 exquisitely carved horses and two superb chariots. It was created in 1922 by the Philapelphia Toboggan Company and originally installed in Idora Park in Youngstown (Ohio). In 1984 the carousel has been fully restored back to its original elegance, by Jane and David Walentas, in their studio in Dumbo. Jane's Carousel was installed in a spectacular pavilion designed by Pritzker Prize winning architect Jean Nouvel. It was opend to the public September 16, 2011

La giostra-carosello più bella al mondo è giusto ai piedi del ponte di Brooklyn, lato Dumbo. La corsa costa solo 2 dollari, e i vostri bambini apprezzeranno l'esperienza. Verificate giorni di chiusura e orari sul sito web.

EMPIRE STATE BUILDING
350 Fifth Ave Midtown West
www.esbnyc.com

Located in the center of Midtown Manhattan, the 86th and 102nd floor observatories provide unforgettable 360° views of New York City and beyond. Whether you're in town for a week or a day, no visit to NYC is complete without experiencing the top of the Empire State Building.

L'Empire State Building è molto più di una semplice vista panoramica. Rappresenta una esperienza coinvolgente all'interno di un simbolo di fama mondiale. Oltre alle terrazze panoramiche, la visita comprende la hall recentemente restaurata, con i suoi meravigliosi soffitti con dipinti Art Déco, la mostra di carattere storico "Il coraggio di sognare", la nuova mostra "Sostenibilità" e un dispositivo audio interattivo. Aperti ogni giorno dell'anno dalle 8:00 alle 2:00 di notte. L'ultimo ascensore sale all'1:15. Armatevi di pazienza: prima di arrivare all'86° piano, dovrete fare circa 1 ora e mezza di fila. Ma ne vale la pena. Biglietti: 26 dollari bambini, 29 adulti.

BROOKLYN'S CHILDREN MUSEUM
145 Brooklyn Avenue
www.brooklynkids.org

A pioneer in education, Brooklyn Children's Museum was the first museum created expressly for children when it was founded in 1899. Its success has sparked the creation of 300 children's museums around the world. With award-winning, hands-on exhibits and innovative use of its collections, the Museum engages children from pre-school to high school in learning adventures. The mission of Brooklyn Children's Museum is to actively engage children in educational and entertaining experiences through innovation and excellence in exhibitions, programs, and use of its collection. The Museum encourages children to develop an understanding of and respect for themselves, others and the world around them by exploring cultures, the arts, science, and the environment. Regular hours: 10am – 5 pm. Closed on Monday. Admission is $9.00 per person and free for Museum members and children under 1 year of age.

Quando fu inaugurato, nel 1899, il Brroklyn Children Museum fu il primo museo creato apposta per i ragazzi. Dopo il suo successo sono sorti nel mondo circa 300 musei per i più giovani. La mission è quella di educare i ragazzi coinvolgendoli in attività culturali, spettacoli, progetti.

MOIRA ANN SMITH PLAYGROUND

Madison Square Park between 24th and 25th Sts

www.madisonsquarepark.org

The Madison Square Park playground was dedicated to NYPD Officer Moira Ann Smith on March 10, 2012. Officer Smith was one of the many officers and emergency responders who answered the call of duty and selflessly gave their lives in order to save others on September 11, 2001.
The award-winning playground is open year-round from 7am to dusk.
Entrances are located just inside the park at Madison Avenue and 25th and 26th Streets.

*Il playground di Madison Square Park fu dedicato all'agente di polizia Moira Ann Smith il 10 Marzo del 2012. L'agente Moira fu uno dei primi a rispondere alle chiamate di emergenza che seguirono all'attacco terroristico dell'11 Settembre 2001.
Questo parco pluripremiato è aperto tutto l'anno dalle 7 del mattino fino all'imbrunire. Le entrate sono situate agli incroci tra la Madison Avenue, la 25sima e la26sima strada.*

TOY'S ARE US, M&M's, FAO SCHWARZ, LEGO'S, DYSNEY STORES

These are not only shops or stores: these are wonders for children and a jump-back in time for their parents. The flagship stores of these brands are a must-see for young and adult, and each of them has something different.
Do not miss the ride on the wheel at Toy's, the magical atmosphere of FAO Schwarz, the pictures with the characters of Dysney, the hundreds colors of M&M's.

Questi non sono negozi, sono meraviglie per i bambini e salti indietro nel tempo per i loro genitori. I flagship stores di questi brand sono tappe imperdibili per grandi e piccini, ed ognuno di loro ha qualcosa di diverso e sorprendente dagli altri. Non perdetevi il giro sulla ruota panoramica da Toy's, la magica atmosfera di Fao Schwarz, le foto con i personaggi di Dysney, il pieno di M&M's.

CONEY ISLAND LUNA PARK

1000 Surf Avenue, Brooklyn

www.lunaparknyc.com

Coney Island is a popular NYC tourist destination. Located just a few short miles east of Manhattan, it presented a perfect seaside getaway for the fast-growing population. Coney Island is home to three rides protected as New York City landmarks listed in the National Register of Historic Places. The Wonder Wheel (1918), now part of Deno's Wonder Wheel Amusement Park, the Coney Island Cyclone roller coaster (1927), owned by the City and operated by Luna Park and the towering Parachute Jump (1938), no longer in action since 1968 but still standing strong since its rousing debut at the 1939 New York World's Fair.

Una delle icone di New York, è il parco giochi più ripreso nei film americani. Per arrivarci sono necessari dai 25 ai 50 minuti di metro (dipende dalla vostra posizione a Manhattan), ma ne vale la pena. Il giro sulla ruota panoramica è d'obbligo. Per i più temerari ci sono altre attrazioni più moderne. Ma andare a Coney Island sarà come fare un tuffo nel passato, in una New York quasi scomparsa.

BRONX ZOO
2003 Southern Boulevard, Bronx
www.bronxzoo.org

Despite its name, this is not just a zoo, but a real amusement park, which offers the Dinosaur Safari, the ride on the Wild Asia Monorail, or the Shuttle, or the ride on camels, the aquarium and the 4-D theater, the Bug Carousel... Stay sure: your kids will have so much to do and see.
Tickets: from $ 21. Children under 2 are free.

A dispetto del suo nome, questo non è solo uno zoo, ma un vero e proprio parco divertimenti, che offre il Safari dei Dinosauri, il giro sulla Wild Asia Monorail o il giro in Shuttle, la corsa sui cammelli, l'acquario e il teatro in 4-D, la Bug Carousel e tanto altro ancora. Insomma, i vostri bambini avranno tanto da fare e da vedere. Biglietti: da 21 dollari. I bambini sotto i 2 anni entrano gratis.

WOLLMAN ICE SKATING RINK IN CENTRAL PARK
Central Park South (59th Street) and 6th Avenue
www.wollmanskatingrink.com

The most beautiful and romantic ice rink in the world opens every year in late October. You can skate admiring the magnificent view, or take lessons in skating and hockey with professional instructors. The rink opens at 10am and close at different times depending on the day of the week.

La pista di ghiaccio più bella e romantica al mondo apre ogni anno a fine ottobre. Potete pattinarci liberamente, ammirando il panorama meraviglioso, oppure prendere lezioni di skating e hockey con istruttori professionisti. La pista apre alle 10 e chiude in orari diversi a seconda dei giorni della settimana.

BOOKS OF WONDER and BARNES&NOBLES
33 East 17th Street - **www.barnesandnoble.com**
18 W 18th St - **www.booksofwonder.com**

Two wonderful bookshops for children and adults, with collective readings, meetings with authors, cultural events. The historical site of B&N is located in the amazing Union Square, while the Books of Wonder is located at the 18 West of the 18th Street (between Fifth and Sixth Avenue) inside the Ladies Mile shopping district.

Due meravigliose librerie per bambini e ragazzi, dove si organizzano letture collettive, incontri con gli autori, eventi culturali. La sede storica di B&N si trova nella vivacissima Union Square, mentre Books of Wonder la trovate al 18 West della 18esima Strada (tra la quinta e la sesta Avenue) all'interno del Ladies Mile shopping district.

Angel of Harlem

"YOU SHOULD GO TO THE CITY OF BLINDING LIGHTS". He just said it out loud, as only he could do, as he was telling me about where he was born and the story of how he met my grandmother. It must have been the seventh or eighth time I heard that story, but I was never tired of listening. You can't tell your grandfather to be quiet. You can't tell him that you already know the ending, especially if telling the story makes him smile again, it makes him happy and it brings back memories of the person he has loved for a lifetime.

"What nonno?"

"You told me they call it like that, right? Your New York, the city of blinding lights?"

"Yes, nonno, they call it like that too, well, they do in that song that I forced you to listen to I don't know how many times ..."

"City of blinding lights" by U2 (from the album "*How to Dismantle an Atomic Bomb*"), not one of their best songs, but for me, it has a special significance, because it's about the city that I love, where I would have liked to live and work, or at least tried do something.

One day, we were on the balcony, and my grandfather asked me: *"Why do you like this song so much?"*

"Because it's about a city that I love."

He looked at me with his big bright eyes, after remaining silent for a moment, and then said: *"If you love her so much, you should let her know, sooner or later."* I smiled, and then we ended up speaking about something else.

"DOVRESTI ANDARE NELLA CITTÀ DELLE LUCI ACCECANTI". La frase la gettò li, come solo lui sapeva fare, mentre mi raccontava del suo paese natale e di come conobbe la nonna. Era la settima o l'ottava volta che sentivo quella storia, ma non mi sarei mai stancato di ascoltarla. Perché un nonno non si può zittire. Non puoi dirgli che già conosci il finale, specie quando la storiella gli fa tornare il sorriso, lo rende felice e gli riporta alla mente la persona che ha amato per una vita.

"Cosa nonno?"

"Mi avevi detto che la chiamano così, vero, la tua New York, la città delle luci accecanti?"

"Si, nonno, la definiscono anche così, almeno in quella canzone che per qualche mese ti ho costretto ad ascoltare non so più quante volte...".

Era "City of blinding lights" degli U2 (dal cd "*How to dismantle an atomic bomb*"), non uno tra i loro pezzi migliori, ma per me aveva un significato particolare, perché era riferita alla città che amavo, in cui mi sarebbe piaciuto vivere e lavorare, o quanto meno fare qualcosa.

Un giorno, eravamo in balcone, il nonno mi chiese: *"Ma perché ti piace cosi tanto questa canzone?"*.

"Perché parla di una città che adoro".

Lui mi squadrò con quegli occhioni vivi e lucidi, restò un attimo in silenzio, poi sentenziò: *"Se la adori così tanto, dovresti farglielo capire, prima o poi"*. Io sorrisi, e poi finimmo col parlare d'altro.

About a year later, my grandfather's health conditions were aggravated, he was 82 years old and his body was starting to give up on him. I had marriage problems with my wife, and even if we both madly loved our two children, we were risking to blow up the invisible shell that protected them. To make matters worse, my business was falling apart: a five year crisis, but especially my two business partners deciding to leave at the first signs of recession. They just thought about saving their interests and leaving. As usual, I thought I would make it alone, but the burden became too heavy and the time to make drastic decisions had arrived.

My grandfather knew everything, as any good old patriarch he didn't even need to ask certain things to know about them. I couldn't hide my state anyway. I was about to enter the tunnel of depression, I was speaking less and less and I had lost my smile and even my ways of joking about everything.

I don't know why, but grandparents always know when to intervene. And above all, they know how to do it with an effect. He started speaking in a roundabout way, from the title of that song, and I don't know how he even still remembered it.

We were at the waterfront, I was pushing him in his wheelchair. It was a wonderful day, sunny but not hot. He had agreed to leave the house, which was unusual, on one condition: *"If I feel that I'm about to pee on myself, we return home immediately."* The walk lasted longer than I had expected, and we stopped to have an ice cream. When he decided that the moment had arrived, he made no effort to find the right words.

"Perhaps it's time to go to the city of blinding lights. Take a break to think. And take these as well."

He pulled out an envelope from his jacket. Inside were 1500 euro.

"I wanted to take nonna on a cruise with these, but her disease was faster. I would come with you, but in a wheelchair I think I would weigh you down. I'd like to see what you find so exciting about that city".

I had tears in my eyes at the thought of the money set aside for his last holiday with my grandmother, who died six months earlier. I tried to hint an answer: *"I can't leave now, nonno, everything will explode."*

His tone was peremptory as usual: *"Nonsense, nothing will explode here. Companies are made and they end. You make others. And the crisis will end sooner or later, money can't disappear. I've seen others, you know, of these... what do they call them now? Recessions? Surely they haven't been as difficult, but in the end, they all finish. And some even did some good to this crazy world. Don't worry, it definitely won't be this trip that ruins your marriage. You can tell the children that you are going for work. Go to New York, and clean up your head. Maybe even your heart."*

Facing words like these, you realize that you can't argue. I hugged him and thanked him. But not enough. Not as much as he deserved. And when I tried to open my mouth he stopped me: *"Now take me home because these diapers don't hold for more than a few hours."*

Era trascorso forse più di un anno da quel dialogo. Le condizioni di salute del nonno si erano aggravate, aveva ormai 82 anni e il fisico non reggeva più. Io ero entrato in crisi con mia moglie, e malgrado amassimo entrambi alla follia i nostri due figli, stavamo rischiando di far saltare il guscio che li proteggeva. Per di più la mia azienda andava a rotoli: cinque anni di crisi, ma soprattutto la fuoriuscita dei due soci, che al primo alito di recessione avevano pensato bene di pararsi il culo e andarsene, si erano fatti sentire. Avevo pensato di farcela da solo, come al solito, ma il fardello era divenuto troppo pesante ed il tempo delle decisioni drastiche era ormai giunto.

Mio nonno sapeva tutto, da buon vecchio patriarca non aveva nemmeno il bisogno di chiedere certe cose per venirne a conoscenza. Io del resto non riuscivo nemmeno più a nascondere il mio stato. Stavo per entrare nel tunnel della depressione, parlavo sempre meno, avevo perso il sorriso e perfino il vizio di scherzare su tutto.

Non so perché, ma i nonni sanno quando devono intervenire. E soprattutto sanno come farlo in maniera convincente. Lui la prese alla larga, partendo dal titolo di quella canzone che, non so come, ancora ricordava.

Eravamo sul lungomare, lui sulla sedia a rotelle, io che lo spingevo. Era una giornata meravigliosa, soleggiata ma non calda. E lui stranamente aveva accettato di uscire da casa, a una condizione: *"Se capisco che me la sto per fare addosso, torniamo immediatamente a casa".* La passeggiata durò più del previsto, e ci fermammo a mangiare un gelato. Quando decise che il momento era arrivato, non fece alcuno sforzo per trovare le parole.

"Forse è venuto il momento di andare nella città delle luci accecanti. Prenditi una pausa di riflessione. E prenditi pure questi".

Tirò fuori dalla giacca una busta da lettera. Dentro c'erano 1500 euro.

"Avrei voluto portarci la nonna in crociera, con questi, ma la sua malattia è stata più veloce. Verrei con te, ma sulla sedia a rotelle penso che ti sarei di peso. Vorrei proprio vedere cosa ci trovi di così eccitante in quella città".

Avevo le lacrime agli occhi, al pensiero di quei soldi messi da parte per l'ultima vacanza con la nonna, scomparsa sei mesi prima. Accennai una risposta: *"Non posso andarmene ora, nonno, qui salta tutto".*

Il suo tono fu perentorio come al solito: *"Stupidaggini, qui non salta proprio nulla. Le aziende nascono e muoiono. Se ne creano altre. E la crisi prima o poi finirà: i soldi non possono scomparire. Ne ho viste altre, sai, di queste... come le chiamano ora? Recessioni? Sicuramente non sono state così dure, ma alla fine, sono tutte finite. E qualcuna ha fatto perfino del bene a questo pazzo mondo. Stai tranquillo, non sarà certo questo viaggio a far saltare il tuo matrimonio. Ai bambini puoi dire che ci vai per lavoro. Vai a New York e ripulisci la tua testa. Magari anche il tuo cuore".*

Ecco, di fronte a parole così, ti rendi conto che non puoi replicare. Lo abbracciai e lo ringraziai. Ma non abbastanza. Non quanto meritava. E quando provai ad aprire bocca mi bloccò subito: *"Ora riportami a casa perché i pannoloni non reggono più di qualche ora".*

I had to go, otherwise I would have betrayed him, and that's the last thing I wanted to do. My grandfather had spent his whole life looking after his children and his grandchildren, and every time he gave me some advice I never regretted listening to him afterwards. I already had two good reasons to go: his "donation" and his words. I spent the night almost sleepless, thinking about how and when to leave. I was still unsure, but in the morning a third reason erased any doubts left. It was a sentence in the book I was reading, "*American Pastoral*" by Philip Roth: "Life is just a short period of time in which we are alive." I turned on the computer and booked the flight and the hotel. I wanted to feel alive.

Twenty days later I landed in New York on a United flight. From the airport, over a mountain of containers, I could see the breathtaking skyline. In the hotel shuttle bus there were nine other people with me, German, Dutch, and American. Some on holiday, a couple on their honeymoon, someone else looking for work. We arrived in the centre of Manhattan at 5pm, and a German, stunned by all the traffic and crowds of people in Times Square, asked the driver: "*Is it rush hour, or is there a problem?*" The black man, with the face of someone who has a joke ready for every question to answer, smiled: "*No, it's like this eight days a week. Welcome to Disney World.*"

Don't get bothered, the first night in New York you never sleep very well. If you're lucky you'll wake up at 6am. My eyes opened at 4:30am, and after trying in every possible way to get them to close again, I decided to go for a run in Central Park, the place I love the most in the Big Apple. I thought that at that time I would only have the company of a few homeless people, maybe some cleaners, but I found myself with dozens of cyclists and runners. There was a whole city already awake in that park. I put my headphones on and started running and listening to jazz. The second best soundtrack. The first, is the one sung by the resident birds in Central Park.

I had decided to try to do what I had not had the courage to do twenty years ago, when it would have been easier: try my luck elsewhere, in a city that felt more like home, exciting and alive. I wasn't ever the countryside type, but I never found the strength to cut that umbilical cord that binds you to your family and to the city where you were born. But then there were the financial and emotional crises. And I had a project that perhaps could work: a book about New York. Yes, I did realize that it wasn't a novelty, and when I entered the beautiful *Barnes&Noble* bookshop in Union Square, as I stood in front of dozens of books about the metropolis, for a moment, I thought about giving up. But I thought my idea was original. And luckily my head was still hard.

Non potevo non partire, l'avrei tradito, ed è l'ultima cosa che avrei voluto fare. Mio nonno aveva speso tutta la sua vita per i suoi figli e i suoi nipoti, e ogni volta che mi aveva dato un consiglio non mi ero mai pentito di averlo seguito. Avevo già due buoni motivi per partire: la sua "donazione" e le sue parole. Passai la notte quasi insonne, a pensare come e quando partire. Restava qualche piccolo dubbio, ma al mattino si profilò un terzo motivo che cancellò ogni dubbio. Me lo fornì una frase del libro che stavo leggendo, "*Pastorale americana*" di Philip Roth: "La vita è solo un breve periodo di tempo nel quale siamo vivi". Accesi il computer e prenotai volo e hotel. Volevo sentirmi vivo.

Venti giorni dopo atterravo a Newark con un volo United. Già dall'aeroporto puoi vedere, oltre la montagna di container, la skyline che toglie il fiato. Nello shuttle che mi accompagnava all'hotel c'erano altre nove persone: tedeschi, olandesi, americani. Qualcuno in vacanza, una coppia in viaggio di nozze, qualcun altro in cerca di lavoro. Arrivati nel caos delle cinque di pomeriggio nel centro di Manhattan, un tedesco, sbalordito per il traffico e la bolgia umana che affolla perennemente Times Square, chiede all'autista: "*È l'ora di punta o c'è qualche problema?*". L'uomo di colore, con la faccia di chi ha pronta una battuta per ogni domanda, accennò un sorriso: "*No, è così otto giorni la settimana. Benvenuti a Disney World*".

Mettetevi l'anima in pace: la prima notte a New York dormirete poco. E se va bene vi sveglierete alle 6. I miei occhi si sono aperti alle 4.30, e dopo aver provato in tutti i modi a farli richiudere, ho deciso che era meglio andare a correre in Central Park, che poi è il posto che più adoro della Grande Mela. Pensavo che a quell'ora sarei stato in compagnia di qualche barbone, magari degli addetti alle pulizie, e invece mi sono ritrovato trai decine di ciclisti e appassionati di running. C'era una intera città già sveglia in quel parco. Ho messo le cuffiette e ho iniziato a correre ascoltando musica jazz. È la colonna sonora più adatta. Dopo quella suonata dagli uccelli residenti a Central Park.

Avevo deciso di provare a fare quello che non avevo avuto il coraggio di fare venti anni prima, quando sarebbe stato tutto più facile: cercare fortuna altrove, in una città che sentissi mia, che fosse elettrizzante e viva. Non ero fatto per la provincia, ma non avevo mai trovato la forza di rompere quel cordone ombelicale che ti lega alla famiglia e alla città in cui si nasce. Ora c'erano le crisi. Quella economica e quella affettiva. E avevo un progetto che forse poteva funzionare: un libro su New York. Si, mi rendevo conto di non proporre una grande novità, e quando entrai nella bellissima libreria *Barnes&Noble* di Union Square, di fronte alle decine di libri dedicati alla metropoli, per un attimo pensai alla resa. Però pensavo di avere un'idea originale. E per fortuna la testa era ancora dura.

The first day at the BookExpoAmerica was a disaster, maybe because I was still tired from the journey and I felt I couldn't do my best. I showed four distributors the mock-up of the book, they all paid me compliments, but no one thought of adding it to their catalogue. At one point of the day it was even hard to understand people's words, and I couldn't make out if they really liked the book or if they were making fun of it. Tired and discouraged, I went to visit a friend who has been living and working in New York for 18 years. It's amazing how you can tell the story of a lifetime, or rather two, whilst having a pizza and a beer. Steve is doing well, a few years ago he bought a house in the East Village, before the prices went up and you could still afford to buy houses here. He has a job he loves, a wife and two beautiful daughters. He is happy, though - from what I understand - to live a decent life here, you need a monthly income of at least $ 5,000. In my world, there are those who live a year with that same amount.

/////

Maybe because I had slept more and better the second night, or because the sun was shining on Manhattan, the second day of appointments turned out to be great: four distributors had offered to put my book in their catalogues. I was only hoping for one, too much grace! And now, somehow, I had to choose who to trust. In these situations, you either have to be lucky or you have to find someone who can help you. But if you don't have time, and I only had a few days, you can only put your trust in luck. I made my choice thanks to another detail: Francesca, a friendly and helpful Italian. She worked in one of the companies that wanted my book and in only an hour, she immersed me in advice. But above all, there was a detail that made the difference. Francesca was born in the same village my grandfather was from. Do you believe in signs and in angels? I do. And sometimes I rely on them.

I was in seventh heaven. I had the opportunity to do something in New York, to make a dream I had decades ago finally come true. A dream I had the first time I set foot in Manhattan. It was my honeymoon. Another life, another world. Before the children, before Ground Zero, before the recession, and many other things.

I decided it was time to celebrate. I arrived at the Flatiron, in Madison Square Park, a place that I prefer to Times Square, because it's more real, less touristy, more like New York. I dove inside *Eataly*, one of the most fashionable places in the city. I reached the terrace bar and asked for a craft beer. Just what I needed, along with some company. I was definitely not alone: there were at least 100 young people and even many adults. An incredible chitchat. Many smiles and lots of drinking.
It had been years since I had last been alone in a bar or restaurant. I had done it too many times in the past. Then one day, while waiting for a pasta dish, I looked at the people around me: single parents, men

Il primo giorno di appuntamenti in fiera, al BookExpoAmerica, fu un disastro, forse perché ero ancora stanco del viaggio e sentivo di non rendere al meglio. Mostrai il mock-up del libro a quattro distributori, tutti mi fecero i complimenti, ma nessuno fu sfiorato dall'idea di inserirlo in catalogo. A un certo punto della giornata facevo perfino fatica a comprendere le parole degli interlocutori, e non capivo se il libro piaceva davvero o se mi prendessero in giro.
Stanco e sfiduciato, andai a trovare un amico che da 18 anni vive e lavora a New York. È incredibile come si riesca a raccontare una vita, anzi due, nel bel mezzo di una pizza e di una birra. A Steve è andata bene, qualche anno fa ha comprato casa nell'East Village, quando le case qui si potevano ancora acquistare, prima che i prezzi raggiungessero vette folli. Oggi Steve ha un lavoro che ama, una moglie e due splendide figlie. È felice, anche se - da quel che ho capito - per vivere qui in maniera dignitosa c'è bisogno di un reddito mensile non inferiore ai 5000 dollari. Mentre nel mio mondo c'è chi, con la stessa cifra, ci vive un anno.

/////

Sarà perché avevo dormito di più e meglio la seconda notte, sarà perché il sole splendeva su Manhattan, il secondo giorno di appuntamenti si rivelò eccezionale: quattro distributori si erano offerti di inserire il mio libro in catalogo. Ne cercavo uno, troppa grazia! E ora in qualche modo dovevo scegliere a quali mani affidarmi. In certe situazioni o hai culo oppure devi trovare qualcuno che ti consiglia bene. Se però non hai tempo, e io avevo solo qualche giorno, ti devi affidare alla fortuna. Scelsi sulla base di un altro dettaglio: in una delle aziende che volevano il mio libro c'era Francesca, un'italiana simpatica e disponibile che in un'ora mi inondò di consigli. Ma c'era, soprattutto, un particolare che faceva la differenza. Francesca era nata nello stesso paese di mio nonno. Credete in certi segnali e negli angeli? Io sì. E a volte mi affido alle loro mani.

Ero al settimo cielo. Avevo la possibilità di fare qualcosa a New York, di realizzare un sogno rimasto nel cassetto per vent'anni. Un sogno nato il primo giorno in cui misi piede a Manhattan. Era il viaggio di nozze. Un'altra vita, un altro mondo. Prima dei figli, prima di Ground Zero, prima della recessione e di tante altre cose.

Decisi che era il caso di festeggiare. Arrivai al Flatiron, in Madison Square Park, una piazza che preferisco a Times Square, perché è più reale, meno turistica, più newyorchese. Mi tuffai dentro Eataly, uno dei posti più in della città. Raggiunsi il bar sulla terrazza e chiesi una birra artigianale. Era quello che ci voleva, insieme ad un po' di compagnia. In effetti non ero solo: nel locale c'erano almeno 100 giovani e anche molti adulti. Un vociare incredibile. Tanti sorrisi e tante bevute.

and women who killed time with their iPads and smartphones. It was all so damn sad. I thought of my wife and my children, and the pleasure of dining with family. Since that day, I don't eat alone in restaurants anymore. I would rather skip a meal. Which isn't that bad after all. For my pockets and my figure.

But in New York it's different, you never feel alone, and anywhere you go, all you need to do is just smile or say "hello" to start speaking with people around you, man or woman makes no difference. It's like this everywhere: in parks, on the street, in restaurants. Especially in bars...

In fact I was alone for just ten minutes, then a black girl, a beautiful black girl, asked if she could sit next to me, because by then the place was packed and there were no more free tables. Her name was Eleanor and I had noticed her as soon as she entered the place. Let's say all the men had noticed her as she walked in. She was about six feet tall, long black hair, high heels, tight jeans on two amazing legs, a white blouse and a blue jacket. A vision. Sat next to me and that was speaking to me.

Now, a man has two types of daydreams when he leaves his adolescence affairs and decides to devote more attention to the other half of the sky: the first is to go to bed with two women, the second (if he's a white man) is having a relationship with a black woman. It's some sort of reversed racism. The curiosity to see what the other side of the river is like.

When Eleanor started talking, I looked into her eyes, occasionally glancing at her full lips and at her open blouse, and I thought: "Really Lord, too much grace today. Nearly a contract and a beautiful woman. All at once. Where's the catch?"

We started to get to know each other, and I discovered that you can tell the story of a lifetime, or rather two, even whilst having a beer and some fried mushrooms. So the pizza isn't strictly necessary to open up to who's in front of you.

Eleanor was divorced, currently single, working in a marketing agency and everything she said sounded like a poem. Evening came, we drank two more beers, and it was soon 10 o'clock. I told her that I was going to stay in New York for a few more days.

"*This is my card, I'd love to see you again.*" She smiled, we shook hands and I thought I would never see her again.

/////

"*How's it going?*"
"*Great, someone is interested in the project.*"
It wasn't Eleanor, but the voice I had spoken to for the past 25 years.
"*I'm sure you'll make it and that things will turn for the best.*" A muffled smile, she didn't hold back a tear, but then hid it, before the children burst through the iPad screen on the Skype call.
A few minutes later, after the children had gone, she was back: "*You're looking well. Maybe this trip will do us good. Nonno is always right.*"
"*Yeah, maybe it will do us good.*"
A glance, a smile, a virtual kiss, many thoughts, a lifetime together

Erano anni che non mi fermavo da solo in un locale o in un ristorante. L'avevo fatto fin troppe volte in passato. Poi un giorno, mentre attendevo il mio piatto di pasta, guardai la gente che mi stava intorno: genitori single, uomini e donne che ammazzavano il tempo maneggiando iPad e smartphone. Era tutto così maledettamente triste. Pensai a mia moglie e ai miei figli, al piacere di stare a tavola con la famiglia. Da quel giorno non mangiai più da solo al ristorante. Piuttosto saltavo i pasti. Il che non era poi così male. Per le tasche e per il fisico.

Ma a New York è diverso, hai la sensazione di non essere mai solo, e in qualsiasi posto entri, basta un sorriso o un "ciao" per attaccare bottone con chi ti sta accanto, uomo o donna che sia non importa. È così ovunque: nei parchi, per strada, al ristorante. Figuriamoci in una birreria...

Infatti rimasi in solitudine solo per una decina di minuti, poi una ragazza di colore, una stupenda ragazza di colore, mi chiese se poteva sedersi accanto a me, perché ormai il locale era strapieno e non c'erano più tavoli liberi. Si chiamava Eleanor e l'avevo notata appena entrata nella sala. Diciamo che l'avevano notata tutti gli uomini presenti nella birreria. Era alta un metro e ottanta circa, aveva lunghi capelli neri, tacchi alti, jeans aderenti su due gambe da urlo, camicetta bianca e giacca blu. Uno spettacolo della natura. Che mi sedeva accanto e mi parlava.

Ora, ci sono due sogni che un uomo fa ad occhi aperti fin da quando lascia gli affari adolescenziali per dedicare maggiore attenzione all'altra metà del cielo: la prima è andare a letto con due donne, la seconda (se è un uomo bianco) è avere una storia con una donna di colore. È una specie di razzismo al contrario. La curiosità di vedere com'è l'altra riva del fiume.

Quando Eleanor iniziò a parlare la guardavo negli occhi, sbirciando di tanto in tanto le sue labbra enormi e la camicetta aperta, e pensavo: "Davvero troppa grazia oggi, Signore. Un quasi contratto e una donna bellissima. Tutto insieme. Dov'è il trucco?".

Iniziammo a raccontarci le nostre storie, e scoprii che si può raccontare una vita, anzi due, anche tra una birra e dei funghi in pastella. Dunque la pizza non è strettamente necessaria per aprirsi a chi ti sta di fronte.

Eleanor era divorziata, al momento single, lavorava in una agenzia di marketing, viveva ad Harlem e ogni cosa che diceva era poesia. Divenne sera, bevemmo altre due birre, si fecero le 10. Le dissi che sarei rimasto a New York ancora per qualche giorno.

"*Questo è il mio biglietto, mi piacerebbe rivederti*".
Sorrise, ci stringemmo la mano e già immaginavo di non rivederla più.

/////

"*Come sta andando?*"
"*Alla grande, c'è qualcuno interessato al progetto.*"
Non era Eleanor, ma la voce con cui parlavo da 25 anni.
"*Sono sicuro che ce la farai e che le cose andranno per il meglio*". Un sorriso smorzato, una lacrima non trattenuta, ma subito nascosta, prima che i bambini irrompessero nello schermo dell'iPad e nella telefonata con Skype.
Qualche minuto dopo, lasciati i bambini, di nuovo lei: "*Ti trovo bene. Forse questo viaggio servirà. Il nonno ha sempre ragione*".
"*Già, forse ci farà bene.*"

that runs in front of your eyes and a big question mark. End a relationship or try to save it? I would not have slept easily that night either. Too many thoughts, too many dreams, and some answers to give myself and my world. I put on my shorts and shoes and went to run around Central Park. I found that at that time there weren't any cyclists or people running. Only an army of dogs led around by their masters. And lots of rats that don't hide when someone passes close by.

/////

It was my second to last day in the city. I had 24 hours to relax and I decided to go for a stroll in Manhattan, with my camera, without schedules or set places to visit. I had breakfast like many New Yorkers have: a coffee and a croissant from the vendor in front of the Metro stop. As I sipped the hot drink (for an Italian it's hard to call it coffee), I skimmed the headlines of a newspaper and read some famous phrases by the poet Maya Angelou, who had died a few hours earlier. I was touched by one of these in particular for its beauty: *"Life is not measured by the number of breaths we take, but by the moments that take your breath away."*

I went to Downtown, I wanted to go to the Memorial Museum and remain breathless before the twin towers' craters. Just as I came out from the underground, my phone rang: *"It's Eleanor, would you like to meet me?"*

I don't know if I lost the air in my lungs, but it was something like that. Half an hour later we were together in front of one of the two giant holes. There were hundreds of people, but you could only hear the roar of the water that slipped into the holes that lead to hell. I closed my eyes and touched the names of those who died in the attack. A shiver or two, the plane crashing, the people sentenced to death falling down, the collapse. It was nearly 15 years ago, but it still felt like it had happened yesterday. It was our generation's war. And it isn't over yet. Who knows if it will ever end?

"You're crying," said Eleanor, surprised. I hugged her. And we stood still, for a few more minutes, in silence. I hadn't lost anyone in the attack. But for those who love New York, that tragedy was like loosing a family member. And every time you think about it, every damn time you see it again in videos, you get emotional and can't help but think of it again. They're feelings that you can't control.

"Enough of this, I'll take you to a nice place."

We walked back up the island, until eighth road, turning towards East Village. We walked for about half an hour, talking about New York, our lives, projects and the future. At one point she said *"We're here."* I looked around and spontaneously said: *"Sorry, but I don't see anything nice."*

"Beautiful things aren't always so obvious, sometimes you have to know how to recognize them, sometimes they are one step away from us but we can't see."

We walked into Cafe Mogador, a place that has a bar and a restaurant,

Uno sguardo, un sorriso, un bacio virtuale, tanti pensieri, una vita insieme che ti scorre davanti e un grande punto interrogativo. Chiudere una storia o tentare di salvarla? Non avrei dormito facilmente neanche quella notte. Troppi pensieri, troppi sogni, e qualche risposta da dare a me stesso e al mio mondo. Misi le scarpe e i pantaloncini e andai a correre intorno a Central Park. Scoprii che a quell'ora non ci sono ciclisti, e nemmeno runner. Solo un esercito di cani portati a spasso dai loro padroni. E molti topi che non fuggono al passaggio degli uomini.

/////

Era il penultimo giorno in città. Avevo 24 ore di relax e me ne sarei andato a zonzo per Manhattan, con la mia macchina fotografica, senza orari e senza meta. Feci colazione come la fanno tanti newyorchesi: un caffè e un croissant acquistato al carretto che staziona davanti alla fermata della metro. Mentre sorseggiavo quella bevanda bollente (per un italiano è difficile chiamarla caffè), scorrevo i titoli di un quotidiano e leggevo alcune frasi celebri della poetessa Maya Angelou, deceduta da poche ore. Una tra queste, in particolare, mi rimase impressa per la sua bellezza: «La vita non si misura dal numero dei respiri che prendiamo, ma dai momenti che ci tolgono il respiro».

Scesi fino a Downtown, volevo andare al Memorial Museum e perdere il respiro davanti ai crateri delle torri gemelle. Appena uscito dalla metropolitana il telefono squillò: *"Sono Eleanor, ti va di vedermi?"*

Non so se persi il respiro, ma era qualcosa di simile. Mezz'ora dopo eravamo insieme davanti ad uno dei due giganteschi hole. C'erano centinaia di persone, ma si udiva solo il silenzio e lo scrosciare dell'acqua che si infilava nei buchi che portano all'inferno. Chiusi gli occhi, sfiorai con la mano i nomi delle persone decedute nell'attentato alle torri gemelle. Un brivido, due, l'aereo che si schianta, i condannati a morte che si gettano dai grattacieli, il crollo. Sono passati quasi 15 anni, ma è come se fosse accaduto ieri. È stata la guerra della nostra generazione. E non è ancora finita. Chissà se finirà mai.

"Stai piangendo", disse Eleanor, sorpresa. La abbracciai. E restammo ancora in silenzio per un paio di minuti. Non avevo perso nessuno nelle torri. Ma per chi ama New York, quella tragedia equivaleva alla perdita di un famigliare. E ogni volta che ci pensi, ogni maledetta volta che lo rivedi in video, ti emozioni e ci ripensi. Sono sensazioni che non puoi fermare.

"Ora basta, ti porto in un bel posto".

Risalimmo l'isola a piedi, fino all'ottava strada, deviando verso l'East Village. Camminammo per più di mezz'ora, parlando di New York, delle nostre vite, dei progetti e del futuro. Ad un certo punto disse *"siamo arrivati"*. Mi guardai intorno e mi venne spontaneo dirle: *"Scusa ma io non vedo niente di bello."*

"Le cose belle non sono sempre così evidenti, a volte bisogna saperle riconoscere, a volte sono ad un passo da noi ma non le vediamo."

Varcammo la soglia del Cafè Mogador, un posto che è un bar, un ristorante, un luogo in cui incontrarsi e scambiare quattro chiacchie-

a place to meet people and have chat. It only took 10 minutes for me to understand what Eleanor meant. It doesn't stand out for its beauty. No doubts that it's nice, it's original, with tagines used as vases, vintage chairs and tables. But it's not a typical New York bar that leaves you speechless: no refined designs, no light effects. The beauty was elsewhere: in the people, in the dishes, the smells and the atmosphere. The beauty was all around us, all you had to do was look for it.

The beauty was speaking to me. And I didn't want to stop listening.

"*What shall we do? Do you like contemporary art?*"

"*I love it,*" I replied, "*well I do, until it becomes incomprehensible, excessive and stupid.*"

"*We can go to the Moma then, today is Friday, and Friday afternoons you can enter for free.*"

We spent a couple of hours among paintings and sculptures, then we had drink at the museum's bar, and then back out, walking, talking, smiling. When you're comfortable with a person time passes by quickly and you don't even realize it. You don't feel tired, you have no desire to stop or go home. I was moved by her, in ecstasy. I hadn't felt like this in a long time, yet I did realize that often we ended up talking about my family, my children.

"*Now I'll take you to try a restaurant that you certainly wouldn't have ever reviewed. But you'll have to be patient.*"

As usual, she made all the decisions. Besides, she was playing at home. And I let her, because for the first time, I didn't have to decide for others, or choose. I just adapted to the situations.

We ended up at the corner between Sixth Avenue and the 53rd street and I quickly realized where she had brought me: a long line of people waiting for their turn, to take a dish served by the Halal Guys, a New York institution, a success thanks to the cheap price (six dollars) and the high quality of food: chicken and rice, accompanied by a delicious white sauce, whose recipe, as tradition has it, is secret and is unknown to the hundreds of New Yorkers that queue there every day.

We ate sitting in the street, whilst still talking about everything and anything. I liked Eleanor, I would have gone to bed with her right away, but I was hoping it wouldn't happen, at least not right away. Because the best moments are the ones before it happens. When you get to know someone. When a new world is revealed to you and you're not sure if you'll like it, but you know you'll certainly enjoy finding out. I was dying to kiss her, and at the same time I didn't want to. She was too beautiful, so damn interesting. I wanted those moments to last as long as possible. But I only had one more day in Manhattan.

"*Time to go, I have to be with my mother for a bit. Since my father isn't with us anymore we drink a cup of tea together before bed. And it's a ritual that I wouldn't miss for anything in the world. Not even for you, although I'd like to stay longer.*" She gave me a kiss on the cheek, and promised that we would see each other again the day after.

I returned to my hotel on foot, 40 streets further south. A long

re. Mi bastarono 10 minuti per comprendere cosa Eleanor volesse dire: quel luogo non ti colpisce per la sua bellezza. È carino, certo. È originale, con le tagine utilizzate come portafiori, le sedie e i tavoli vintage. Ma non è il tipico locale newyorchese che ti lascia a bocca aperta: nessun design ricercato, nessuna luce ad effetto. La bellezza era altrove: nelle persone, nei piatti, nei profumi e nell'aria. La bellezza era intorno a noi, bastava solo saperla cogliere.

La bellezza mi parlava. Ed io non volevo smettere di ascoltarla.

"*Che facciamo? Ti piace l'arte contemporanea?*"

"*La adoro*", risposi, "*almeno fino a quando non diventa incomprensibile, eccessiva e stupida.*"

"*Allora andiamo al Moma, oggi è venerdì e il pomeriggio si entra gratis.*"

Trascorremmo un paio d'ore tra quadri e sculture, poi un aperitivo al bar del museo, e di nuovo fuori, a camminare, parlare, sorridere. Quando stai bene con una persona il tempo scorre in fretta e nemmeno te ne accorgi. Non accusi stanchezza, non hai nessuna voglia di fermarti o tornare a casa. Ero trasportato da lei, in estasi. Era da tempo che non mi sentivo così bene, eppure mi rendevo conto che spesso finivamo col parlare della mia famiglia, dei miei figli.

"*Ora ti faccio provare un ristorante che di certo non avresti mai recensito. Dovrai avere solo un po' di pazienza.*"

Come al solito era lei a prendere l'iniziativa. Del resto giocava in casa. E a ma piaceva lasciarla fare: per la prima volta non ero tenuto a decidere per altri, o a scegliere. Mi adeguavo e basta.

Finimmo all'angolo tra la sesta Avenue e la 53esima strada e compresi subito dove mi aveva portato: una lunga fila di gente attendeva il suo turno per prendere il piatto servito dagli Halal Guys, una istituzione newyorchese, un successo dettato dal prezzo economico (sei dollari) e dalla bontà del cibo: riso col pollo, accompagnato da una deliziosa salsa bianca la cui ricetta, come tradizione vuole, è segreta e ignota alle centinaia di newyorchesi che ogni giorno fanno la fila.

Mangiammo seduti per strada, continuando a parlare di tutto e del nulla. Eleanor mi piaceva, ci sarei andato a letto subito, ma speravo che non accadesse, almeno non subito. Perché i momenti più belli sono quelli precedenti. Quelli della scoperta e della conoscenza. Quando un mondo nuovo ti si svela non sei certo che ti piacerà, ma di certo ti piacerà scoprirlo. Morivo dalla voglia di baciarla, e allo stesso tempo non volevo farlo. Era troppo bella, stramaledettamente interessante. E volevo che quei momenti durassero a lungo. Ma restava un solo giorno da trascorrere a Manhattan.

"*È ora di andare, devo stare un po' con mia madre. Da quando mio padre non c'è più usiamo bere un thè insieme, prima di andare a letto. Ed è un rito che non voglio perdere per nulla al mondo. Nemmeno per te, anche se mi piacerebbe restare ancora insieme.*"

Mi diede un bacio sulla guancia, e promise che ci saremmo rivisti il giorno dopo.

Tornai in hotel a piedi: 40 strade più a Sud. Una camminata lunghissima tra luci e grattacieli, ristoranti e bar pieni di gente, barboni e topi, auto della polizia e camion dei vigili del fuoco che sfrecciano da una parte all'altra dell'isola a tutte le ore. Ero felice e pensieroso. Arrivai a letto talmente stanco ed eccitato che fu difficile addormentarsi.

walk among lights and skyscrapers, full restaurants and bars, homeless people and rats, police cars and fire engines whizzing from one part of the island to the other. I was happy and pensive. I went to bed so tired and excited that it was difficult to fall asleep.

/////

"*I took a day off work, I couldn't leave you all alone. I'll come to pick you up and we can have lunch together. Okay?*"
The answer was obvious. I would have wanted to say: I can't wait, I've been thinking of you all night and I'm already ready and waiting in the lobby. But in these cases, pride and male stupidity, made me say something else. "*Of course, I'll finish breakfast and get ready.*"
As she walked in, and was coming up the escalator, more or less everyone turned to look at her. I sat transfixed in my chair, like an imbecile. She wore an extraordinary elegant white sheath dress. High heels, sunglasses that held back her hair, white nail varnish, a good perfume.
"*Good morning, you look like you didn't get much sleep.*"
"*You're beautiful,*" I said, as I risked giving her a kiss on the cheek that was happily returned. We left the hotel and on the road I noticed a bus that said "Have a nice day." Have you ever thought you might be dreaming? Everything seemed so perfect, so unreal. I was afraid I would wake up at any moment, but the dream continued, for another whole day.
She took me to "The Five Leaves", a small place in Greenpoint (Brooklyn), for a Saturday brunch. I told her that I loved looking at New York from Dumbo, under the Brooklyn Bridge, so we stayed there, sat on the steps in front of the carousel, admiring the skyline and talking like two teenagers in love. Last time I had been there was with my wife and children, and of course I couldn't help but tell her, and she didn't seem to mind. We returned to Manhattan and stopped in Washington Square Arch, where a couple of her friends that were part of Theatre Company would be performing in the afternoon. It was a fun show, they were all dressed in white, and they seemed to be part of the "Guilty remnant" sect from the Leftovers series. She introduced me to all of them and we went for a drink together, then she said that we had to leave because we were invited to dinner.
"*It was a lie, I wanted to be alone with you, in the most beautiful place in New York.*"
She led me to High Line, a former elevated railway in the Meatpacking District, turned into a walk path surrounded by nature: an urban renewal intervention that should teach the world and that perhaps could only have been made here. Thanks to this intervention, a rough and abandoned area in the neighbourhood had become the coolest place in Manhattan, full of fashionable bars and trendy shops. We visited some clothes and design shops, then a book shop, and finally went up the High Line. She took my hand, not as you take your partner's hand, but as you do to give confidence to a child. She found two free wooden sunbeds and we lay down to watch the sunset over New York. We felt the last hours go by relentlessly and the words began to leave space for silence. Even our smiles vanished, replaced by melancholy

/////

"*Ho preso un giorno di vacanza, non potevo lasciarti solo. Vengo a prenderti e pranziamo insieme. Ti va?*"
La risposta era scontata. Avrei dovuto dirle: non vedo l'ora, ho pensato a te tutta la notte e sono già pronto nella hall, aspettavo la tua chiamata. Ma in questi casi l'orgoglio, o la stupidità maschile, ti impongono parole diverse. "*Certo che mi va, finisco di fare colazione e sono pronto.*"
Quando entrò nella hall, salendo le scale mobili, più o meno tutti i presenti si girarono a guardarla. Io restai pietrificato sulla poltrona, come un imbecille. Aveva un tubino bianco di un'eleganza straordinaria. Tacchi alti, occhiali da sole a tenere i capelli, smalto bianco, un buon profumo.
"*Buongiorno, sembri uno che ha dormito poco.*"
"*Sei bellissima*", le dissi, azzardando un bacio sulla guancia che venne ricambiato senza problemi. Uscimmo dall'hotel e sulla strada notai un bus con la scritta "Have a nice day". Vi è mai capitato di pensare di sognare? Sembrava tutto perfetto, tutto irreale. Temevo di svegliarmi da un momento all'altro, e invece il sogno continuò ancora, per un giorno intero.
Mi portò al Five Leaves, un piccolo locale a Greenpoint (Brooklyn), per il brunch del sabato. Le dissi che amavo restare a guardare New York da Dumbo, sotto il ponte di Brooklyn, e restammo a parlare lì, sugli scalini davanti alla giostra per i bambini, ammirando la skyline e continuando a parlare come due ragazzi innamorati. Ero stato in quel posto l'ultima volta con mia moglie e i due ragazzi, e ovviamente non potei fare a meno di raccontarlo, e lei non sembrava disturbata dalla cosa. Ritornammo a Manhattan per fermarci in Washington Square Arch, dove una compagnia teatrale in cui c'erano un paio di sue amiche si sarebbe esibita di pomeriggio. Fu uno spettacolo divertente, erano tutti vestiti di bianco, sembravano i membri della setta dei "Colpevoli sopravvissuti" della serie Leftovers. Me li presentò tutti e andammo a bere qualcosa insieme, poi lei disse che li dovevamo lasciare perché eravamo invitati a cena.
"*Era una bugia, volevo stare sola con te, nel posto più bello di New York*".
Mi condusse alla High Line, l'ex ferrovia sopraelevata nel Meatpacking District, trasformata in passeggiata nel verde: un intervento di recupero urbanistico che ha fatto scuola nel mondo e che forse poteva avvenire solo qui. Grazie a quell'intervento, una zona malfamata e abbandonata si era trasformata nel quartiere più cool di Manhattan, pieno di locali alla moda e di negozi trendy. Ne visitammo alcuni, di abbigliamento e di design, poi una libreria, infine salimmo sulla High Line. Mi prese per mano, non come si prende un compagno, ma come si dà fiducia ad un bambino. Scorse due lettini di legno liberi e ci sdraiammo ad ammirare il tramonto su New York. Sentivamo le ultime ore scorrere inesorabili e le parole iniziavano a lasciare sempre più spazio ai silenzi. Anche i sorrisi svanivano, sostituiti dalla malinconia e dalla tristezza.
"*Dormi con me stanotte.*" Lo dissi guardando il cielo e stringendole la mano. Non era una domanda ma un'implorazione. Mi voltai verso di

and sadness.

"*Sleep with me tonight.*" I said as I was looking at the sky and holding her hand. It wasn't much of a question but more of a plea. I turned to her and realized that a tear was running down her cheek. This time it was her crying. We kissed. And there was no one around us anymore. Only me, her, and New York. No noises, no voices, no thoughts.

We were embraced and silent, for at least an hour, because heaven doesn't need any shallow words. Then she interrupted the ecstasy.

"*I can't, you still have her in your heart. You can tell by how much you speak about her. And how you speak about her. It wouldn't be right. Although it certainly would be lovely. We are two angels who met too late. But you will always be in my heart, even if we've just met.*"

She had the power to always surprise me and leave me speechless. We said goodbye at the hotel entrance. A hug, one last kiss, and another tear. "*I'll be waiting for you here in a few months, I want an autographed copy of the book.*"

/////

At the airport I found the other half of my world waiting for me. She had a sad face. She hugged me gave me a kiss, something that hadn't happened for months. Then she said: "*He's very bad.*" She took me immediately to my grandfather's house. He was in bed, it was very serious. It was hard for him to breathe. In the hope of making him feel a bit better, they told him that I had arrived, and he opened his eyes just long enough to check it was true. I hinted a smile, but I was already crying. I held him close and whispered in his ears: "*It went well. You were right, as usual.*" He found the strength to give me a pat on the back. "*I knew it. Did you think your nonno didn't know?*"

/////

My grandfather died that night. I still think he had wanted to wait for me for a final farewell, before reaching for my grandmother to take her on their cruise. As he had planned, the trip to New York changed my life. I found myself, my wife and my family again, I had new ideas, new dreams and new projects. I lost a very important person, but that person had made me regain my whole life and my loved ones.

As for Eleanor, it's obvious that sometimes I think of her. But I have never written emails or called her on the phone. I'm not an angel, but maybe she really was. Or at least I like to think of her as so.

lei e mi accorsi che una lacrima le accarezzava il volto. Questa volta era lei a piangere. Ci baciammo. E tutto intorno non c'era più nessuno. Solo io, lei e New York. Nessun rumore, nessuna voce, nessun pensiero.

Restammo in silenzio, abbracciati, per almeno un'ora, perché il paradiso non ha bisogno di parole superflue. Poi fu lei a interrompere l'estasi. "*Non posso, hai ancora lei nel cuore. Lo si capisce da quanto ne parli. E da come ne parli. Non sarebbe giusto. Anche se sicuramente sarebbe bello. Diciamo che siamo due angeli che si sono incontrati troppo tardi. Ma resterai sempre nel mio cuore, anche se ci sei appena entrato.*" Aveva il potere di sorprendermi sempre e di lasciarmi muto. Ci salutammo all'ingresso dell'hotel. Un abbraccio, l'ultimo bacio, un'altra lacrima. "*Ti aspetto qui tra qualche mese, voglio una copia del libro. Autografata.*"

/////

In aeroporto trovai ad attendermi l'altra metà del mio mondo. Aveva un volto triste. Mi abbracciò mi diede un bacio, cosa che non accadeva da mesi. Poi disse: "*Sta molto male*". Mi portò subito a casa del nonno. Era sul letto, molto grave. Respirava a fatica. Quando, nella speranza che si riprendesse un po', gli dissero che ero arrivato, aprì gli occhi quanto bastava per controllare che non lo stessero prendendo in giro. Abbozzai un sorriso, ma già piangevo. Lo strinsi forte a me e gli sussurrai nelle orecchie: «*È andata bene. Come sempre avevi ragione*». Trovò la forza di darmi una pacca sulla spalla. "*Lo sapevo. Pensavi che tuo nonno non lo sapesse?*"

/////

Il nonno morì quella stessa notte. Ancora oggi continuo a pensare che mi avesse voluto aspettare per l'ultimo saluto, prima di raggiungere la nonna e portarla in crociera. Quel viaggio a New York, come aveva immaginato, cambiò il corso della mia vita. Ritrovai mia moglie e la famiglia, ritrovai la voglia e le idee, nuovi sogni e nuovi progetti. Avevo perso una persona importantissima, ma quella persona mi aveva fatto ritrovare la mia vita e i miei affetti. Quanto ad Eleanor, è ovvio che ogni tanto penso a lei. Ma non le ho scritto mail. Non l'ho chiamata al telefono. Io non sono un angelo, ma forse lei lo era davvero. O almeno mi piace pensarlo.

Mo Foulavand
Neuro-Ophthalmogy
NYU Langone Hospital

What do you like of New York and New Yorkers?
I love the energy and the spirit that you get from the city. New York is a vibrant city, New Yorkers have a reputation of being rude and aggressive but they have big hearts once you get to know them. They are actually very caring and protective of their city and in moments of crises they have showed a lot of solidarity. New Yorkers are a community of people that have come from all over the world, with different cultures and traditions, who have chosen to work and live together, and I think it's truly wonderful.
Your favourite restaurants?
I'm Iranian, so I appreciate good Persian food. Ravagh Restaurant, has truly authentic Persian cuisine. I also love ABC Kitchen: the food is delicious and the restaurant has a very special design Blue Hill also has good food and nice atmosphere.
A place for shopping?
Definitely Soho and the West Village, where you can find little boutiques and locale artists. But I also shop at Barney and Charles Tyrwhitt. For home decor, I always find beautiful things at Abc Carpet.
Your favourite place in the city?
Central Park is my favourite place to walk or to bike. I'm city person but I love the idea that in the middle of the city you can experience so much nature, trees and lakes, in every corner you can be entertained by dancers, singers, musicians, painters in the heart of New York.

(italian text at page 363)

› Sivan Askayo
FOTOGRAFA

Cosa ti piace di New York?
Il dinamismo e l'energia. E poi è una città che ad un fotografo offre sempre nuovi stimoli visuali. Qui non mi annoio mai e trovo sempre ispirazione.

Cosa non ami?
L'inverno troppo freddo. E lo stare schiacciati l'uno all'altro in metro.

I "tuoi" ristoranti?
Cafe Gitane in Mott Street, Nolita, un ristorante franco-marocchino. Buvette Gastroteque nel West Village, un bistrot francese. E Eataly, nel Flatiron district.

Dove fai shopping?
Da B&H per fotocamere e accessori professionali per il mio lavoro. Da McNally Jackson per i libri. J. Crew e Anthropologie per i vestiti.

Un posto da non perdere per i turisti?
"Sleep no more", ma non voglio dire altro. Dovete andarci.

Il tuo posto preferito?
Il Meatpacking district e la High line.

› Trisha Krauss
ILLUSTRATRICE

Cosa ti piace dei newyorchesi?
Il loro sense of humour e la capacità di lavorare o giocare dando sempre il massimo. New York è stata la città più divertente in cui ho vissuto e quella in cui ho più lavorato.

Il tuo ristorante preferito?
Bar Piti, un classico, ma anche un ottimo posto per trascorrere una calda sera d'estate. molto vicino al posto in cui sono solita risiedere, nel West Village.

Il posto migliore per lo shopping?
Century 21 ha ottime occasioni di design. Da Bergdorf Goodman per i grandi classici.

La zona che più ami?
Il West Village, ovviamente.

Un turista non può perdersi...
La High Line nel Meat Packing District. Il Tenement Museum nel Lower East Side. La passeggiata sul Brooklyn Bridge. La spesa da Zabar's nell'upper West Side seguita da un picnic a Central Park.

Qual è il tuo prossimo progetto/sogno?
Finire le illustrazioni di un libro per Random House US e poi scrivere e realizzare illustrazioni per altri libri. Fuori dal lavoro, sogno di ristrutturare una vecchia casa di bambole. E poi vorrei un mese senza alcun progetto, per vedere come ci si sente.

› Ornella Fado
CONDUTTRICE TV

Calabrese trapiantata negli States, Ornella Fado conduce la trasmissione "Brindiamo" sul canale NYCTV.

Qual è il tuo quartiere preferito a NY?
Vivo nell'Upper West Side da 20 anni e lo adoro. Sono a due passi dal Lincoln Center, da Central Park e dal fiume.

Cosa non ti piace di New York?
Mi piace ogni cosa di questa città. Amo l'energia che sento ogni volta che cammino per le sue strade. Qui mi sento a casa.

Qual è il tuo ristorante preferito?
Grazie al mio lavoro ne conosco tanti e me ne piacciono diversi: La Masseria e SD26 tra gli italiani. Buddakan nel Meatpacking district e Apples Bee.

Un posto per fare shopping?
Mi piace fare acquisti da Saks, sulla quinta strada: sono loro a fornirmi gli abiti per lo show. Adoro anche Michael's, negozio di arte e design, perché mi piace dipingere.

Qual è il tuo prossimo progetto/sogno?
Ho appena festeggiato i primi 10 anni di "Brindiamo". Pensiamo ai prossimi 10!

› Albin Konopka
MUSICISTA - COMPOSITORE

Cosa ti piace di New York?
New York è tuttora la capitale del mondo. Mi piace la diversità etnica. Mi piace andare in Chinatown o in Little Russia in Brighton Beach. Vivo in quel che rimane della parte spagnola di Harlem. Adoro andare in un negozio di Little India che vende centinaia di erbe e spezie... E poi abbiamo i più grandi teatri e se ami la musica questo è il posto in cui stare. Mi spiace per il West End londinese.

E cosa non ti piace?
Troppa spazzatura per strada, e poi non sopporto l'inquinamento acustico: troppo abuso di sirene. E poi non mi piace il fatto che i newyorchesi pensano di avere il meglio di tutto. like about New York and New Yorkers?

I tuoi ristoranti preferiti?
Don Antonio's per la pizza. Thai Market per il thailandese, The Curry Club per l'indiano, Gallagher's per le bistecche. Edi and The Wolf per un interessante fusion austriaco.

E per lo shopping?
Internet!

I tuoi posti preferiti in città?
High Line e la la North Woods section di Central Park. Alcuni musei: Met, Moma, The Frick, Natural History. E Times Square.

Un turista deve vedere...?
Il 9/11 Memorial, anche solo per rispetto. E ovviamente la High Line.

Cosa sogni?
Faccio quel che amo fare, sono un musicista. Sono contento di non avere un ufficio, ho una famiglia stupenda e sono amato. Sto già vivendo il mio sogno.

› Daniela Kucher
BLOGGER E FOTOGRAFA

Qual è la tua zona preferita di NY?
Tutta la città senza differenze. Adoro il suo continuo cambiamento.

E cosa non ti piace?
Che i newyorchesi vadano sempre di fretta.

Il tuo ristorante preferito?
La Esquina, un messicano a Nolita.

E per lo shopping?
Sono sempre a caccia di sconti, e dunque mi affido a Racked.com

La tua zona preferita?
D'estate Prospect Park con le sue performance di musicisti. Quando sei lì dimentichi di trovarti nella città più frenetica del mondo.

Un posto da non perdere?
Il mio blog "First Generation Fashion": l'ho aperto proprio per aiutare le persone a scoprire il lato culturale di New York partendo dal punto di vista di chi vive in città.

Il tuo prossimo progetto?
Far diventare il blog il mio lavoro.

› Bobby Seeger
MOTORCYCLE MANUFACTURER

Cosa ami di New York?
La città vecchia, la sporcizia, la gente.

Il tuo ristorante preferito?
Oficina Latina in Prince st. e Peasant in Elizabeth st. A Brooklyn I eat at Jimmy's Diner on Union ave.

Il tuo best place per lo shopping?
Genuine Motorworks a Brooklyn, so che lì posso trovare ciò che cerco.

Il tuo posto preferito?
Mi piace scorazzare in moto di notte, attraversare i ponti da Est a Ovest della città.

Un luogo da non perdere?
Sedetevi in mezzo ai ponti di Brooklyn e guardate le navi.

› Chiemi Nakai
PIANISTA - COMPOSITRICE

Cosa ti attrae di New York?
E' la capitale mondiale della musica che amo.

Cosa non ti piace?
I freddi e lunghi inverni.

I tuoi ristoranti preferiti?
Oficina Latina in Manhattan and Geido, a Flatbush, Brooklyn.

Lo shopping?
A Union Square e China Town.

I luoghi del cuore?
Meatpacking district, West Village, Soho.

Cosa non bisogna perdersi a New York?
Meatpacking district, downtown Brooklyn, la musica live.

Your next project/dream?
Nuovi cd, nuova musica, nuovi concerti.

› Jeryl Brunner
GIORNALISTA - SCRITTRICE

I newyorchesi sono un gruppo unito e si sacrificano tanto pur di vivere qui: poco spazio, case piccole, traffico e rumore. Ma ne vale la pena!

Cosa non ti piace di New York?
Il poco spazio, le case piccole, il rumore. E i costi alti.

I tuoi ristoranti?
Fred's at Barneys. Rotisserie Georgette. Luigi's.

E per lo shopping?
The Sunday flea market a Columbus Avenue.

Un posto che ami.
Central Park e la passeggiata in bici lungo il fiume Hudson.

Cosa non devono perdersi i turisti?
L'opportunità di andare a teatro.

Il tuo prossimo progetto?
Migliorare e ancora migliorare.

› Mo Foulavand
NEURO-OFTALMOLOGO

Amo lo spirito e l'energia che la città infonde. I newyorkesi sono passano per rudi e aggressivi, ma hanno un grande cuore, sono solidali e amano e proteggono la loro città.

Il ristorante favorito?
Sono iraniano, quindi dico il Ravagh Restaurant, autentica cucina persiana. Amo anche ABC Kitchen, cibo delizioso e atmosfera fantastica.

Dove fa shopping?
Soho e il West Village, con le loro piccole boutique e gliartisti locali. Ma vado anche da Barney and Charles Tyrwhitt. Per l'home decor, trovo sempre qualcosa di carino da Abc Carpet.

Il suo luogo del cuore?
Central Park per bici e passeggiate. Adoro il fatto che pur stando nel centro della metropoli puoi trascorrere qualche ora in mezzo alla natura e agli alberi, godendoti spettacoli e performance di ballerini, musicisti, pittori e cantanti.

Recipes
indice ricette

Appetizer › Antipasto

A

Arepa › 258

B

Baby artichokes salad
Insalata di carciofini › 82
Beef bulgogi tacos
Tacos di manzo bulgogi › 241
Black rice salad
Insalata di riso nero › 302
Brass ale beer waffles
Waffle alla birra › 225

C

Carbonara flatbread › 310
Cassoncini, portobella filling, prosciutto › 60
Cheese pie › 209
Cold eggplant salad
Insalata fredda di melanzane › 89
Cucumber and yogurt gazpacho
Gazpacho di cetriolo e yogurt › 98

F

Fried gnocco
Gnocco fritto › 196
Fried Pickles
Cetrioli fritti › 205

G

Grilled bacon
Bacon alla griglia › 108
Grilled wild octopus
Polpo alla griglia › 172

H

Hamachi, chinese salted black beanse
Hamachi e fagioli neri cinesi salati › 192
Horiatiki (Greek salad)
Horiatiki (insalata greca) › 262
Hummus › 70

K

Kebbe krass › 92
Kyoto crunchy sloppy joes 239

L

Lamb meatballs
Polpette di agnello › 158

Lobster roll
Panino all'aragosta › 166
Lobster tempura
Tempura di aragosta › 117

M

Marinated beets
Barbabietole marinate › 129
Melon gazpacho, cottage cheese
Gazpacho di melone con formaggio cottage › 150
Mouhamarra › 95
Mozzarella in carrozza › 272

O

Octopus and chickpea salad
Polpo e insalata di ceci › 248

P

Pan roasted squid
Calamari arrosto (con anguria) › 192
Piemontese-style crostino with carne cruda
Crostino Piemontese con carne cruda › 162
Pizza tartufata
Truffled Pizza › 198
Polpettine di vitello › 296

R

Razor clams with fennel and chiles
Cannolicchi con finocchio e peperoncino › 138

S

Scallop ceviche with peaches, ginger and thai basil › 254
Shrimp scampi
Gamberoni scampi › 133
Smoked salmon tacos
Tacos di salmone affumicato › 66
Spicy carrots
Carote piccanti › 128
Spicy papaya salad mixed with grilled pork
Insalata di papaya piccante con maiale grigliato › 290
Spicy sashimi salad › 240
Sympetherio salad
Insalata Sympetherio › 244

T

Tabouli salad
Insalata Tabouli › 73
Terra Mare › 234
Tosta de Boquerón › 282
Tuna tartare
Tartare di tonno › 122

W

Watermelon salad › 302
Wild striped bass tiradito
Tiradito di spigola selvaggia › 146

Entrees › Piatto Principale

A

Afro asian american gumbo
Gumbo afro asiatico americano › 301
Agnolotti, lemon ricotta, shrimp, salsa verde pesto
Agnolotti, ricotto al limone, gamberi, pesto salsa verde › 59
Artic chair
Salmerino Alpino › 157

B

Benedict royale › 226
Braised lamb shank
Stinco d'agnello brasato › 70
Branzino › 286
Bucatini all'amatriciana › 125

C

Cernia alla mugnaia › 122
Charlie Bird farro salad › 139
Chivito › 258
Churrasco and chimichurri › 180
Crispy chicken
Pollo croccante › 134
Crispy duck wings
Ali di anatra croccanti › 218
Crispy softshell crab
Granchio croccante › 118

D

Diver caught scallops
Capesante in salsa piccante › 191
Diver scallops, avocado salad
Capesante e insalata di avocado › 306

F

Fermented corn sauce
Salsa di mais fermentato › 67
Free range chicken › 175
Fried chicken
Pollo Fritto › 310

G

General tsao's lobster
L'aragosta del Generale Tsao › 254
Gnocchi alla sorrentina › 230
Grilled branzino
Branzino alla griglia › 250
Grilled cobia with white asparagus, artichokes hearts and aioli
Pesce cobia alla griglia con asparagi bianchi › 179
Grilled rack of lamb › 118

L

Lamb Biryani
Agnello Biryani › **76**
Lamb Stew
Stufato di agnello › **208**
Lobster ceviche › **146**
Lobster ravioli
Ravioli di aragosta › **168**
Lobster with summer beans and dill › **104**
Low country shrimp
Gamberetti low country › **313**

M

Moussaka › **265**
Mussels and beer
Cozze e birra › **202**

N

Nali Ki Nihari (Lamb shank) › **78**
Nuestra paella › **281**

O

Oxtail Oden
Coda di bue Oden › **113**

R

Roasted chathamcodfish nicoise
Merluzzo arrosto, spinaci e olive › **85**

S

Sa Poak Gai Tod Der (Der styled deep fried chicken thigh) › **292**
Sea scallops, corn cobs and maitake mushrooms
Capesante, funghi e granturco › **316**
Shahi Tukda (Awadhi Saffron Bread Pudding) › **78**
Shakshuka › **88**
Shrimp Burger › **218**
Spaghetti alla chitarra › **197**
Spaghetti al pomodoro › **297**
Spaghetti con fagiolini › **214**
Steamed mussels › **186**

V

Veal ravioli
Ravioli di vitello › **152**

W

Whole flounder with mixed nuts › **162**

Z

Zucchini and heirloom tomato lasagna
Lasagne di zucchine e pomodori Heirloom › **276**

Dessert › Dolce

A

Apple pie › **215**

B

Banana cheesecake › **85**
Banofee pie
Tortino Banofee › **158**
Bittersweet chocolate souffle
Soufflè di cioccolato fondente › **152**
Bomboloni › **60**

C

Carrot cake
Tortino alle carote › **108**
Cherry pie › **166**
Chocoba › **95**
Chocolate Bruno
Mousse al cioccolato › **112**
Chocolate cake
Dessert al cioccolato › **198**

F

Flan with dulce de leche › **180**
Fried Oreos › **205**

G

Green tea mille crepe
Millecrepes al tè verde › **117**

H

Homemade greek yogurt
Yogurt "greco" › **250**

M

Mango flan
Flan di mango › **282**
Mixed berry parfait
Parfait di bacche miste › **175**

N

Namoura › **73**
New York cheesecake with passionfruit coulis
and almond struesel › **54**

P

Panna Cotta Thai Tea
Panna Cotta al tè tailandese › **292**
Pistachio semifreddo with warm chocolate sauce › **306**

R

Ricotta cheesecake › **226**
Ricotta pancakes › **186**

S

Sour cherry pie
Torta di visciole › **210**
Summer Strawberries › **64**

T

Tiramisù › **125**
Triple chocolate mousse
Tripla mousse al cioccolato › **142**
Turon › **268**
Twice baked, upside down comte cheese soufflé
Soufflé capovolto di formaggio comte cotto due volte › **101**

Z

Zeppole alla Nutella › **273**

publisher › editore

www.nextbook.it

ITALY

Via Rosmini 21 - 72100 Brindisi
tel. +39 (0) 389 7965 348

info@nextbook.it

PHOTO CREDITS › Crediti Fotografici

pag. 52 › Ph courtesy 21 Club

pag. 87 › Ania Gruca

pag. 97 › L. Hughes

pag. 102-103 › Francesco Tonelli

pag. 106-107 › Ph courtesy ESQuared Hospitality

pag. 111 › Ph courtesy Blue Ribbon Sushi Izakaya

pag. 130-131 › Gary Landsman

pag. 136-138-139 › Noah Fecks

pag. 140 › Sebastian Lucrecio

pag. 149 › Thomas Loof

pag. 161 › Virginia Rollison

pag. 170-175 › Marc Lins and Daniel Krieger

pag. 183 › Gregory Pescia

pag. 222 › Gary Landsman

pag. 228-229 › Ken Goodman

pag. 232 › Noel Sutherland

pag. 242-243-245 › Paul Johnson

pag. 247 › Ph courtesy MP Taverna

pag. 253 › Paul Johnson

pag. 257-258 › Mirko Viola

pag. 267 › Justine Dungo

pag. 275 › Ph courtesy Pure Food and Wine

pag. 279 › Ph courtesy Salinas

pag. 285 › Ph courtesy Seasonal

pag. 299 › Ph courtesy The Cecil

pag. 308-309 › Nathan Rawlinson

pag. 314 › Thomas Schauer

› Some photographs of the sections Shoopping, Family attractions, Cheap Eats, Hotels are taken from the websites of the companies reviewed in the book.

› Alcune foto delle sezioni Shoopping, Family attractions, Cheap Eats, Hotels sono state estrapolate dai siti web delle aziende recensite nel libro.

SAN MARZANO

www.cantinesanmarzano.com